尾田栄一郎

Some people think that hot things have to be eaten while they're hot, or they'll lose their delicious flavor. But surely there are more people who cool down their food before eating it. So shouldn't we have a special name for people who can eat piping hot food? How about calling them "*racy tongues*"? I envy people like that, so I picked an embarrassing name.

　　　-Eiichiro Oda, 2003

In Japan, people who can't eat hot foods are said to have a *neko jita*, a cat's tongue. --Editor

Eiichiro Oda began his manga career at the age of 17, when his one-shot cowboy manga **Wanted!** won second place in the coveted Tezuka manga awards. Oda went on to work as an assistant to some of the biggest manga artists in the industry, including Nobuhiro Watsuki, before winning the Hop Step Award for new artists. His pirate adventure **One Piece**, which debuted in **Weekly Shonen Jump** in 1997, quickly became one of the most popular manga in Japan.

ONE PIECE VOL. 29
SKYPIEA PART 6

SHONEN JUMP Manga Edition

STORY AND ART BY EIICHIRO ODA

English Adaptation/Megan Bates
Translation/Masumi Matsumoto, HC Language Solutions Inc.
Touch-up Art & Lettering/John Hunt
Design/Sean Lee
Supervising Editor/Yuki Murashige
Editor/Yuki Takagaki

Printed in the U.S.A.

Published by VIZ Media, LLC
P.O. Box 77010
San Francisco, CA 94107

10 9
First printing, February 2010
Ninth printing, December 2021

viz.com

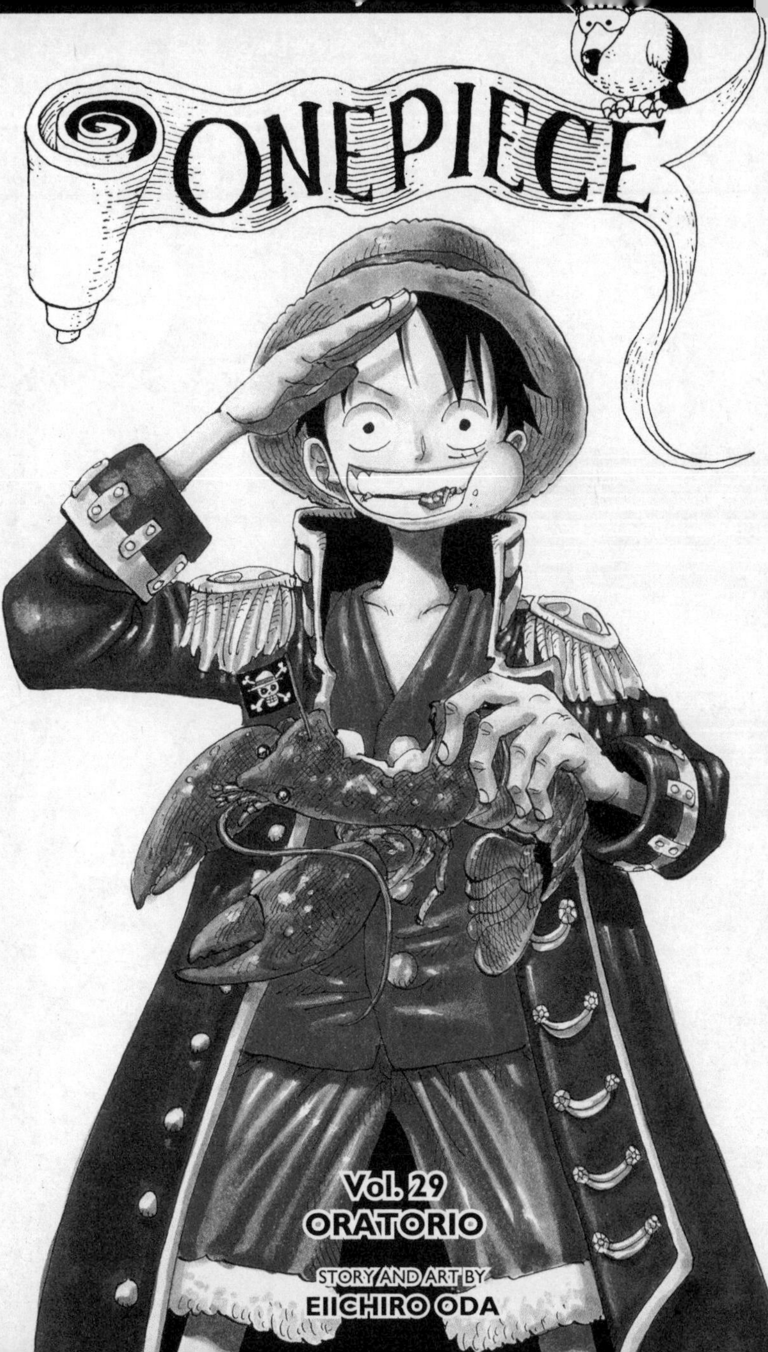

ONE PIECE

Vol. 29
ORATORIO

STORY AND ART BY
EIICHIRO ODA

The Shandians

The warriors and natives of Upper Yard. They're fighting to regain control of their homeland, which was taken over by the current Kami Eneru.

Wyper

Kamakiri

Braham

Genbo

Raki

Aisa

The Former Kami

"Sky Knight" Ganfor

Conis

The Straw Hats

Boundlessly optimistic and able to stretch like rubber, he is determined to become King of the Pirates.

Monkey D. Luffy

A former bounty hunter and master of the "three-sword" style. He aspires to be the world's greatest swordsman.

Roronoa Zolo

A thief who specializes in robbing pirates. Nami hates pirates, but Luffy convinced her to be his navigator.

Nami

A village boy with a talent for telling tall tales. His father, Yasopp, is a member of Shanks's crew.

Usopp

The big-hearted cook (and ladies' man) whose dream is to find the legendary sea, the "All Blue."

Sanji

A blue-nosed man-reindeer and the ship's doctor.

Tony Tony Chopper

A mysterious archaeologist with the power to sprout limbs anywhere. She's the newest member of the Straw Hat crew.

Nico Robin

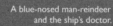

Monkey D. Luffy started out as just a kid with a dream—to become the greatest pirate in history! Stirred by the tales of pirate "Red-Haired" Shanks, Luffy vowed to become a pirate himself. That was before the enchanted Devil Fruit gave Luffy the power to stretch like rubber, at the cost of being unable to swim—a serious handicap for an aspiring sea dog. Undeterred, Luffy set out to sea and recruited some crewmates—master swordsman Zolo; treasure-hunting thief Nami; lying sharpshooter Usopp; the high-kicking chef Sanji; Chopper, the walkin' talkin' reindeer doctor; and the mysterious archaeologist Robin.

The crew's next destination is Skypiea, an island in the clouds ruled over by the powerful Kami Eneru. As soon as they arrive, they get arrested for trespassing and are put on trial, after which Nami and half the crew are led away to be sacrificed! While the gang faces some fearful challenges put up by the locals, Nami makes an amazing discovery—Upper Yard, the only place among the sky islands made of soil, is actually the other half of Jaya, the island back on the ground! Which means it's also the location of the fabled city of gold, El Dorado! Having freed themselves, the crew begins the search for treasure. But they soon find themselves caught in a battle between Eneru's army and the Shandian natives fighting to reclaim the island. Eneru predicts, "In three hours, only five people will remain alive." What will happen in his "survival game"?

Kami's Forces

They suddenly appeared with an army from one of the islands in the sky and took over Upper Yard. They now reign over Skypiea.

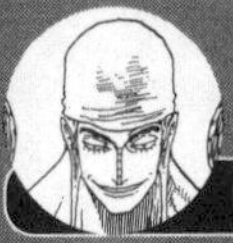

Skypiea's one and only Kami

Kami Eneru

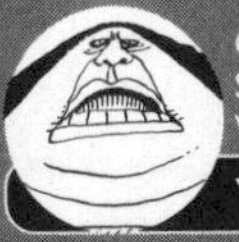

Commander of Skypiea's Heavenly Warriors

Yama

Skypiea Vassals

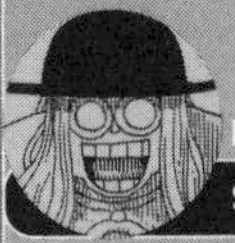

Ball Challenge

Satori of the Forest

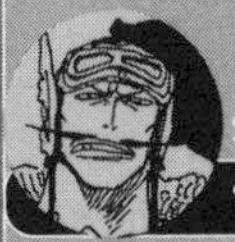

String Challenge

"Sky Rider" Shura

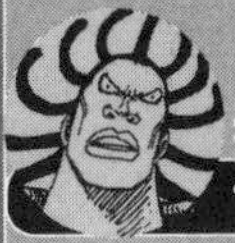

Swamp Challenge

"Sky Boss" Gedatsu

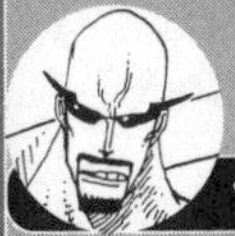

Iron Challenge

"Sky Breeder" Ohm

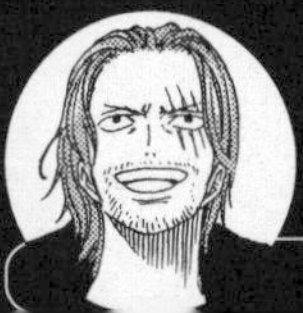

A pirate that Luffy idolizes. Shanks gave Luffy his trademark straw hat.

"Red-Haired" Shanks

SKYPIEA

ONE PIECE

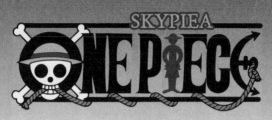

Vol. 29
Oratorio

CONTENTS

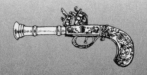

Chapter 265:
PIRATE ROBIN VS. HEAVENLY WARRIORS COMMANDER YAMA

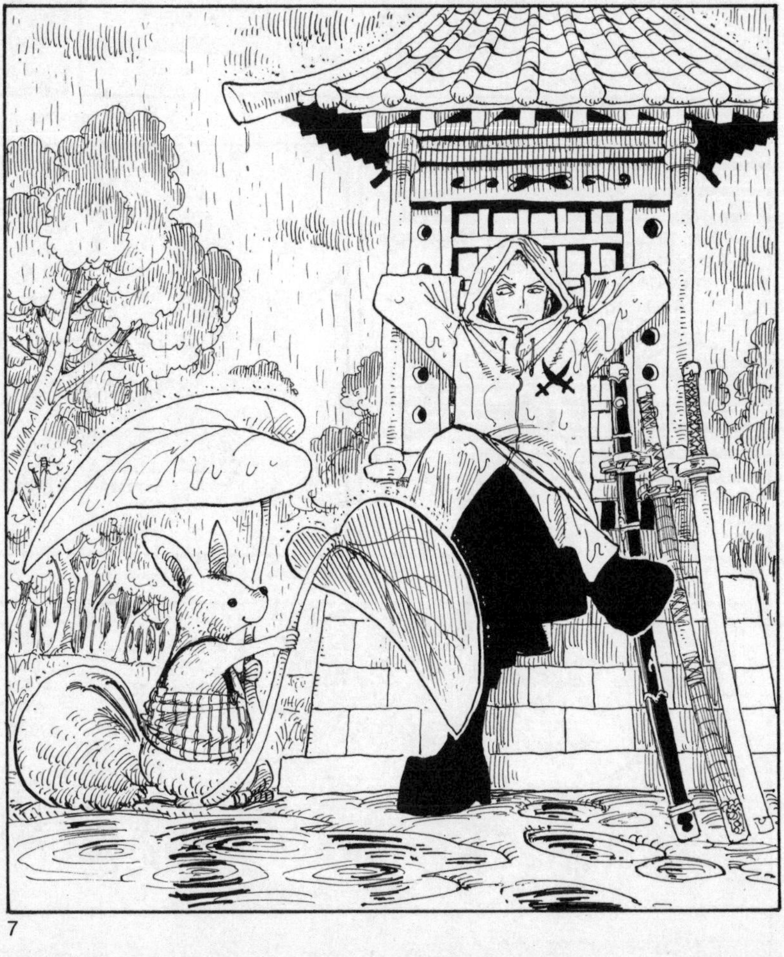

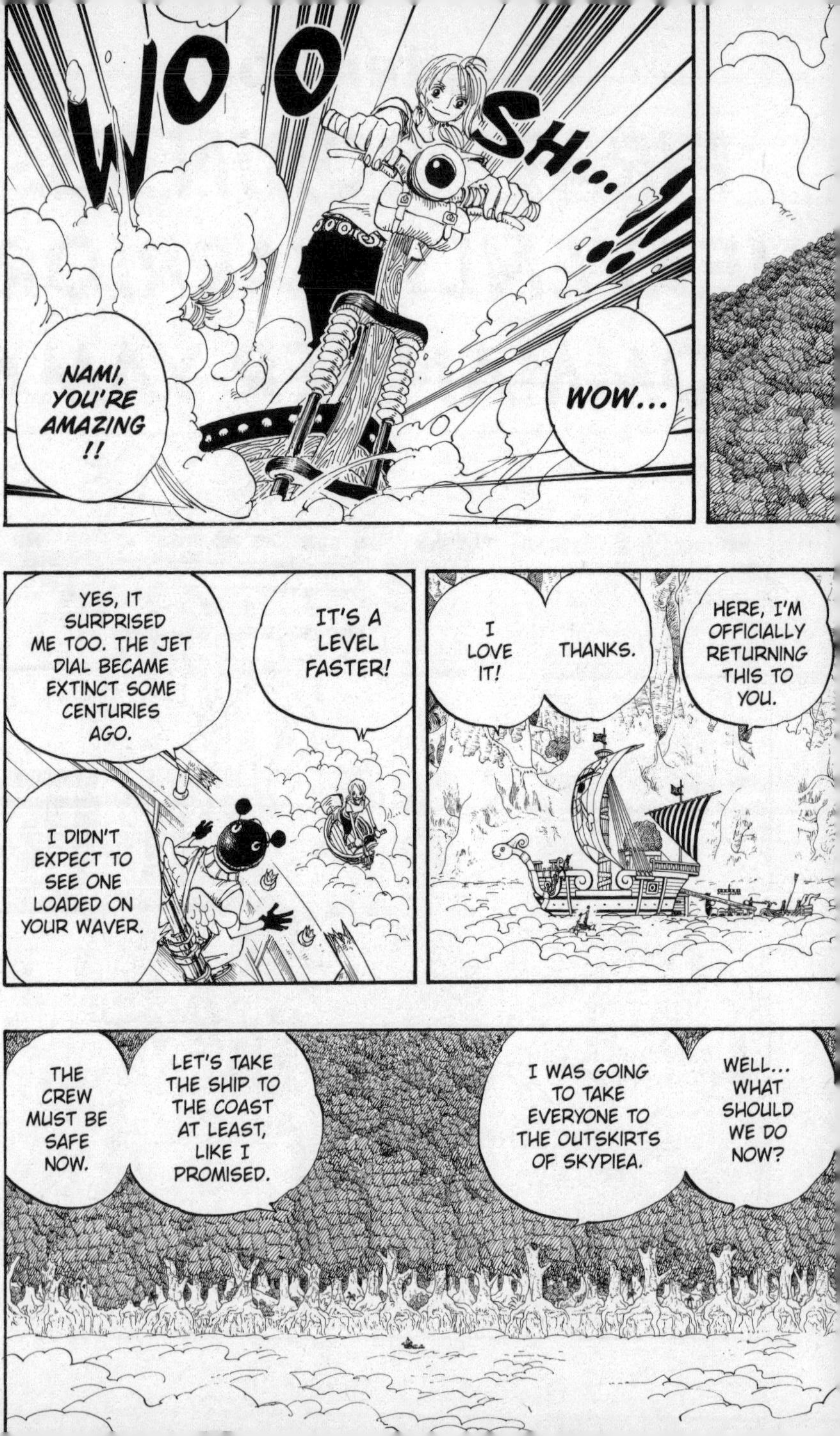
WOOOSH...!!
WOW...
NAMI, YOU'RE AMAZING !!
HERE, I'M OFFICIALLY RETURNING THIS TO YOU.
THANKS.
I LOVE IT!
IT'S A LEVEL FASTER!
YES, IT SURPRISED ME TOO. THE JET DIAL BECAME EXTINCT SOME CENTURIES AGO.
I DIDN'T EXPECT TO SEE ONE LOADED ON YOUR WAVER.
WELL... WHAT SHOULD WE DO NOW?
I WAS GOING TO TAKE EVERYONE TO THE OUTSKIRTS OF SKYPIEA.
LET'S TAKE THE SHIP TO THE COAST AT LEAST, LIKE I PROMISED.
THE CREW MUST BE SAFE NOW.

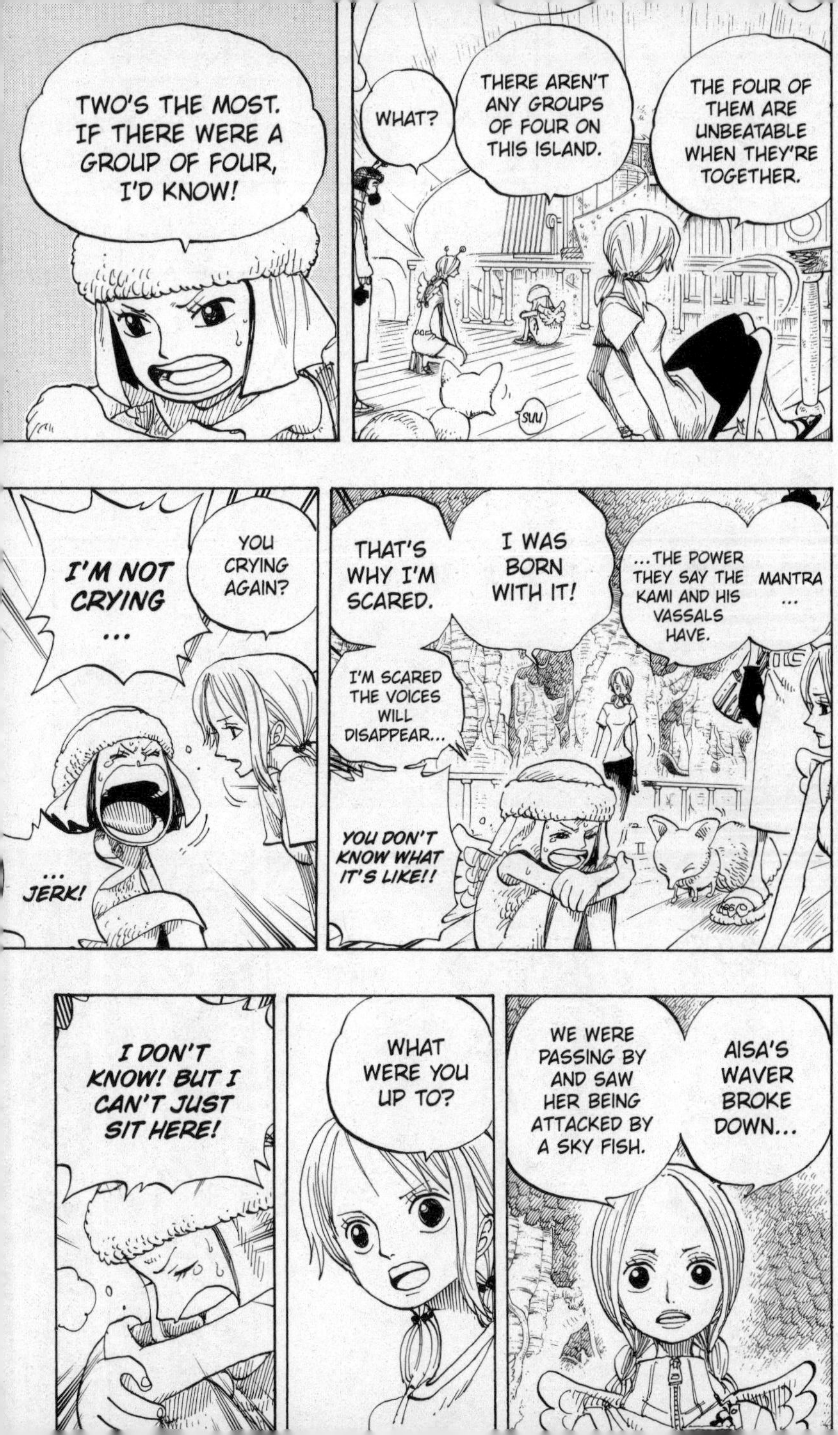
THE FOUR OF THEM ARE UNBEATABLE WHEN THEY'RE TOGETHER.
THERE AREN'T ANY GROUPS OF FOUR ON THIS ISLAND.
WHAT?
SUU
TWO'S THE MOST. IF THERE WERE A GROUP OF FOUR, I'D KNOW!
MANTRA ...
...THE POWER THEY SAY THE KAMI AND HIS VASSALS HAVE.
I WAS BORN WITH IT!
THAT'S WHY I'M SCARED.
I'M SCARED THE VOICES WILL DISAPPEAR...
YOU DON'T KNOW WHAT IT'S LIKE!!
YOU CRYING AGAIN?
I'M NOT CRYING ...
... JERK!
AISA'S WAVER BROKE DOWN...
WE WERE PASSING BY AND SAW HER BEING ATTACKED BY A SKY FISH.
WHAT WERE YOU UP TO?
I DON'T KNOW! BUT I CAN'T JUST SIT HERE!

EVERYONE...

RAKI...

...

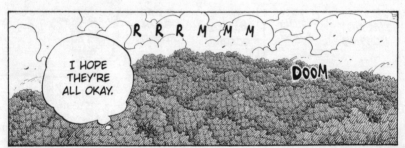

RRRMMM

I HOPE THEY'RE ALL OKAY.

DOOM

MY BACKPACK'S OUTSIDE...

PHEW... NOW WHAT?

GURGLE

KLATTA...

SPLSH

SPLASH

GURGLE...

...AND THE TREES ARE ROTTING, SO THERE'S NO FRUIT.

KLATTA...

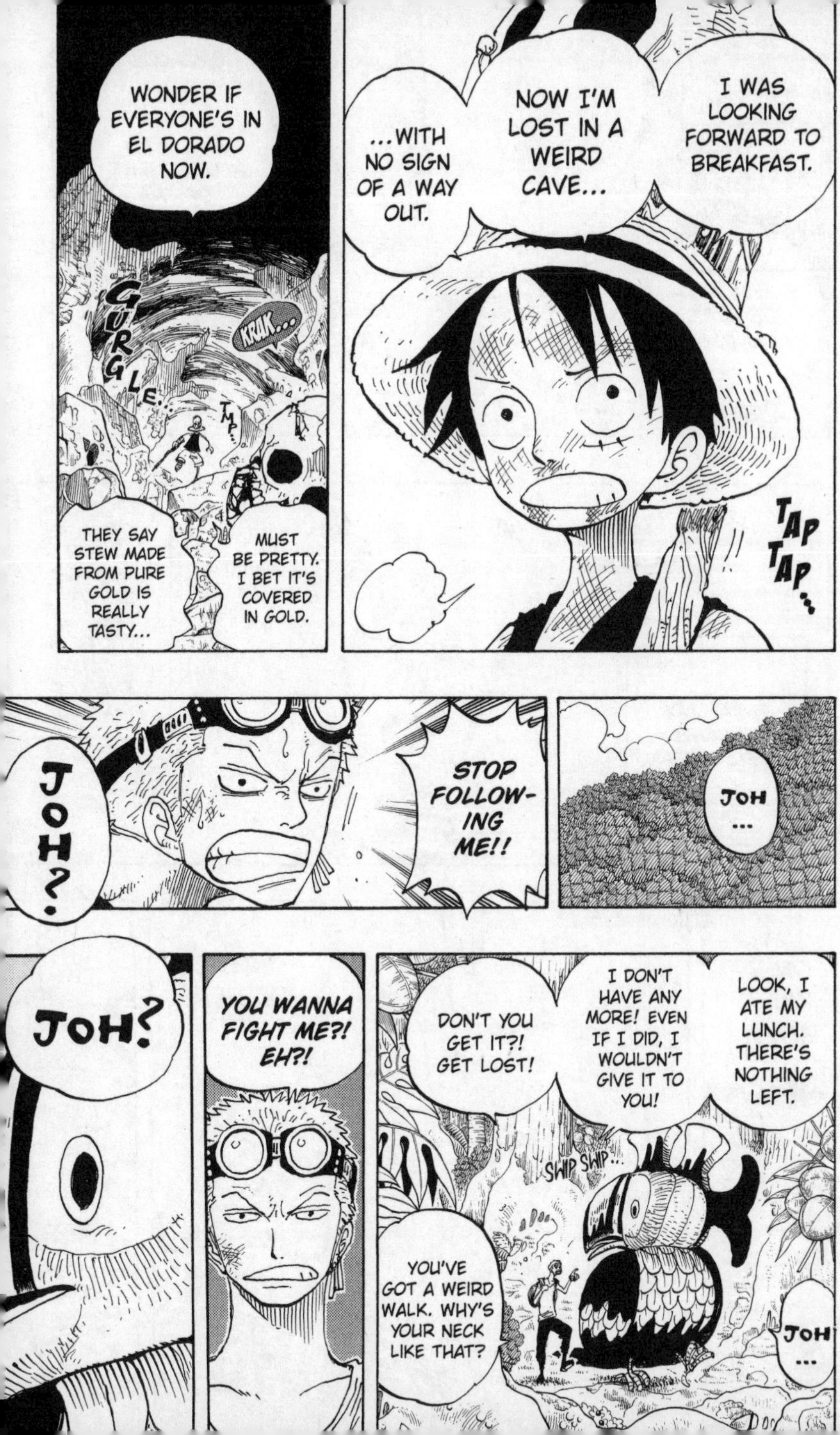
I WAS LOOKING FORWARD TO BREAKFAST.
NOW I'M LOST IN A WEIRD CAVE...
...WITH NO SIGN OF A WAY OUT.
TAP TAP...
WONDER IF EVERYONE'S IN EL DORADO NOW.
GURGLE...
KRAK...
TMP...
MUST BE PRETTY. I BET IT'S COVERED IN GOLD.
THEY SAY STEW MADE FROM PURE GOLD IS REALLY TASTY...
JOH...
STOP FOLLOWING ME!!
JOH?
LOOK, I ATE MY LUNCH. THERE'S NOTHING LEFT.
I DON'T HAVE ANY MORE! EVEN IF I DID, I WOULDN'T GIVE IT TO YOU!
DON'T YOU GET IT?! GET LOST!
SWIP SWIP...
JOH...
YOU'VE GOT A WEIRD WALK. WHY'S YOUR NECK LIKE THAT?
YOU WANNA FIGHT ME?! EH?!
JOH?

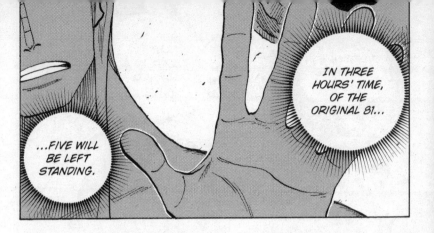

IN THREE HOURS' TIME, OF THE ORIGINAL 81...
...FIVE WILL BE LEFT STANDING.
ONLY AN HOUR REMAINS BEFORE THE TIME STATED IN KAMI ENERU'S PROPHECY.
SHF
SHF
THERE ARE CURRENTLY 25 SURVIVORS.
...
KAMI ENERU... THAT'S IMPOS-SIBLE!!
WHY'S HE HERE ?!
SHF
SHF
I'M GONNA KILL HIM!!

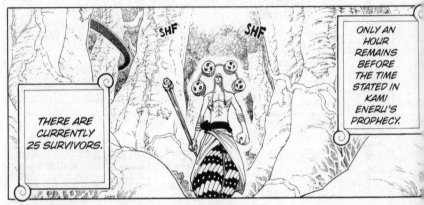

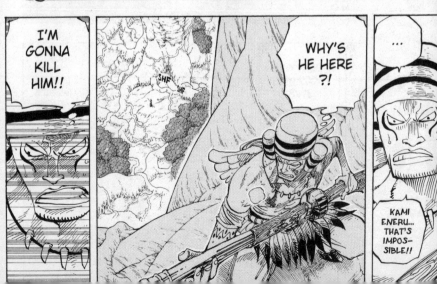

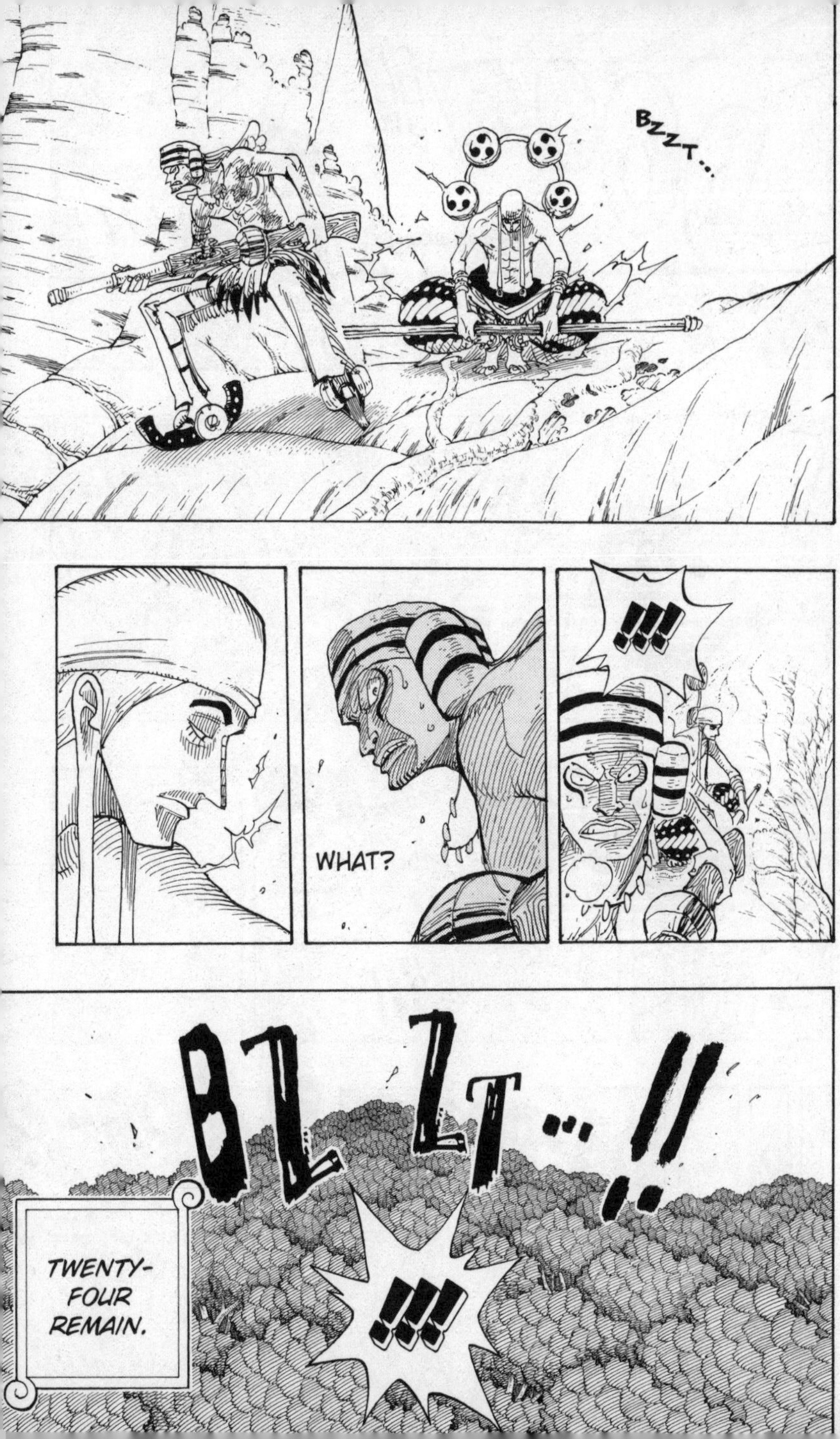
BZZZT...
!!!
WHAT?
TWENTY-FOUR REMAIN.
BZZT...!!
!!!

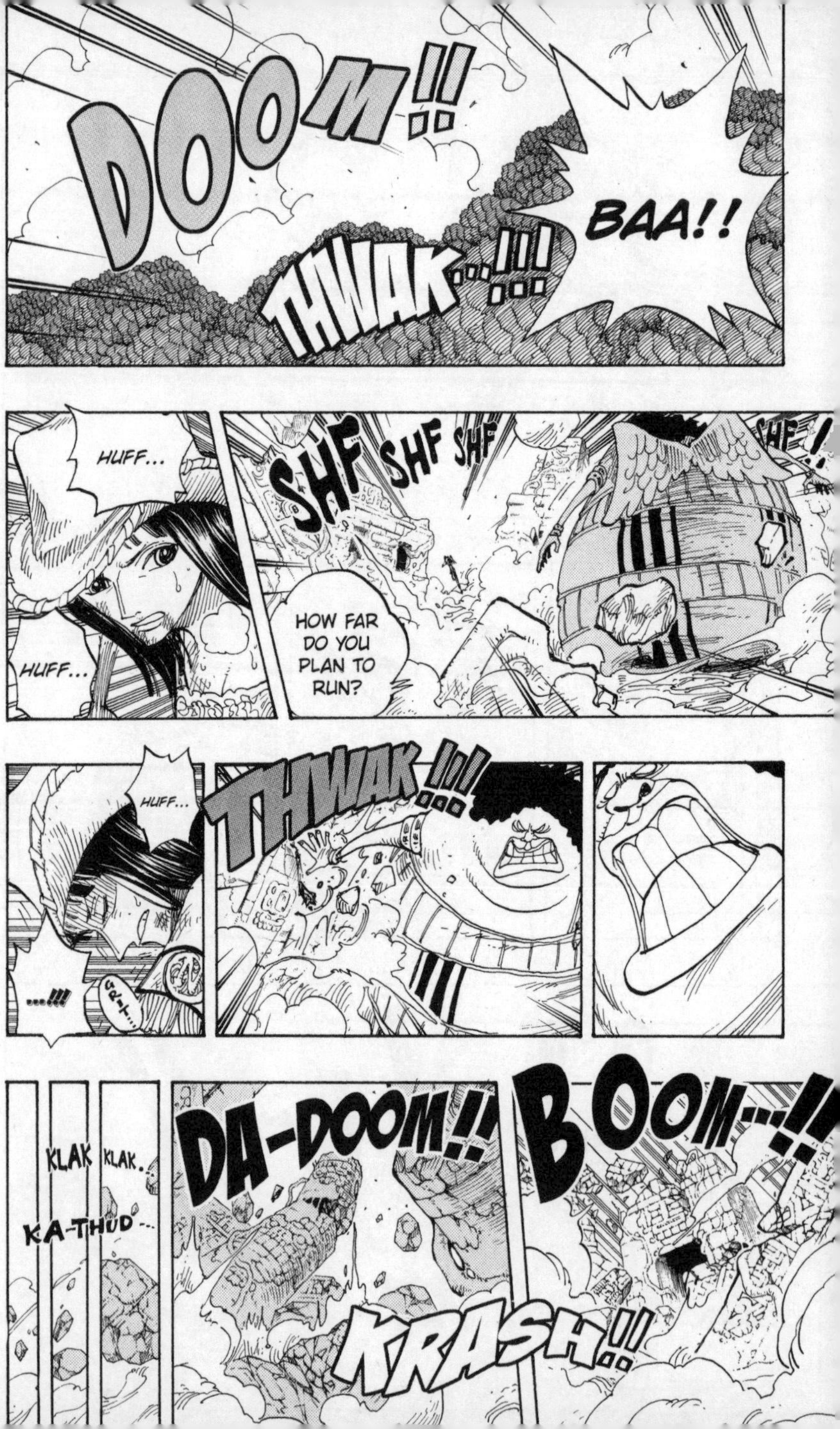
DOOM!!
BAA!!
THWAK...!!!
SHF SHF SHF SHF!
HOW FAR DO YOU PLAN TO RUN?
HUFF...
HUFF...
THWAK!!!
HUFF...
...!!!
GRIT...
BOOM--!!
KRASH!!
DA-DOOM!!
KLAK KLAK..
KA-THUD...

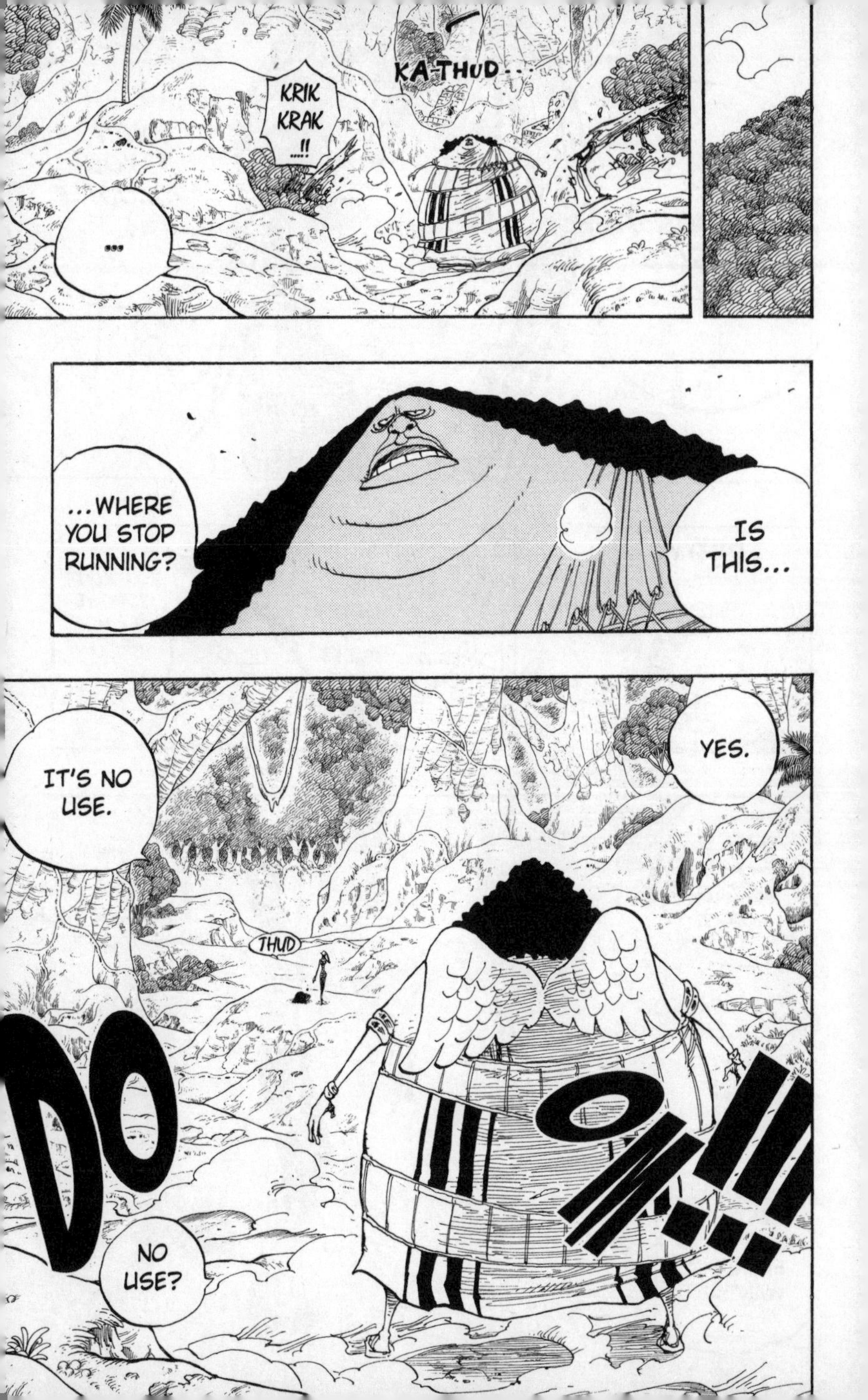

KA-THUD...
KRIK KRAK ...!!
...
IS THIS...
...WHERE YOU STOP RUNNING?
YES.
IT'S NO USE.
THUD
DOON!!
NO USE?

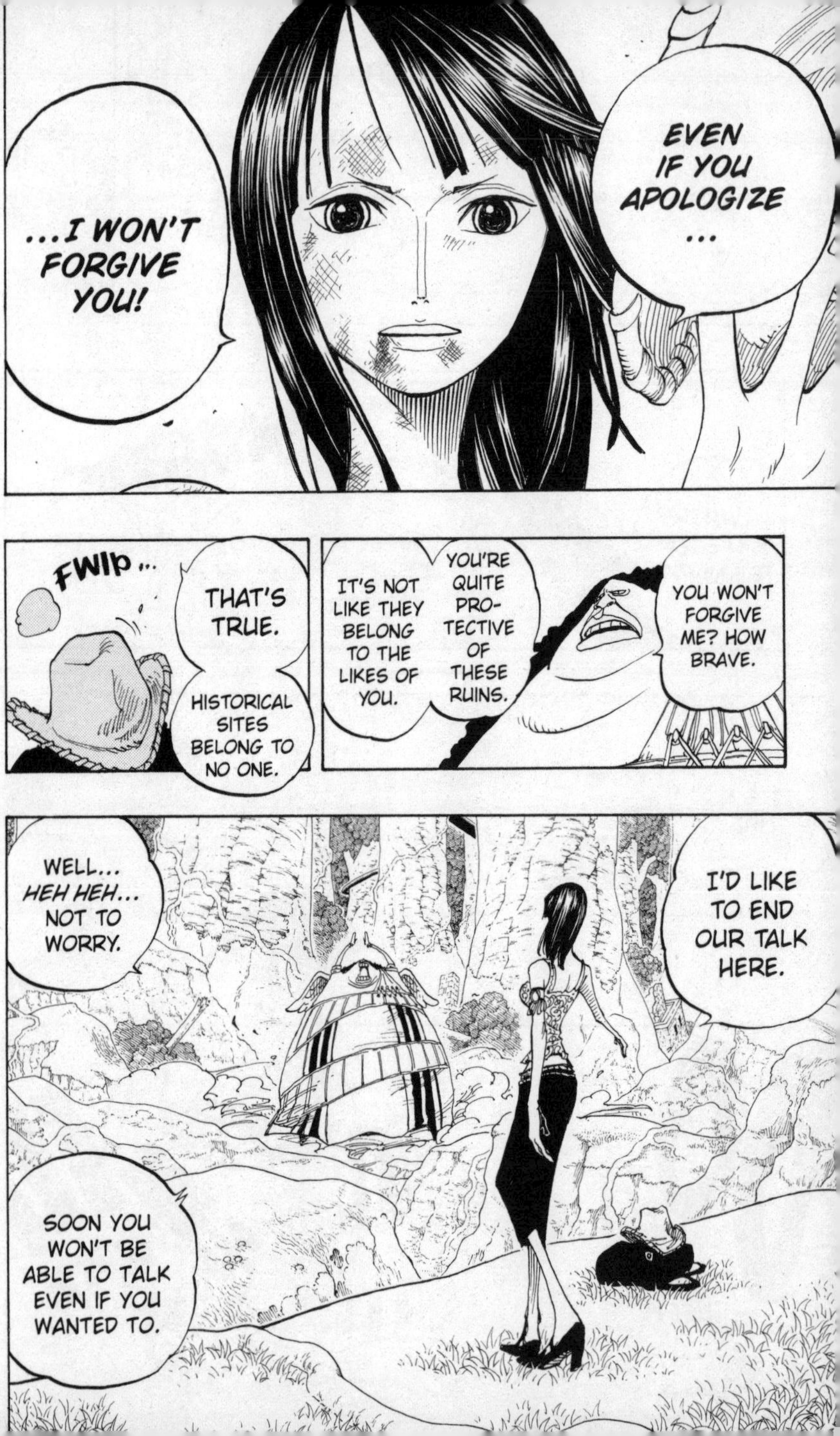
EVEN IF YOU APOLOGIZE ...
...I WON'T FORGIVE YOU!
YOU WON'T FORGIVE ME? HOW BRAVE.
YOU'RE QUITE PRO-TECTIVE OF THESE RUINS.
IT'S NOT LIKE THEY BELONG TO THE LIKES OF YOU.
FWIP...
THAT'S TRUE.
HISTORICAL SITES BELONG TO NO ONE.
I'D LIKE TO END OUR TALK HERE.
WELL... HEH HEH... NOT TO WORRY.
SOON YOU WON'T BE ABLE TO TALK EVEN IF YOU WANTED TO.

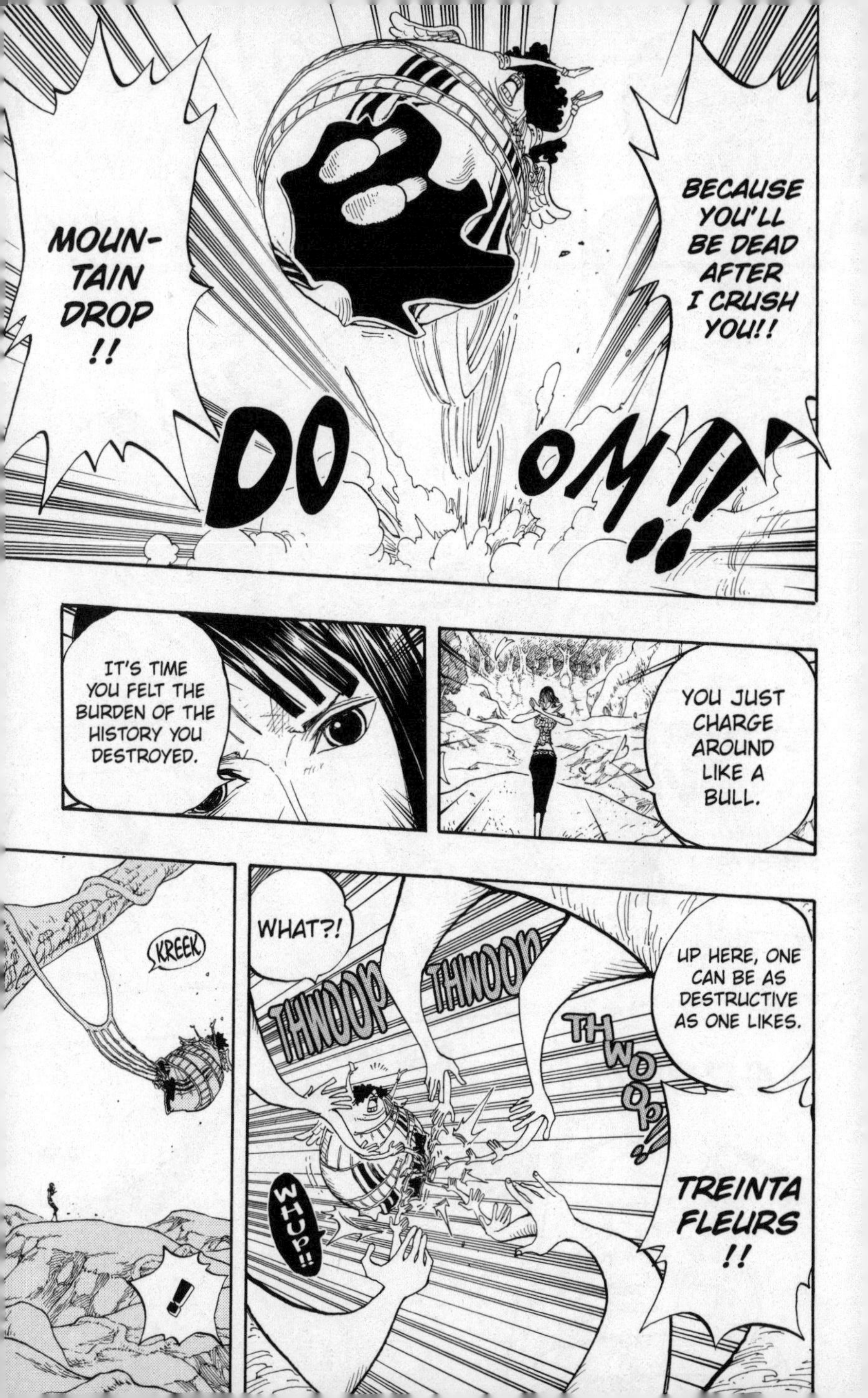
BECAUSE YOU'LL BE DEAD AFTER I CRUSH YOU!!
MOUN-TAIN DROP!!
DOOM!!
YOU JUST CHARGE AROUND LIKE A BULL.
IT'S TIME YOU FELT THE BURDEN OF THE HISTORY YOU DESTROYED.
UP HERE, ONE CAN BE AS DESTRUCTIVE AS ONE LIKES.
TREINTA FLEURS!!
THWOOP!!
THWOOP
THWOOP
WHAT?!
WHUP!!
KREEK
!

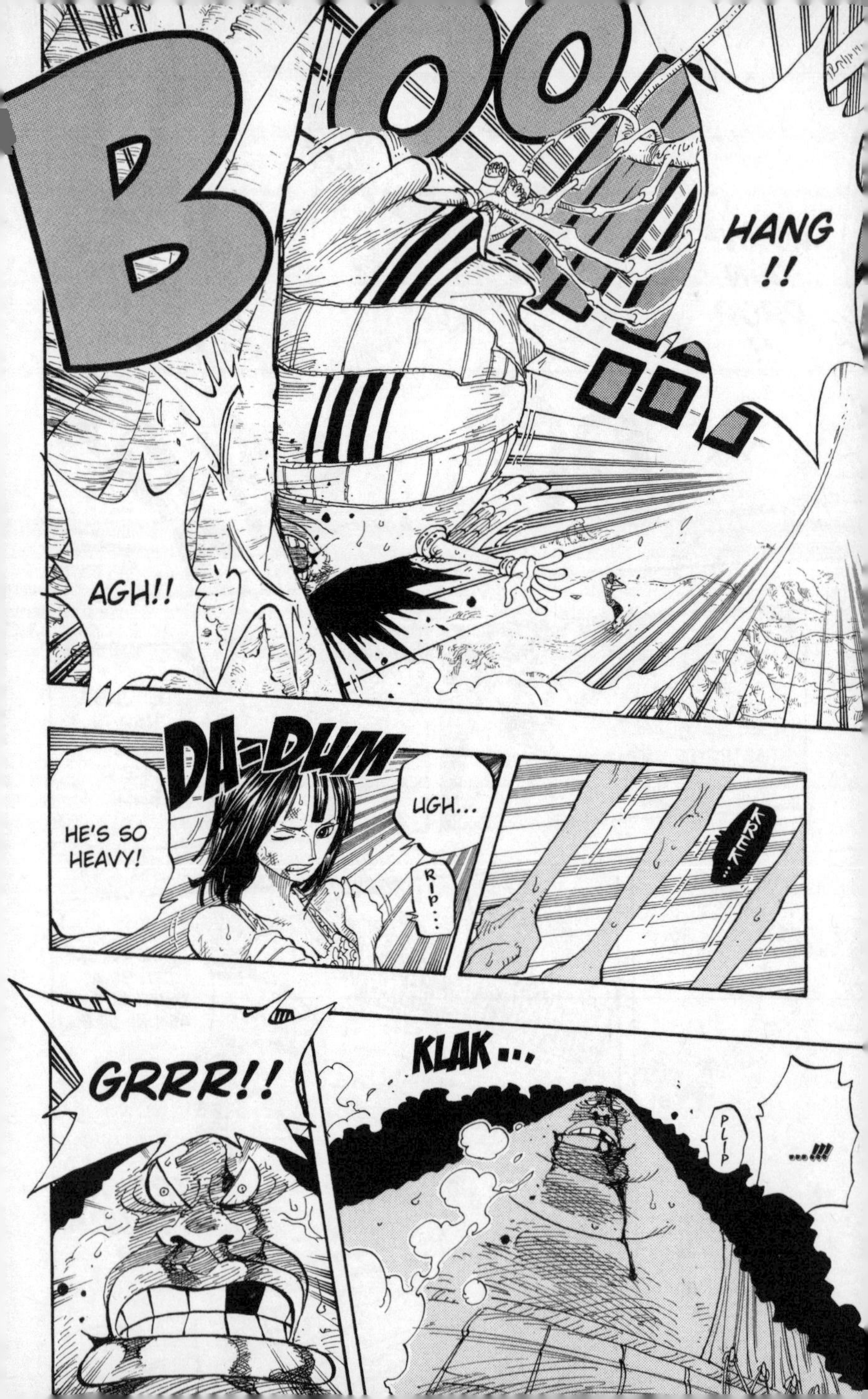
HANG !!
AGH!!
KREK...
UGH...
DA-DUM
RIP...
HE'S SO HEAVY!
...!!!
PLIP
KLAK...
GRRR!!

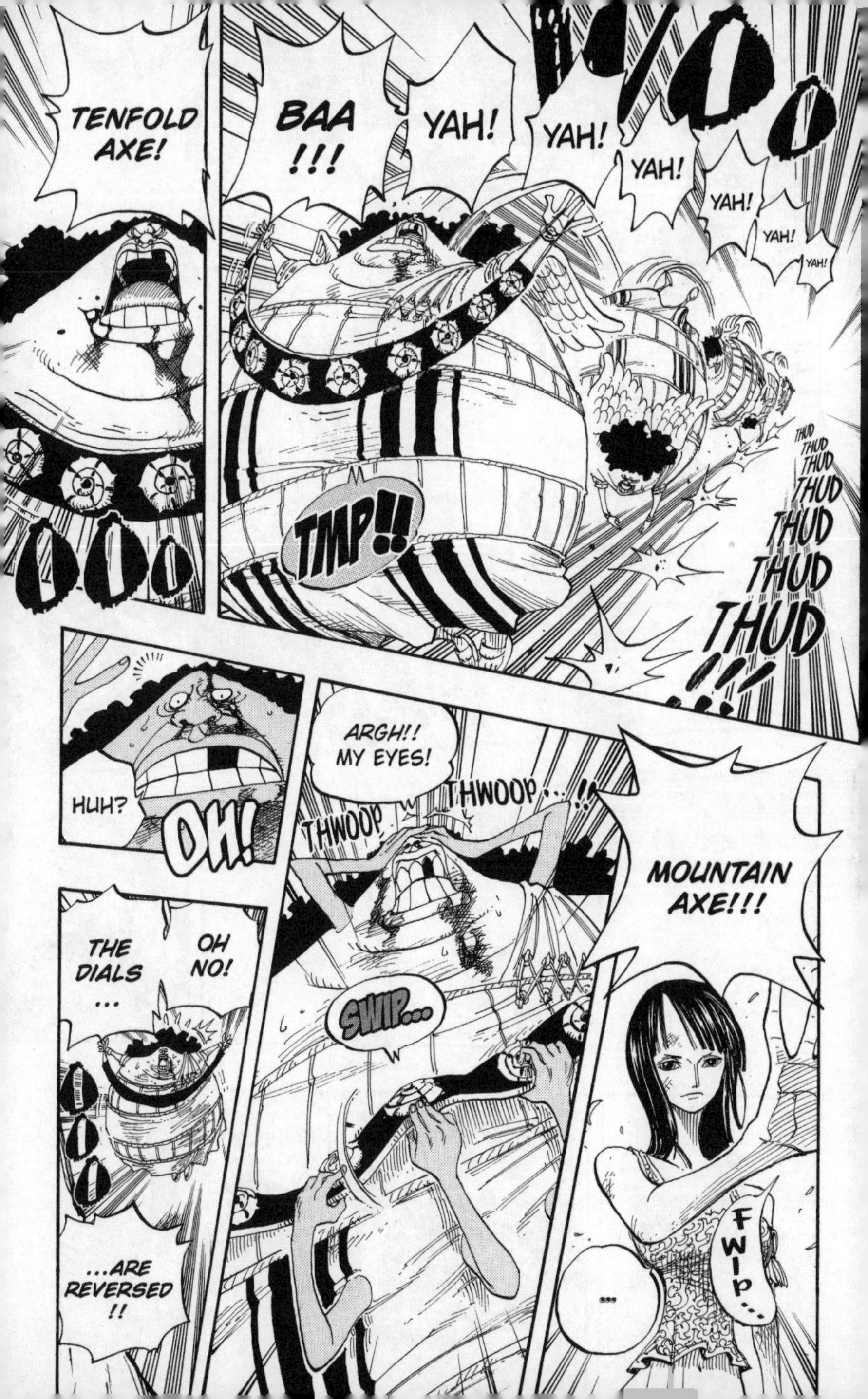
BAA!!!
YAH!
YAH!
YAH!
YAH!
YAH!
YAH!
TMP!!
THUD THUD THUD THUD THUD THUD THUD!!!
TENFOLD AXE!
MOUNTAIN AXE!!!
FWIP...
...
ARGH!! MY EYES!
THWOOP...!!
THWOOP
SWIP...
HUH?
OH!
OH NO!
THE DIALS...
...ARE REVERSED!!

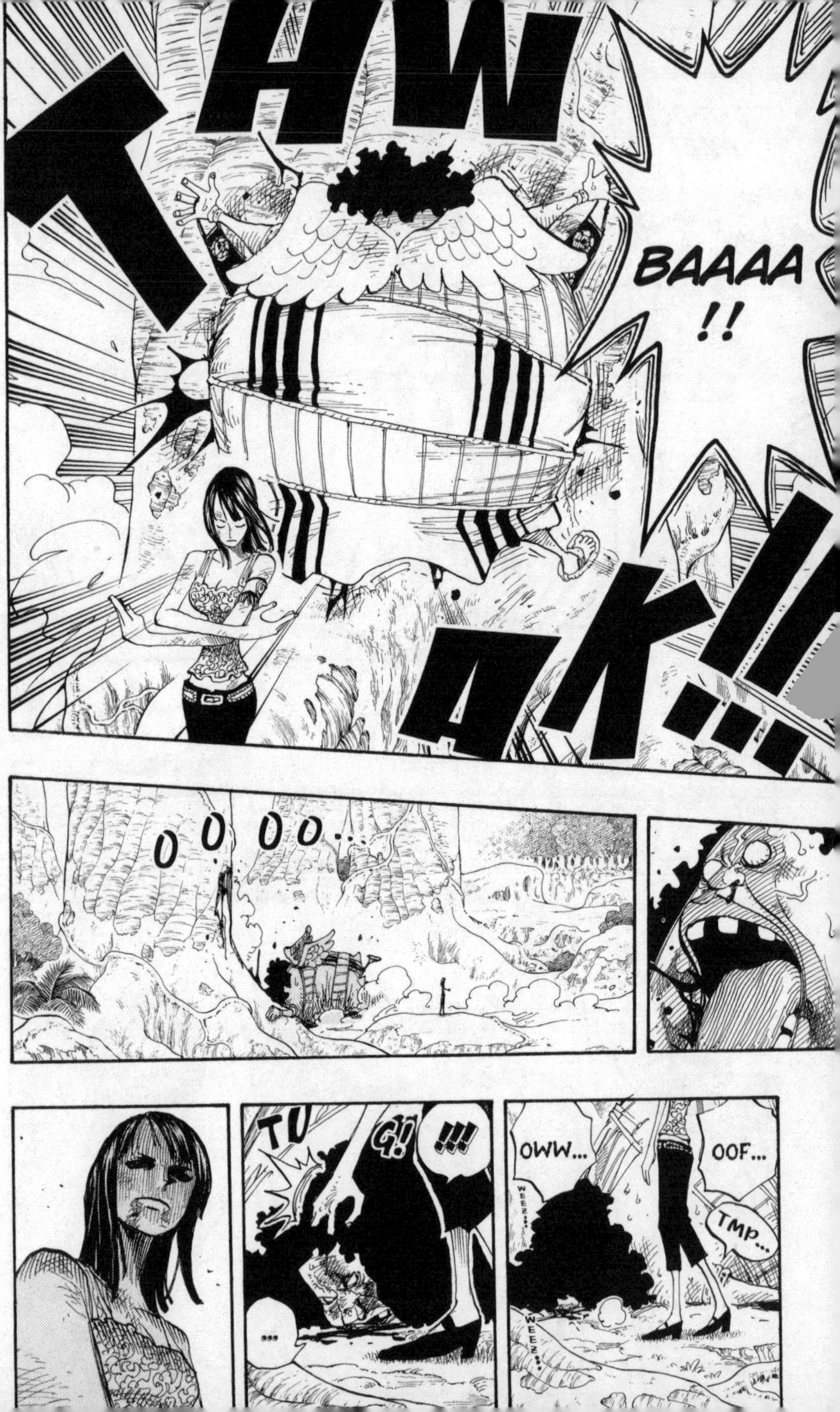
THW
BAAAA !!
ACK!!
OOOO...
OOF...
TMP...
OWW...
WEEZ...
WEEZ...
TU
G!
!!!
...

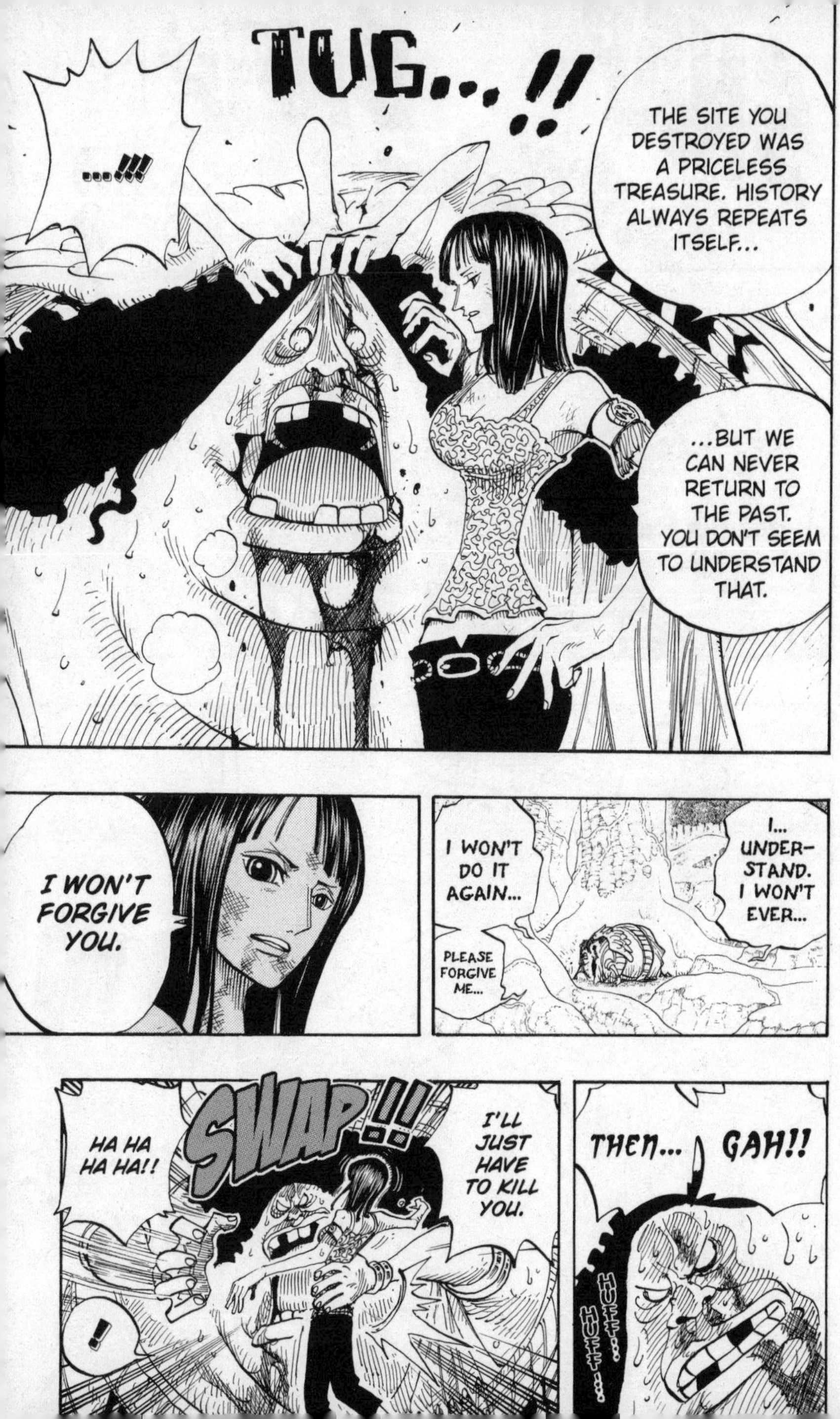
TUG...!!
THE SITE YOU DESTROYED WAS A PRICELESS TREASURE. HISTORY ALWAYS REPEATS ITSELF...
...!!!
...BUT WE CAN NEVER RETURN TO THE PAST. YOU DON'T SEEM TO UNDERSTAND THAT.
I... UNDER-STAND. I WON'T EVER...
I WON'T DO IT AGAIN...
PLEASE FORGIVE ME...
I WON'T FORGIVE YOU.
THEN... GAH!!
HUFF... HUFF...
SWAP!!
I'LL JUST HAVE TO KILL YOU.
HA HA HA HA!!
!

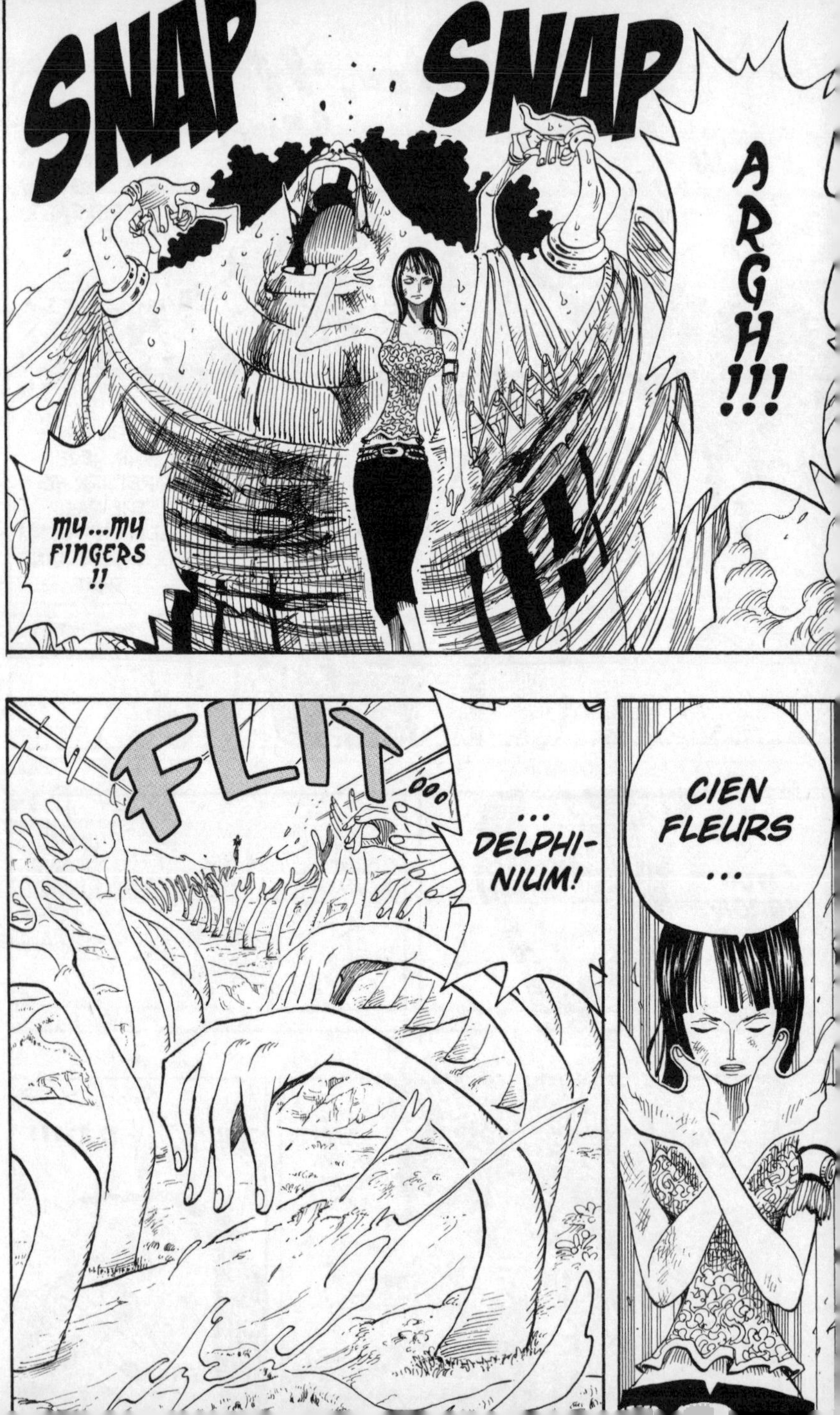
SNAP
SNAP
ARGH!!!
MY...MY FINGERS !!
CIEN FLEURS ...
FLIT
... DELPHI-NIUM!

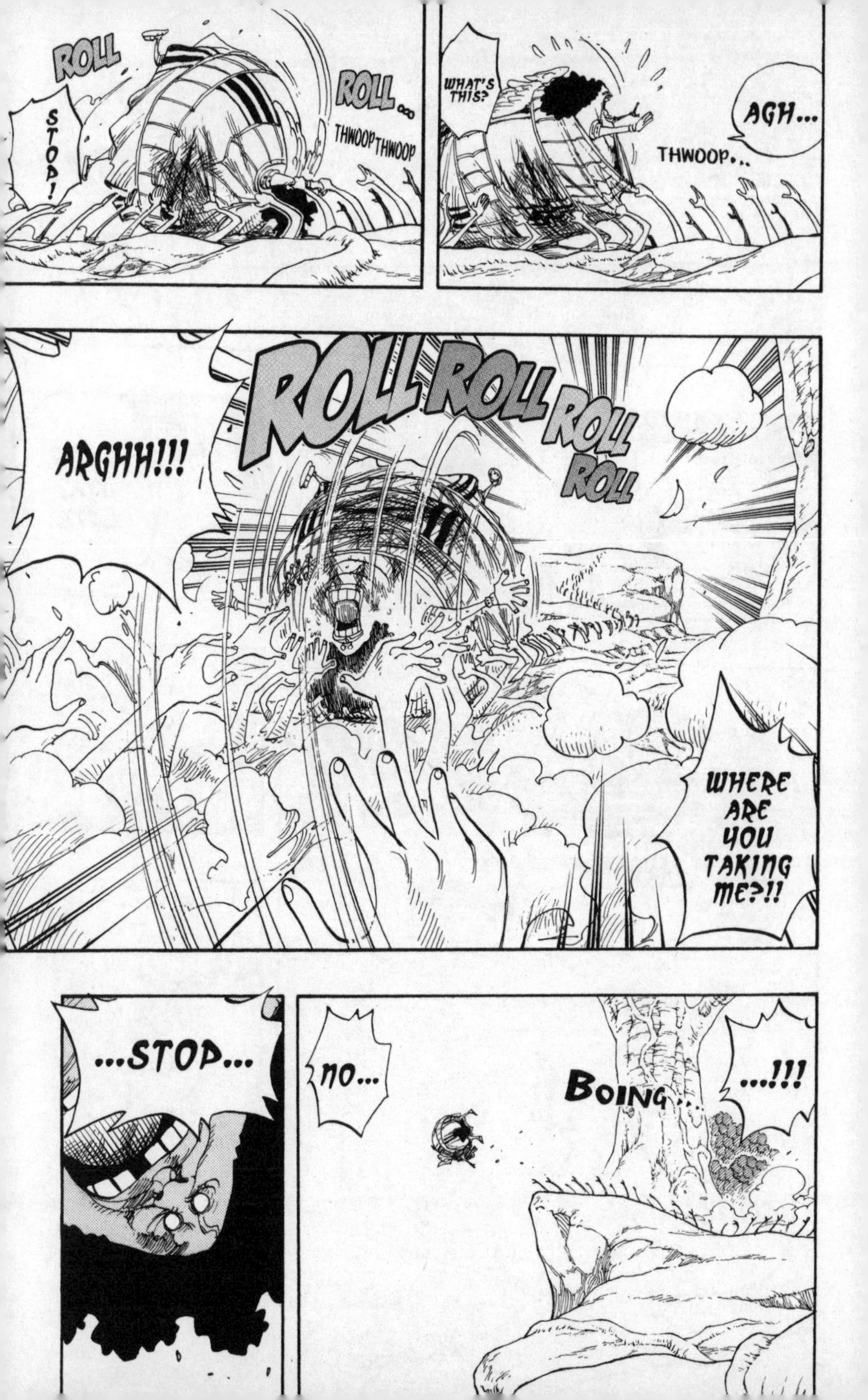
AGH...
WHAT'S THIS?
THWOOP...
ROLL...
THWOOP THWOOP
ROLL
STOP!
WHERE ARE YOU TAKING ME?!!
ROLL ROLL ROLL ROLL
ARGHH!!!
...!!!
BOING...
no...
...STOP...

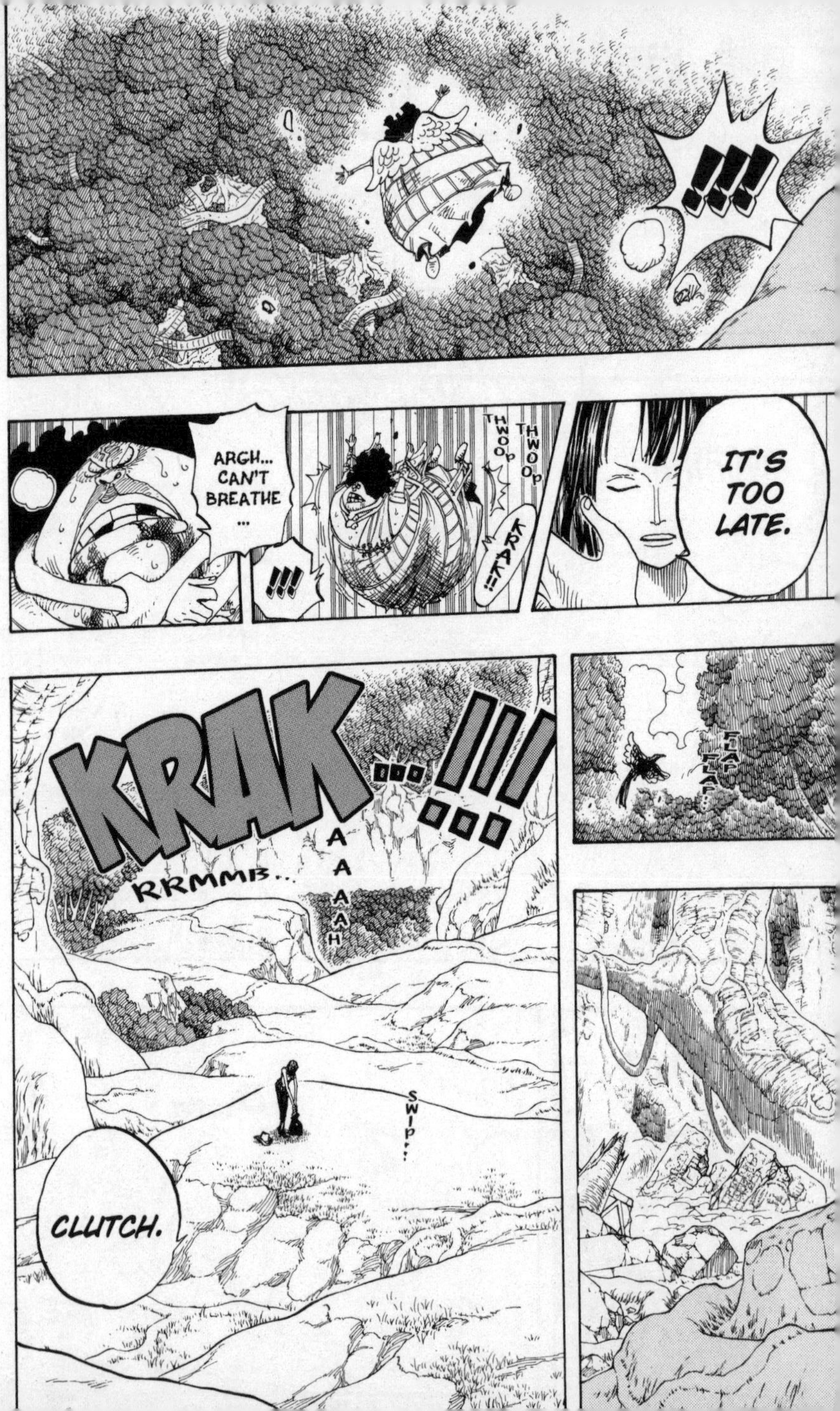
!!!
IT'S TOO LATE.
THWOOP THWOOP
KRAK!!
!!!
ARGH... CAN'T BREATHE ...
FLAP FLAP...
KRAK...!!!...!
RRMMB...
AAAAAH
SWIP..
CLUTCH.

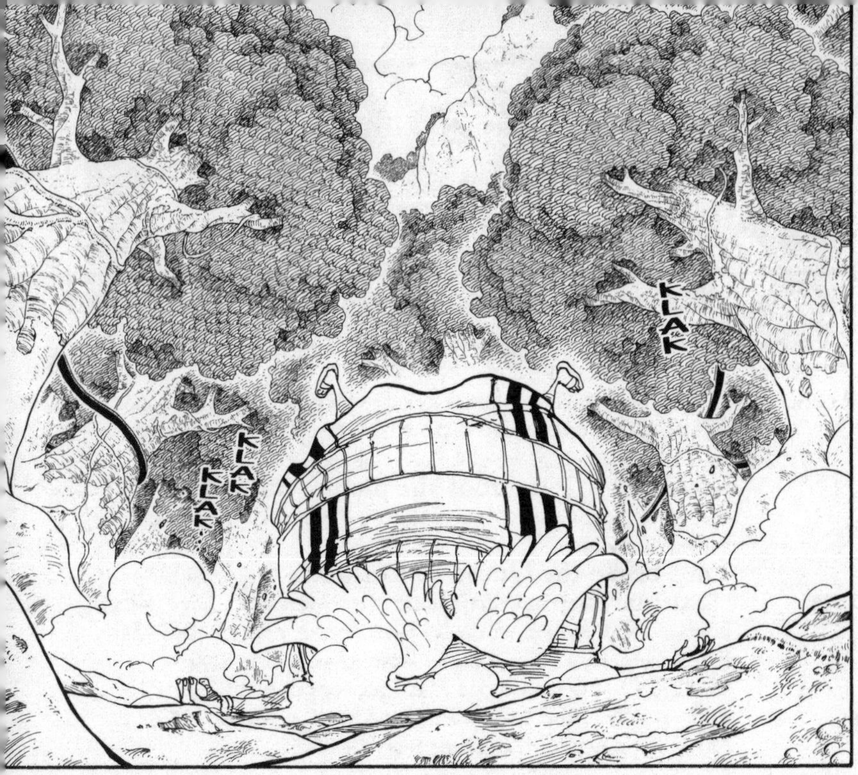
KLAK
KLAK
KLAK...

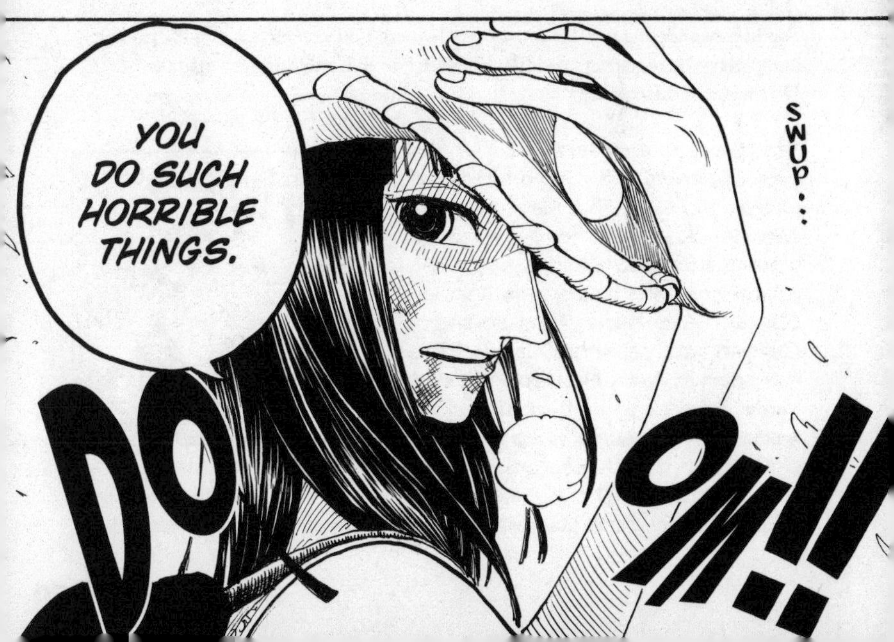
SWUP...
YOU DO SUCH HORRIBLE THINGS.
DOOM!!

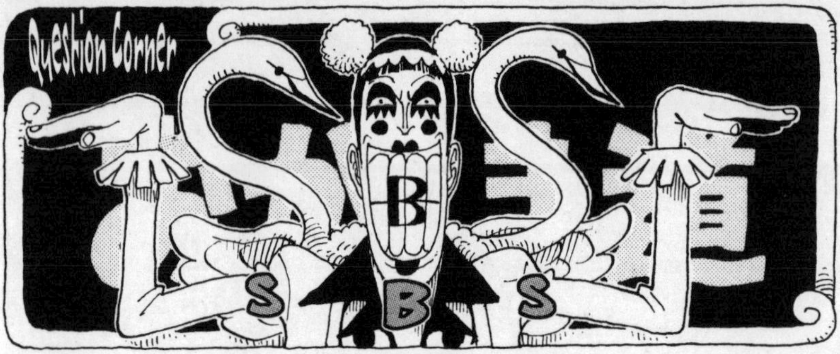
Question Corner
B
S
B
S

KANJI BEHIND MR. 2 BON CLAY: OH COME MY WAY

Reader: At Jump Festa 2003, when someone asked "Why is Zolo so awesome?" you answered, **"Because he's just like me,"** putting the Japanese voice actor for Zolo, Kazuya Nakai, on the spot.

You need to get out of the picture immediately.

Okay, now that Eiichiro Oda is gone, we can begin the Question Corner without further ado.

Let's begin the Question Corner!!

Oda: I had totally forgotten about that moment. Jump Festa is an annual event in Japan held at the end of the year. It's huge and lots of fun. I hear that more than 100,000 people attend the two-day event. There's even a remarkable One Piece musical. It's amazing. Now, let's begin the Question Corner.

Q: Hello, Oda Sensei!
I've been wondering this for some time: Is there a difference between the captains in the Navy Headquarters and the Auxiliary Navy? Is one stronger than the other? Do they train differently?

--The Big Brother in the Room

A: Yes, there is a difference. The Navy Headquarters are a super elite group within the Navy. The Navy representatives who appear in the plaza in → volume 11 are lieutenants, sub-lieutenants and ensigns. If former Captain "Axe-Hand" Morgan and Captain Nezumi from Nami's village had been at Navy Headquarters, they might have been in that battle. A good rule of thumb is to keep in mind that there is a three-rank difference between the Navy Headquarters and the Auxiliary. Captains in the Auxiliary would be lieutenants, and sub-captains would be sub-lieutenants, etc.

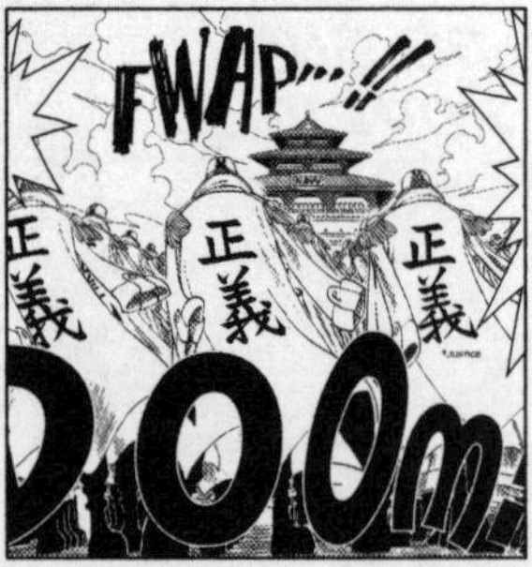
FWAP...!!
正義
正義
正義

Chapter 266:
PIRATE CHOPPER VS. VASSAL OHM

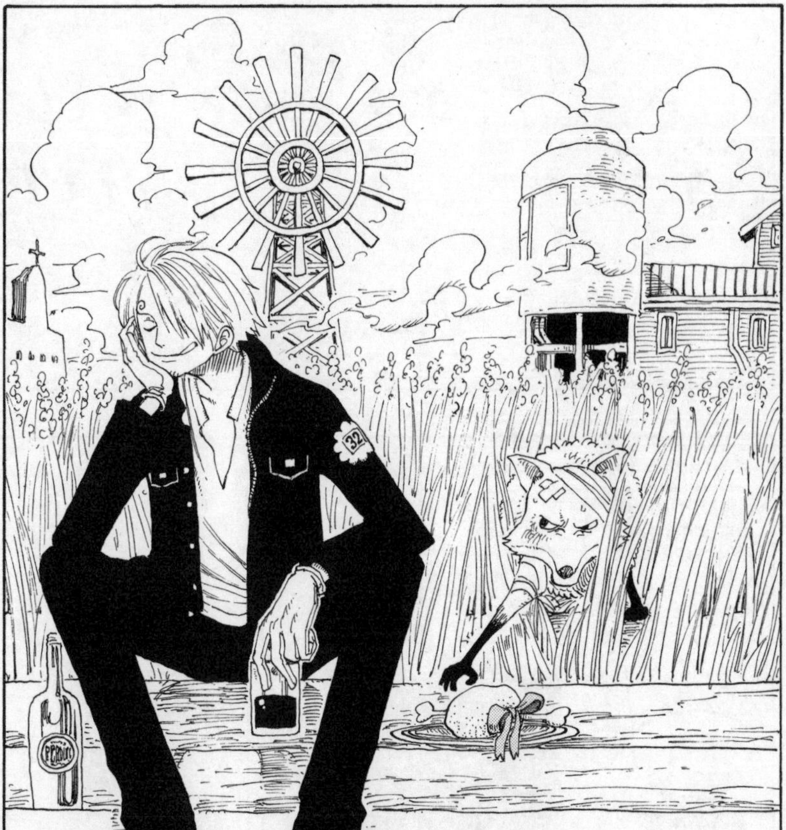

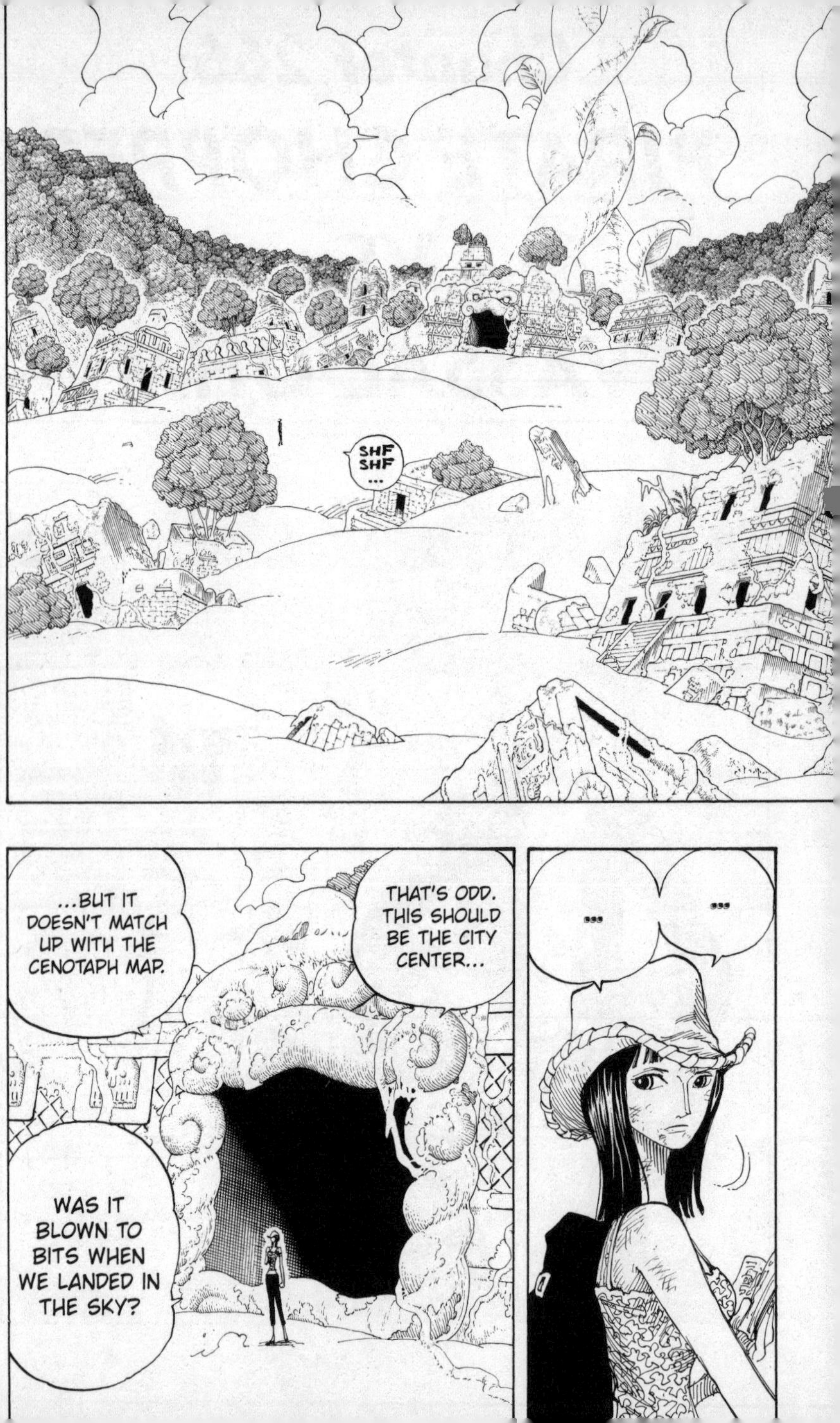
SHF SHF ...
...
...
THAT'S ODD. THIS SHOULD BE THE CITY CENTER...
...BUT IT DOESN'T MATCH UP WITH THE CENOTAPH MAP.
WAS IT BLOWN TO BITS WHEN WE LANDED IN THE SKY?

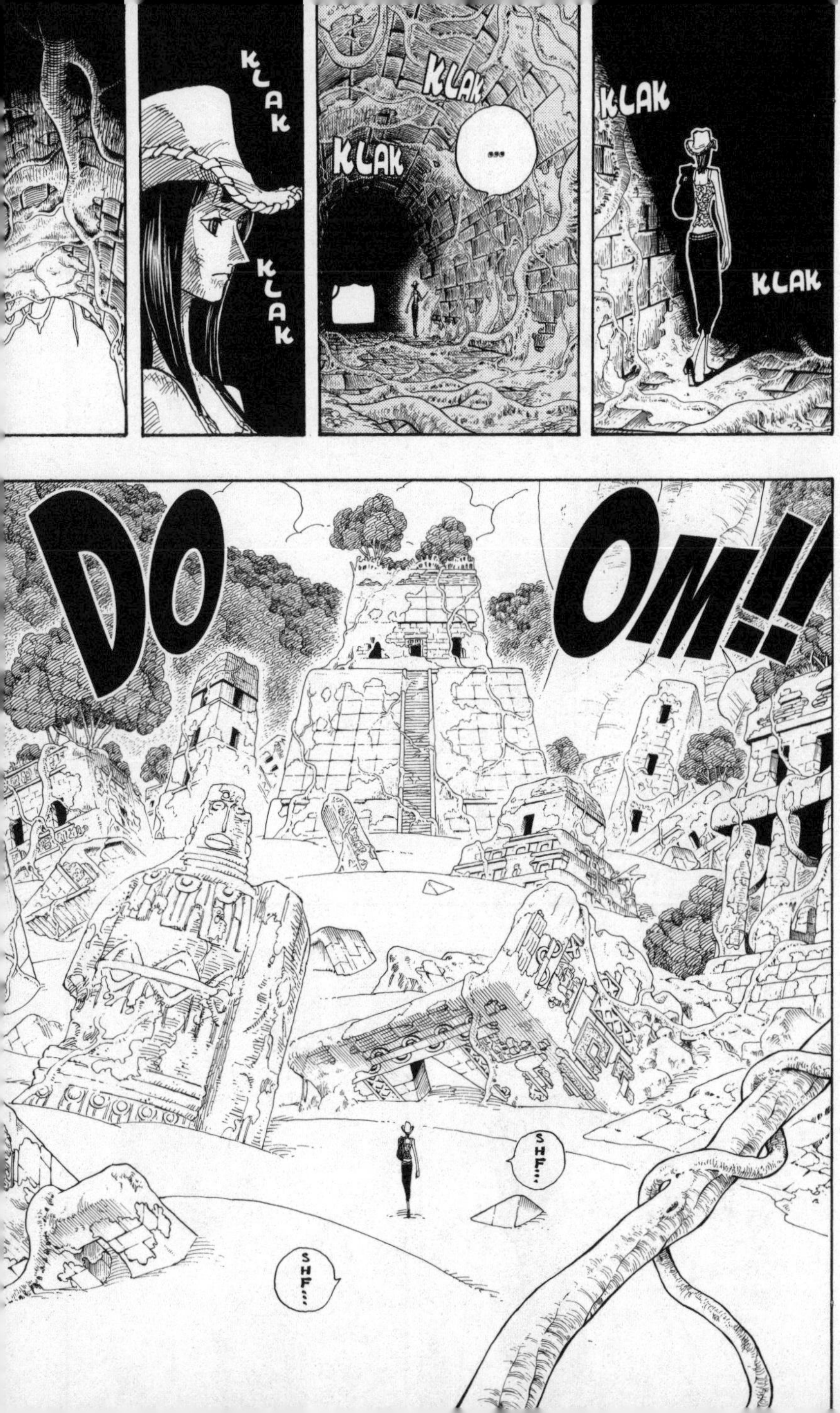
KLAK
KLAK
KLAK
KLAK
...
KLAK
KLAK
DOOM!!
SHF...
SHF...

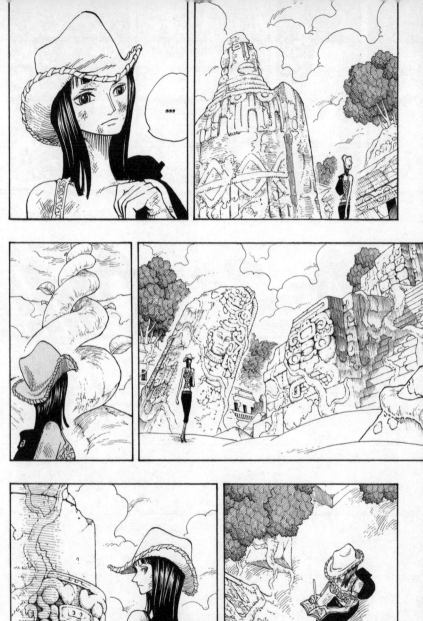

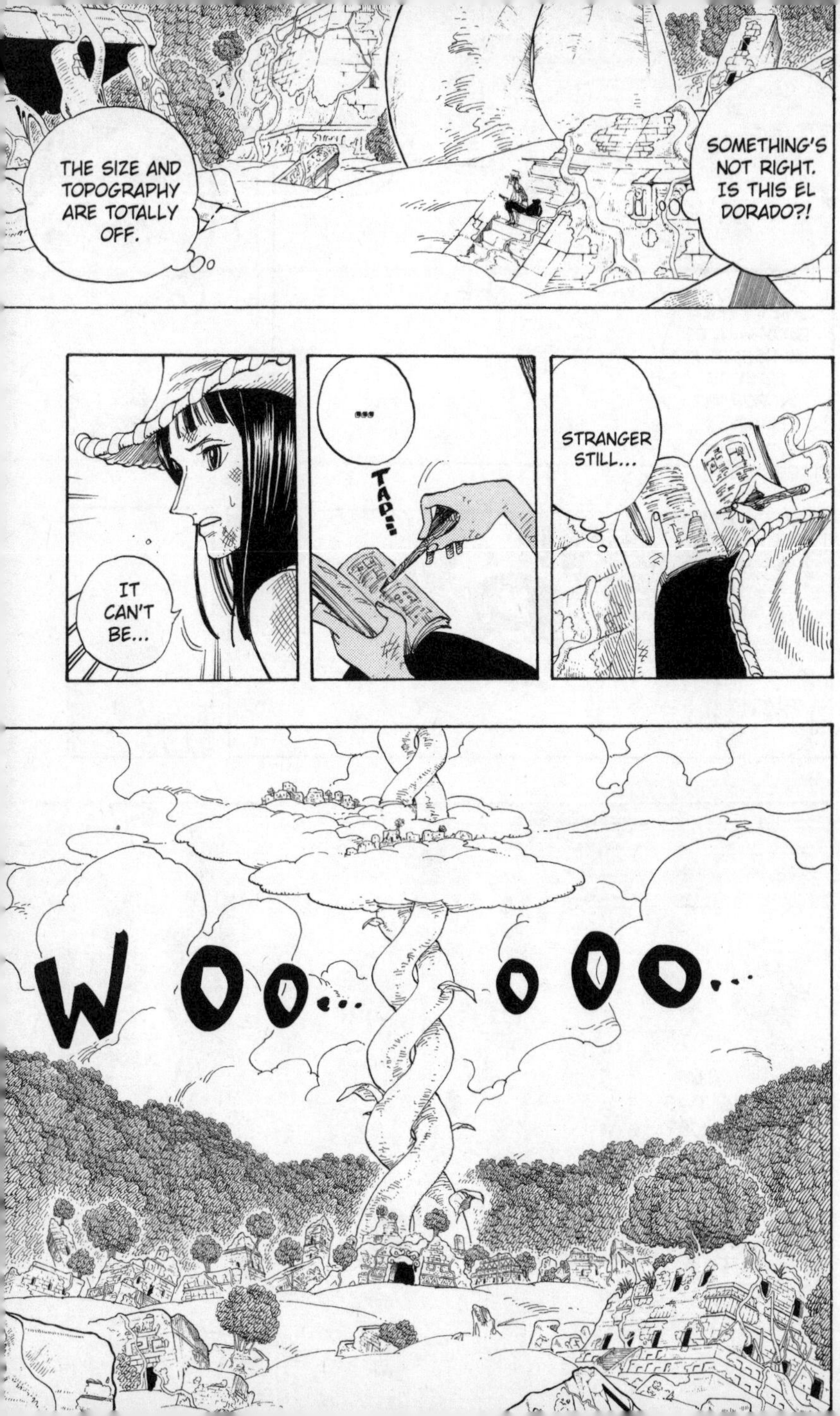
SOMETHING'S NOT RIGHT. IS THIS EL DORADO?!
THE SIZE AND TOPOGRAPHY ARE TOTALLY OFF.
STRANGER STILL...
...
TAP!!
IT CAN'T BE...
WOO... OOO...

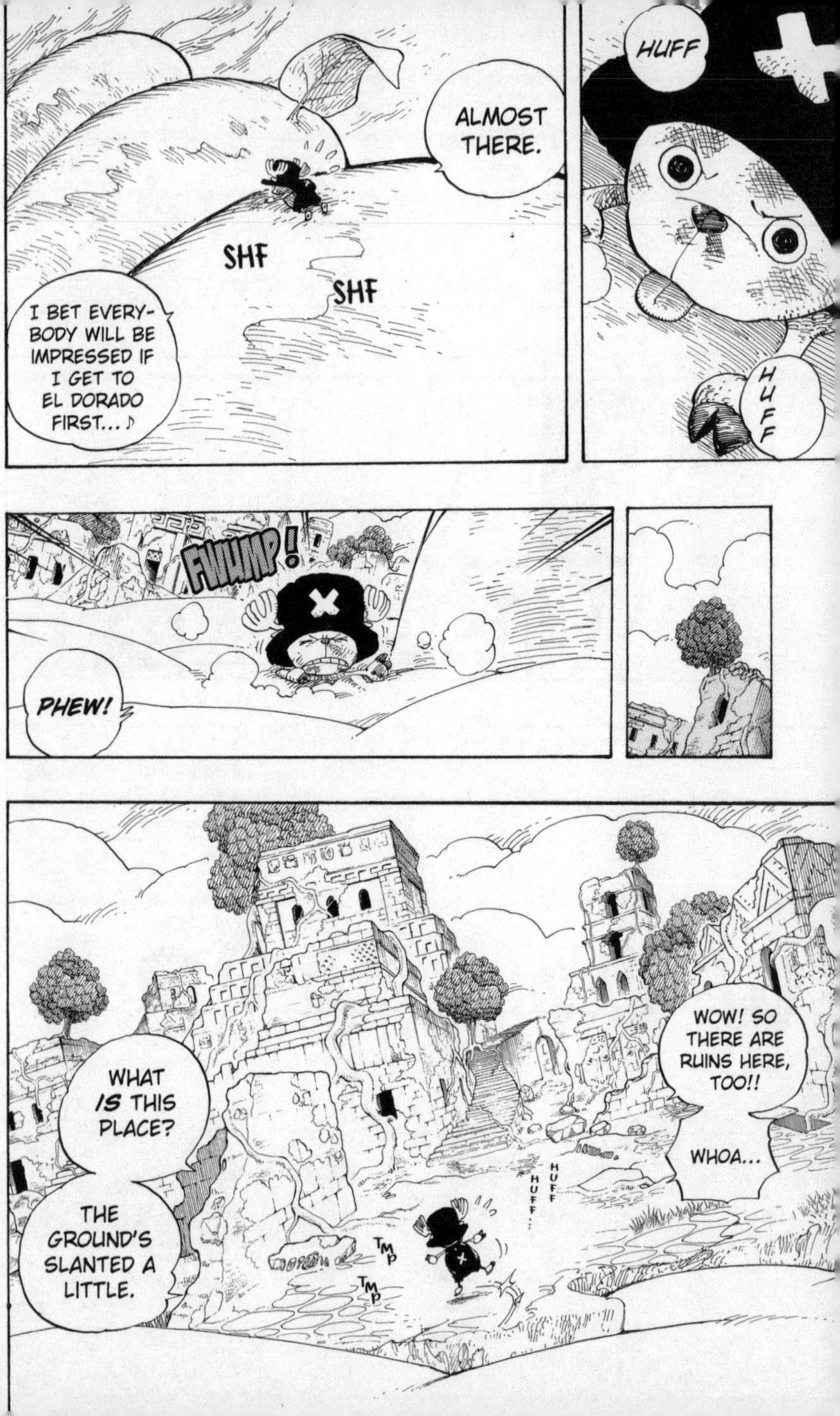
HUFF
HUFF
ALMOST THERE.
SHF
SHF
I BET EVERYBODY WILL BE IMPRESSED IF I GET TO EL DORADO FIRST...♪
FWUMP!
PHEW!
WOW! SO THERE ARE RUINS HERE, TOO!!
WHOA...
HUFF HUFF...
WHAT IS THIS PLACE?
TMP
TMP
THE GROUND'S SLANTED A LITTLE.

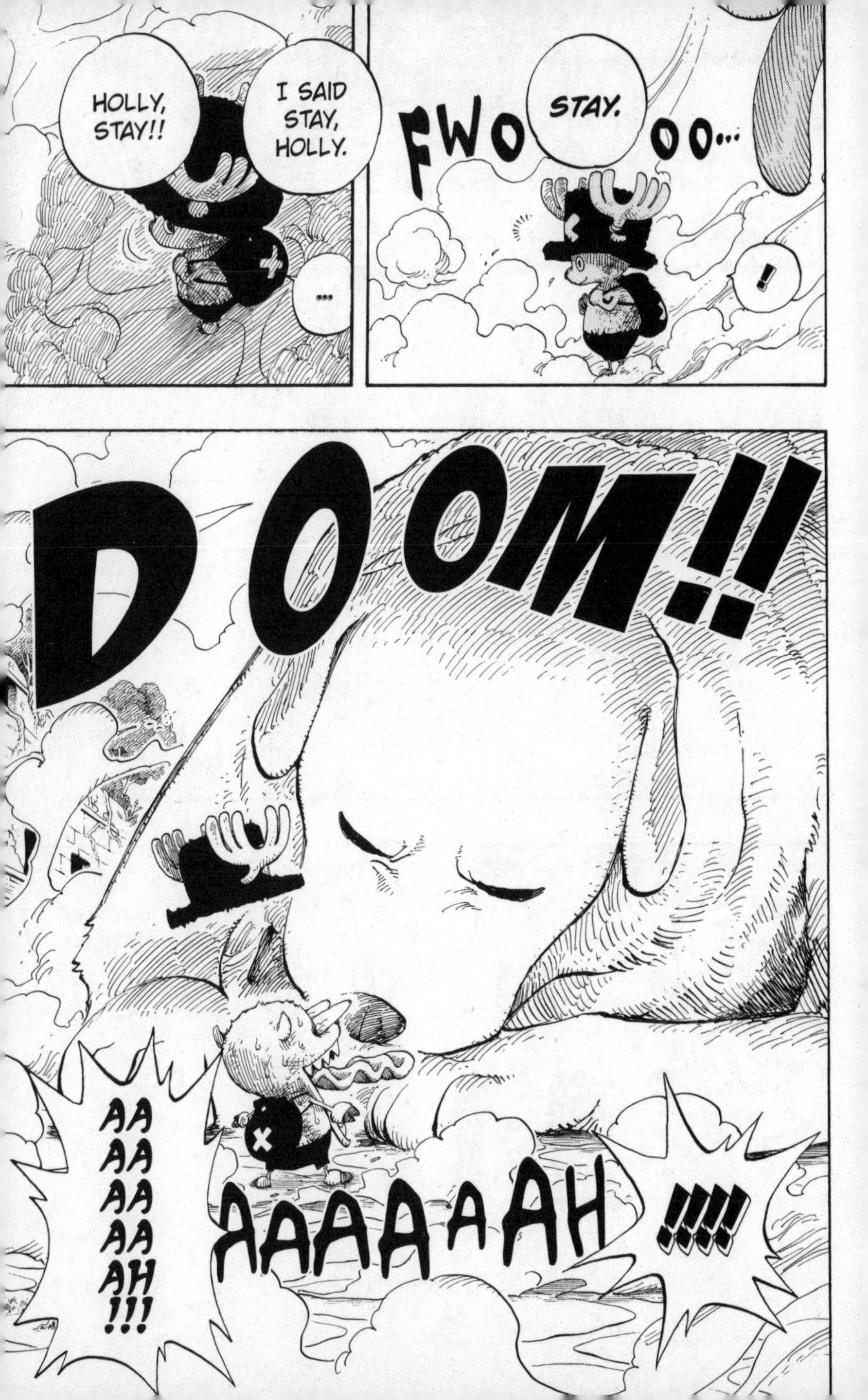

STAY.
FWOOOO...
!
I SAID STAY, HOLLY.
HOLLY, STAY!!
...
DOOM!!
AAAAAAH!!!!
AAAAAAAAAAH!!!

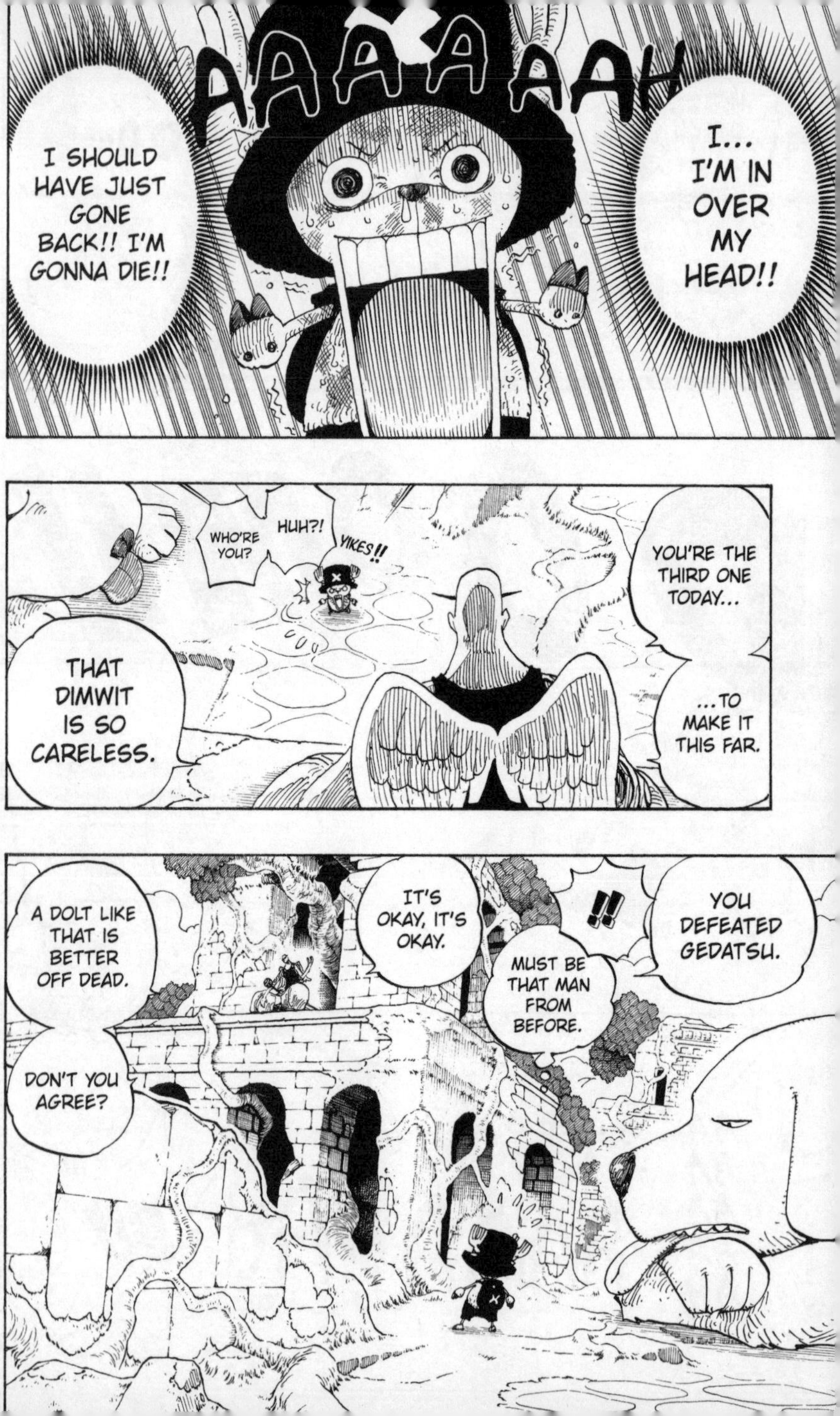
AAAAAH
I... I'M IN OVER MY HEAD!!
I SHOULD HAVE JUST GONE BACK!! I'M GONNA DIE!!
YOU'RE THE THIRD ONE TODAY...
...TO MAKE IT THIS FAR.
YIKES!!
HUH?!
WHO'RE YOU?
THAT DIMWIT IS SO CARELESS.
YOU DEFEATED GEDATSU.
!!
MUST BE THAT MAN FROM BEFORE.
IT'S OKAY, IT'S OKAY.
A DOLT LIKE THAT IS BETTER OFF DEAD.
DON'T YOU AGREE?

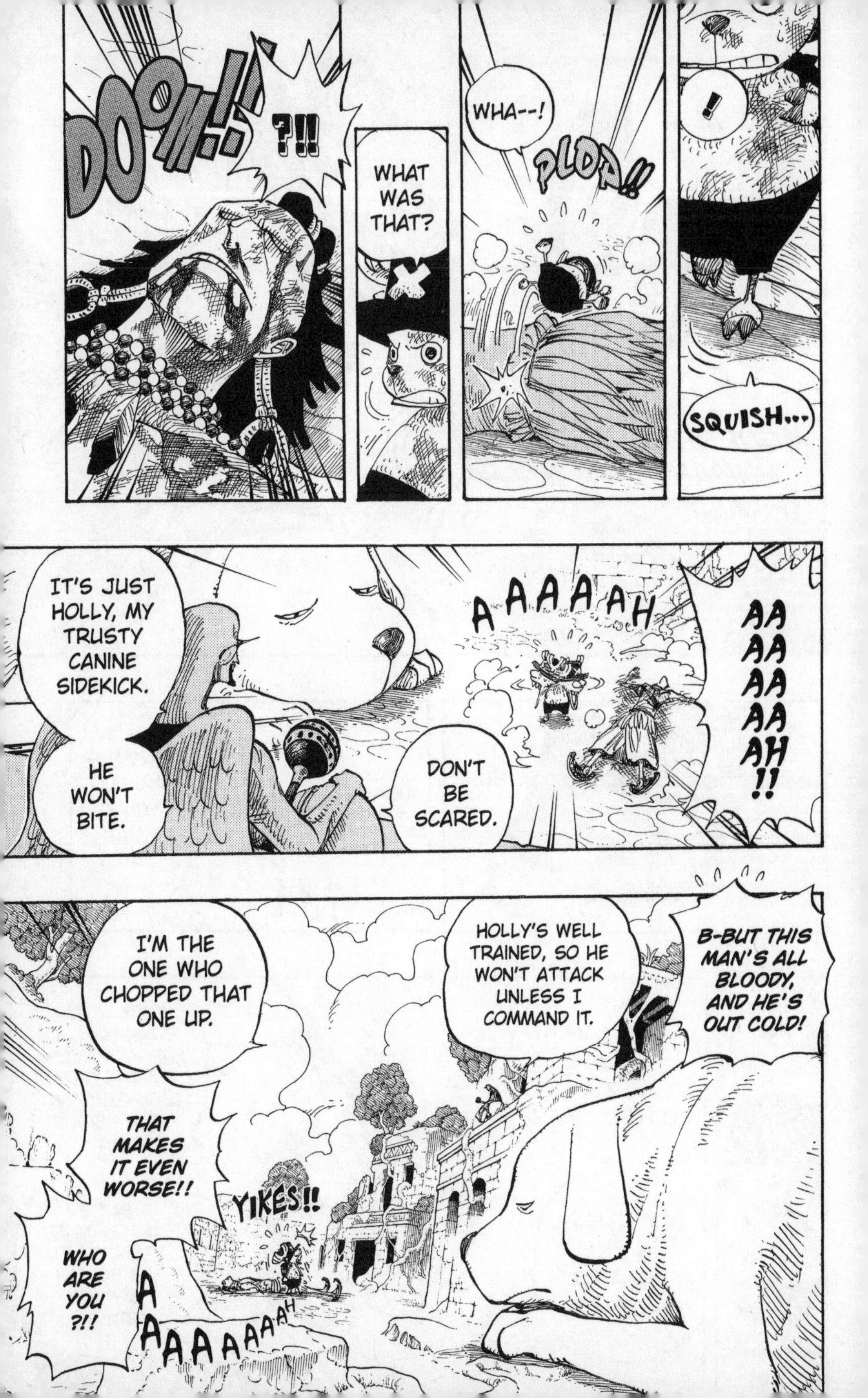
!
SQUISH...
WHA--!
PLOP!!
WHAT WAS THAT?
DOOM!!
?!!
AAAAAAAAAH!!
AAAAAH
IT'S JUST HOLLY, MY TRUSTY CANINE SIDEKICK.
DON'T BE SCARED.
HE WON'T BITE.
B-BUT THIS MAN'S ALL BLOODY, AND HE'S OUT COLD!
HOLLY'S WELL TRAINED, SO HE WON'T ATTACK UNLESS I COMMAND IT.
I'M THE ONE WHO CHOPPED THAT ONE UP.
THAT MAKES IT EVEN WORSE!!
YIKES!!
WHO ARE YOU?!!
AAAAAAAAAH

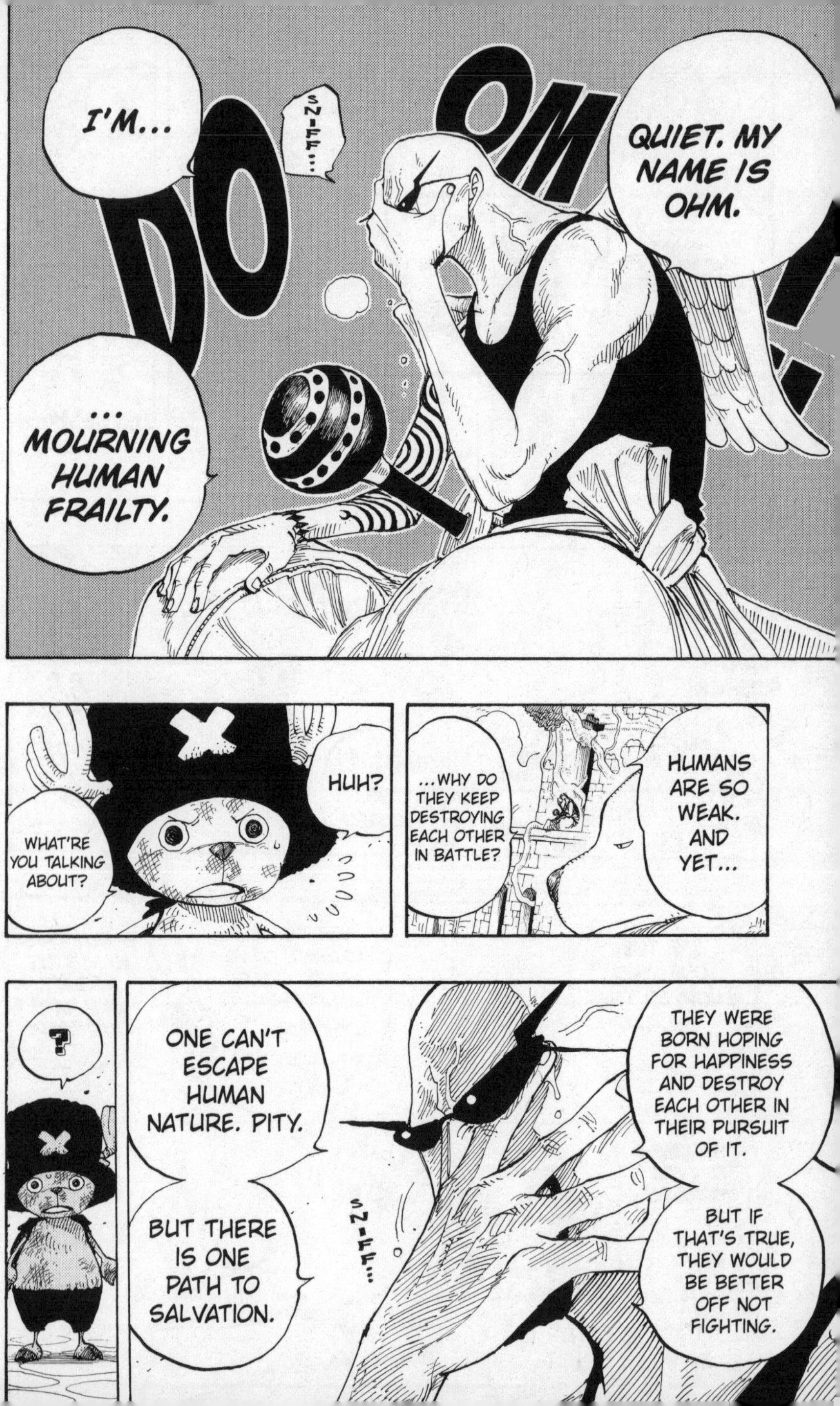
QUIET. MY NAME IS OHM.
DOOM!!
SNIFF...
I'M...
...MOURNING HUMAN FRAILTY.
HUMANS ARE SO WEAK. AND YET...
...WHY DO THEY KEEP DESTROYING EACH OTHER IN BATTLE?
HUH?
WHAT'RE YOU TALKING ABOUT?
THEY WERE BORN HOPING FOR HAPPINESS AND DESTROY EACH OTHER IN THEIR PURSUIT OF IT.
BUT IF THAT'S TRUE, THEY WOULD BE BETTER OFF NOT FIGHTING.
SNIFF...
ONE CAN'T ESCAPE HUMAN NATURE. PITY.
BUT THERE IS ONE PATH TO SALVATION.
?

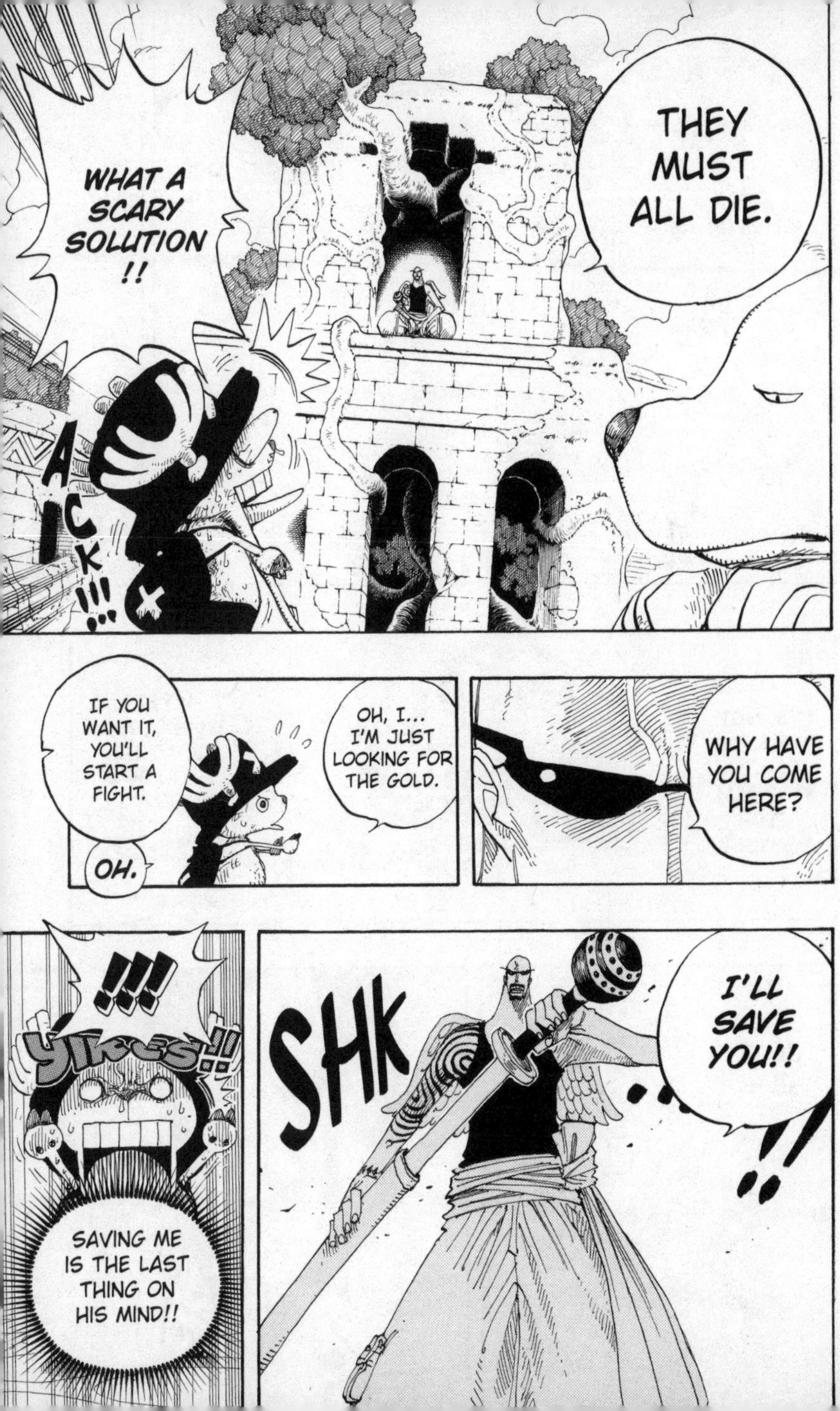
THEY MUST ALL DIE.
WHAT A SCARY SOLUTION !!
ACK!!!
WHY HAVE YOU COME HERE?
OH, I... I'M JUST LOOKING FOR THE GOLD.
IF YOU WANT IT, YOU'LL START A FIGHT.
OH.
I'LL SAVE YOU!!
SHK
...!!
!!!
YIKES!!
SAVING ME IS THE LAST THING ON HIS MIND!!

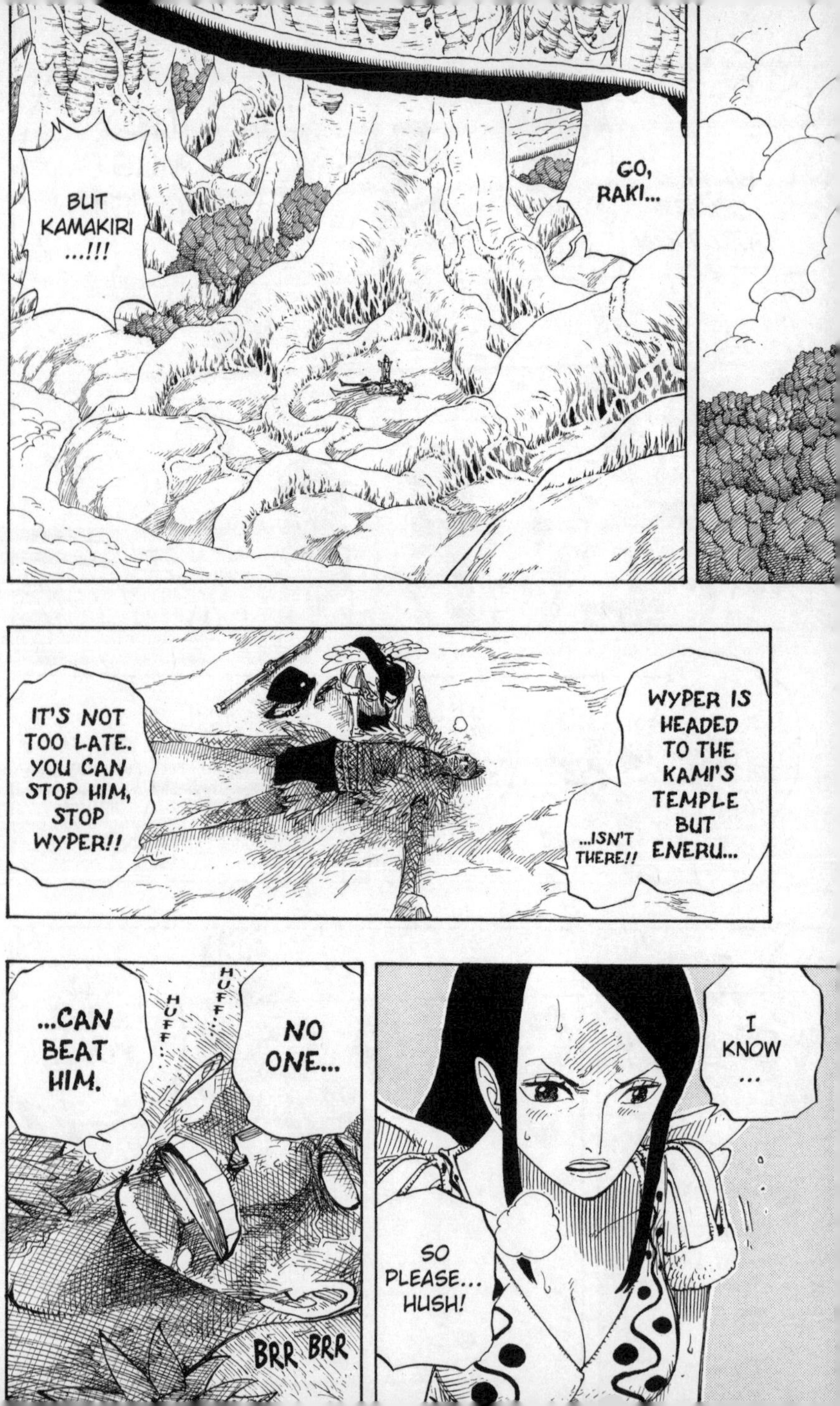
GO, RAKI...
BUT KAMAKIRI ...!!!
WYPER IS HEADED TO THE KAMI'S TEMPLE BUT ENERU...
...ISN'T THERE!!
IT'S NOT TOO LATE. YOU CAN STOP HIM, STOP WYPER!!
I KNOW ...
SO PLEASE... HUSH!
NO ONE...
HUFF HUFF...
...CAN BEAT HIM.
BRR BRR

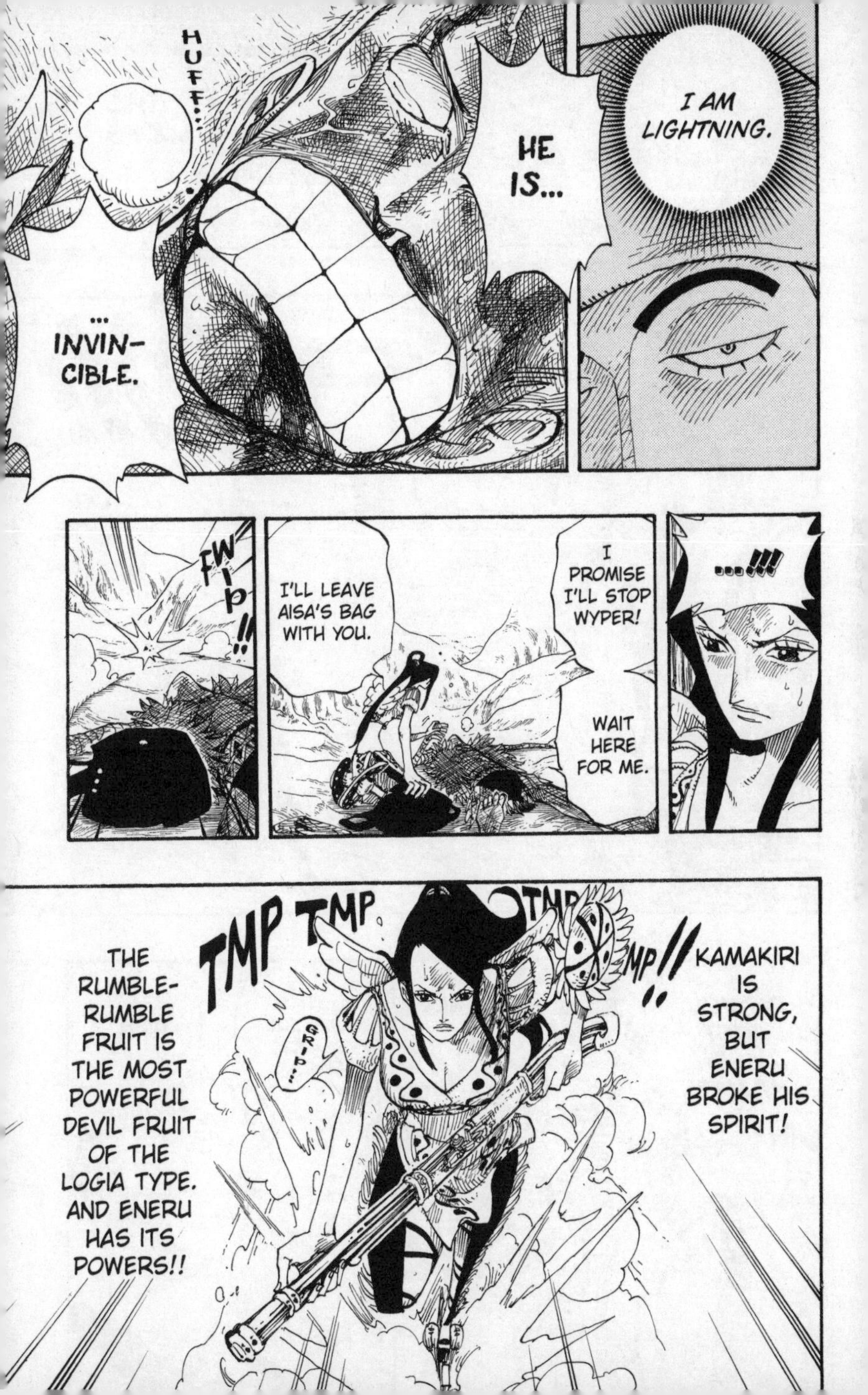
I AM LIGHTNING.
HE IS...
HUFF...
... INVINCIBLE.
...!!!
I PROMISE I'LL STOP WYPER!
I'LL LEAVE AISA'S BAG WITH YOU.
WAIT HERE FOR ME.
FWIP!!
KAMAKIRI IS STRONG, BUT ENERU BROKE HIS SPIRIT!
TMP TMP TMP TMP!!
GRIP!!
THE RUMBLE-RUMBLE FRUIT IS THE MOST POWERFUL DEVIL FRUIT OF THE LOGIA TYPE. AND ENERU HAS ITS POWERS!!

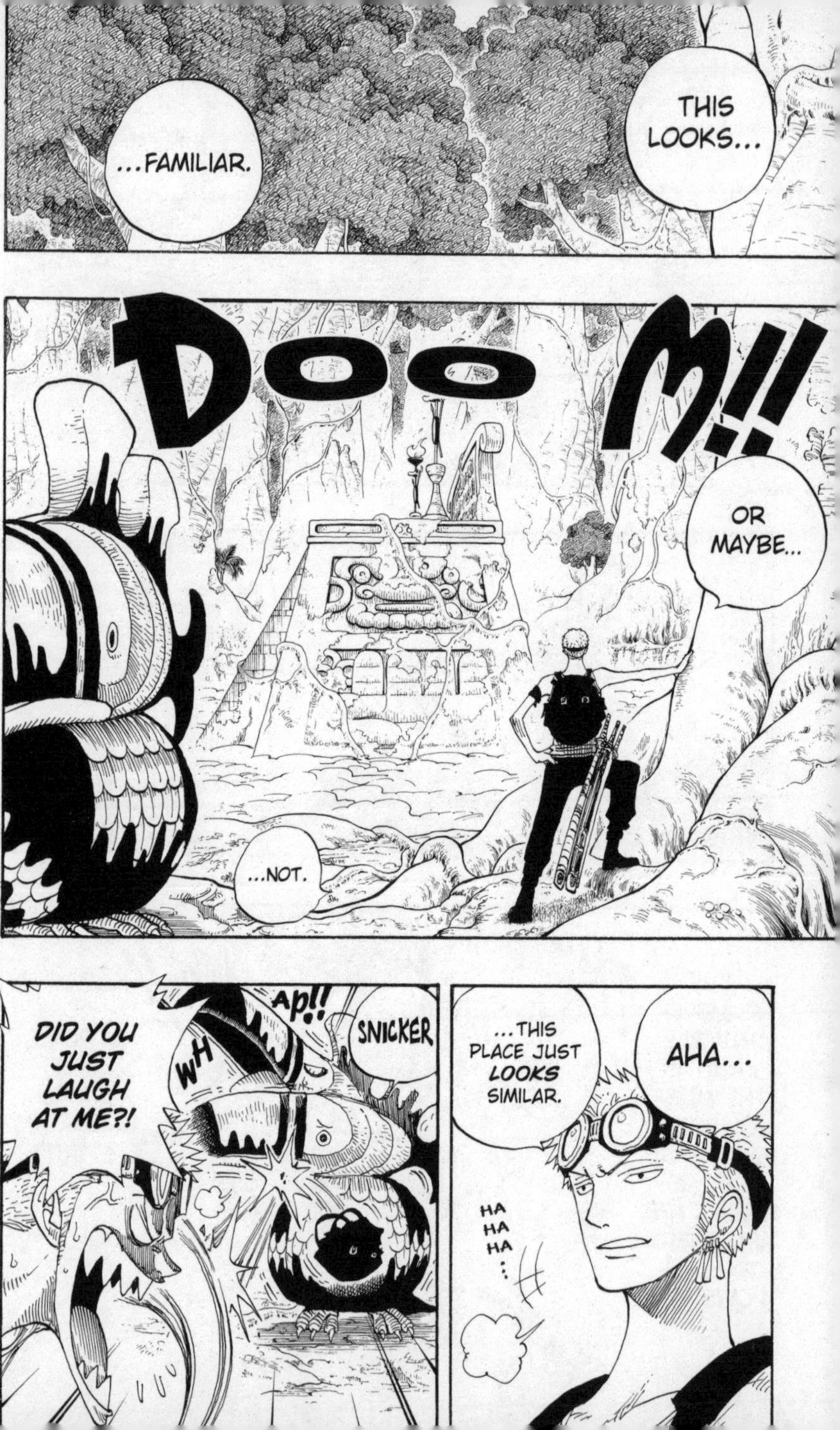

THIS LOOKS...
...FAMILIAR.
DOOM!!
OR MAYBE...
...NOT.
AHA...
...THIS PLACE JUST LOOKS SIMILAR.
HA HA HA...
SNICKER
WHAP!!
DID YOU JUST LAUGH AT ME?!

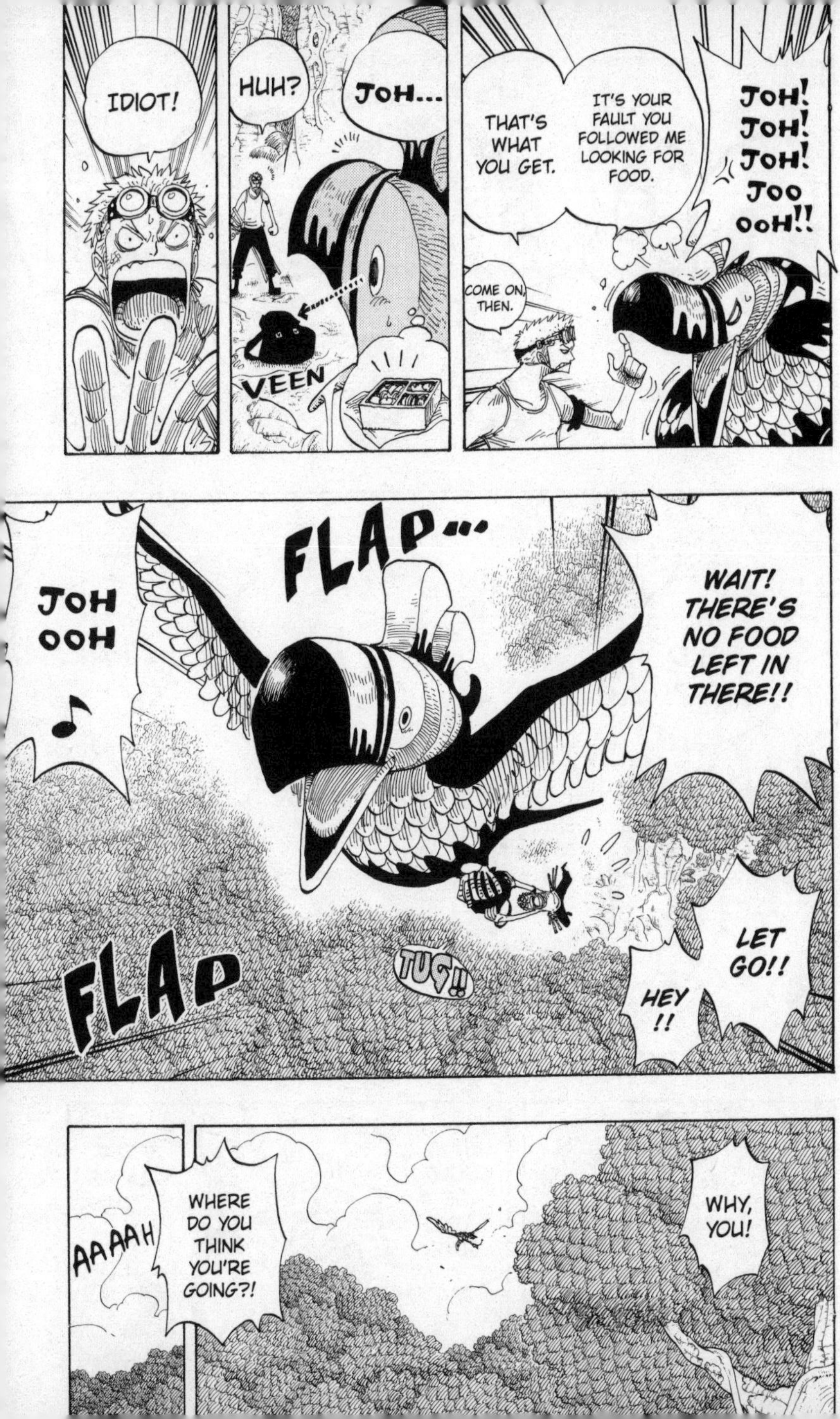
JOH! JOH! JOH! JOO OOH!!
IT'S YOUR FAULT YOU FOLLOWED ME LOOKING FOR FOOD.
THAT'S WHAT YOU GET.
COME ON, THEN.
JOH...
HUH?
VEEN
IDIOT!
WAIT! THERE'S NO FOOD LEFT IN THERE!!
FLAP...
JOH OOH
LET GO!!
HEY !!
TUG!!
FLAP
WHY, YOU!
WHERE DO YOU THINK YOU'RE GOING?!
AAAAH

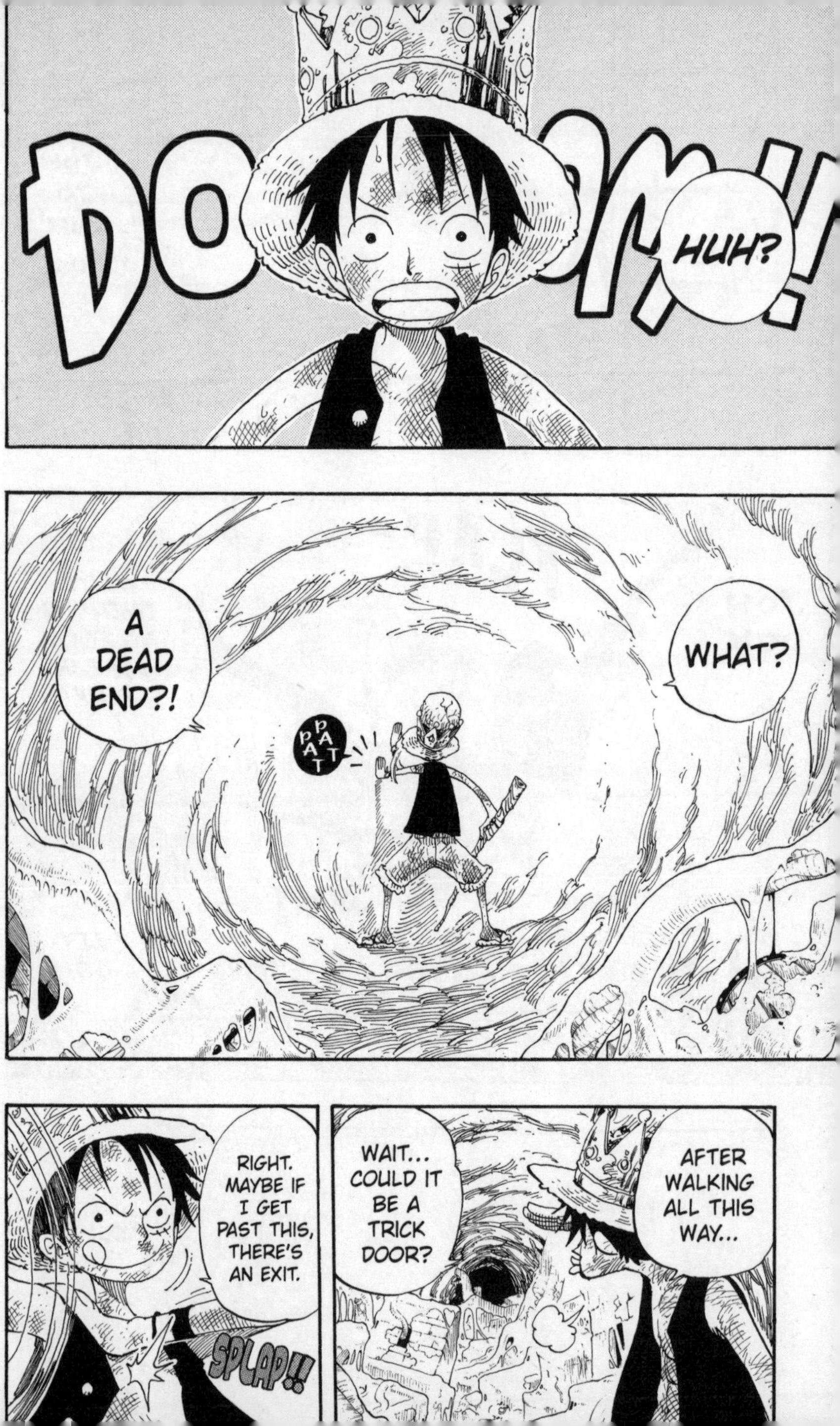
HUH?
WHAT?
PAT PAT
A DEAD END?!
AFTER WALKING ALL THIS WAY...
WAIT... COULD IT BE A TRICK DOOR?
RIGHT. MAYBE IF I GET PAST THIS, THERE'S AN EXIT.
SPLAP!!

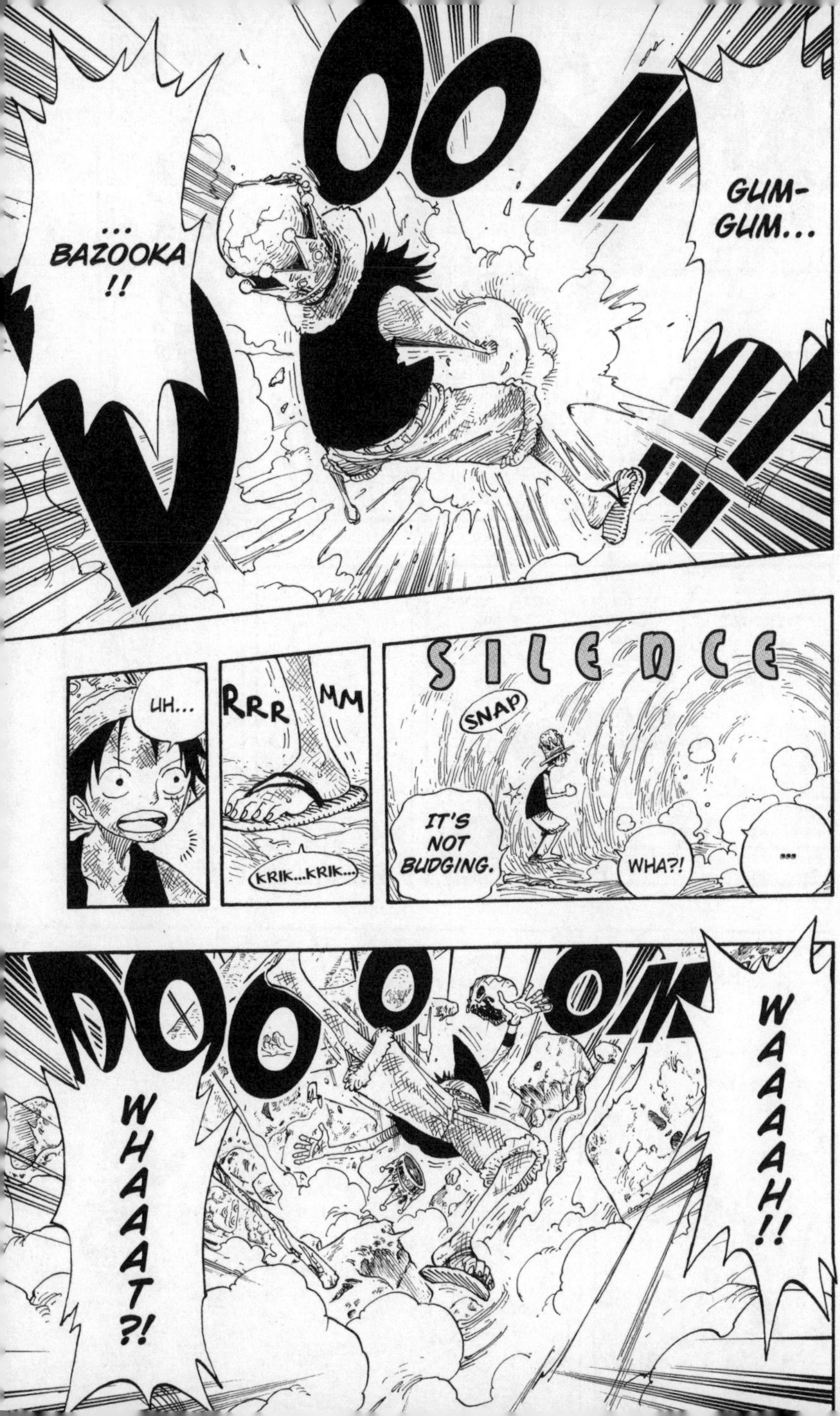
GUM-GUM...
... BAZOOKA!!
SILENCE
SNAP
...
WHA?!
IT'S NOT BUDGING.
RRR MM
KRIK...KRIK...
UH...
WAAAAAH!!
WHAAAAT?!

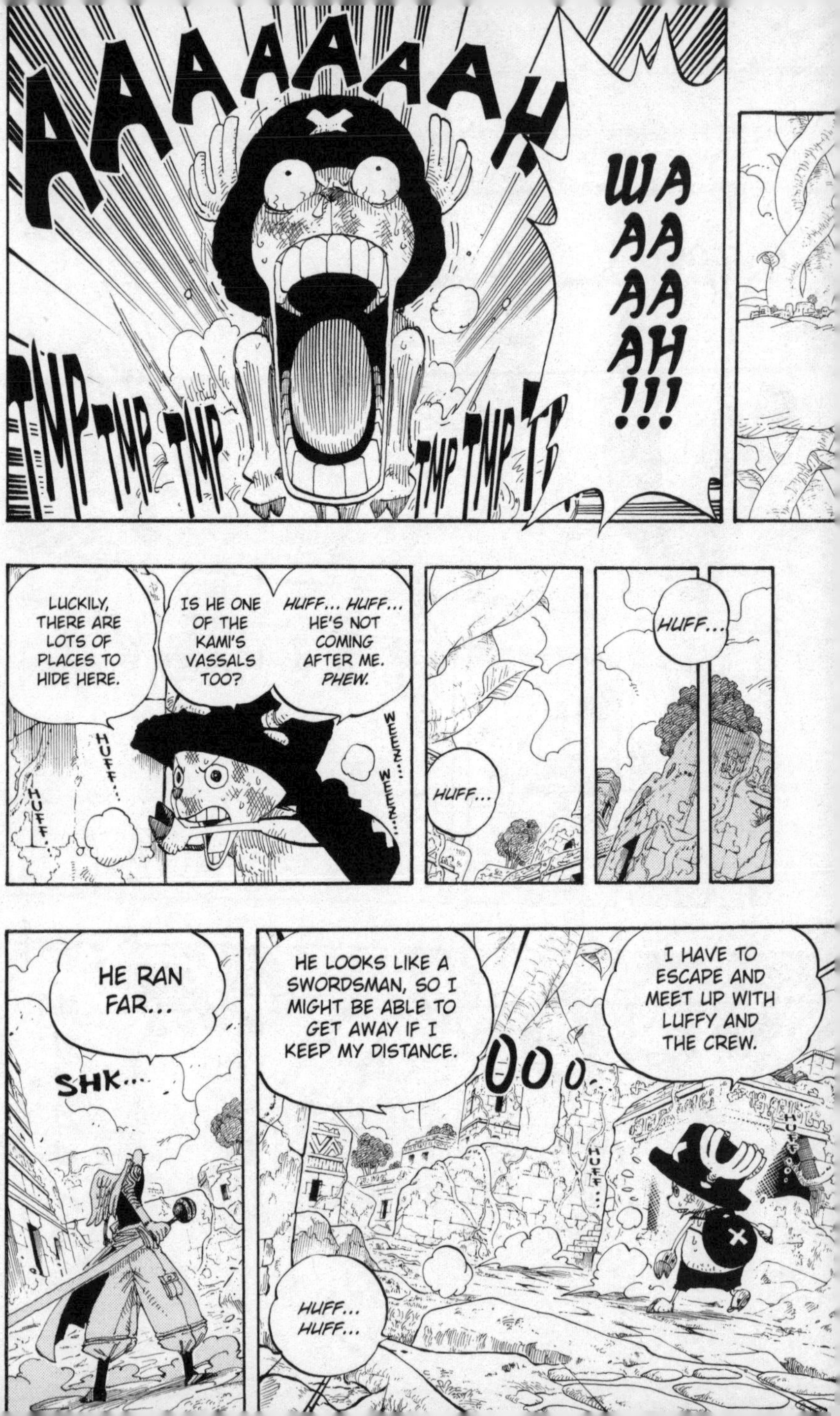
AAAAAAAH
WAAAAAAH!!!
TMP TMP TB
TMP TMP TMP
HUFF...
HUFF...
HUFF... HUFF... HE'S NOT COMING AFTER ME. PHEW.
IS HE ONE OF THE KAMI'S VASSALS TOO?
LUCKILY, THERE ARE LOTS OF PLACES TO HIDE HERE.
WEEZ... WEEZ...
HUFF... HUFF...
I HAVE TO ESCAPE AND MEET UP WITH LUFFY AND THE CREW.
HUFF... HUFF...
HUFF...
OOO
HE LOOKS LIKE A SWORDSMAN, SO I MIGHT BE ABLE TO GET AWAY IF I KEEP MY DISTANCE.
HUFF... HUFF...
HE RAN FAR...
SHK...

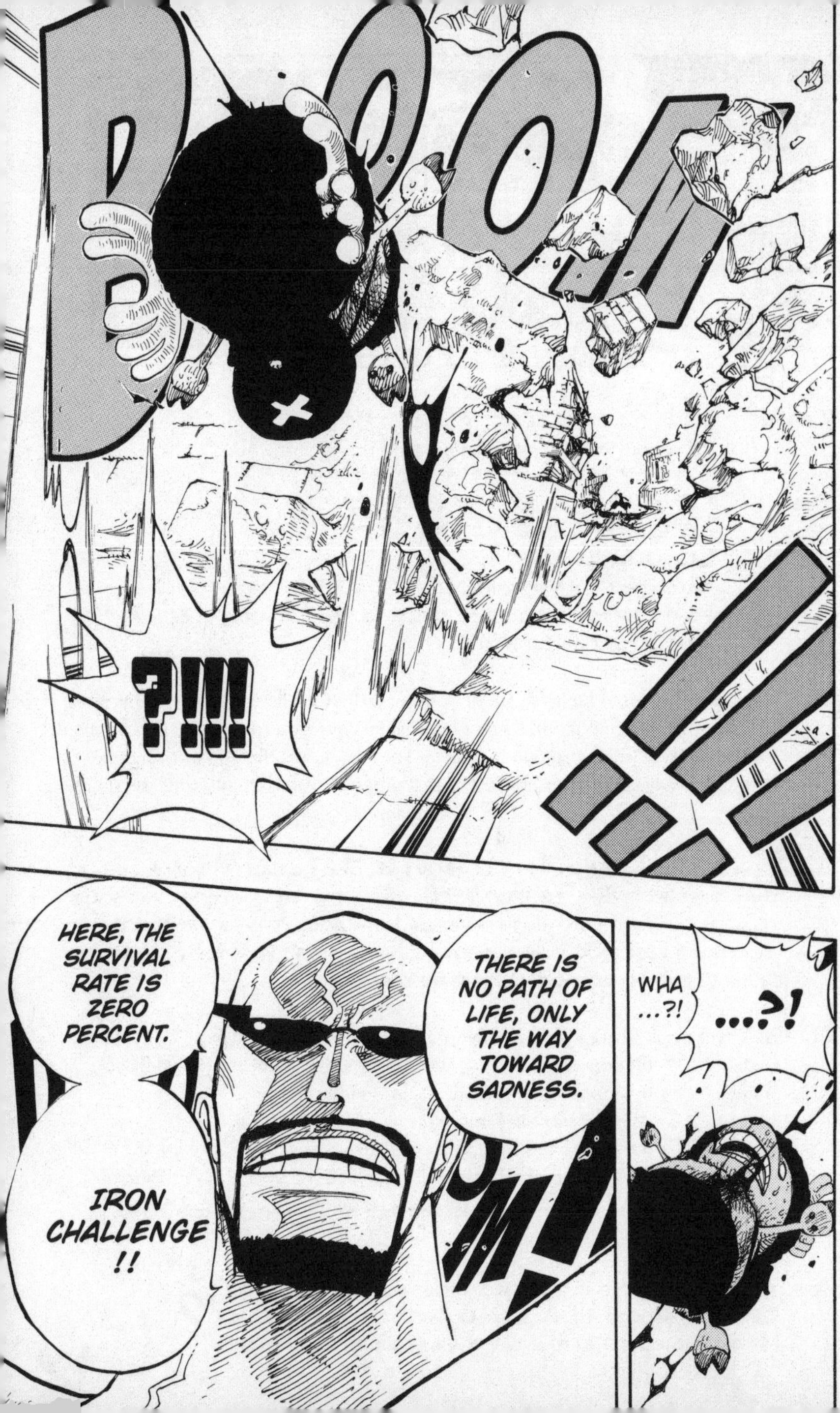
BOOM
?!!!
WHA ...?!
...?!
THERE IS NO PATH OF LIFE, ONLY THE WAY TOWARD SADNESS.
HERE, THE SURVIVAL RATE IS ZERO PERCENT.
IRON CHALLENGE !!

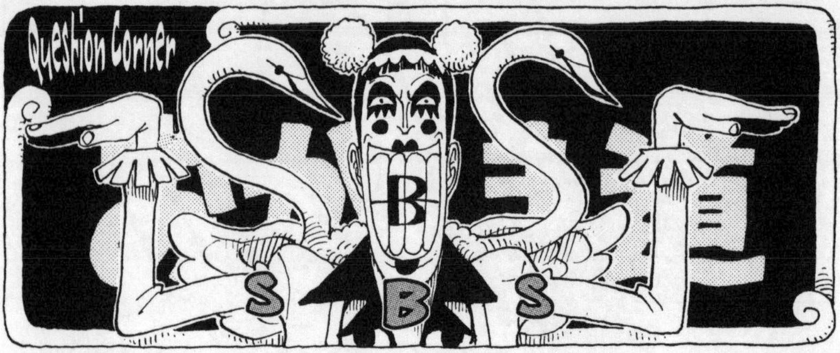
Question Corner
B
SBS

Reader: La la ~~~ La la ~~~ La la ~~~♪
"Kita no Kunikara" by Masashi Sada*
*This is a melancholy song about life in the northern island of Hokkaido.--Ed.

Oda: La la ~~~ La la ~~~ La la ~~~
La la ~~~ La la ~~~ La la ~~~♪
Lu lu lu lu lu ~~!!
Ugh, enough already!!
I can't believe you made me sing that. Though I do love "Kita no Kunikara."

Q: Hi, nice to meet you! I'm a big fan of your work. I always listen to the radio at work, and the other day on Nippon Radio I heard a quiz question for Makoto Kitano about a unique type of snow that falls in France. The answer was that the snow is pink! Did you already know about this and is that why you worked it into your storyline?
--Ayumino Chopper

A: Pink snow, huh? Yes, I knew about it. The reason it's pink is that dust attaches to iron particles in the air, causing the snow to look pink or red. This happened in France. In Vienna there were also cases of yellow snow. Sometimes the mischief caused by air pollution creates fantastic scenery.

Q: Hi, Oda Sensei. I have a question about the Kami's vassals in Skypiea.
Gedatsu => the concept of freeing oneself of earthly problems in Buddhism
Shura => the realm of the semi-divine in Buddhism
Satori => enlightenment in Buddhism
Yama => the lord of the afterlife in Buddhism
Did you choose religious names because the storyline takes place in the realm of a kami (god)? Also, if you could, would you please let me know where Ohm's name comes from?

A: Yes, that's right. I'm not religious, so I winged it.
"Om" is a sacred Hindu symbol, written like this: ॐ
My apologies to all the spiritual readers out there.

Chapter 267: MARCH

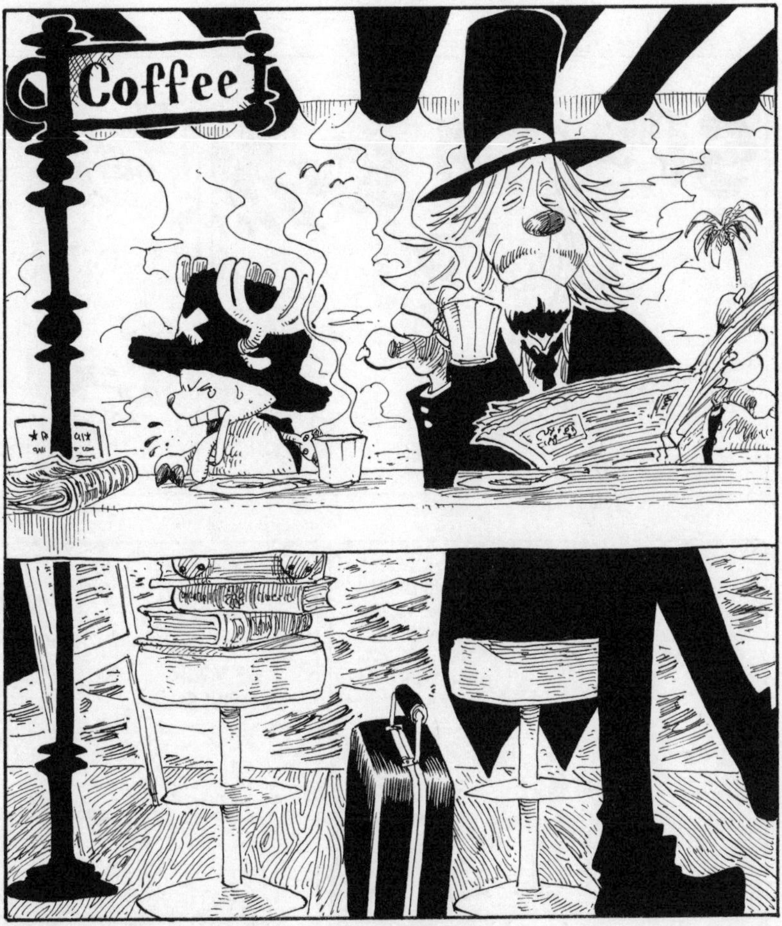
Coffee

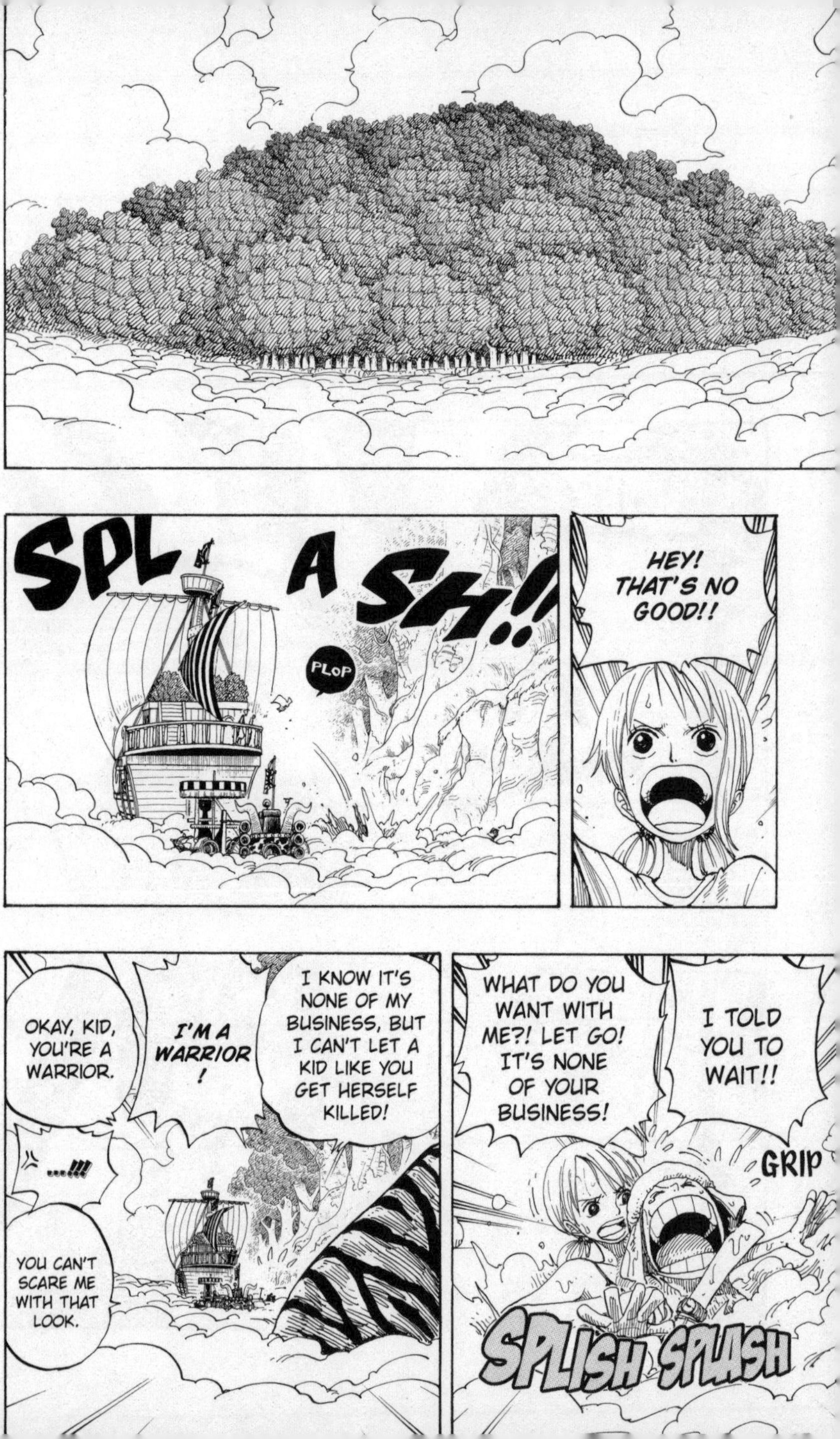
HEY! THAT'S NO GOOD!!
SPLASH!!
PLOP
I TOLD YOU TO WAIT!!
WHAT DO YOU WANT WITH ME?! LET GO! IT'S NONE OF YOUR BUSINESS!
GRIP
SPLISH SPLASH
I KNOW IT'S NONE OF MY BUSINESS, BUT I CAN'T LET A KID LIKE YOU GET HERSELF KILLED!
I'M A WARRIOR!
OKAY, KID, YOU'RE A WARRIOR.
...!!!
YOU CAN'T SCARE ME WITH THAT LOOK.

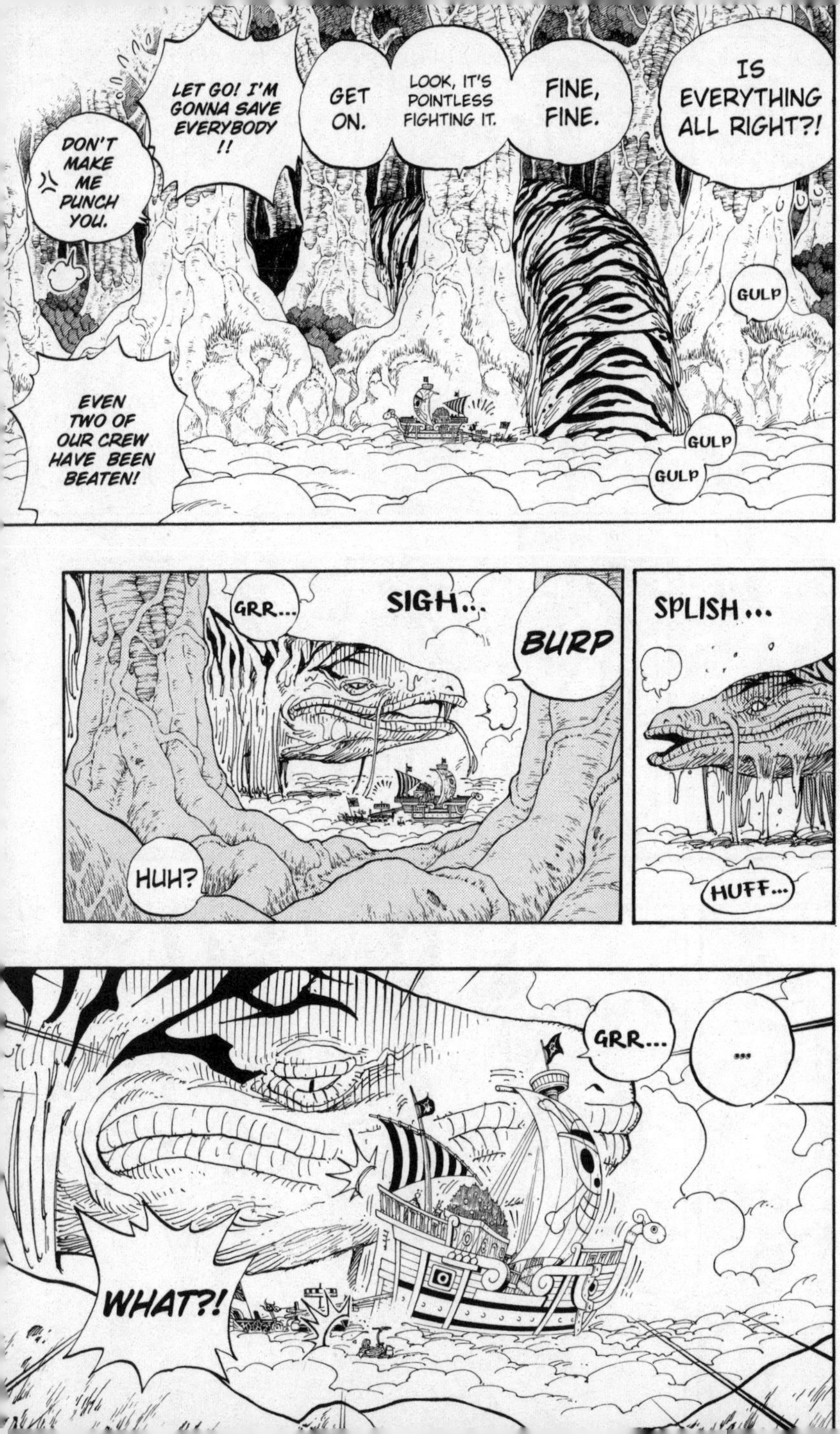
IS EVERYTHING ALL RIGHT?!
FINE, FINE.
LOOK, IT'S POINTLESS FIGHTING IT.
GET ON.
LET GO! I'M GONNA SAVE EVERYBODY!!
DON'T MAKE ME PUNCH YOU.
GULP
GULP
GULP
EVEN TWO OF OUR CREW HAVE BEEN BEATEN!
SPLISH...
HUFF...
BURP
SIGH...
GRR...
HUH?
...
GRR...
WHAT?!

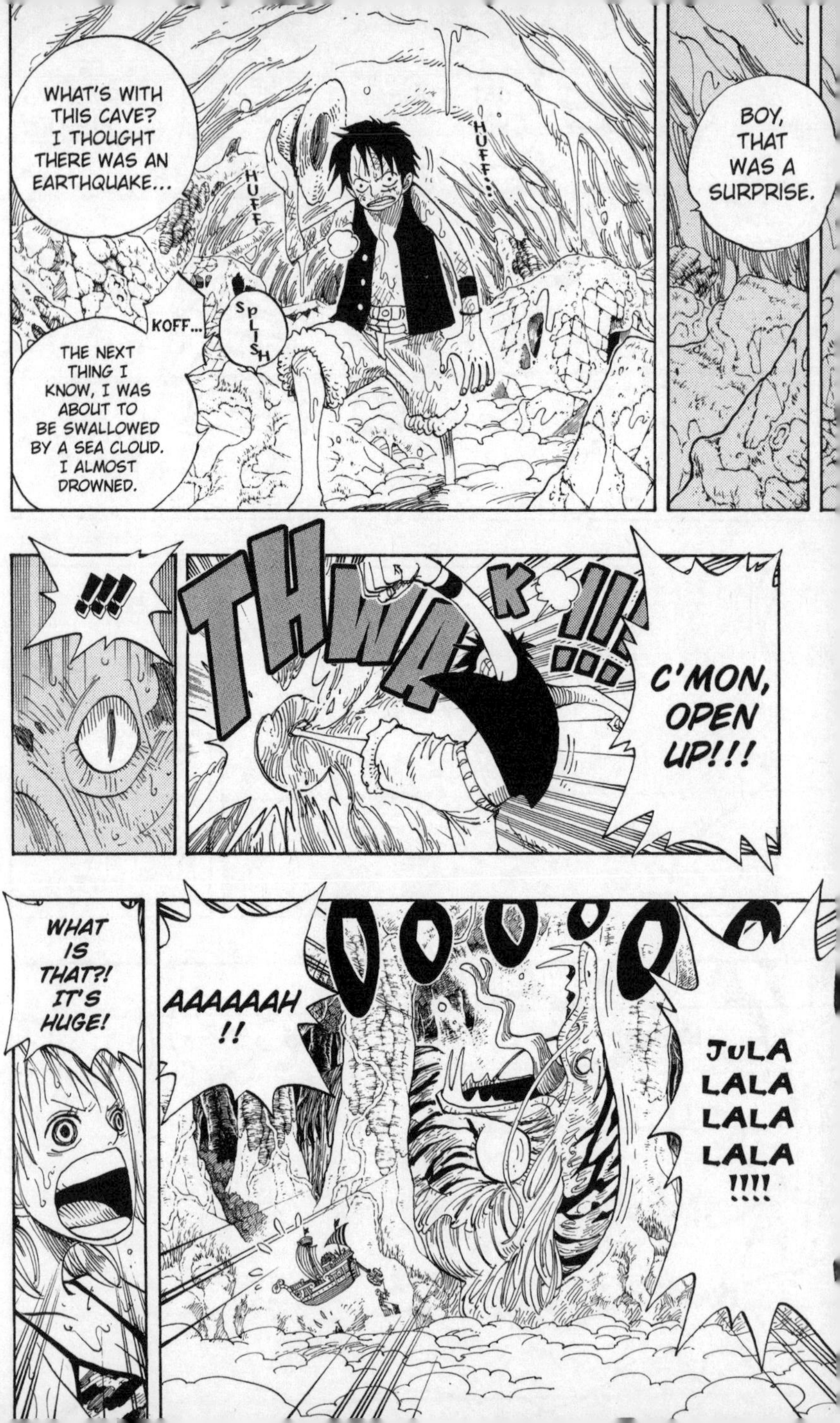

BOY, THAT WAS A SURPRISE.
HUFF...
HUFF
WHAT'S WITH THIS CAVE? I THOUGHT THERE WAS AN EARTHQUAKE...
KOFF...
SPLISH
THE NEXT THING I KNOW, I WAS ABOUT TO BE SWALLOWED BY A SEA CLOUD. I ALMOST DROWNED.
C'MON, OPEN UP!!!
THWAK!!!
!!!
JULA LALA LALA LALA!!!!
AAAAAAH!!
WHAT IS THAT?! IT'S HUGE!

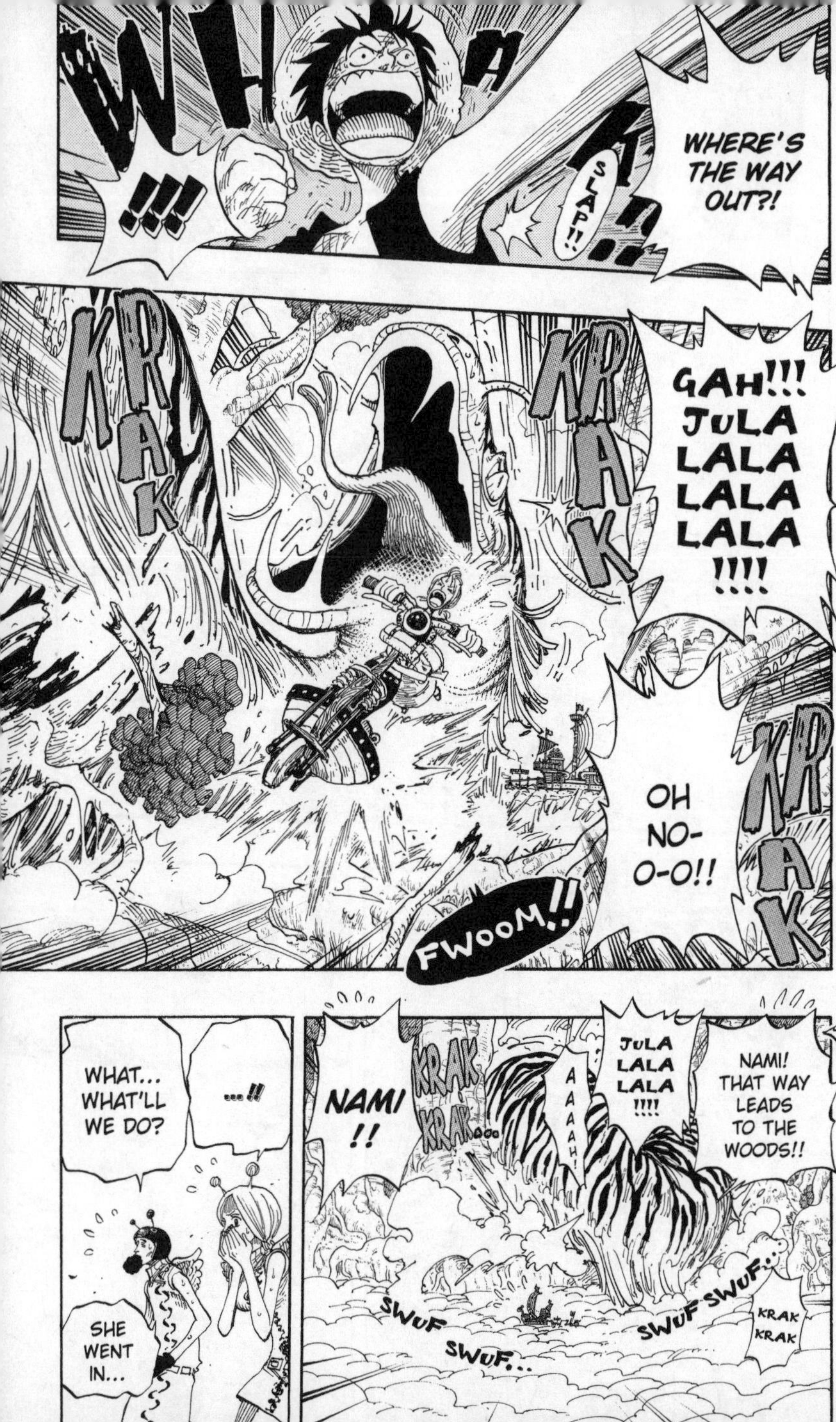
WHA
!!!
WHERE'S THE WAY OUT?!
SLAP!!
GAH!!! JULA LALA LALA LALA!!!!
KRAK
KRAK
KRAK
OH NO-O-O!!
FWOOM!!
NAMI! THAT WAY LEADS TO THE WOODS!!
JULA LALA LALA!!!!
AAAAH!
NAMI!!
KRAK KRAK...
SWUF SWUF...
KRAK KRAK
SWUF
SWUF...
...!!
WHAT... WHAT'LL WE DO?
SHE WENT IN...

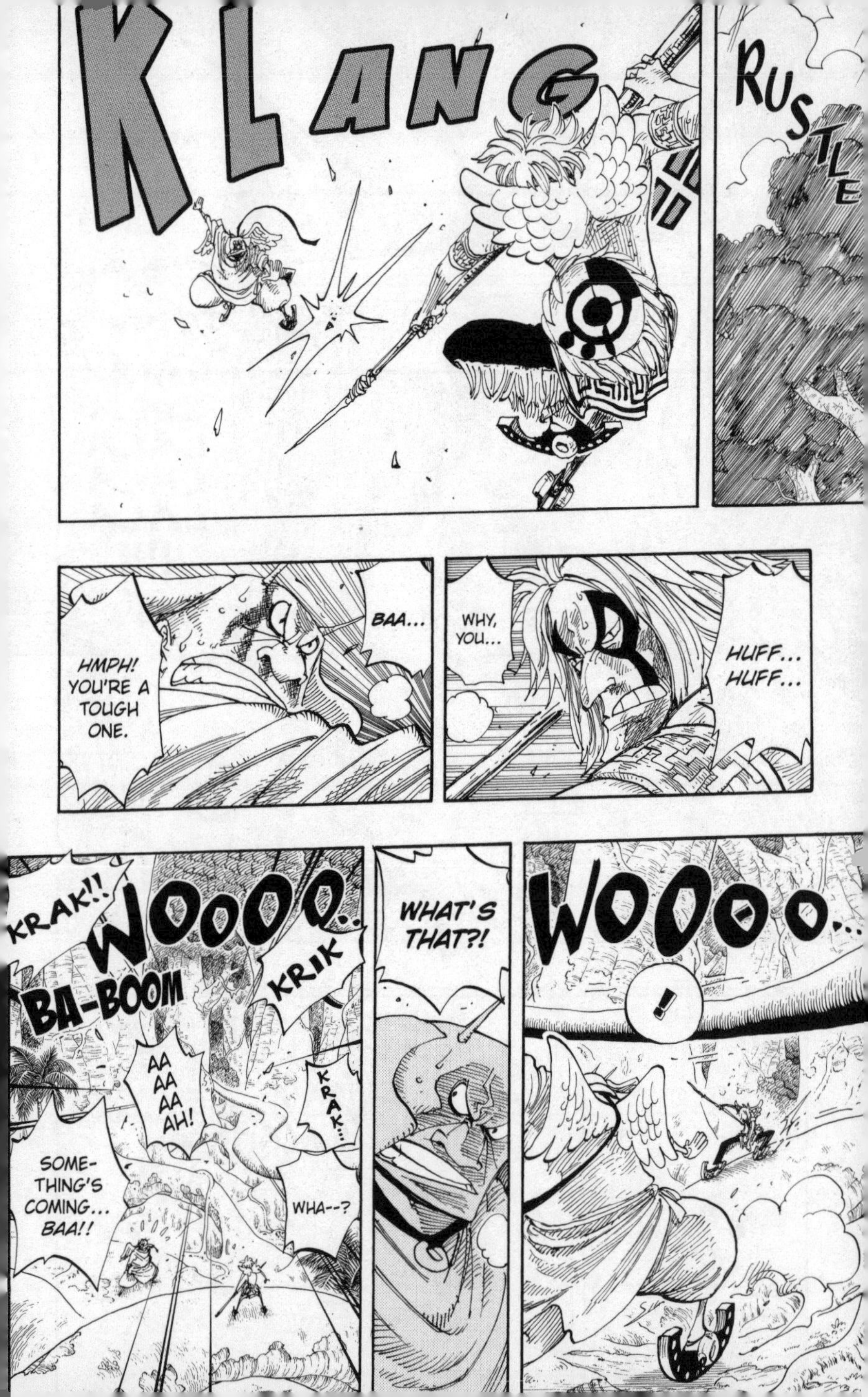
RUSTLE
KLANG
WHY, YOU...
HUFF... HUFF...
BAA...
HMPH! YOU'RE A TOUGH ONE.
WOOOO...
!
WHAT'S THAT?!
WOOOO..
KRIK
KRAK!!
BA-BOOM
KRAK...
AAAAAAAH!
WHA--?
SOME-THING'S COMING... BAA!!

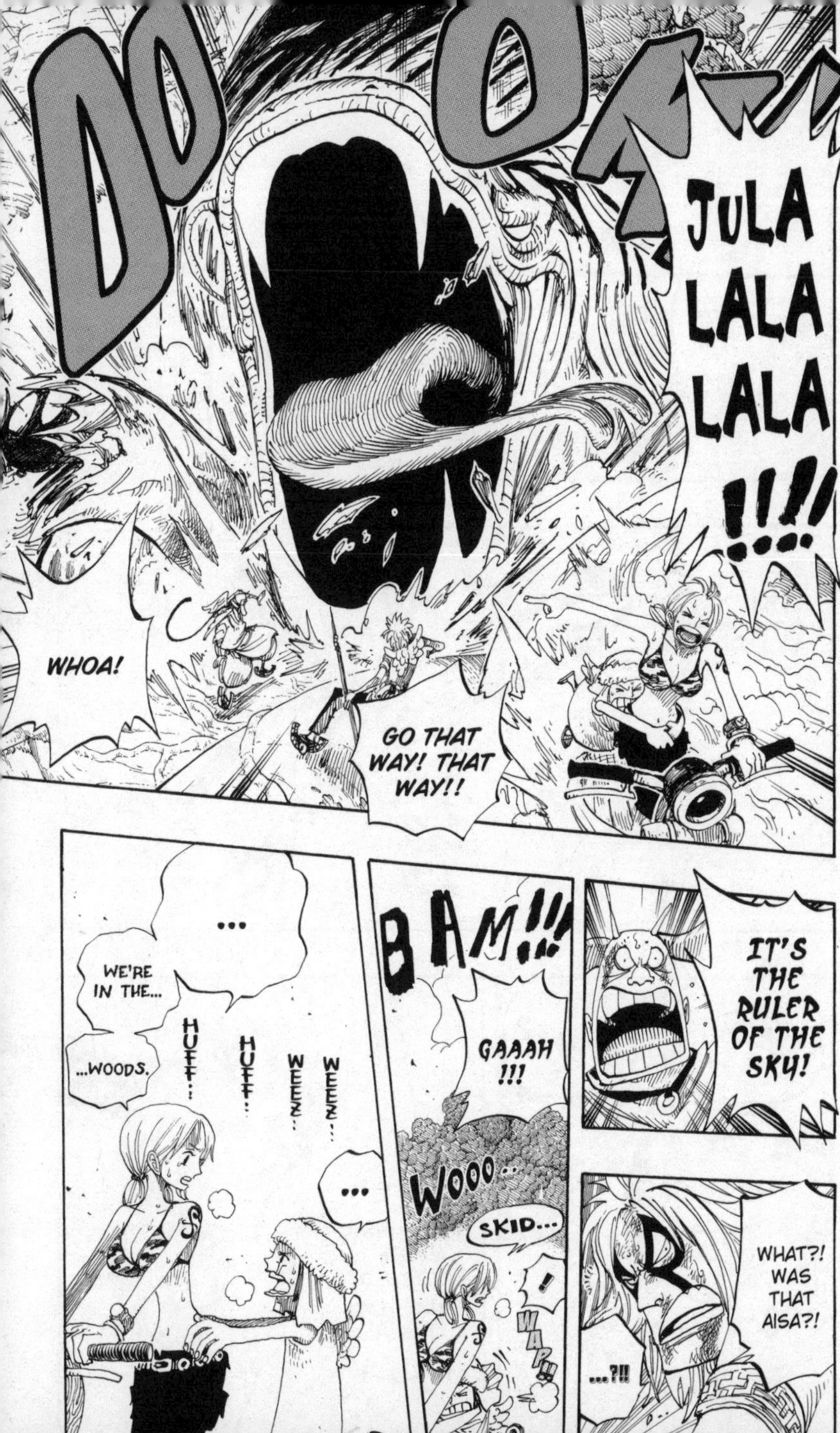
DOOM!
JULA LALA LALA!!!!
GO THAT WAY! THAT WAY!!
WHOA!
IT'S THE RULER OF THE SKY!
WHAT?! WAS THAT AISA?!
...?!!
BAM!!!
GAAAH!!!
WOOO..
SKID...
!
WAP!!
...
WE'RE IN THE...
...WOODS.
HUFF HUFF WEEZ WEEZ
...

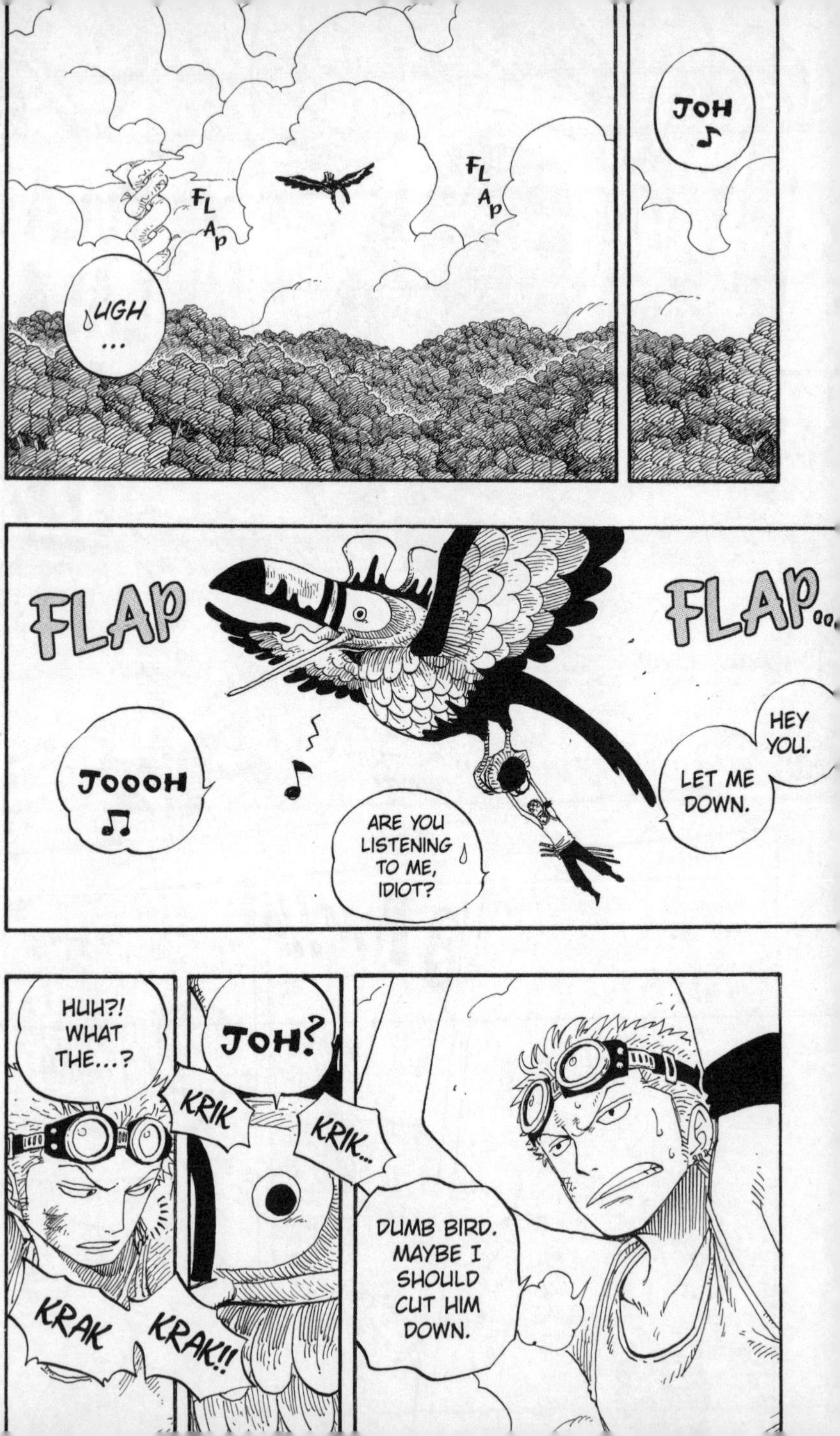
JOH ♪
FLAP
FLAP
UGH ...
FLAP...
HEY YOU.
LET ME DOWN.
FLAP
ARE YOU LISTENING TO ME, IDIOT?
JOOOH ♫
DUMB BIRD. MAYBE I SHOULD CUT HIM DOWN.
JOH?
KRIK
KRIK...
HUH?! WHAT THE...?
KRAK
KRAK!!

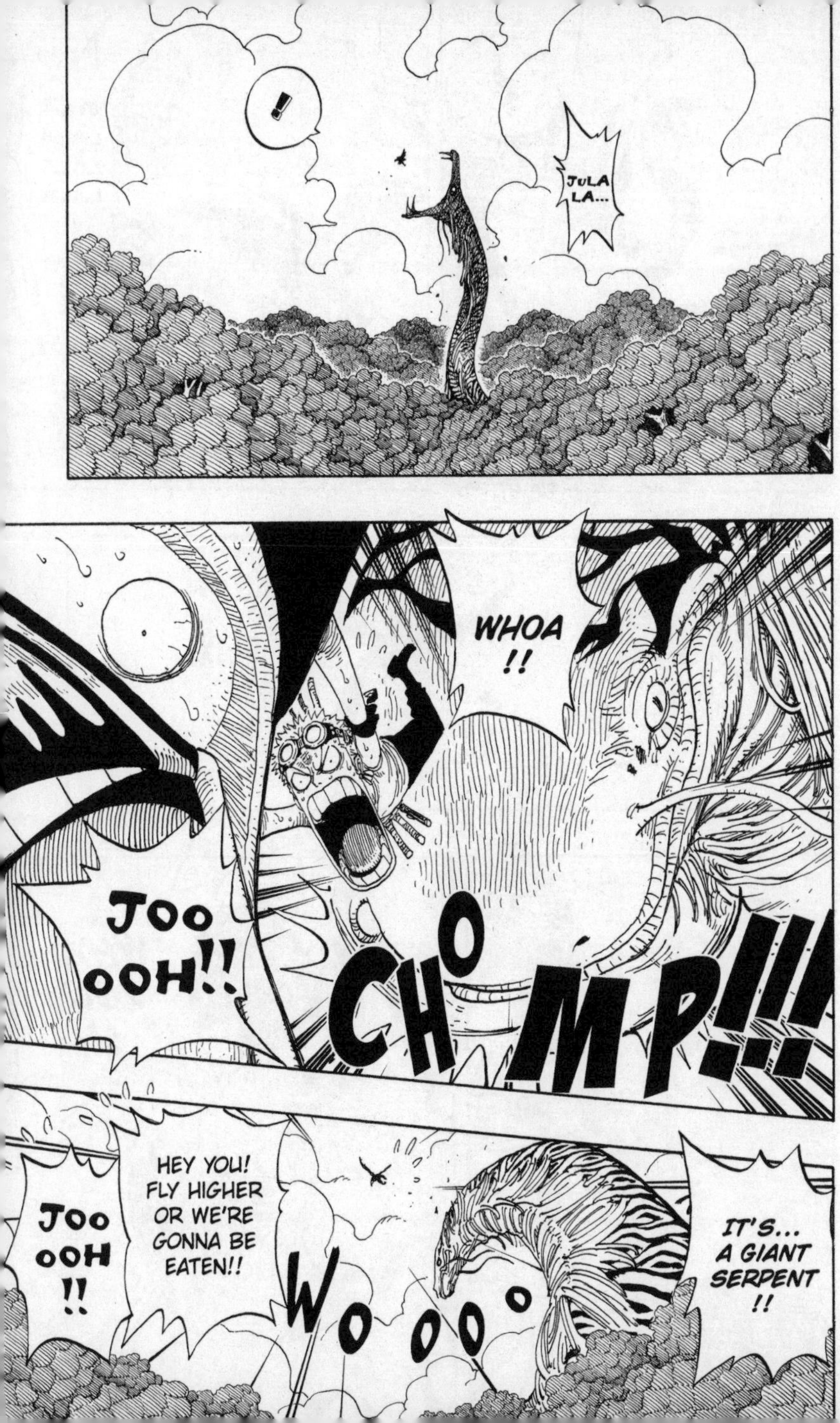
JULA LA...
!
WHOA !!
CHOMP!!!
JOO OOH!!
IT'S... A GIANT SERPENT !!
WOOOO
HEY YOU! FLY HIGHER OR WE'RE GONNA BE EATEN!!
JOO OOH !!

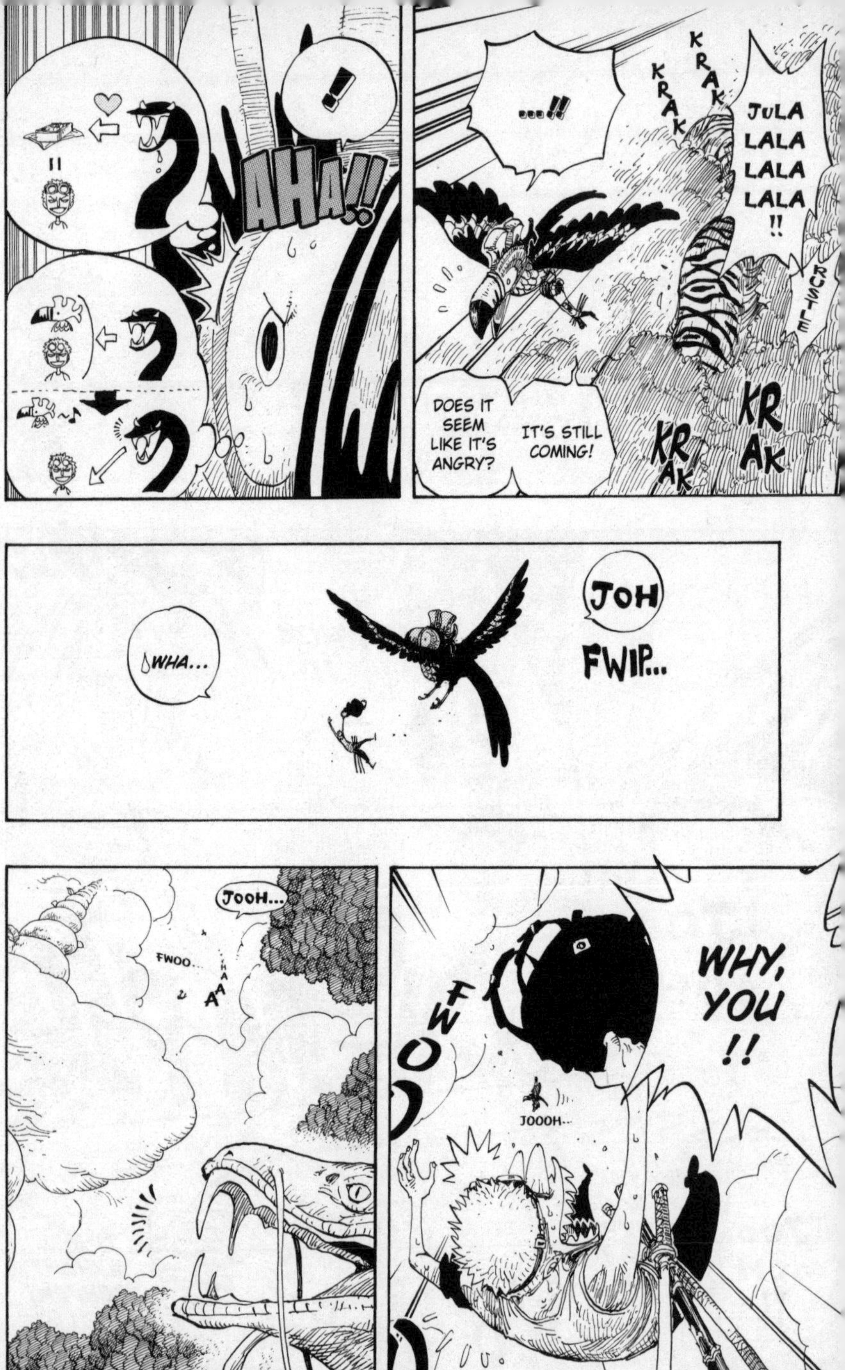
...!!
KRAK
KRAK
JULA LALA LALA LALA !!
RUSTLE
KRAK
KRAK
IT'S STILL COMING!
DOES IT SEEM LIKE IT'S ANGRY?
!
AHA!!
JOH
FWIP...
WHA...
WHY, YOU !!
FWOO
JOOOH...
JOOH...
FWOO...
HAAA

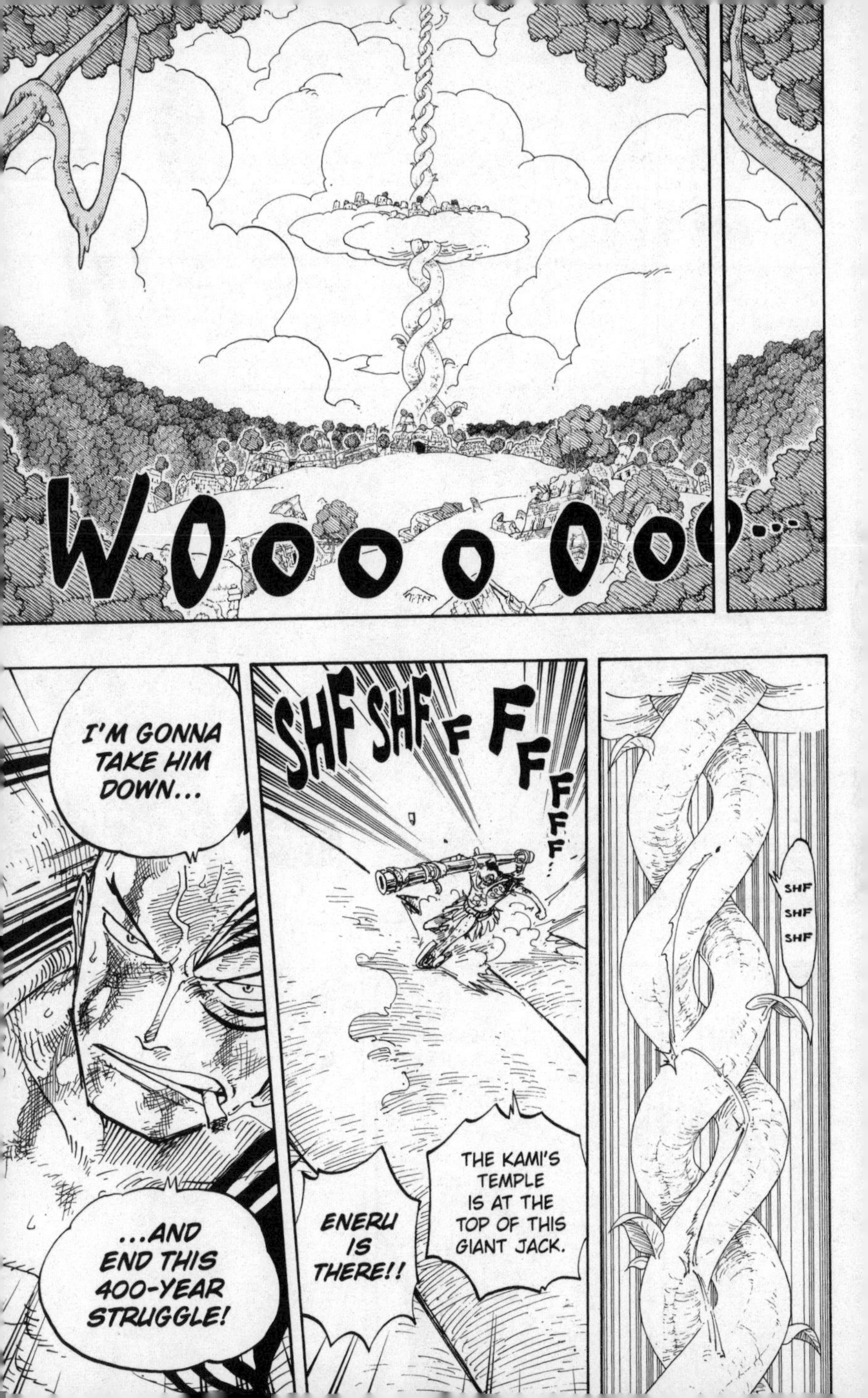
WOOOO OOO...
SHF
SHF
SHF
SHF SHF F FFFFF...
THE KAMI'S TEMPLE IS AT THE TOP OF THIS GIANT JACK.
ENERU IS THERE!!
I'M GONNA TAKE HIM DOWN...
...AND END THIS 400-YEAR STRUGGLE!

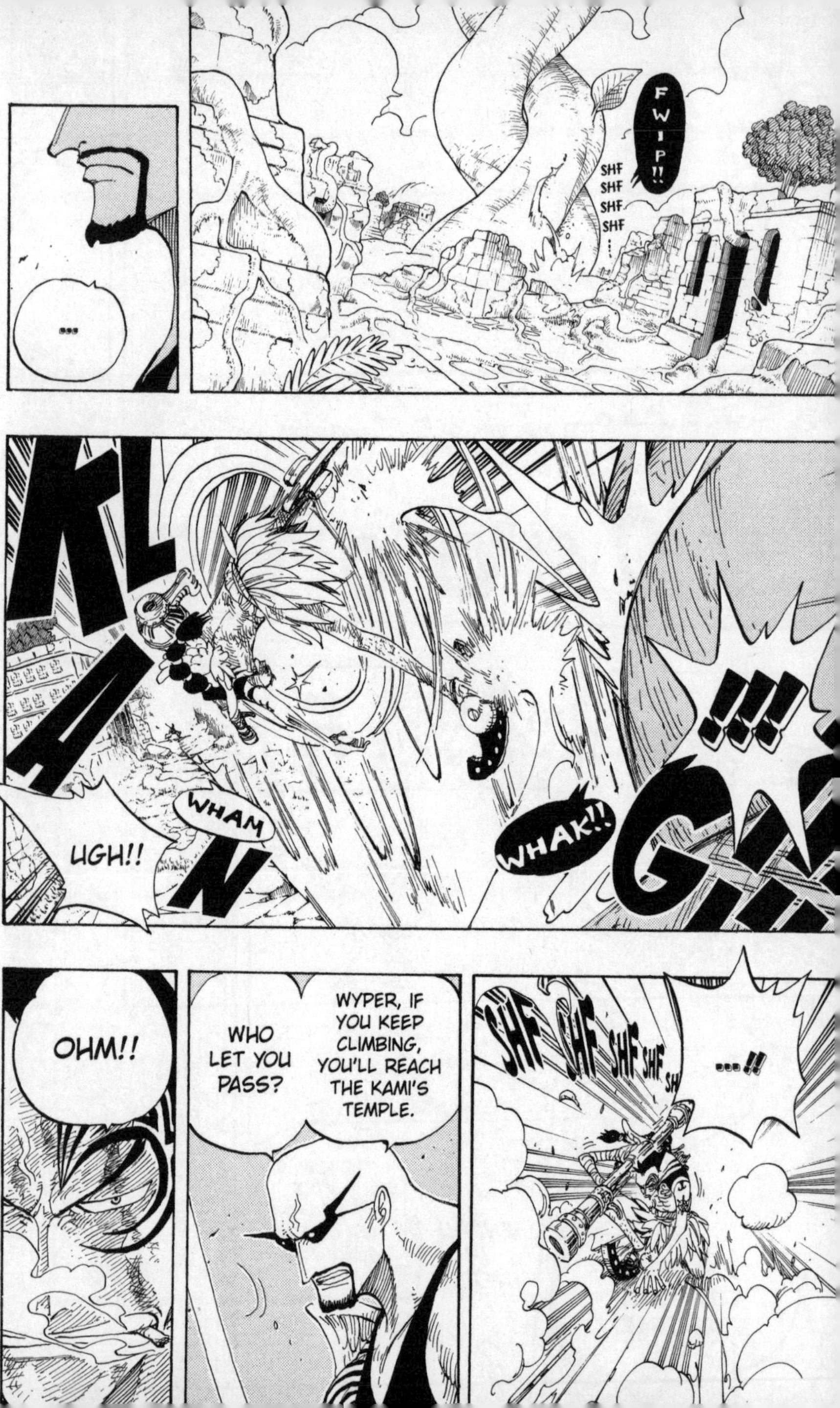
FWIP!!
SHF SHF SHF SHF...
...
WHAK!!
WHAM
UGH!!
SHF SHF SHF SHF SH
...!!
WYPER, IF YOU KEEP CLIMBING, YOU'LL REACH THE KAMI'S TEMPLE.
WHO LET YOU PASS?
OHM!!

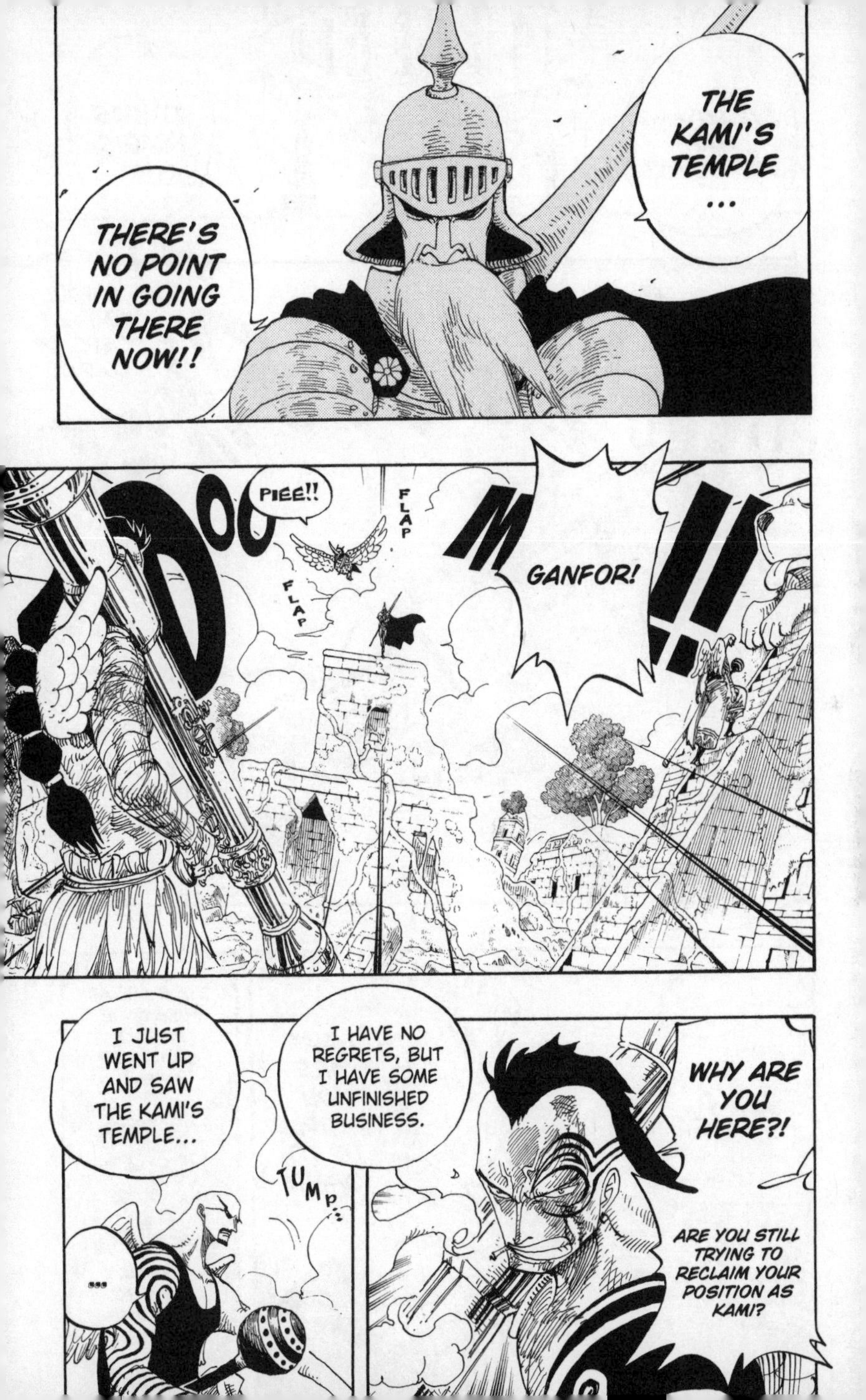
THE KAMI'S TEMPLE ...
THERE'S NO POINT IN GOING THERE NOW!!
GANFOR!
FLAP
FLAP
PIEE!!
DOO
WHY ARE YOU HERE?!
ARE YOU STILL TRYING TO RECLAIM YOUR POSITION AS KAMI?
I HAVE NO REGRETS, BUT I HAVE SOME UNFINISHED BUSINESS.
I JUST WENT UP AND SAW THE KAMI'S TEMPLE...
TUMP
...

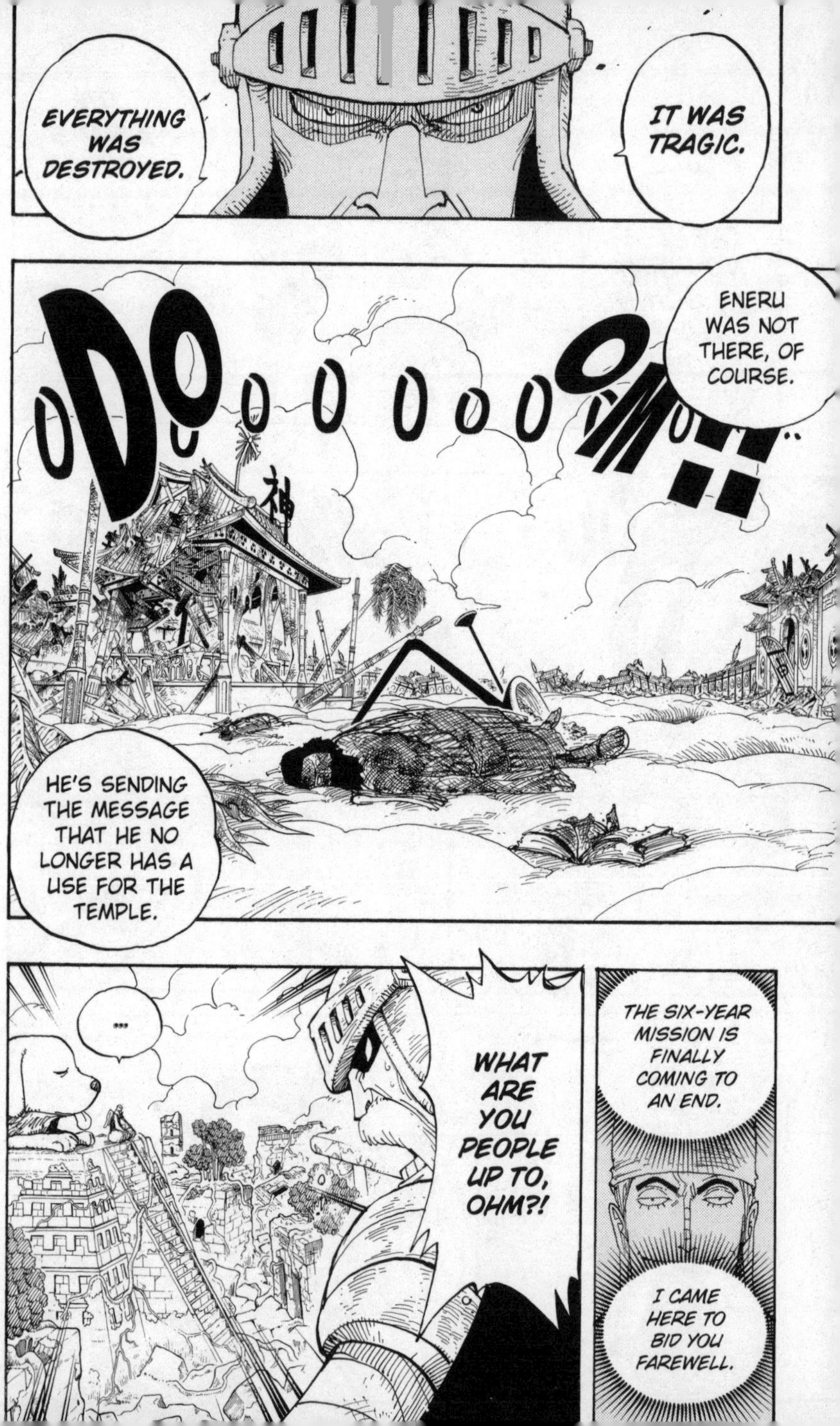
IT WAS TRAGIC.
EVERYTHING WAS DESTROYED.
ENERU WAS NOT THERE, OF COURSE.
DOOOOOOOOOOM!!
HE'S SENDING THE MESSAGE THAT HE NO LONGER HAS A USE FOR THE TEMPLE.
THE SIX-YEAR MISSION IS FINALLY COMING TO AN END.
I CAME HERE TO BID YOU FAREWELL.
WHAT ARE YOU PEOPLE UP TO, OHM?!
...

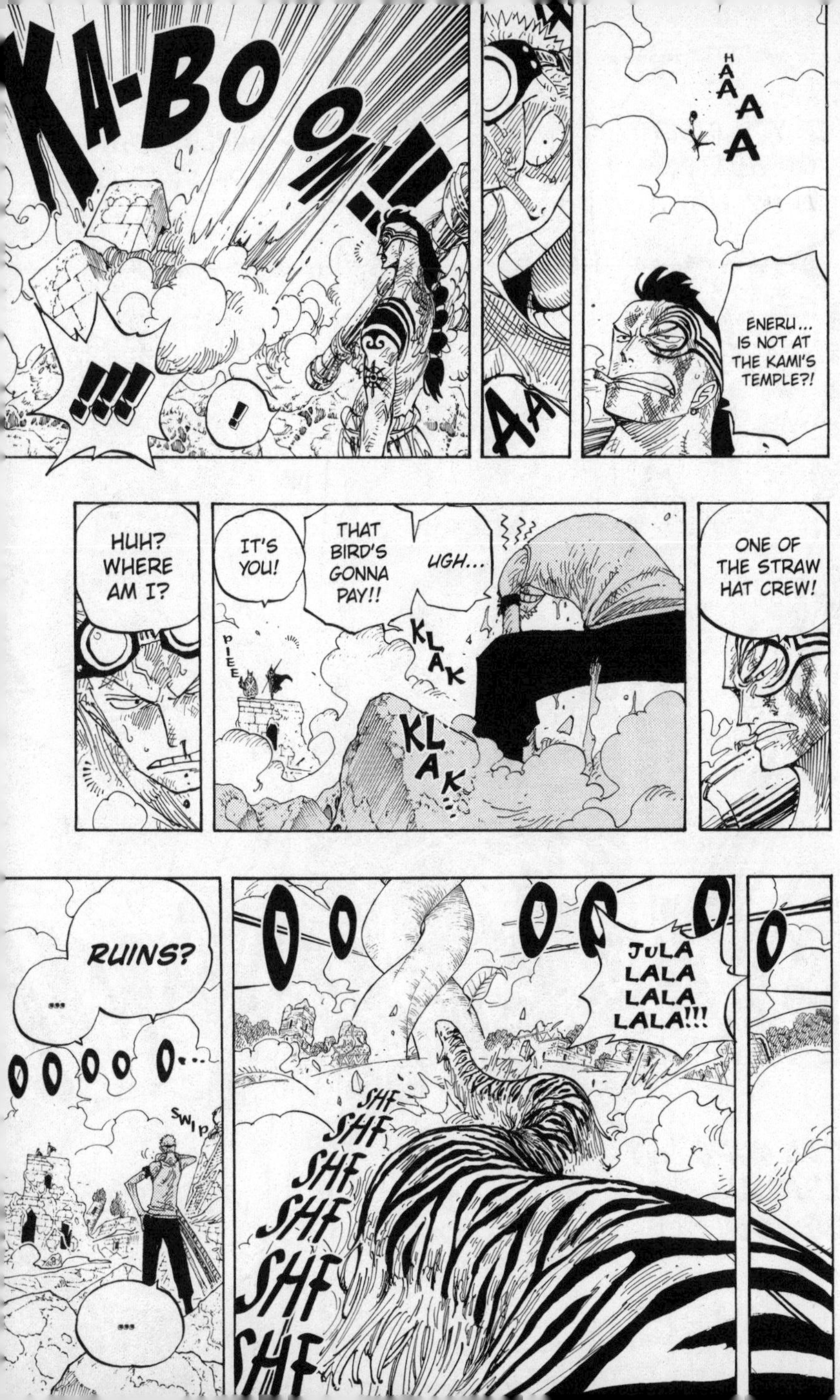
HAAAA
ENERU... IS NOT AT THE KAMI'S TEMPLE?!
AA
KA-BOOM!!!
!!!
!
ONE OF THE STRAW HAT CREW!
UGH...
THAT BIRD'S GONNA PAY!!
IT'S YOU!
KLAK
KLAK
PIEE
HUH? WHERE AM I?
O
O O O O O
JULA LALA LALA LALA!!!
SHF SHF SHF SHF SHF SHF
RUINS?
...
OOOO O...
SWIP
...

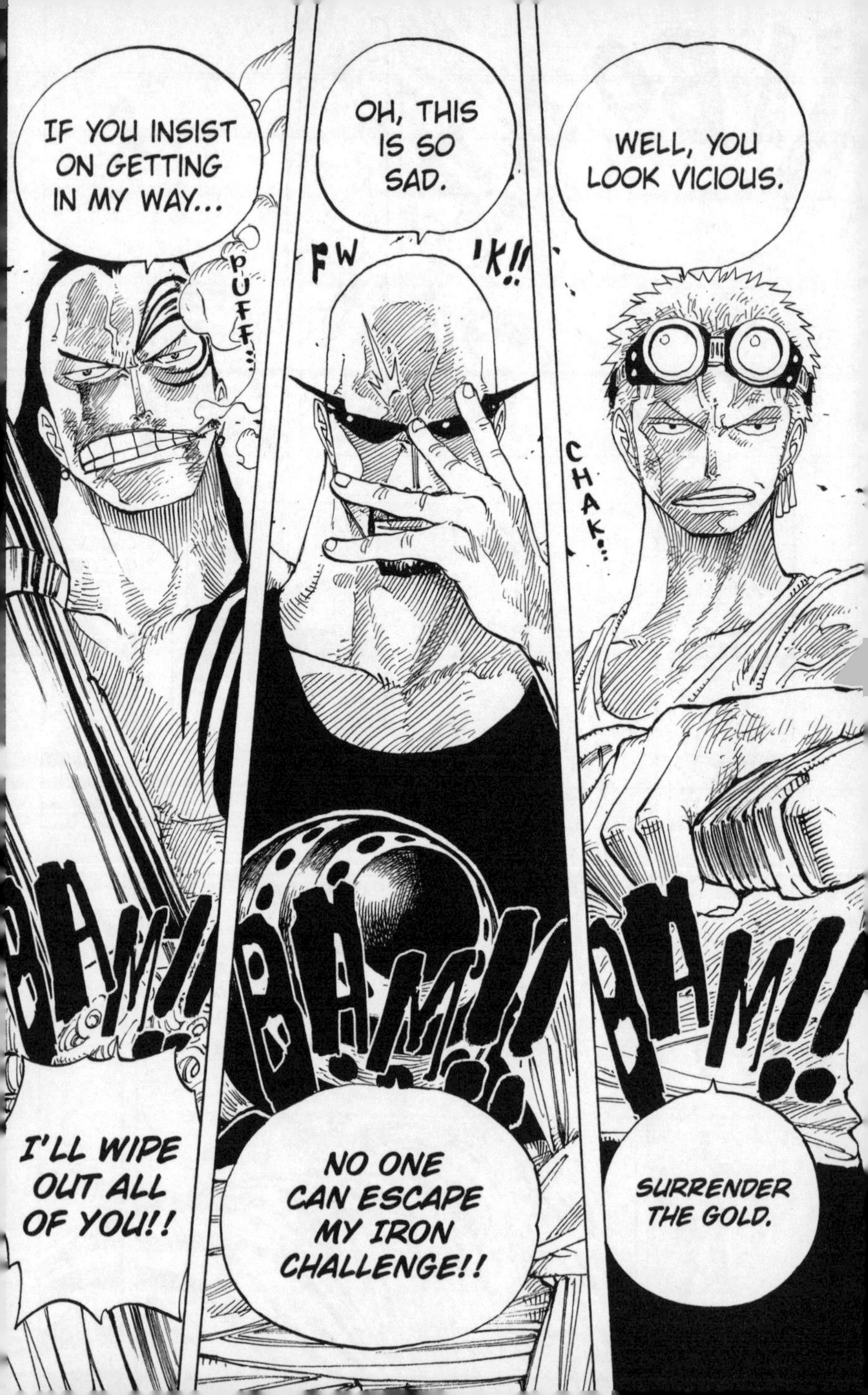
WELL, YOU LOOK VICIOUS.
CHAK..
BAM!!
SURRENDER THE GOLD.
OH, THIS IS SO SAD.
FWIK!!
BAM!!
NO ONE CAN ESCAPE MY IRON CHALLENGE!!
IF YOU INSIST ON GETTING IN MY WAY...
PUFF..
BAM!!
I'LL WIPE OUT ALL OF YOU!!

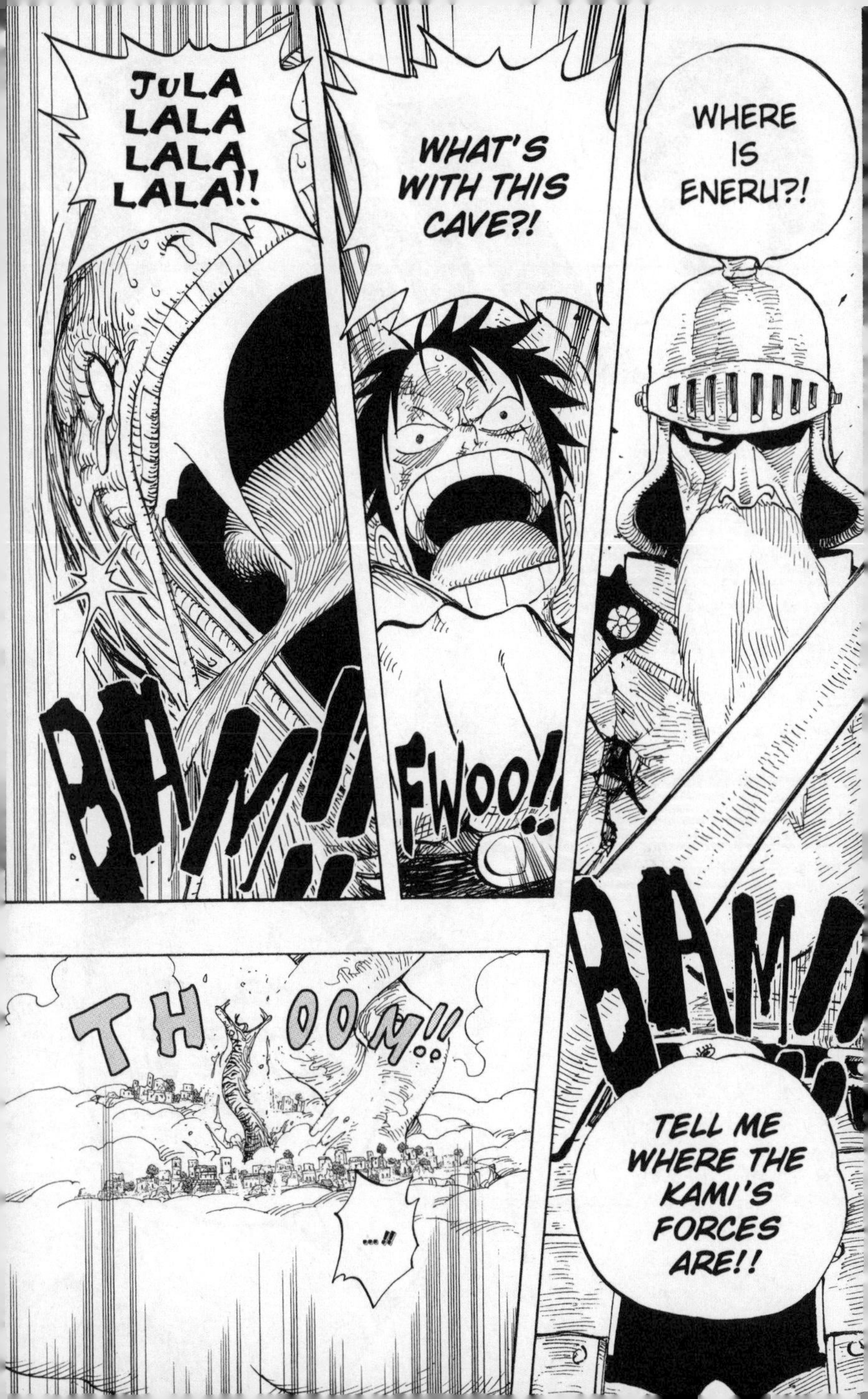
WHERE IS ENERU?!
BAM!!
TELL ME WHERE THE KAMI'S FORCES ARE!!
WHAT'S WITH THIS CAVE?!
FWOO!!
JULA LALA LALA LALA!!
BAM!!
THOOM!!
...!!

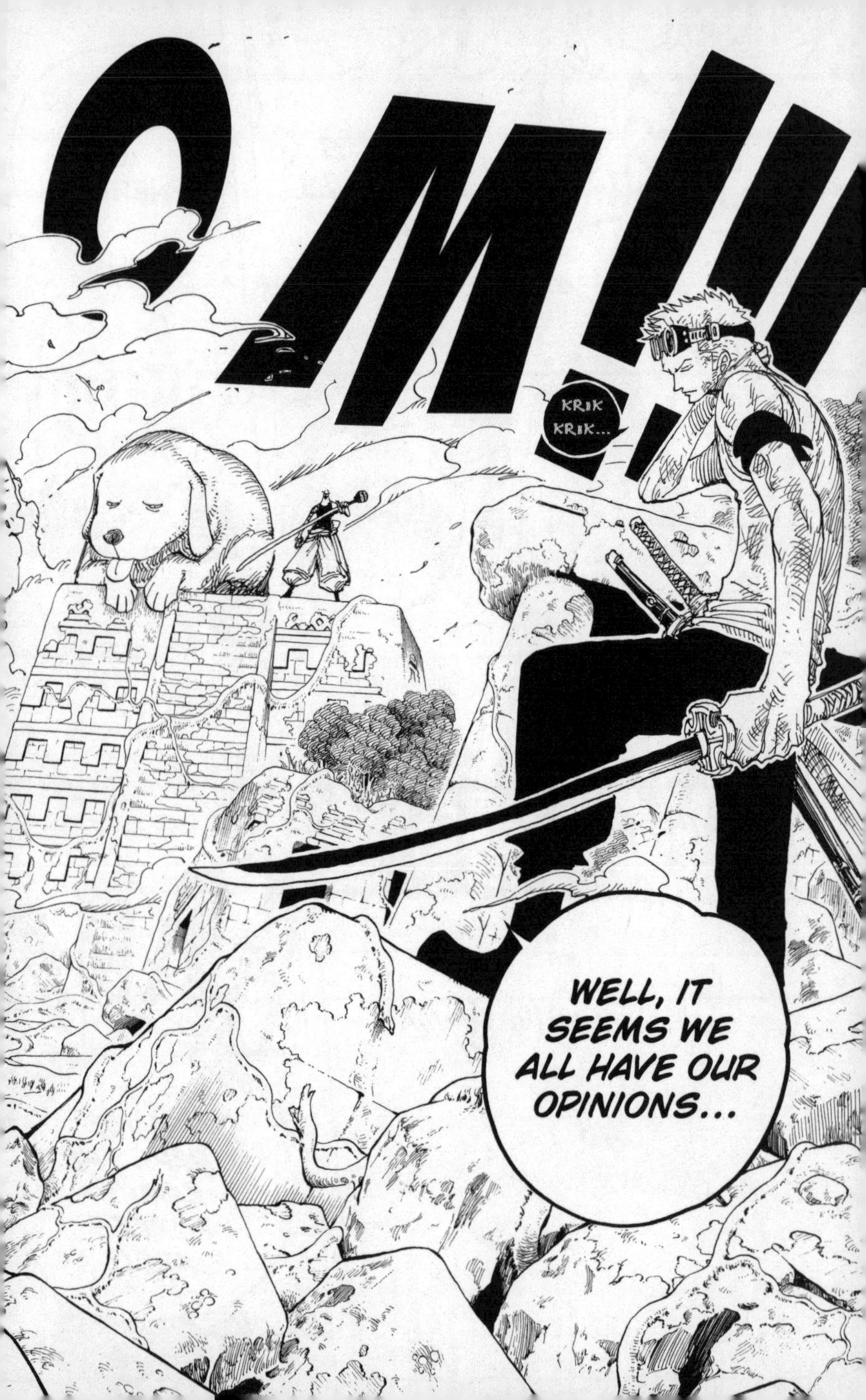
OM!!!
KRIK KRIK...
WELL, IT SEEMS WE ALL HAVE OUR OPINIONS...

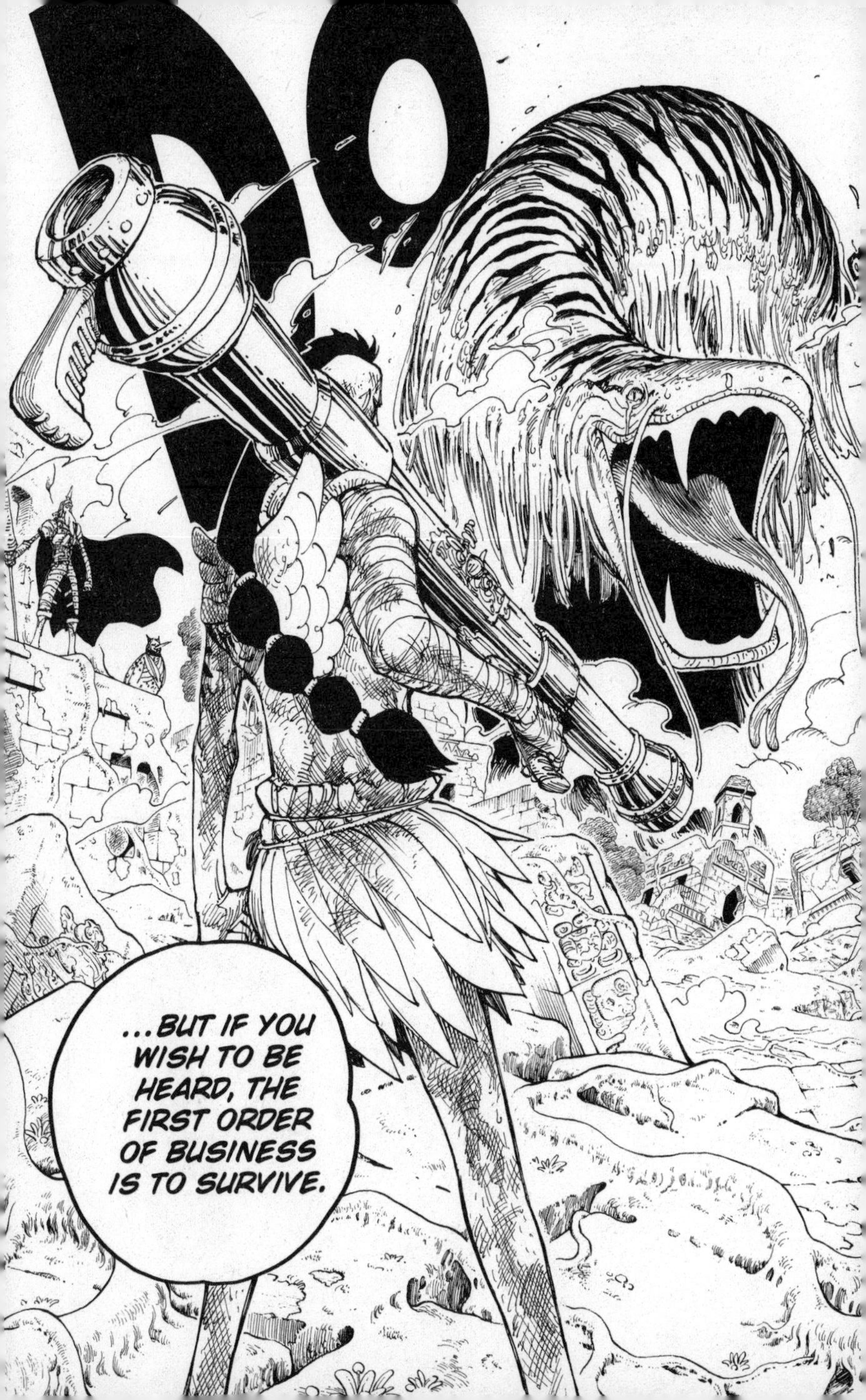
DO
...BUT IF YOU WISH TO BE HEARD, THE FIRST ORDER OF BUSINESS IS TO SURVIVE.

Chapter 268: SUITE

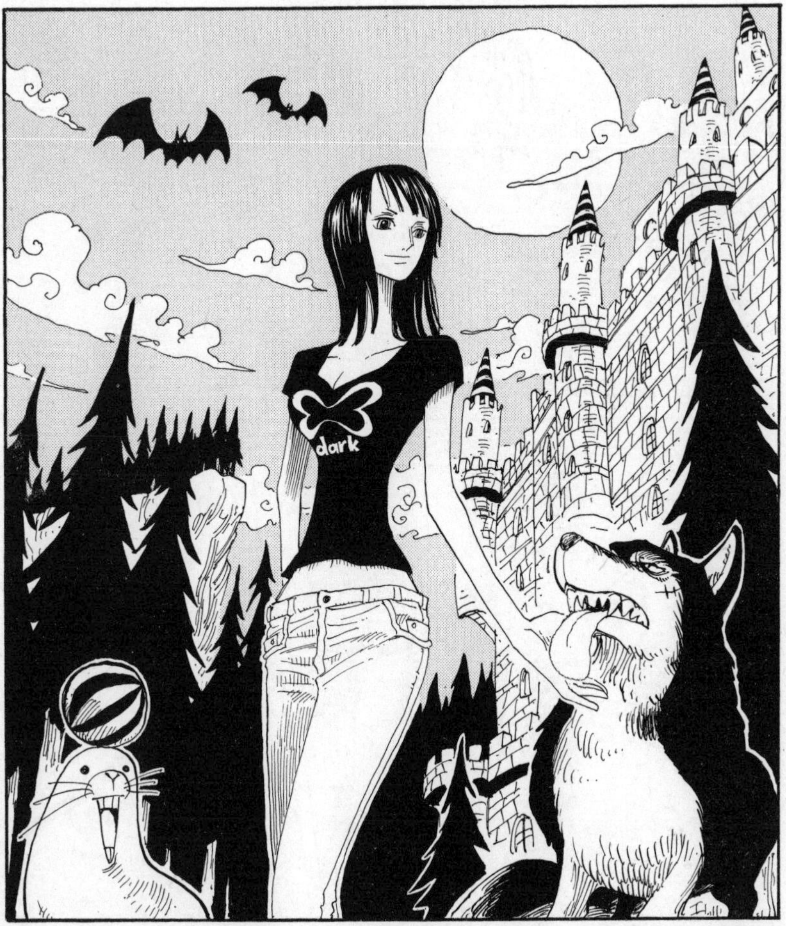
dark

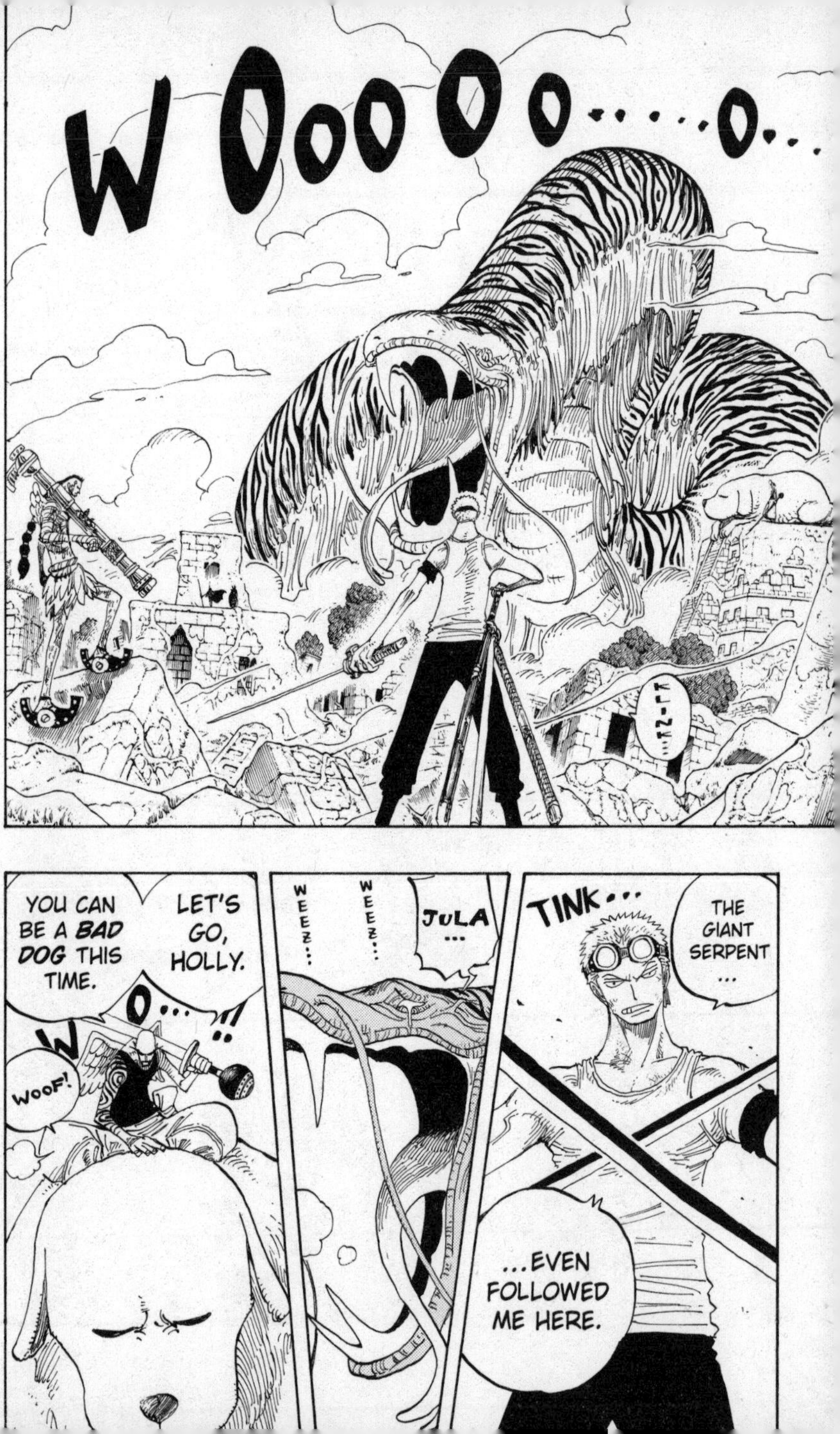
WOOOOO.....O...
KLINK...
TINK...
THE GIANT SERPENT ...
...EVEN FOLLOWED ME HERE.
WEEZ...
WEEZ...
JULA ...
LET'S GO, HOLLY.
YOU CAN BE A BAD DOG THIS TIME.
WO...!!
WOOF!

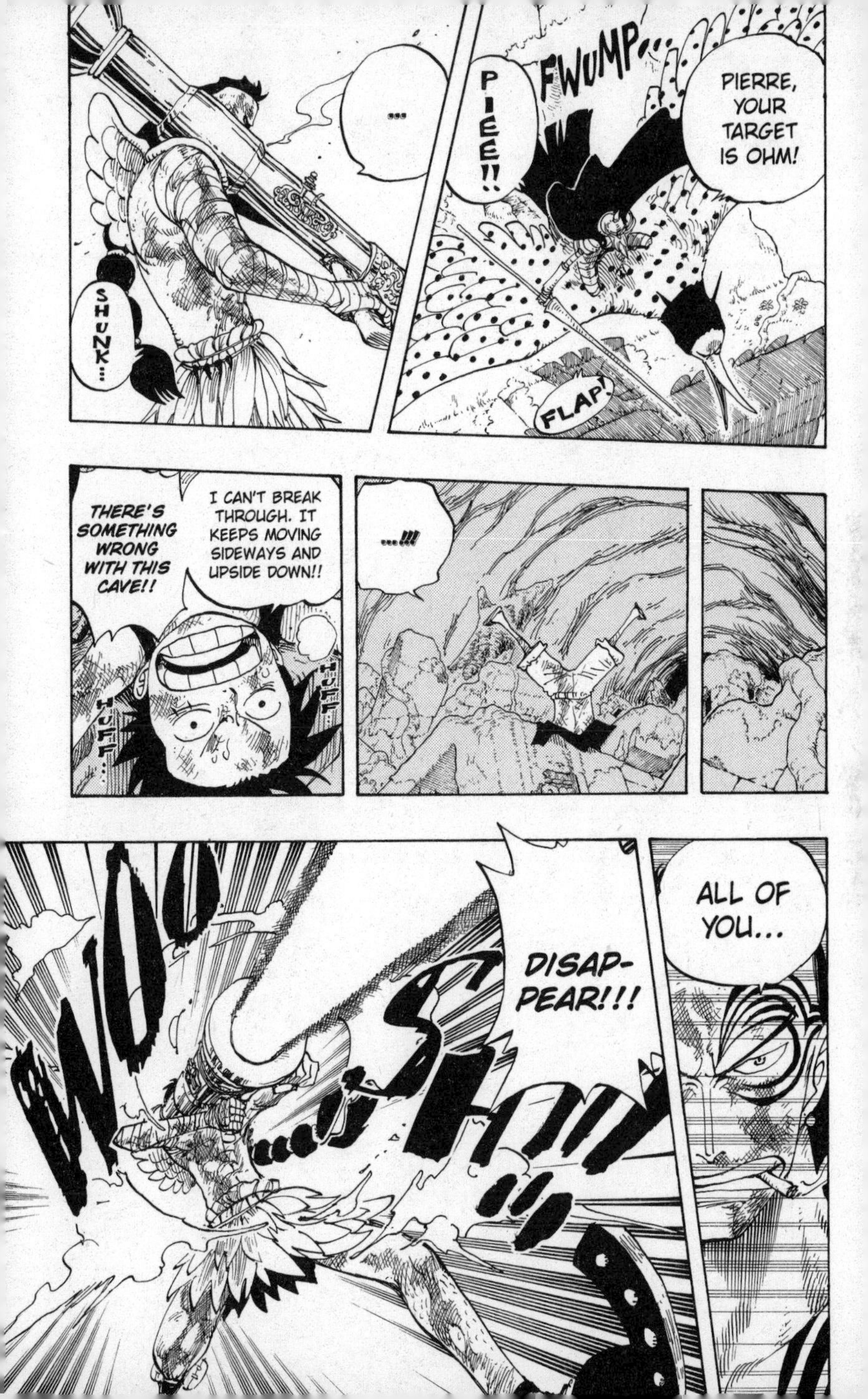
PIERRE, YOUR TARGET IS OHM!
FWUMP...
PIEE!!
FLAP!
...
SHUNK...
...!!!
I CAN'T BREAK THROUGH. IT KEEPS MOVING SIDEWAYS AND UPSIDE DOWN!!
THERE'S SOMETHING WRONG WITH THIS CAVE!!
HUFF...
HUFF...
ALL OF YOU...
DISAP-PEAR!!!

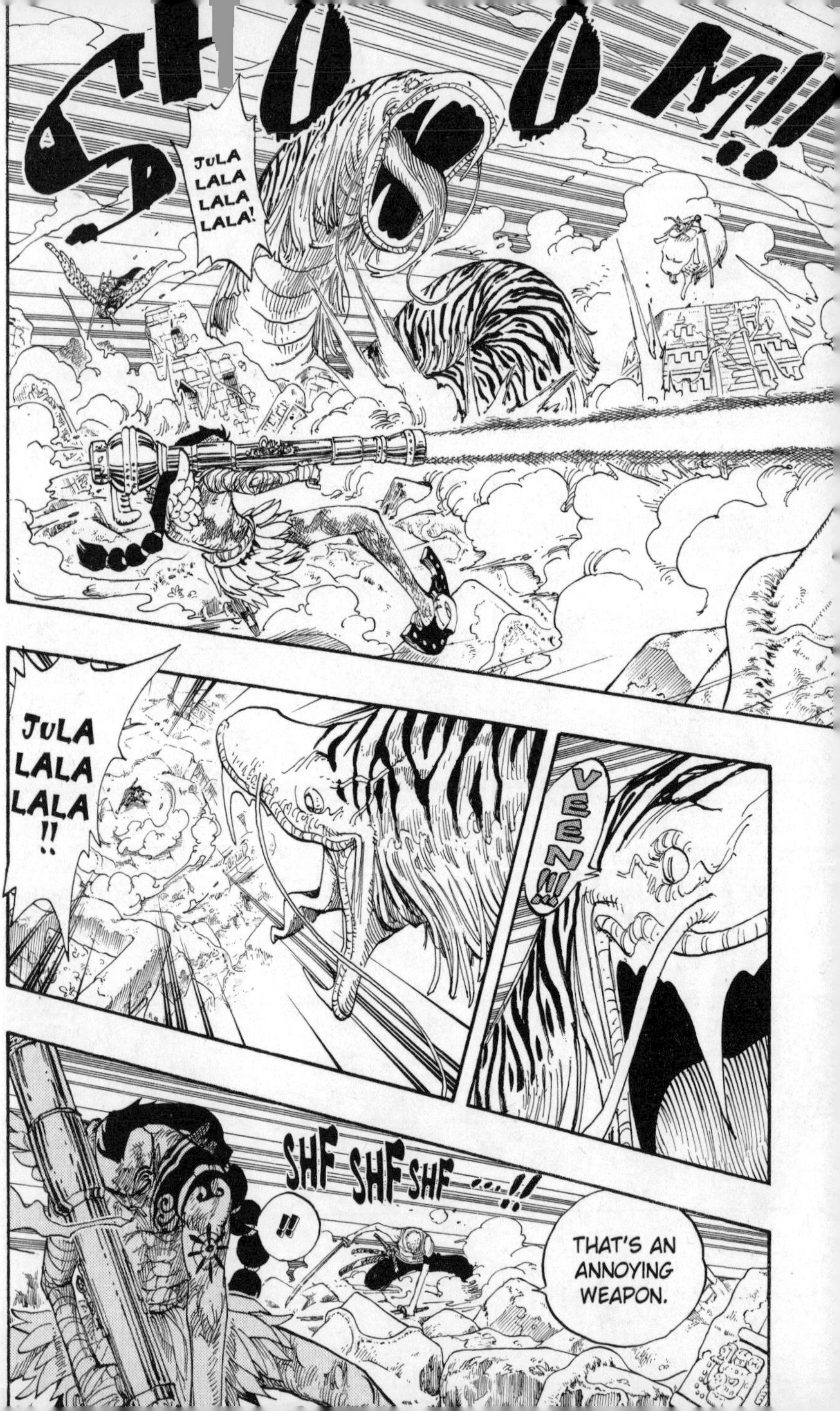
SHOOOM!!
JULA LALA LALA LALA!
VEEN!!!
JULA LALA LALA!!
THAT'S AN ANNOYING WEAPON.
SHF SHF SHF ...!!
!!

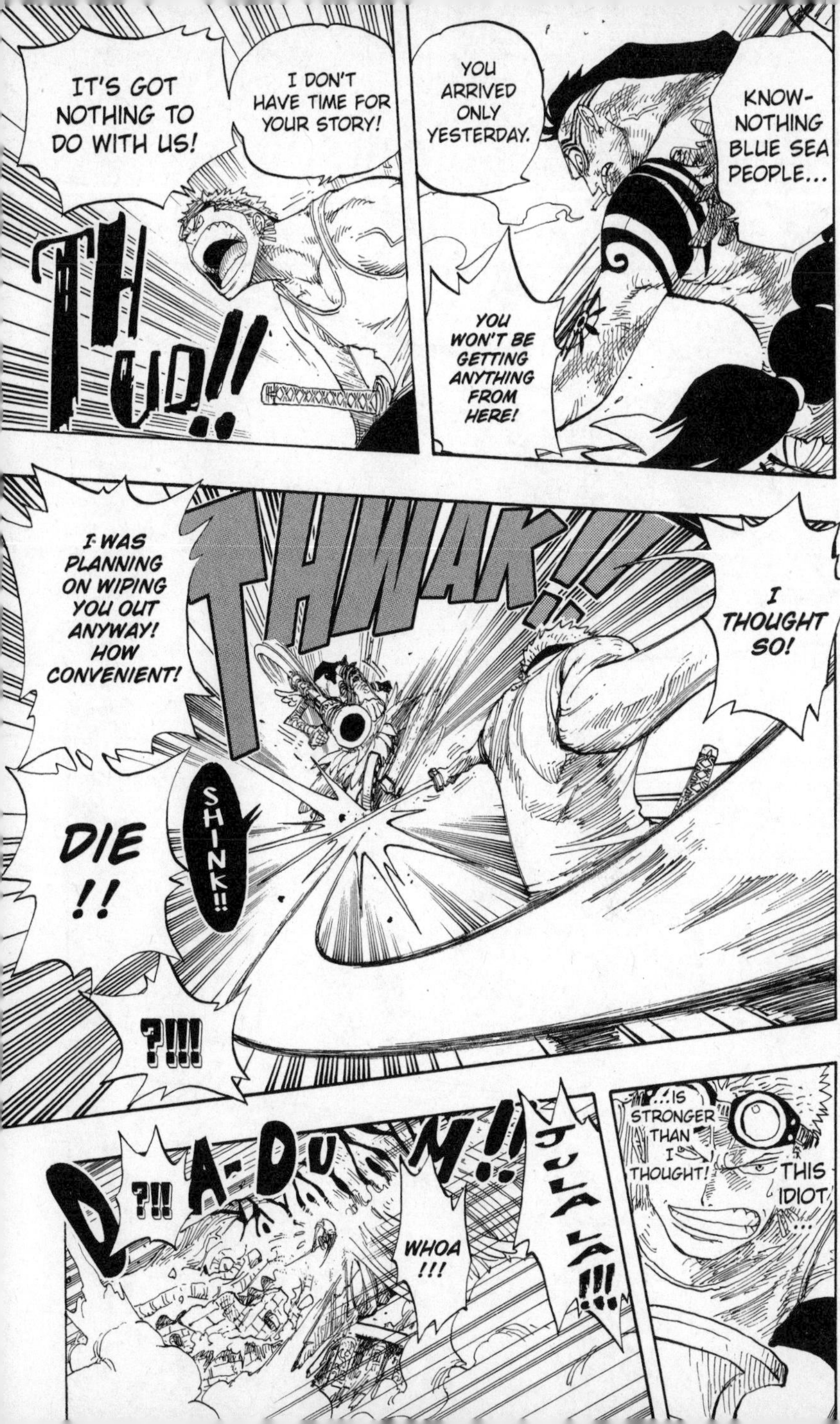
KNOW-NOTHING BLUE SEA PEOPLE...
YOU ARRIVED ONLY YESTERDAY.
YOU WON'T BE GETTING ANYTHING FROM HERE!
I DON'T HAVE TIME FOR YOUR STORY!
IT'S GOT NOTHING TO DO WITH US!
THUD!!
I THOUGHT SO!
THWAK!!
I WAS PLANNING ON WIPING YOU OUT ANYWAY! HOW CONVENIENT!
SHINK!!
DIE!!
?!!!
THIS IDIOT...
...IS STRONGER THAN I THOUGHT!
JULA LA!!!
WHOA!!!
?!!
DA-DUMM!!

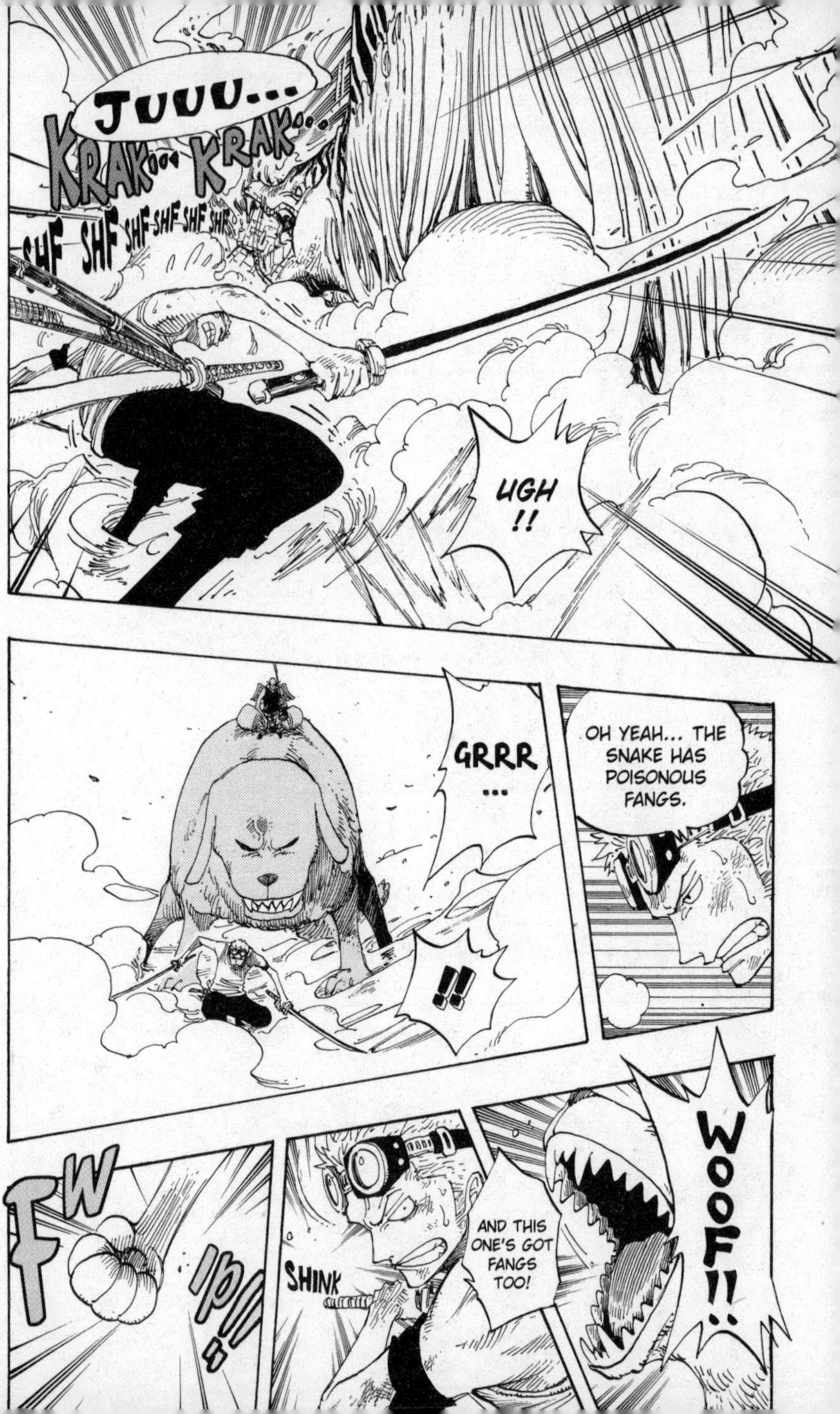
JUUU...
KRAK... KRAK...
SHF SHF SHF SHF SHF SHF
UGH !!
OH YEAH... THE SNAKE HAS POISONOUS FANGS.
GRRR ...
!!
WOOF!!
AND THIS ONE'S GOT FANGS TOO!
SHINK
FWIP!!

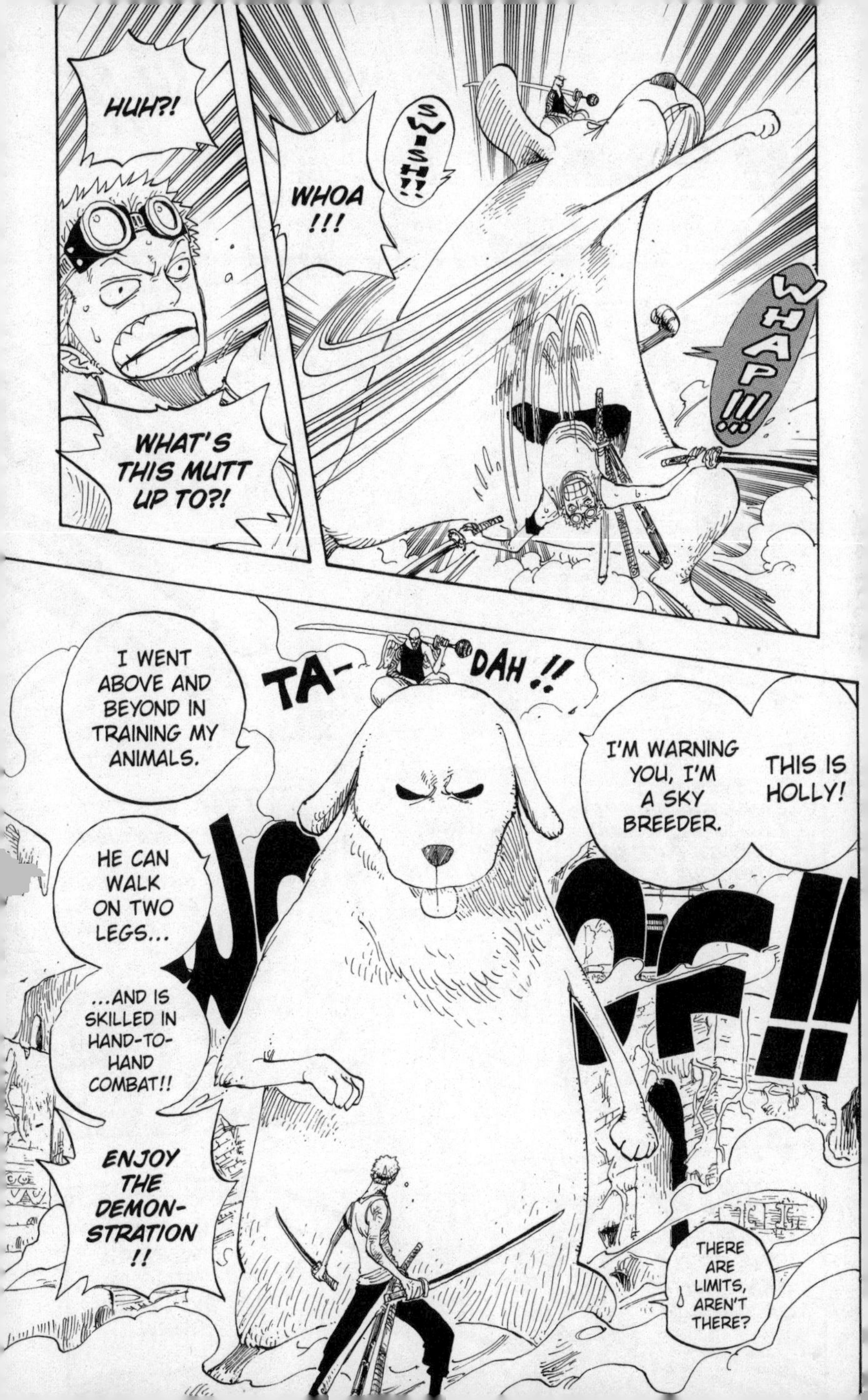
SWISH!!
WHOA !!!
WHAP!!!
HUH?!
WHAT'S THIS MUTT UP TO?!
TA-DAH!!
THIS IS HOLLY!
I'M WARNING YOU, I'M A SKY BREEDER.
I WENT ABOVE AND BEYOND IN TRAINING MY ANIMALS.
HE CAN WALK ON TWO LEGS...
...AND IS SKILLED IN HAND-TO-HAND COMBAT!!
ENJOY THE DEMONSTRATION!!
THERE ARE LIMITS, AREN'T THERE?

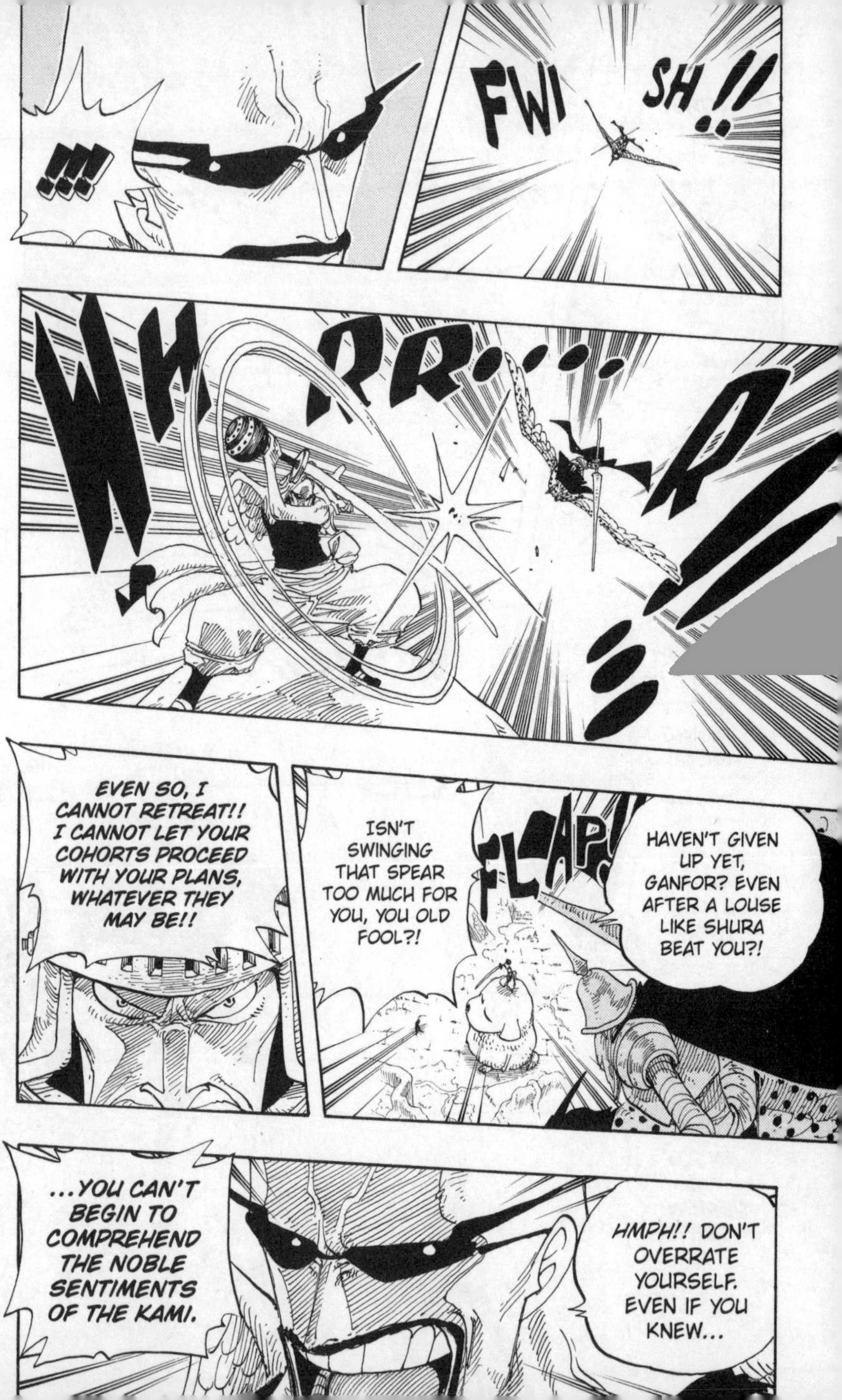
FWISH!!
!!!
WHRR....R!!
HAVEN'T GIVEN UP YET, GANFOR? EVEN AFTER A LOUSE LIKE SHURA BEAT YOU?!
FLAP!
ISN'T SWINGING THAT SPEAR TOO MUCH FOR YOU, YOU OLD FOOL?!
EVEN SO, I CANNOT RETREAT!! I CANNOT LET YOUR COHORTS PROCEED WITH YOUR PLANS, WHATEVER THEY MAY BE!!
HMPH!! DON'T OVERRATE YOURSELF. EVEN IF YOU KNEW...
...YOU CAN'T BEGIN TO COMPREHEND THE NOBLE SENTIMENTS OF THE KAMI.

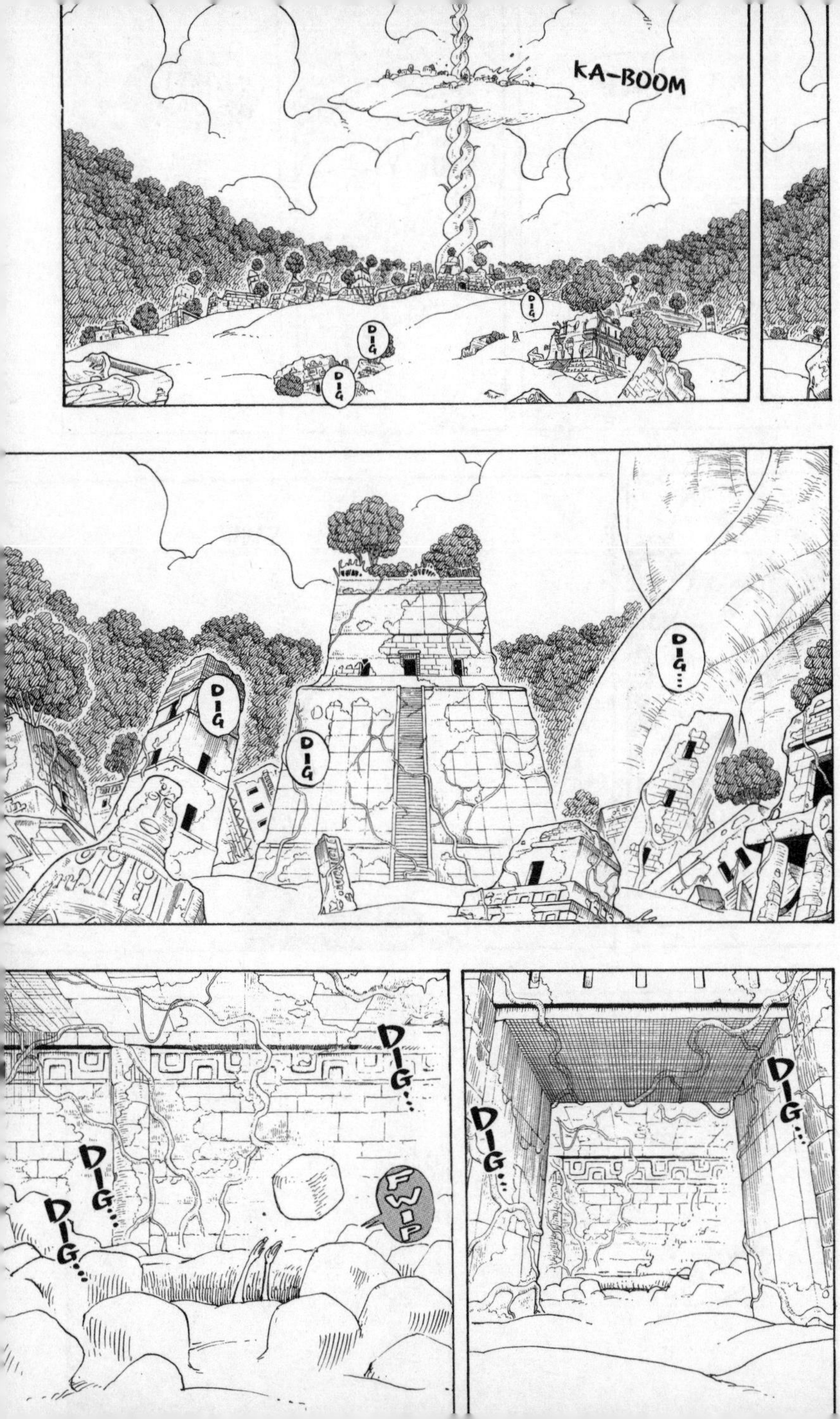
KA-BOOM
DIG
DIG
DIG
DIG...
DIG
DIG
DIG...
DIG...
DIG...
FWIP
DIG...
DIG...

FWIP

SWUF...

SHUNK...

WOBBLE

!

...

FWIP

PHEW
...

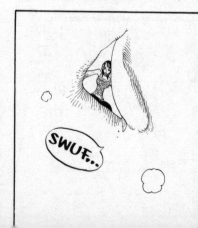

SWUF...

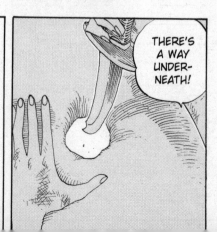

THERE'S A WAY UNDER-NEATH!

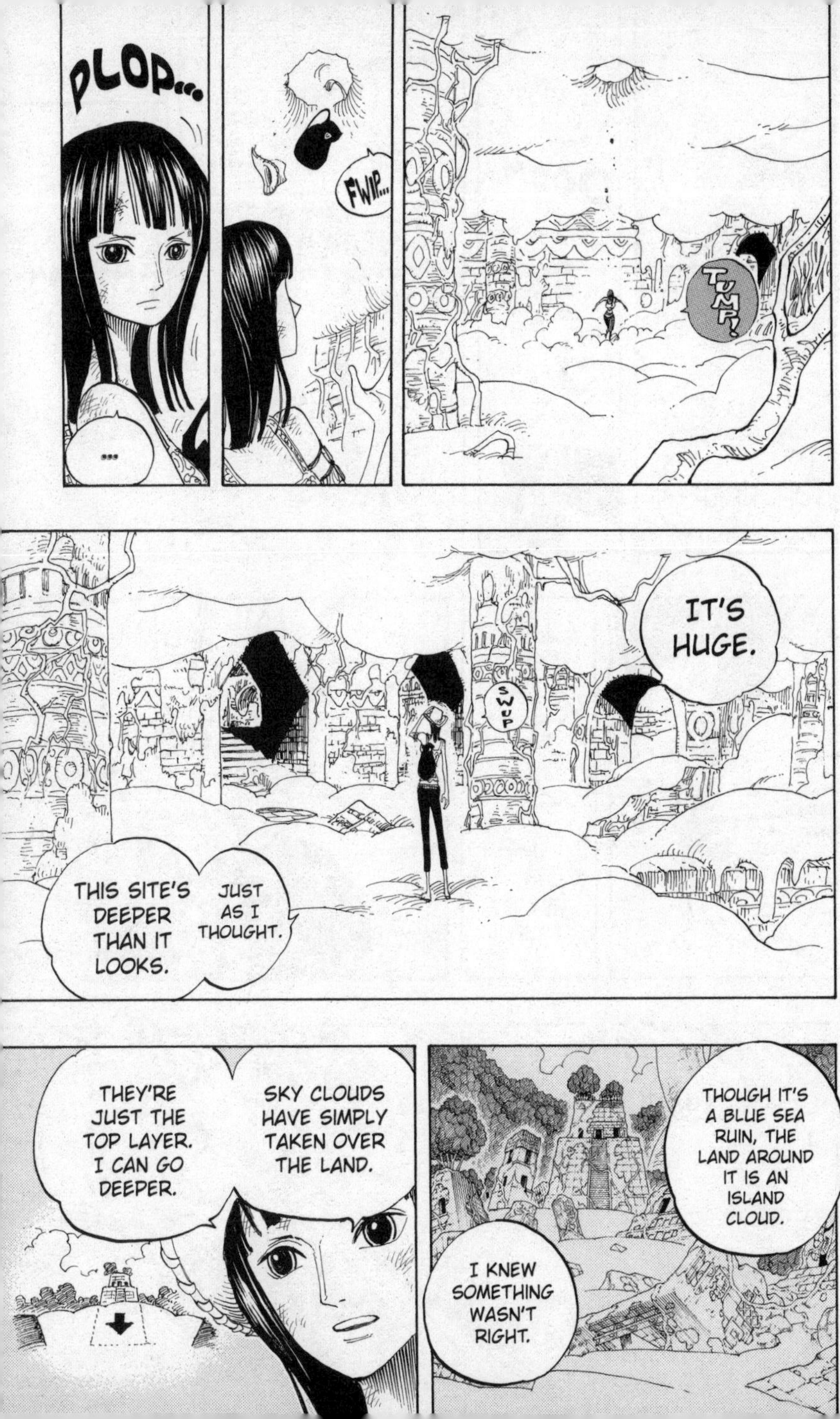
TUMP!
FWIP...
PLOP...
...
IT'S HUGE.
SWUP
JUST AS I THOUGHT.
THIS SITE'S DEEPER THAN IT LOOKS.
THOUGH IT'S A BLUE SEA RUIN, THE LAND AROUND IT IS AN ISLAND CLOUD.
I KNEW SOMETHING WASN'T RIGHT.
SKY CLOUDS HAVE SIMPLY TAKEN OVER THE LAND.
THEY'RE JUST THE TOP LAYER. I CAN GO DEEPER.

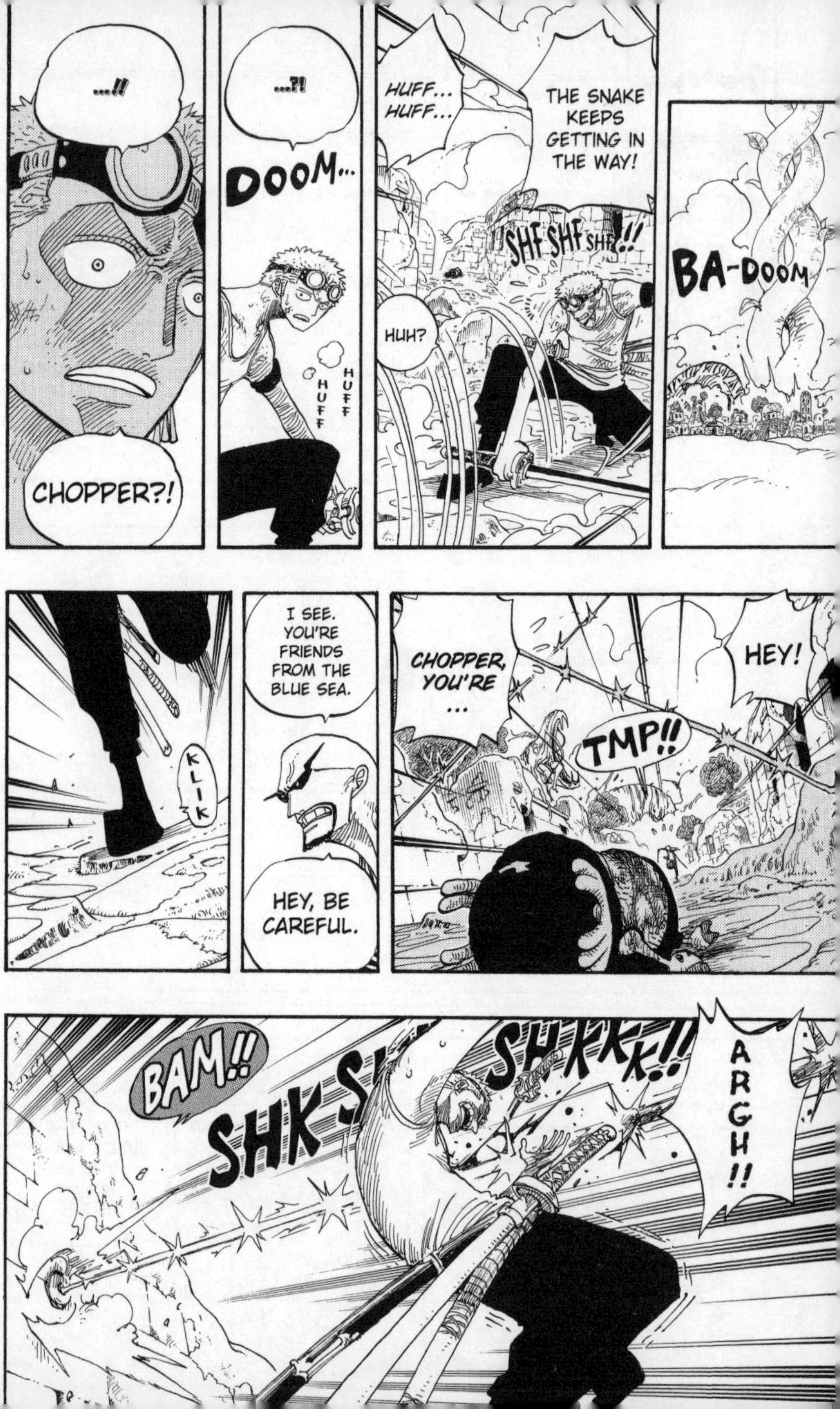
BA-DOOM
HUFF... HUFF...
THE SNAKE KEEPS GETTING IN THE WAY!
SHF SHF SHF!!
HUH?
...?!
DOOM...
HUFF HUFF
...!!
CHOPPER?!
HEY!
CHOPPER, YOU'RE ...
TMP!!
I SEE. YOU'RE FRIENDS FROM THE BLUE SEA.
HEY, BE CAREFUL.
KLIK
ARGH!!
SHRKKK!!
BAM!!
SHK-S

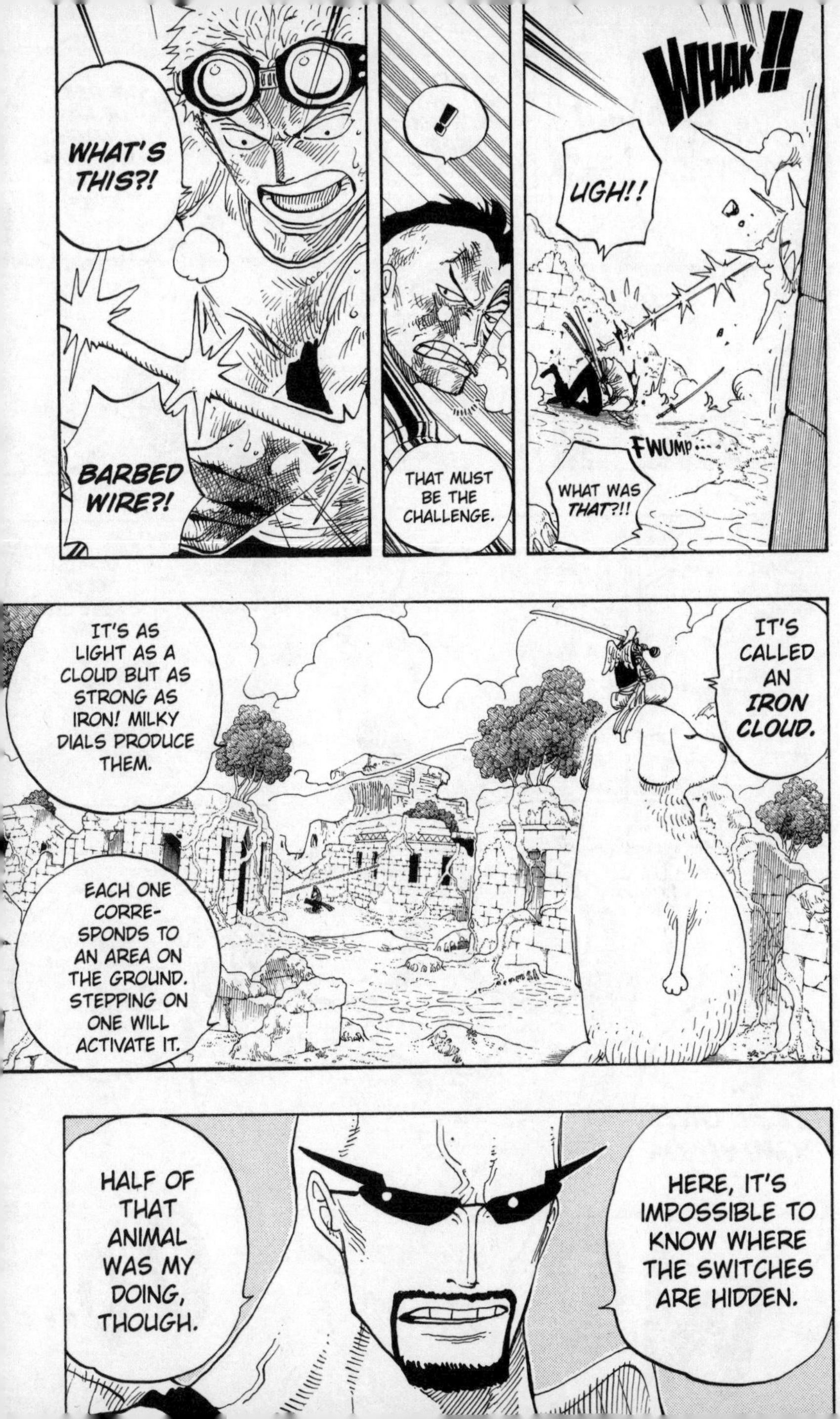
WHAK!!
UGH!!
FWUMP...
WHAT WAS THAT?!!
!
THAT MUST BE THE CHALLENGE.
WHAT'S THIS?!
BARBED WIRE?!
IT'S CALLED AN IRON CLOUD.
IT'S AS LIGHT AS A CLOUD BUT AS STRONG AS IRON! MILKY DIALS PRODUCE THEM.
EACH ONE CORRE-SPONDS TO AN AREA ON THE GROUND. STEPPING ON ONE WILL ACTIVATE IT.
HERE, IT'S IMPOSSIBLE TO KNOW WHERE THE SWITCHES ARE HIDDEN.
HALF OF THAT ANIMAL WAS MY DOING, THOUGH.

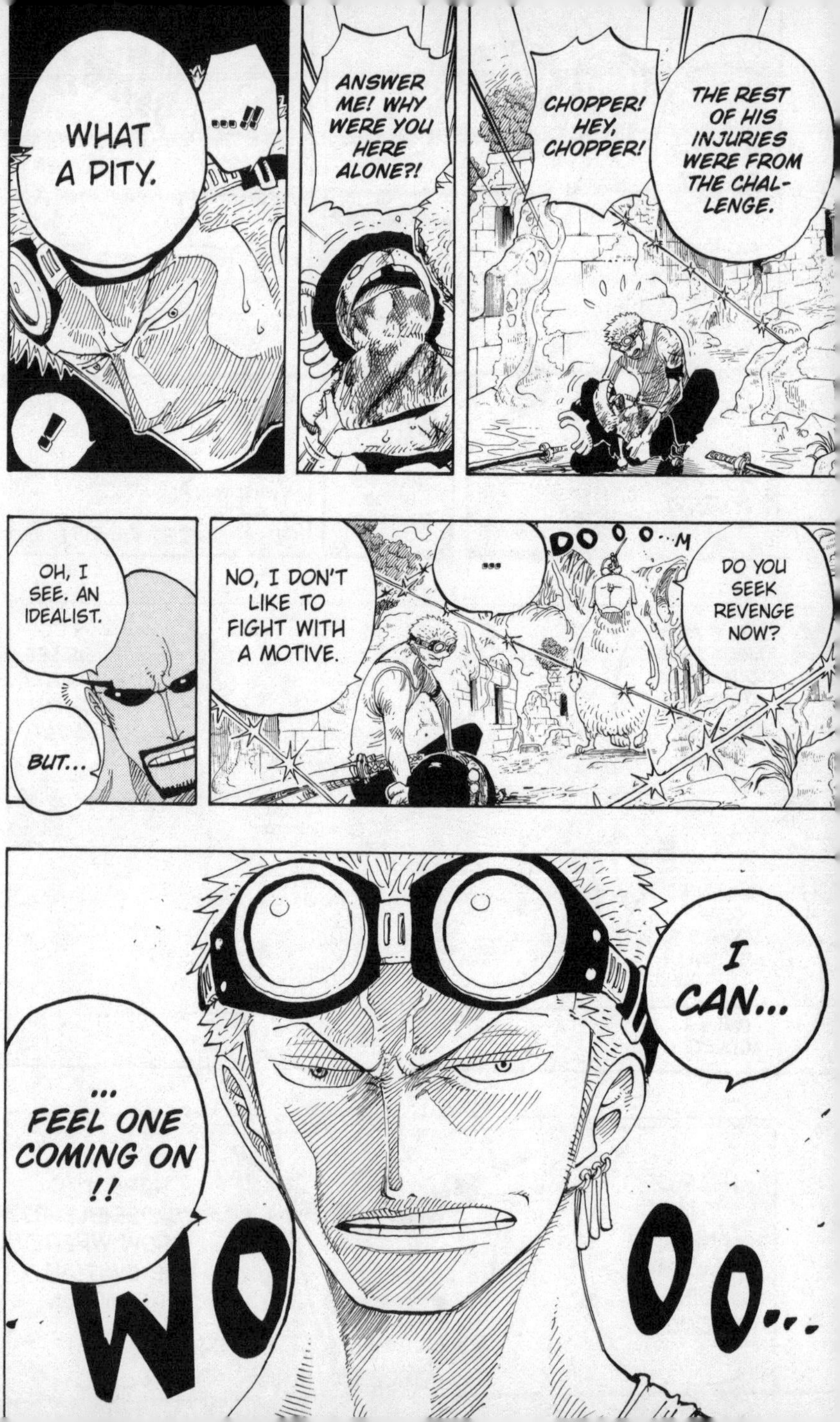
THE REST OF HIS INJURIES WERE FROM THE CHAL-LENGE.
CHOPPER! HEY, CHOPPER!
ANSWER ME! WHY WERE YOU HERE ALONE?!
...!!
WHAT A PITY.
!
DO YOU SEEK REVENGE NOW?
DO O O...M
...
NO, I DON'T LIKE TO FIGHT WITH A MOTIVE.
OH, I SEE. AN IDEALIST.
BUT...
I CAN...
... FEEL ONE COMING ON !!
WO
OO...

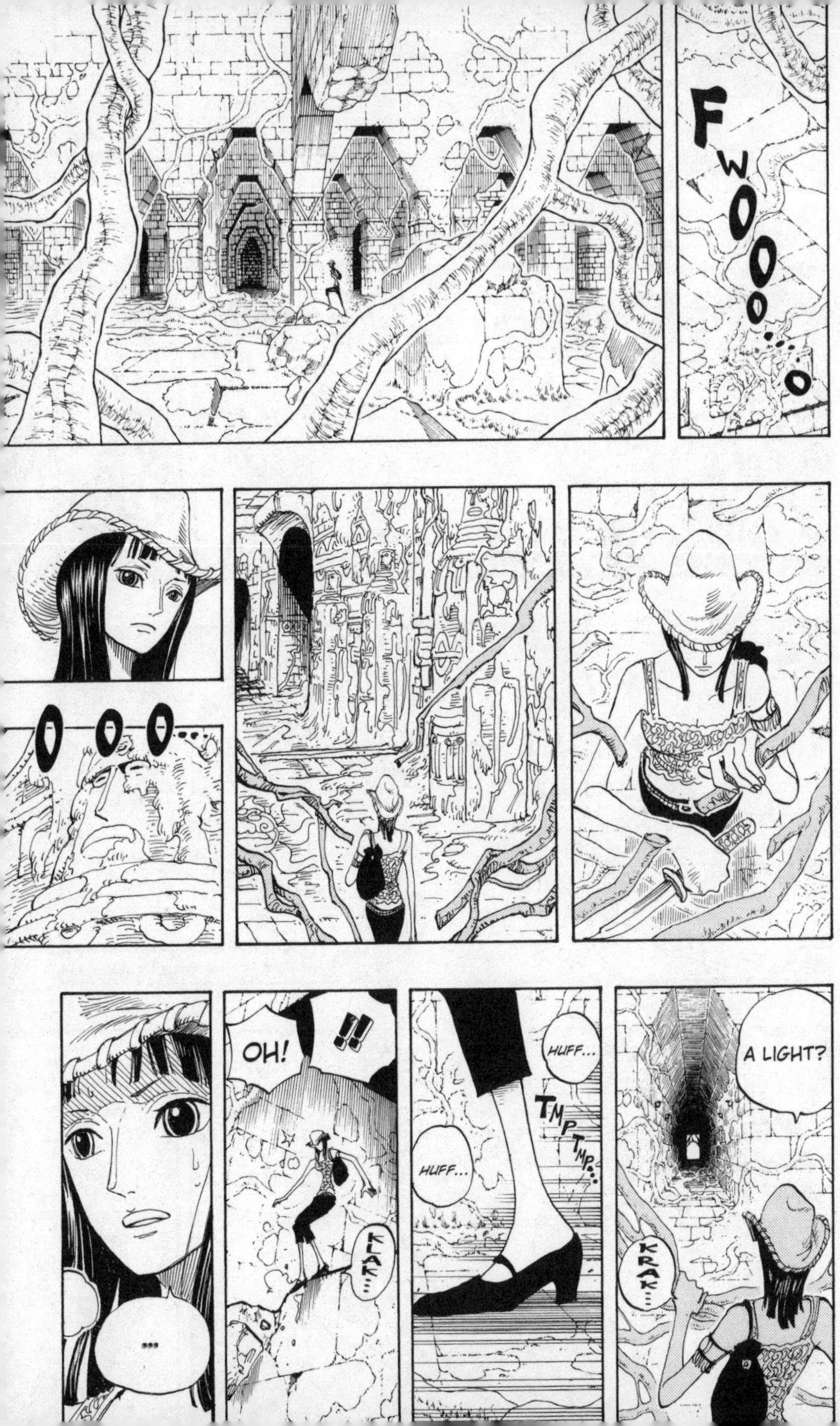
FWOOO...O
OOO...
A LIGHT?
KRAK...
HUFF...
TMP TMP...
HUFF...
OH!
!!
KLAK...
...

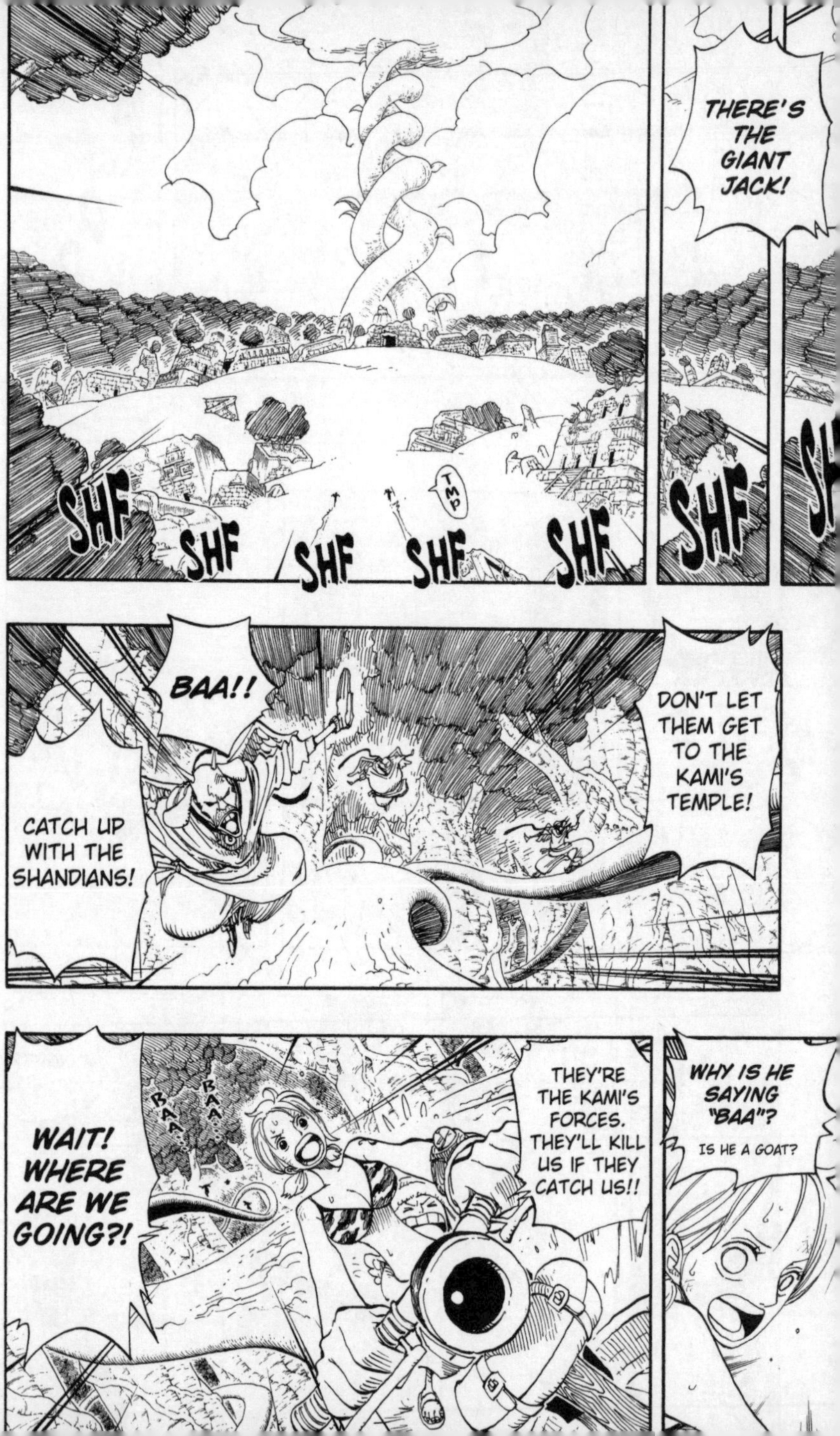
THERE'S THE GIANT JACK!
SHF
SHF
TMP
SHF
SHF
SHF
SHF
SHF
DON'T LET THEM GET TO THE KAMI'S TEMPLE!
BAA!!
CATCH UP WITH THE SHANDIANS!
WHY IS HE SAYING "BAA"?
IS HE A GOAT?
THEY'RE THE KAMI'S FORCES. THEY'LL KILL US IF THEY CATCH US!!
BAA
BAA
WAIT! WHERE ARE WE GOING?!

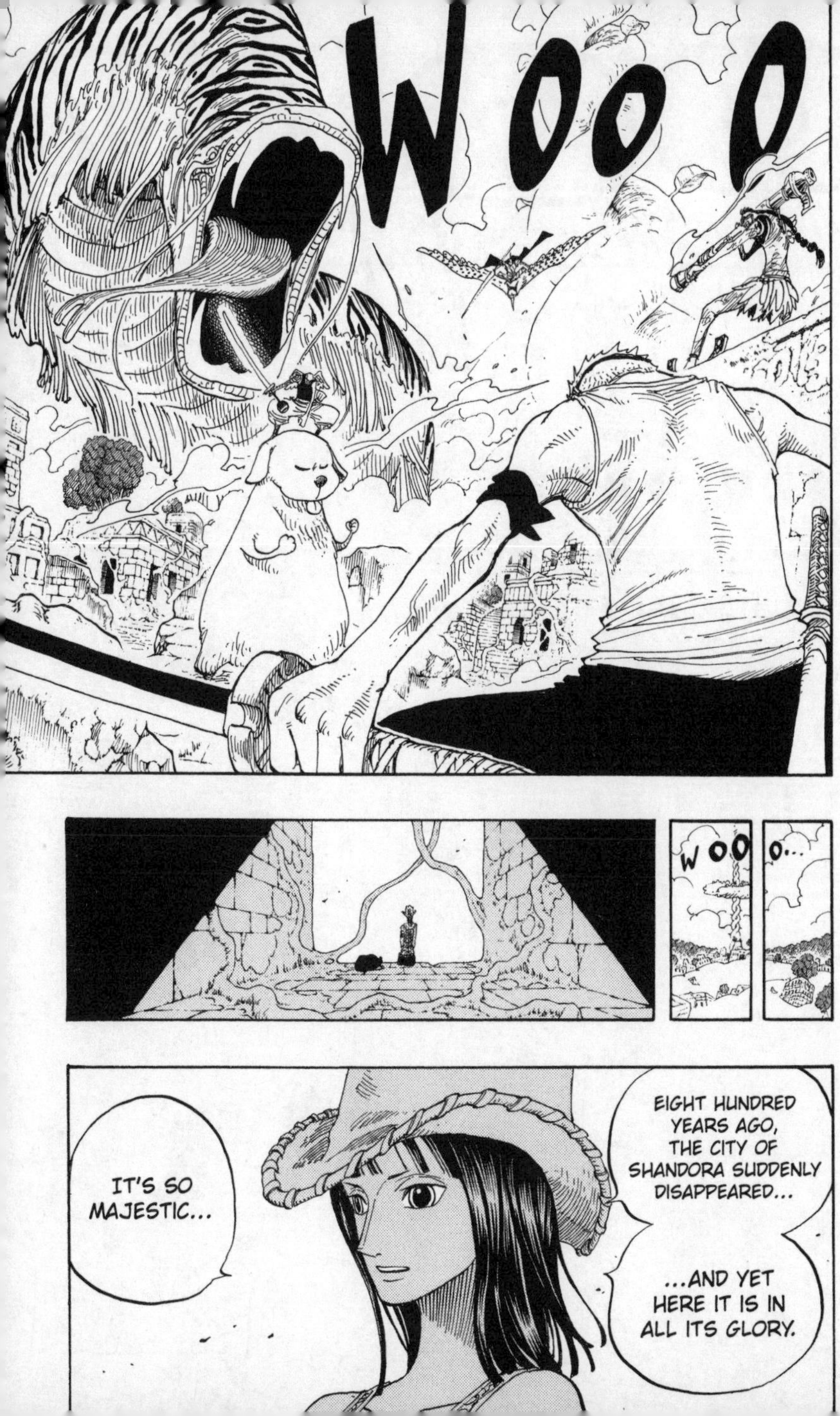
WOOO
WOO
O...
EIGHT HUNDRED YEARS AGO, THE CITY OF SHANDORA SUDDENLY DISAPPEARED...
...AND YET HERE IT IS IN ALL ITS GLORY.
IT'S SO MAJESTIC...

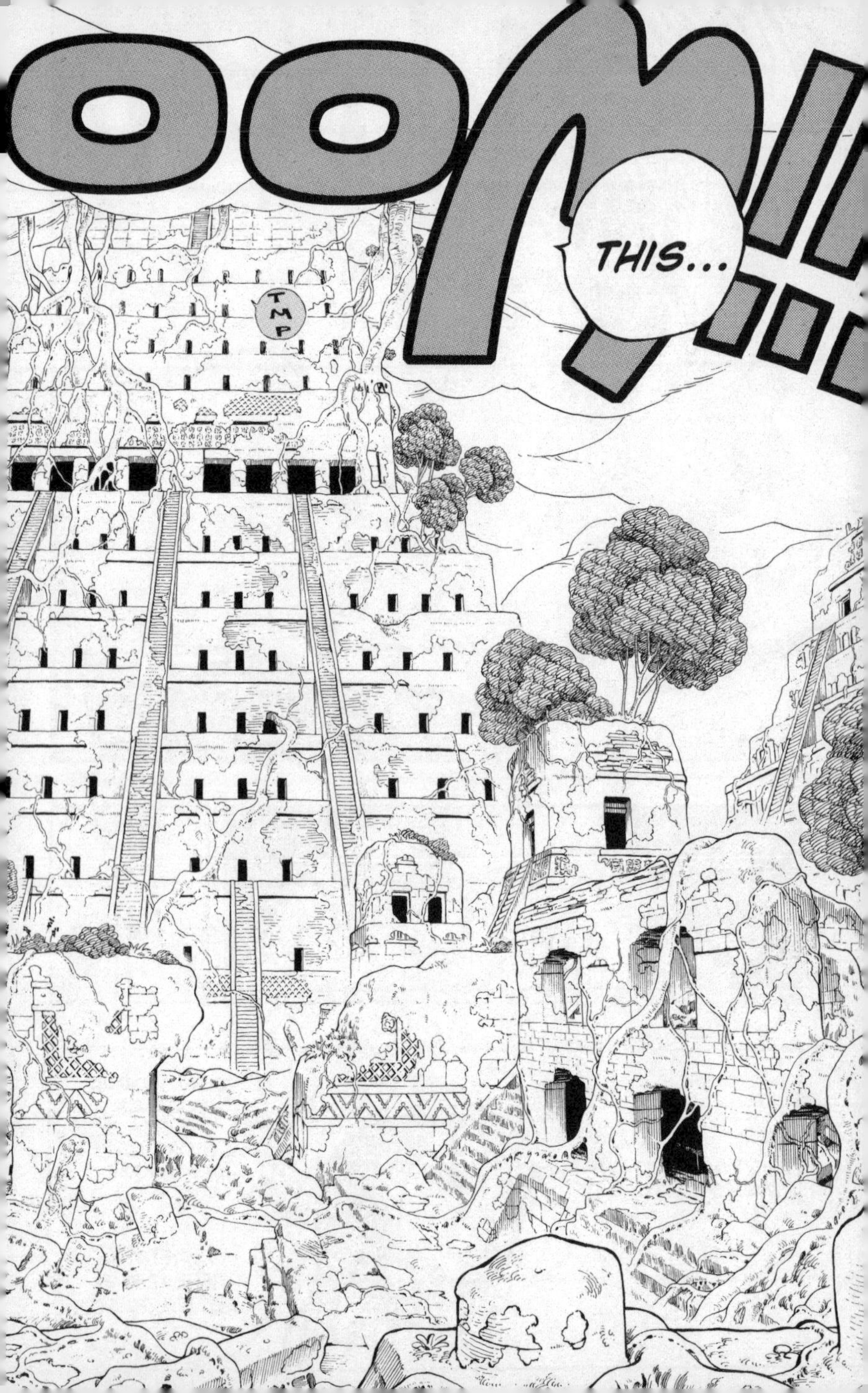
OOM!!
THIS...
TMP

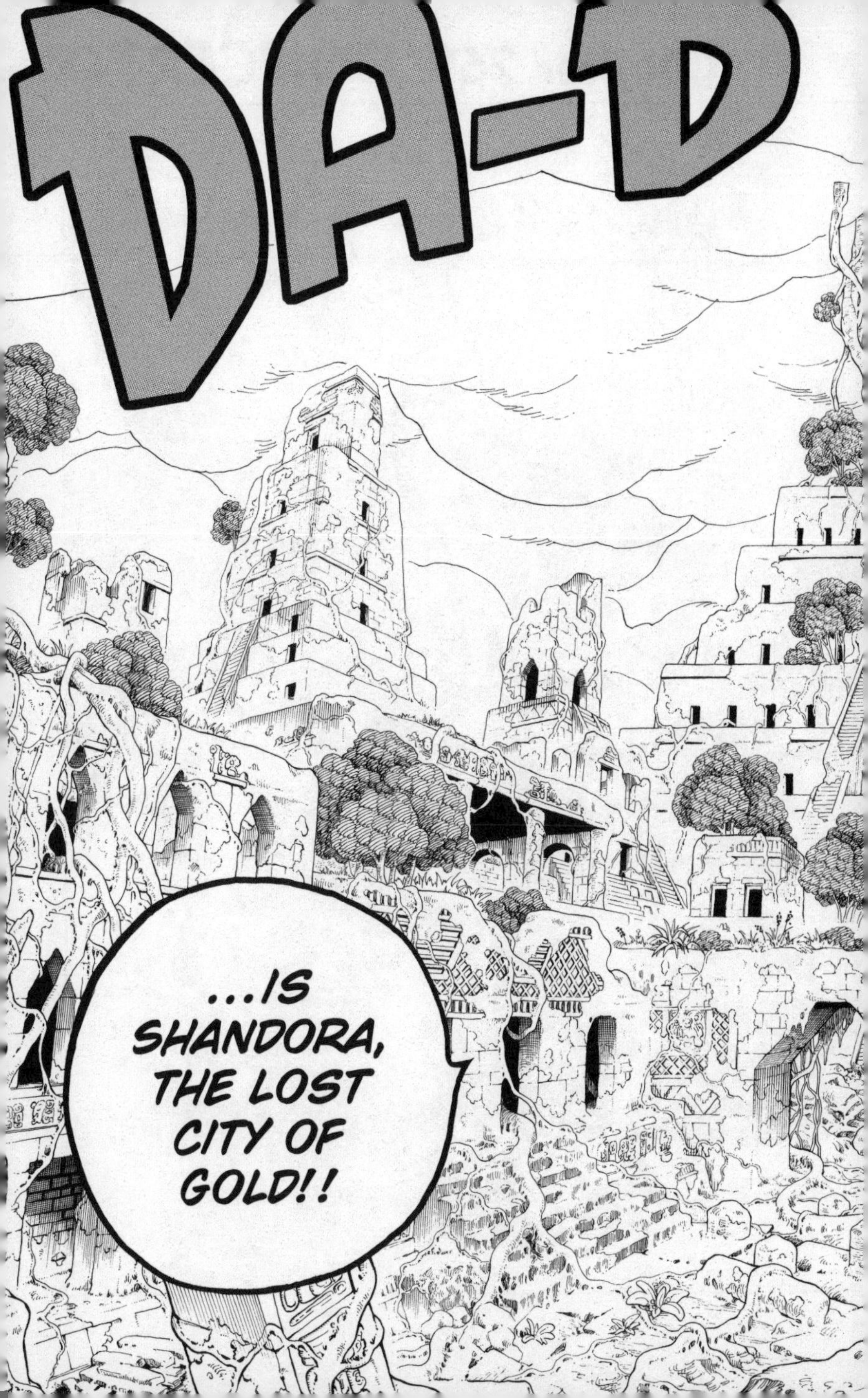
DA-D
...IS SHANDORA, THE LOST CITY OF GOLD!!

Chapter 269: CONCERTO

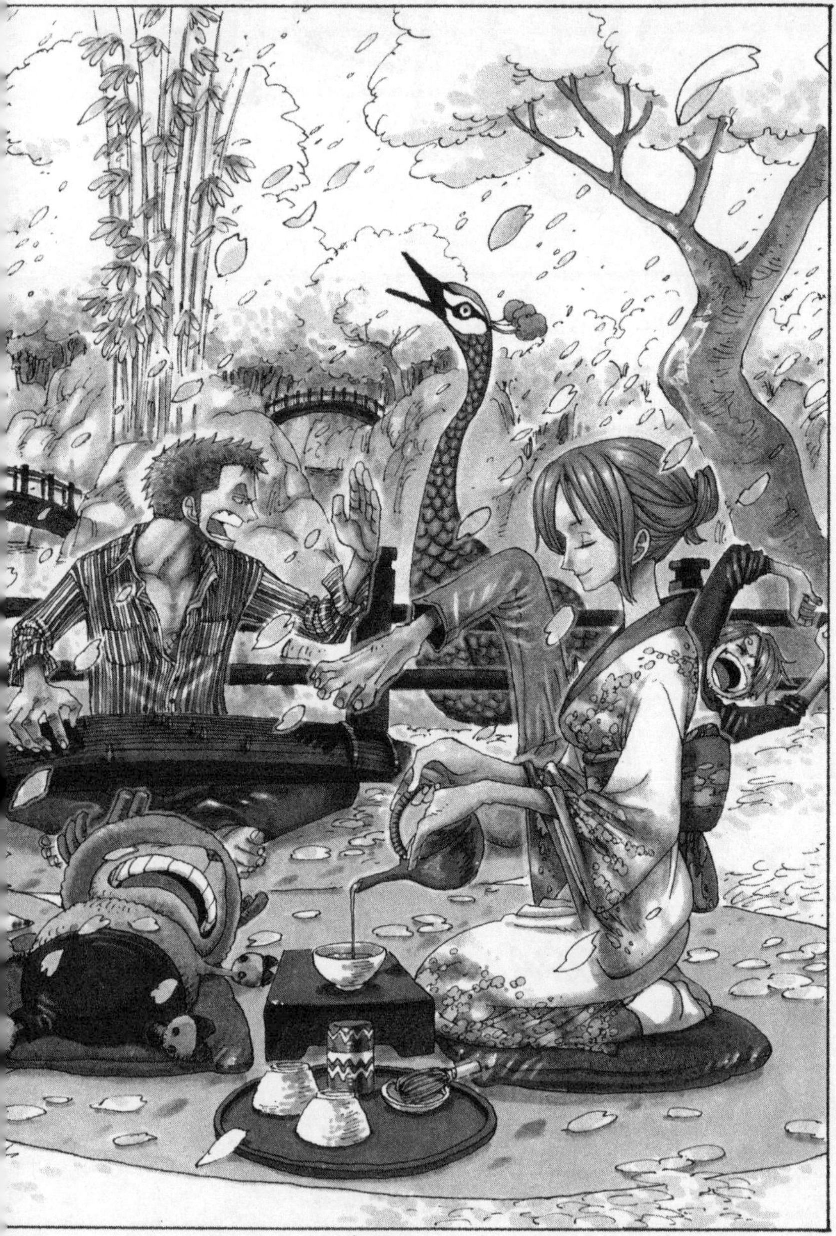

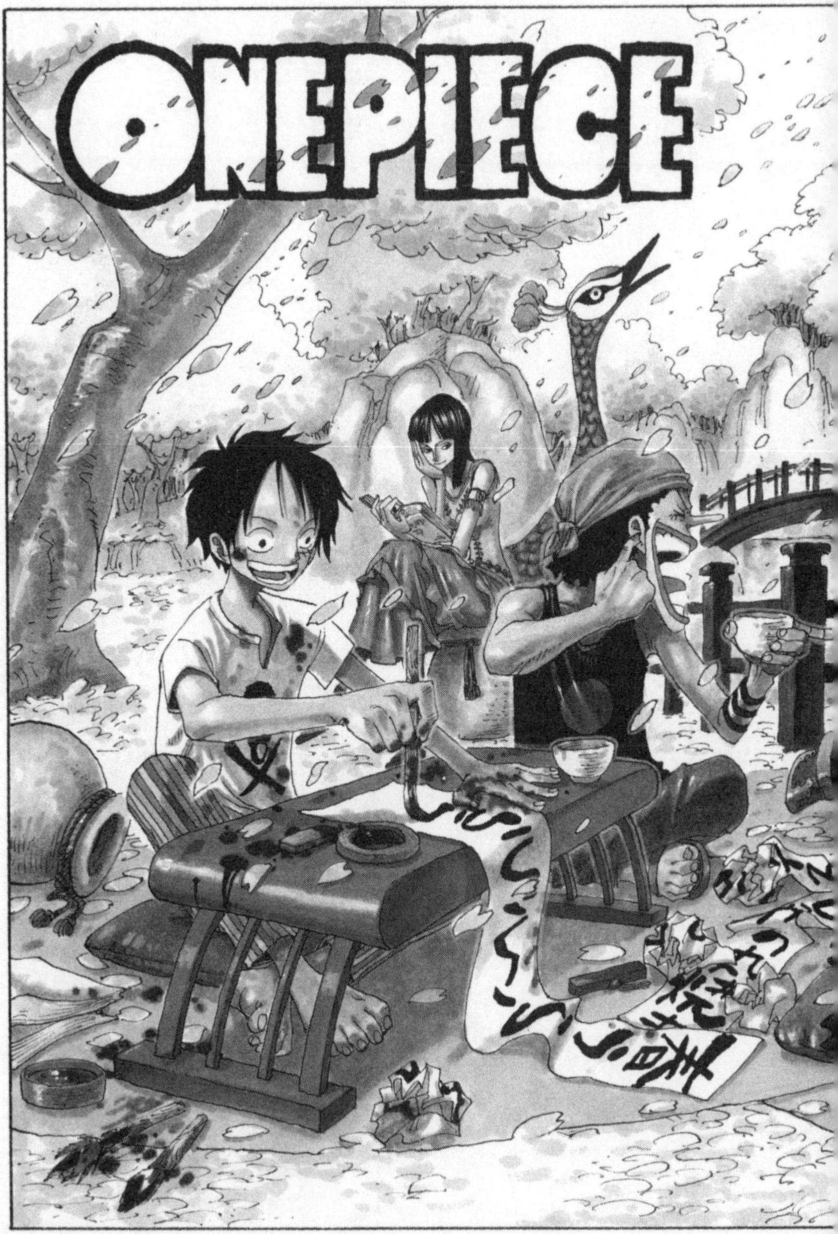
ONE PIECE

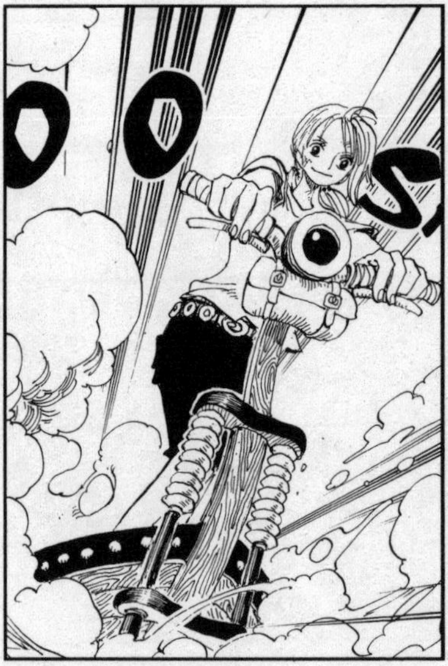
OOS

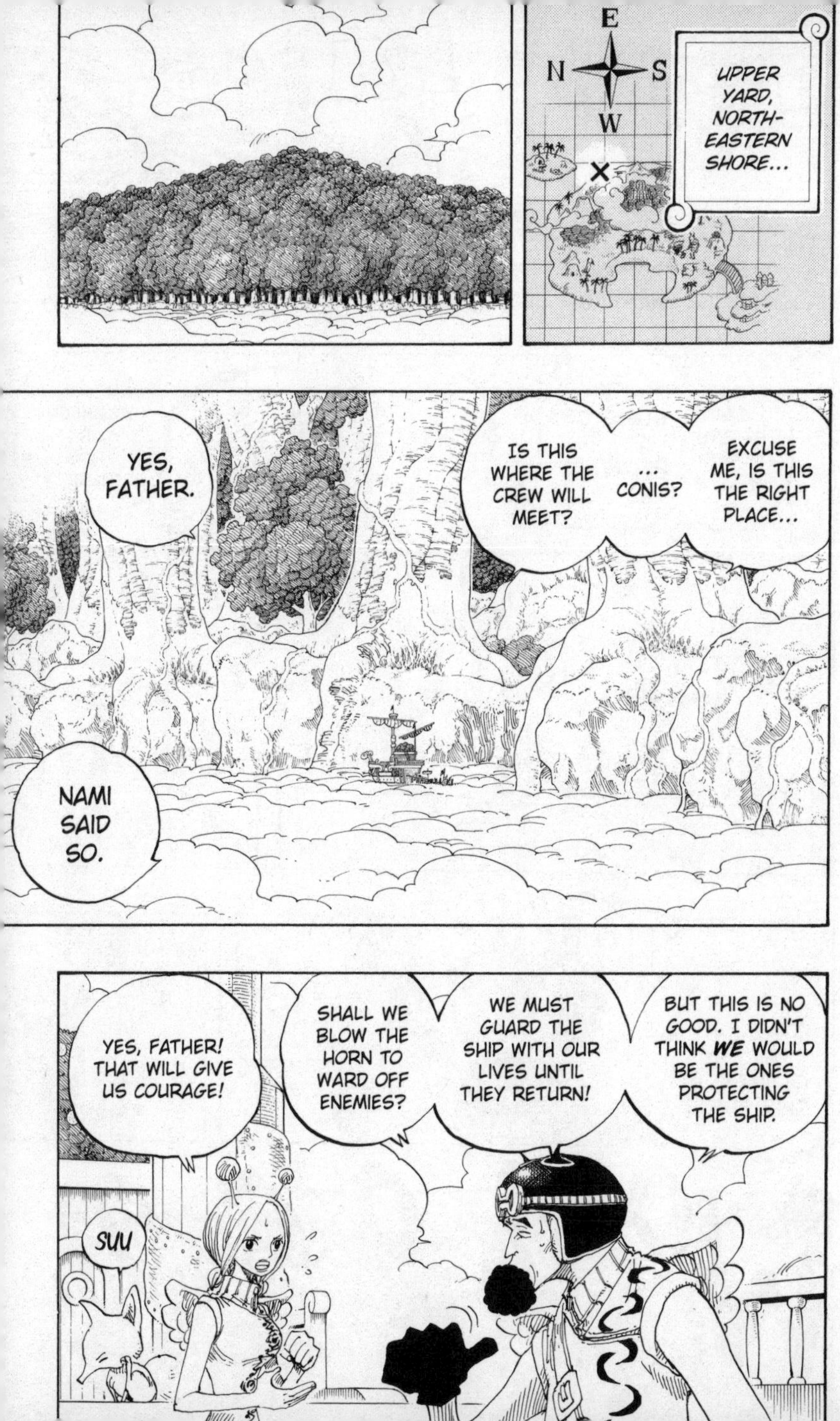
UPPER YARD, NORTH-EASTERN SHORE...
E
N
S
W
EXCUSE ME, IS THIS THE RIGHT PLACE...
... CONIS?
IS THIS WHERE THE CREW WILL MEET?
YES, FATHER.
NAMI SAID SO.
BUT THIS IS NO GOOD. I DIDN'T THINK ***WE*** WOULD BE THE ONES PROTECTING THE SHIP.
WE MUST GUARD THE SHIP WITH OUR LIVES UNTIL THEY RETURN!
SHALL WE BLOW THE HORN TO WARD OFF ENEMIES?
YES, FATHER! THAT WILL GIVE US COURAGE!
SUU

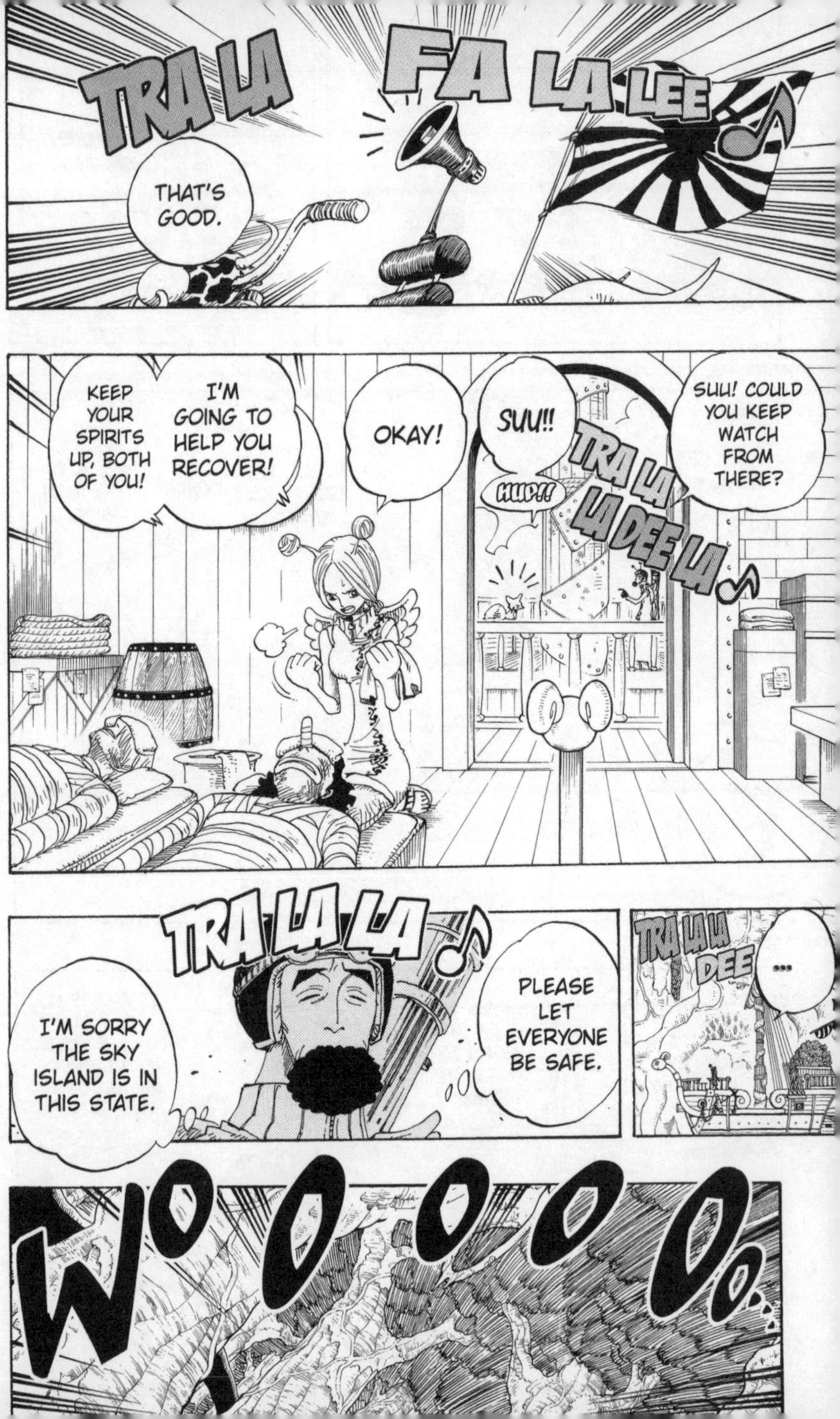
TRA LA FA LA LA LEE
THAT'S GOOD.
SUU! COULD YOU KEEP WATCH FROM THERE?
TRA LA LA DEE LA
SUU!!
HUP!!
OKAY!
I'M GOING TO HELP YOU RECOVER!
KEEP YOUR SPIRITS UP, BOTH OF YOU!
TRA LA LA DEE
...
TRA LA LA
PLEASE LET EVERYONE BE SAFE.
I'M SORRY THE SKY ISLAND IS IN THIS STATE.
WOOOOO

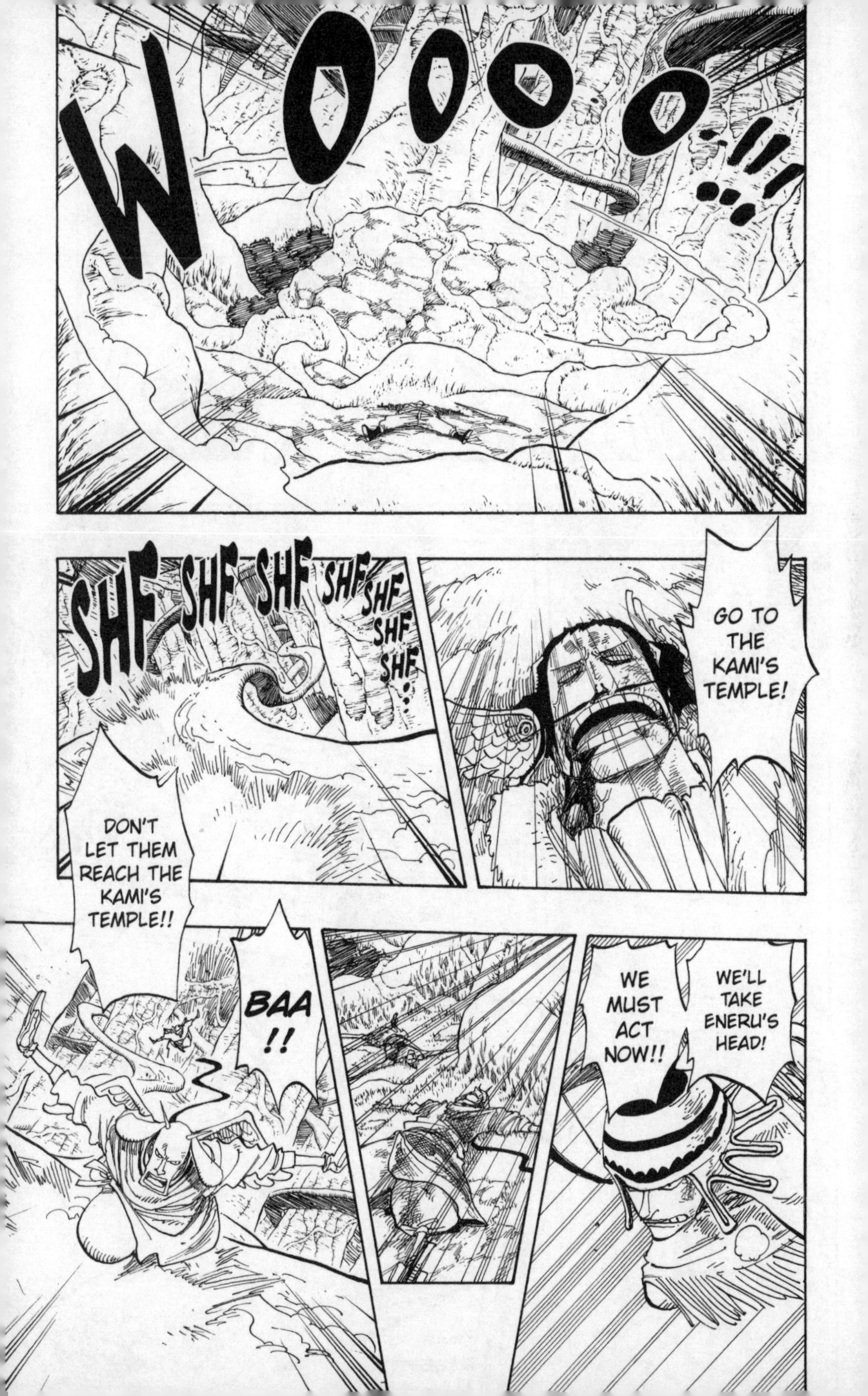
WOOOO...!!!
GO TO THE KAMI'S TEMPLE!
SHF SHF SHF SHF SHF SHF SHF...
WE'LL TAKE ENERU'S HEAD!
WE MUST ACT NOW!!
DON'T LET THEM REACH THE KAMI'S TEMPLE!!
BAA!!

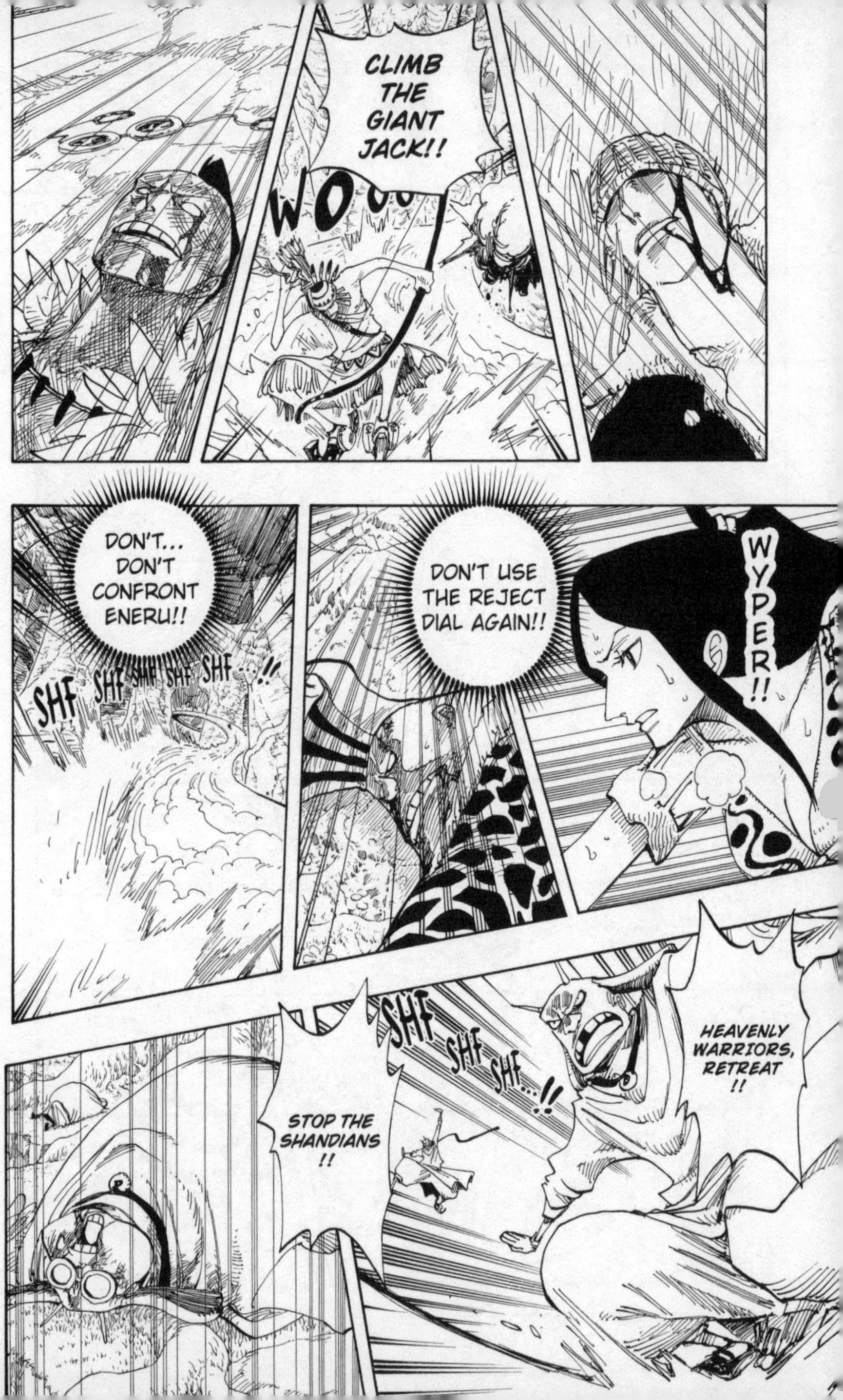
CLIMB THE GIANT JACK!!
WOO
WYPER!!
DON'T USE THE REJECT DIAL AGAIN!!
DON'T... DON'T CONFRONT ENERU!!
SHF SHF SHF SHF SHF...!!
HEAVENLY WARRIORS, RETREAT!!
SHF SHF SHF...!!
STOP THE SHANDIANS!!

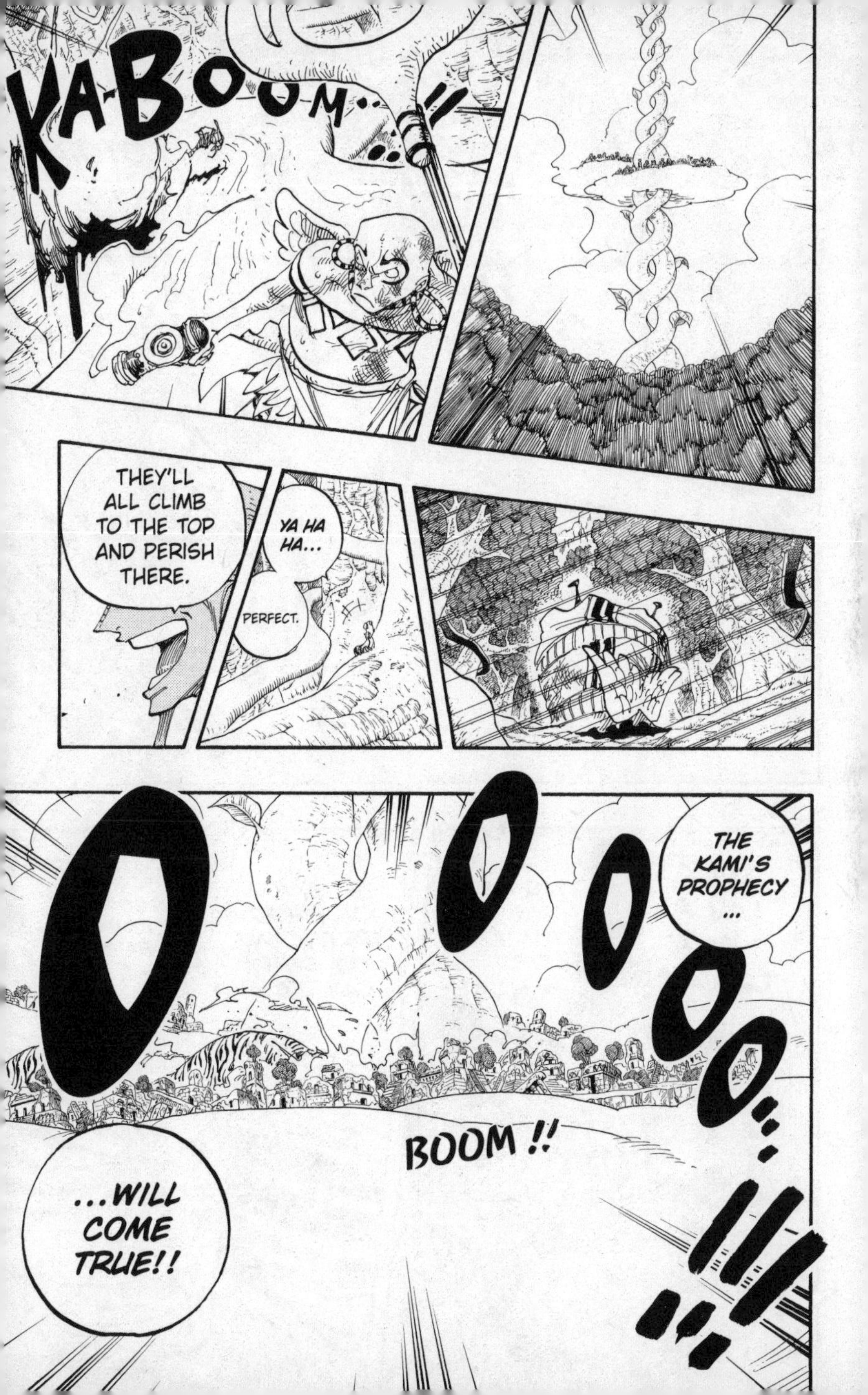
KA-BOOM...!!
YA HA HA...
PERFECT.
THEY'LL ALL CLIMB TO THE TOP AND PERISH THERE.
THE KAMI'S PROPHECY ...
OOOOO...!!!
BOOM!!
...WILL COME TRUE!!

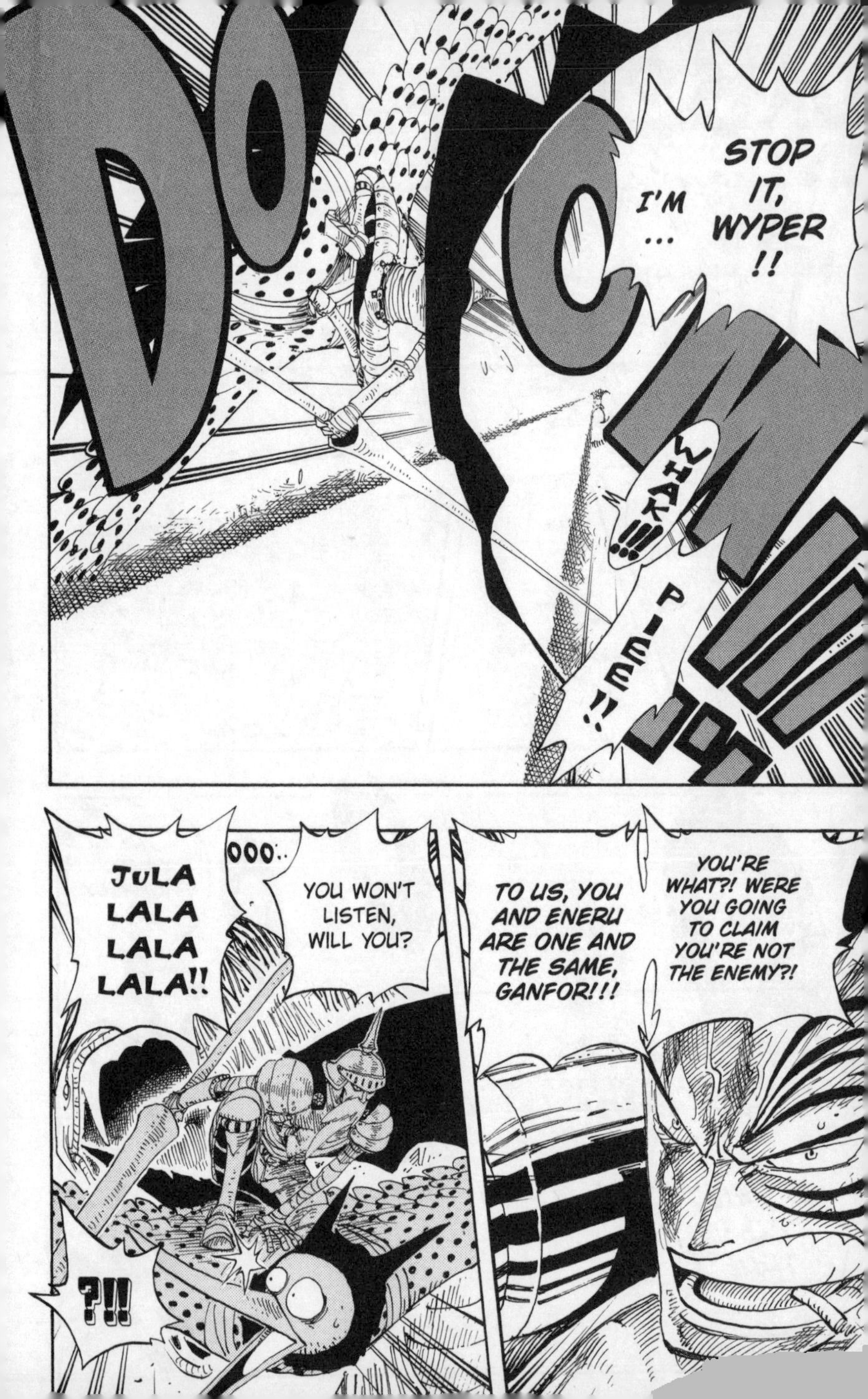
STOP IT, WYPER!!
I'M ...
WHAK!!!
PIEE!!
YOU'RE WHAT?! WERE YOU GOING TO CLAIM YOU'RE NOT THE ENEMY?!
TO US, YOU AND ENERU ARE ONE AND THE SAME, GANFOR!!!
YOU WON'T LISTEN, WILL YOU?
OOO..
JULA LALA LALA LALA!!
?!!

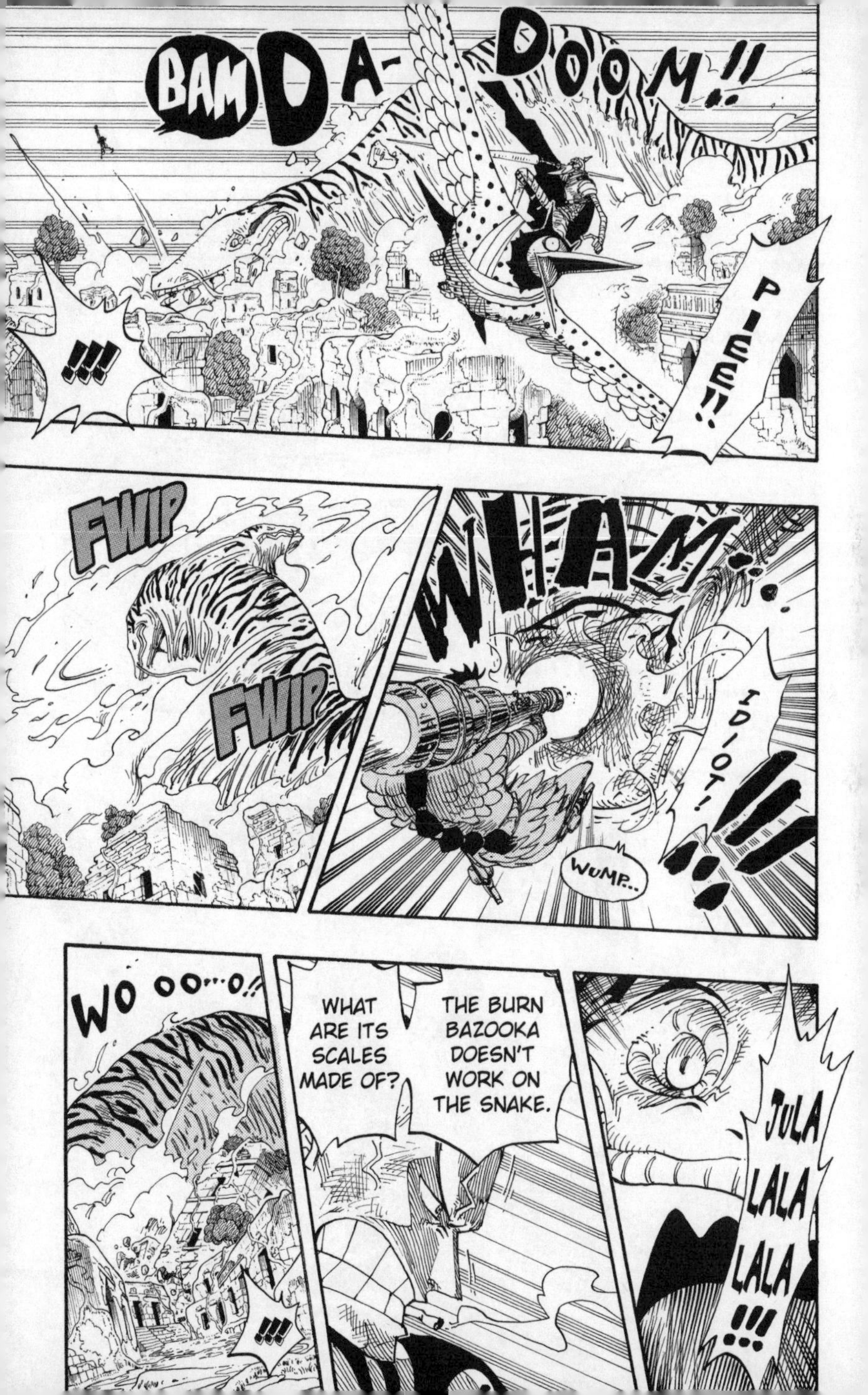
BAM
DA-DOOM!!
PIEE!!
!!!
WHAM!!
I-DI-OT!
!!!
WUMP...
FWIP
FWIP
JULA LALA LALA!!!
THE BURN BAZOOKA DOESN'T WORK ON THE SNAKE.
WHAT ARE ITS SCALES MADE OF?
WO OO...O!!
!!!

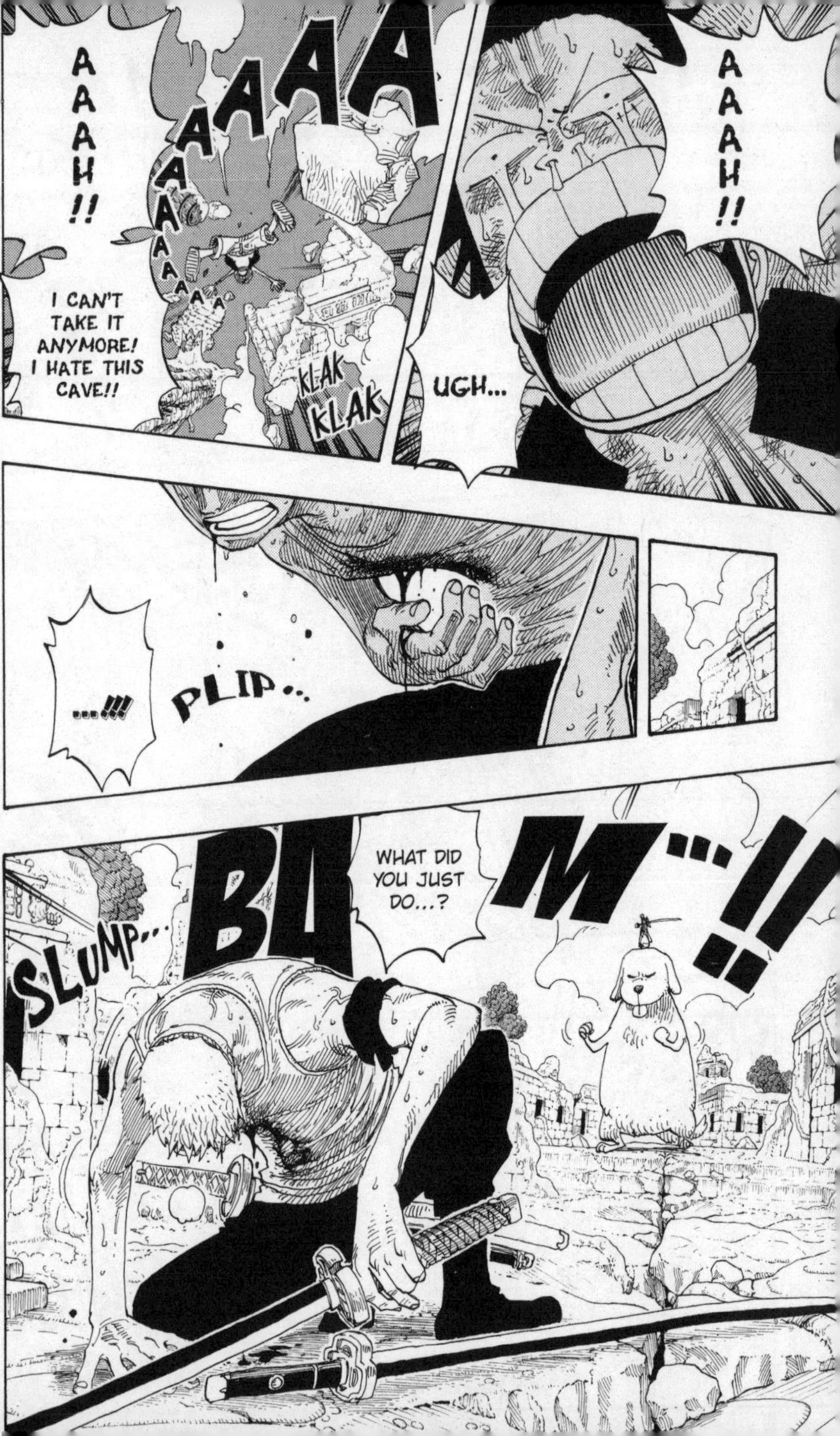
AAAAH!!
UGH...
AAAAH!!
I CAN'T TAKE IT ANYMORE! I HATE THIS CAVE!!
KLAK KLAK
...!!!
PLIP...
BAM...!!
WHAT DID YOU JUST DO...?
SLUMP...

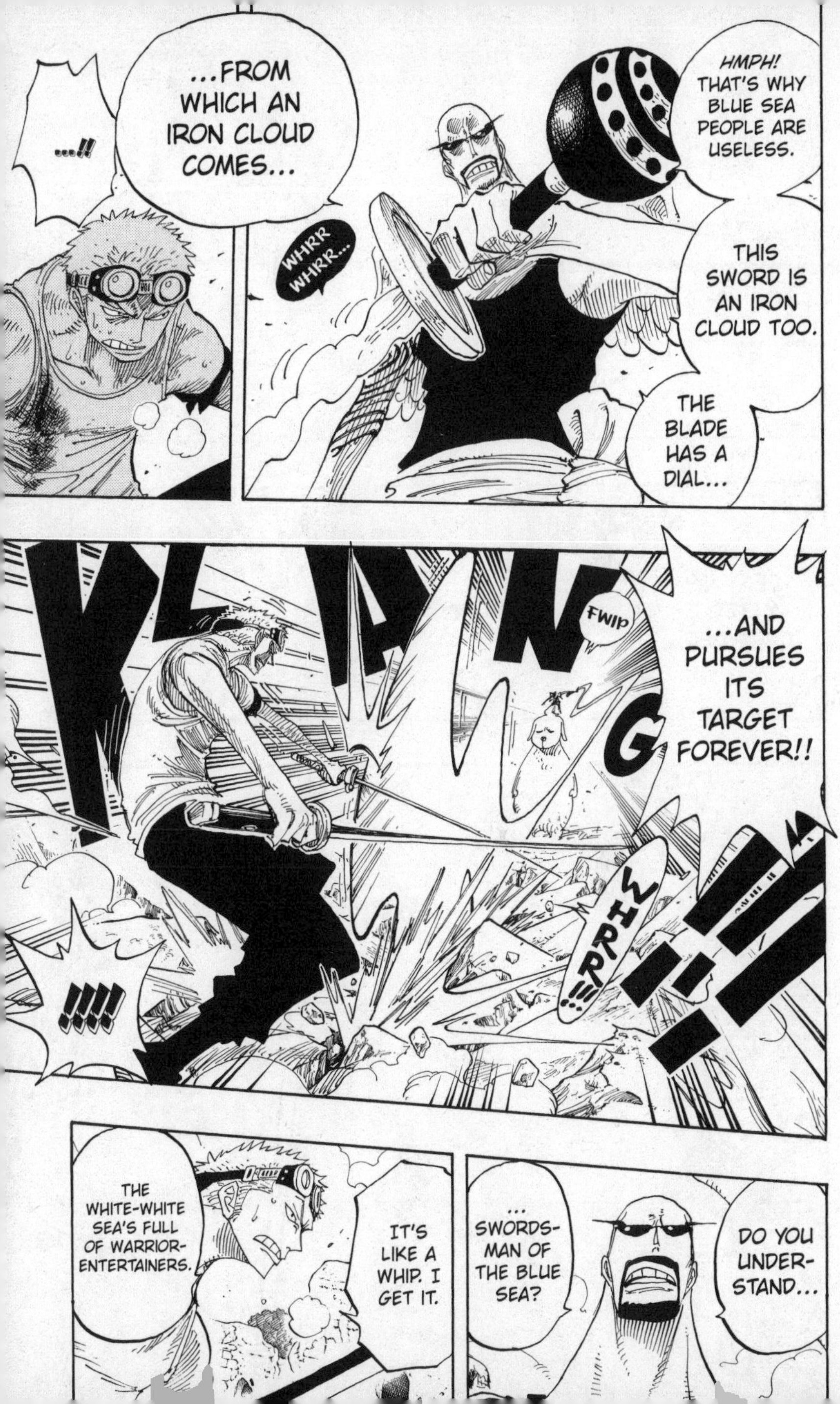
HMPH! THAT'S WHY BLUE SEA PEOPLE ARE USELESS.
THIS SWORD IS AN IRON CLOUD TOO.
WHRR WHRR...
THE BLADE HAS A DIAL...
...FROM WHICH AN IRON CLOUD COMES...
...!!
...AND PURSUES ITS TARGET FOREVER!!
FWIP
WHRR!!!
!!!!
DO YOU UNDER-STAND...
... SWORDS-MAN OF THE BLUE SEA?
IT'S LIKE A WHIP. I GET IT.
THE WHITE-WHITE SEA'S FULL OF WARRIOR-ENTERTAINERS.

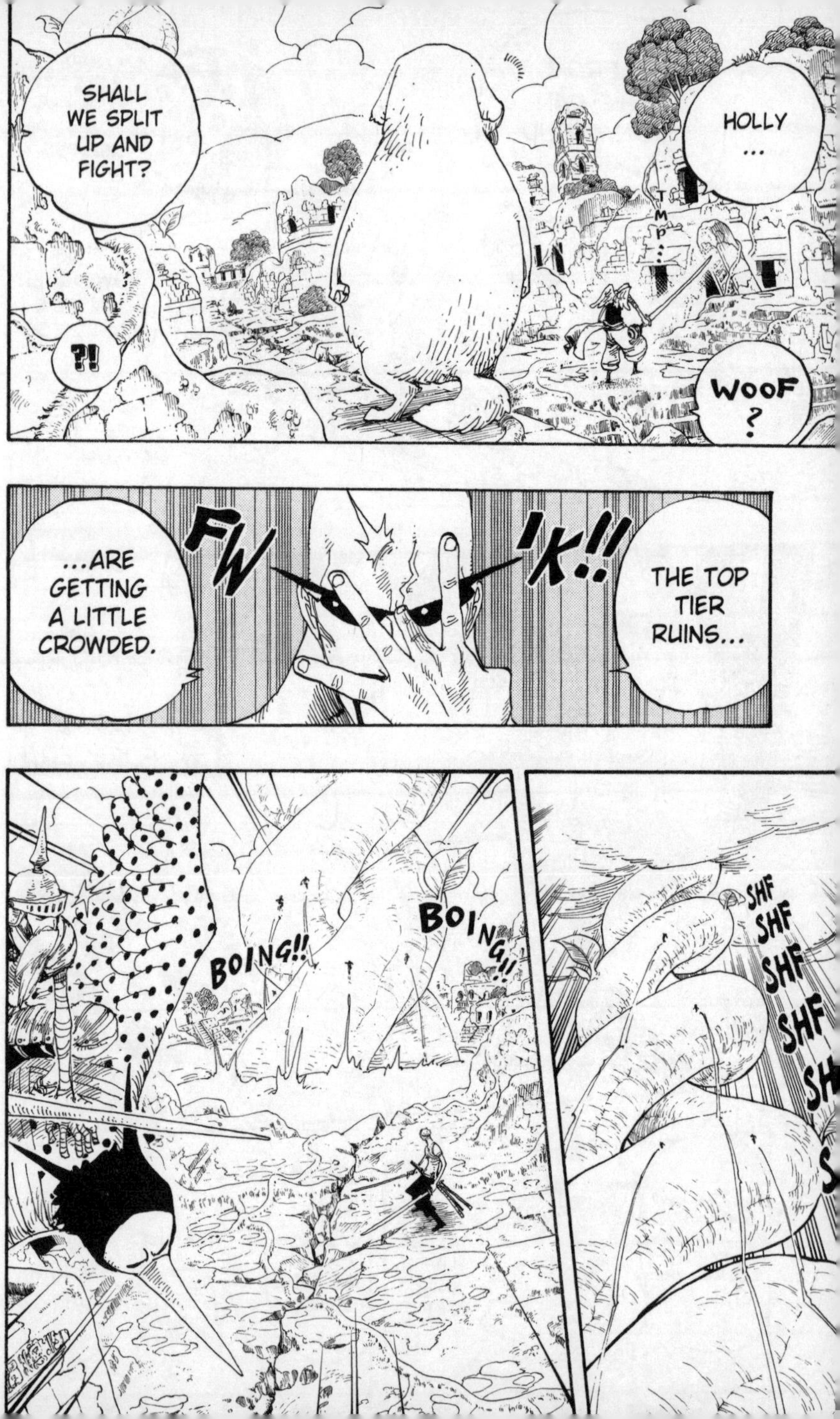
HOLLY ...
TMP...
WOOF ?
SHALL WE SPLIT UP AND FIGHT?
?!
THE TOP TIER RUINS...
FWK!!
...ARE GETTING A LITTLE CROWDED.
SHF SHF SHF SHF SH
BOING!!
BOING!!

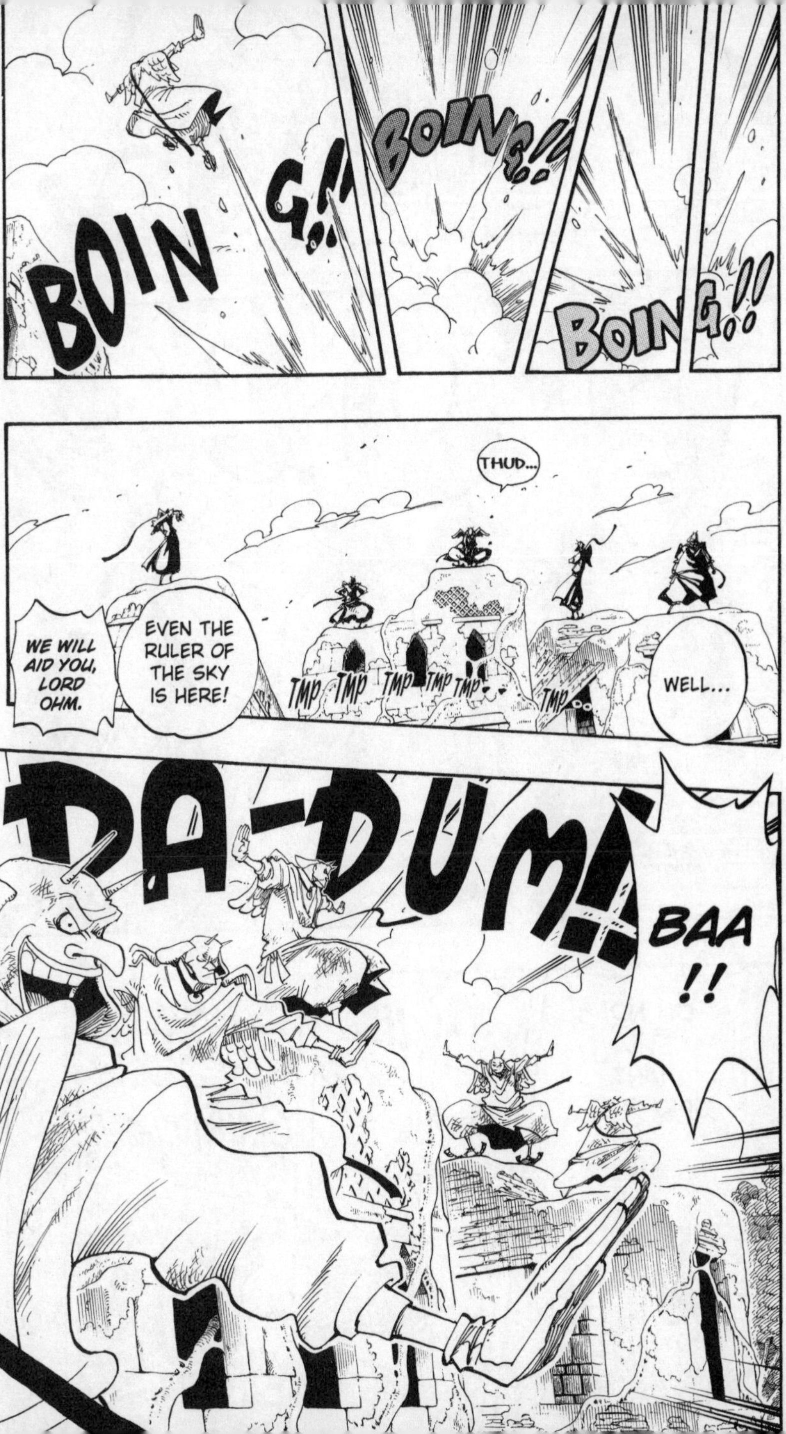
BOING!!
BOING!!
BOIN G!!
THUD...
WELL...
TMP
TMP
TMP
TMP
TMP
TMP
EVEN THE RULER OF THE SKY IS HERE!
WE WILL AID YOU, LORD OHM.
BAA !!
DA-DUM!!

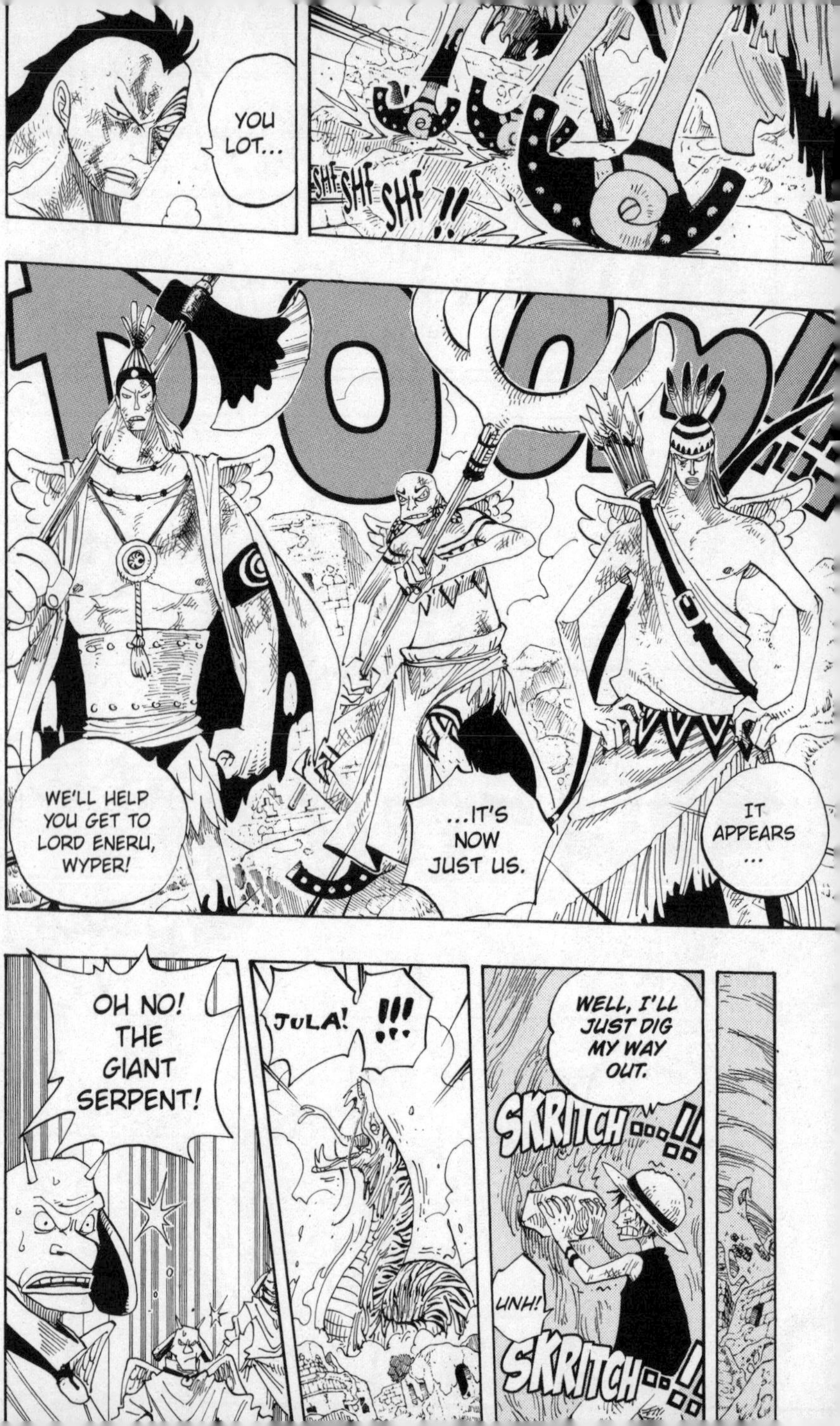
SHF SHF SHF !!
YOU LOT...
DOOM
IT APPEARS ...
...IT'S NOW JUST US.
WE'LL HELP YOU GET TO LORD ENERU, WYPER!
WELL, I'LL JUST DIG MY WAY OUT.
SKRITCH...!!
UNH!
SKRITCH...!!
!!!
JULA!
OH NO! THE GIANT SERPENT!

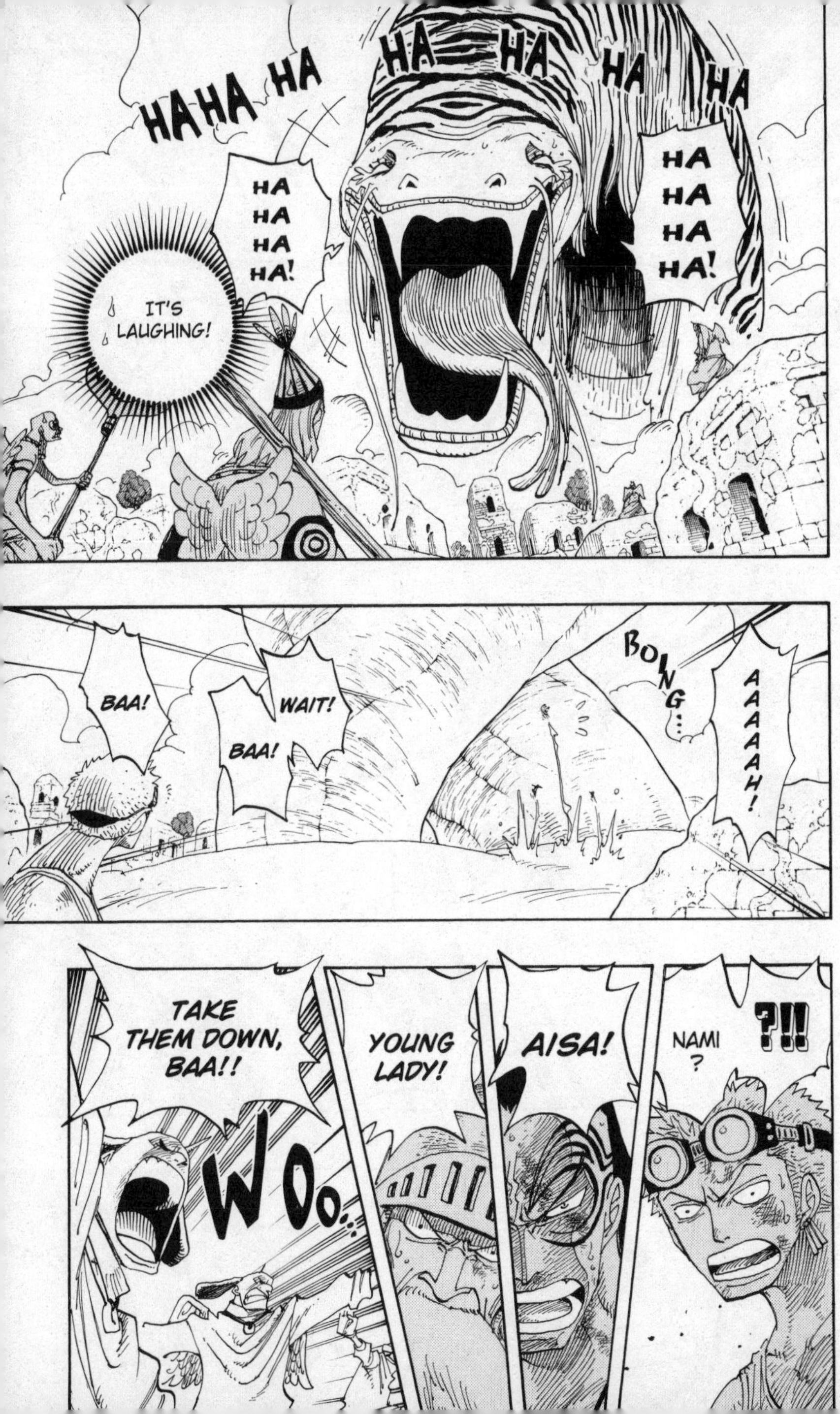
HA HA HA HA
HA HA HA HA!
HAHA HA
HA HA HA HA!
IT'S LAUGHING!
AAAAAAH!
BOING...
WAIT!
BAA!
BAA!
NAMI?
?!!
AISA!
YOUNG LADY!
TAKE THEM DOWN, BAA!!
WOO...

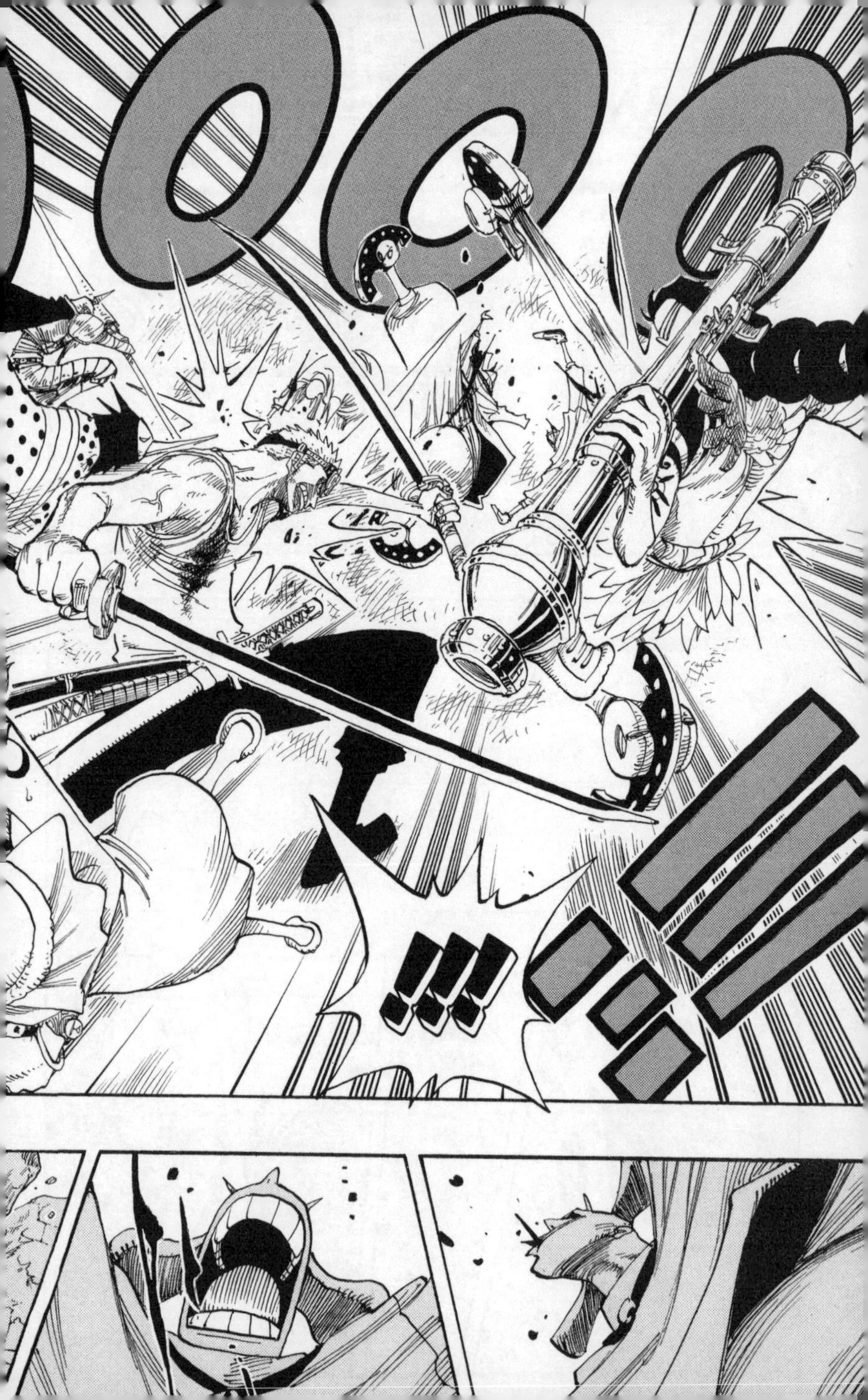
!!!

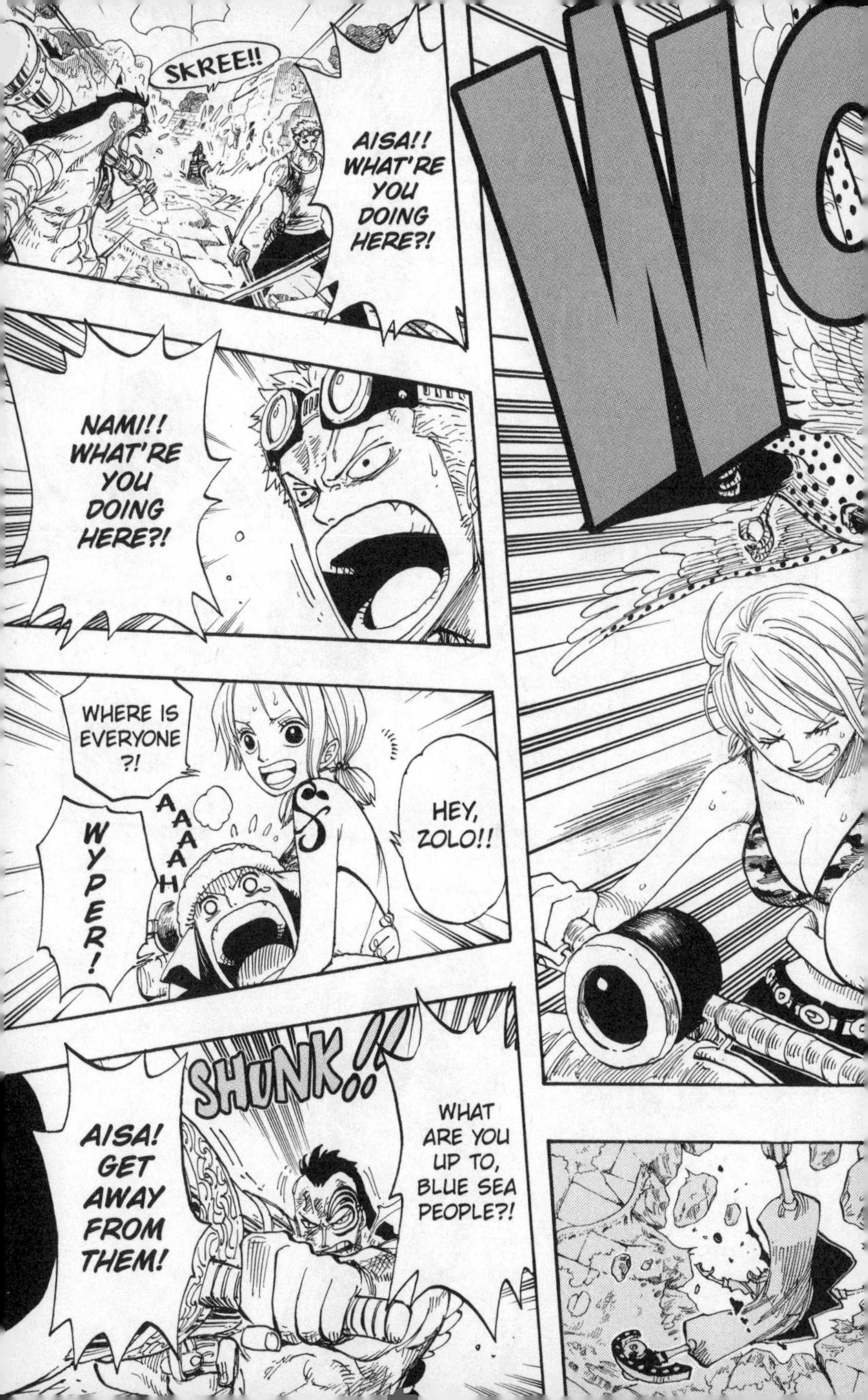
WO
SKREE!!
AISA!! WHAT'RE YOU DOING HERE?!
NAMI!! WHAT'RE YOU DOING HERE?!
HEY, ZOLO!!
WHERE IS EVERYONE ?!
AAAAH
WYPER!
SHUNK
WHAT ARE YOU UP TO, BLUE SEA PEOPLE?!
AISA! GET AWAY FROM THEM!

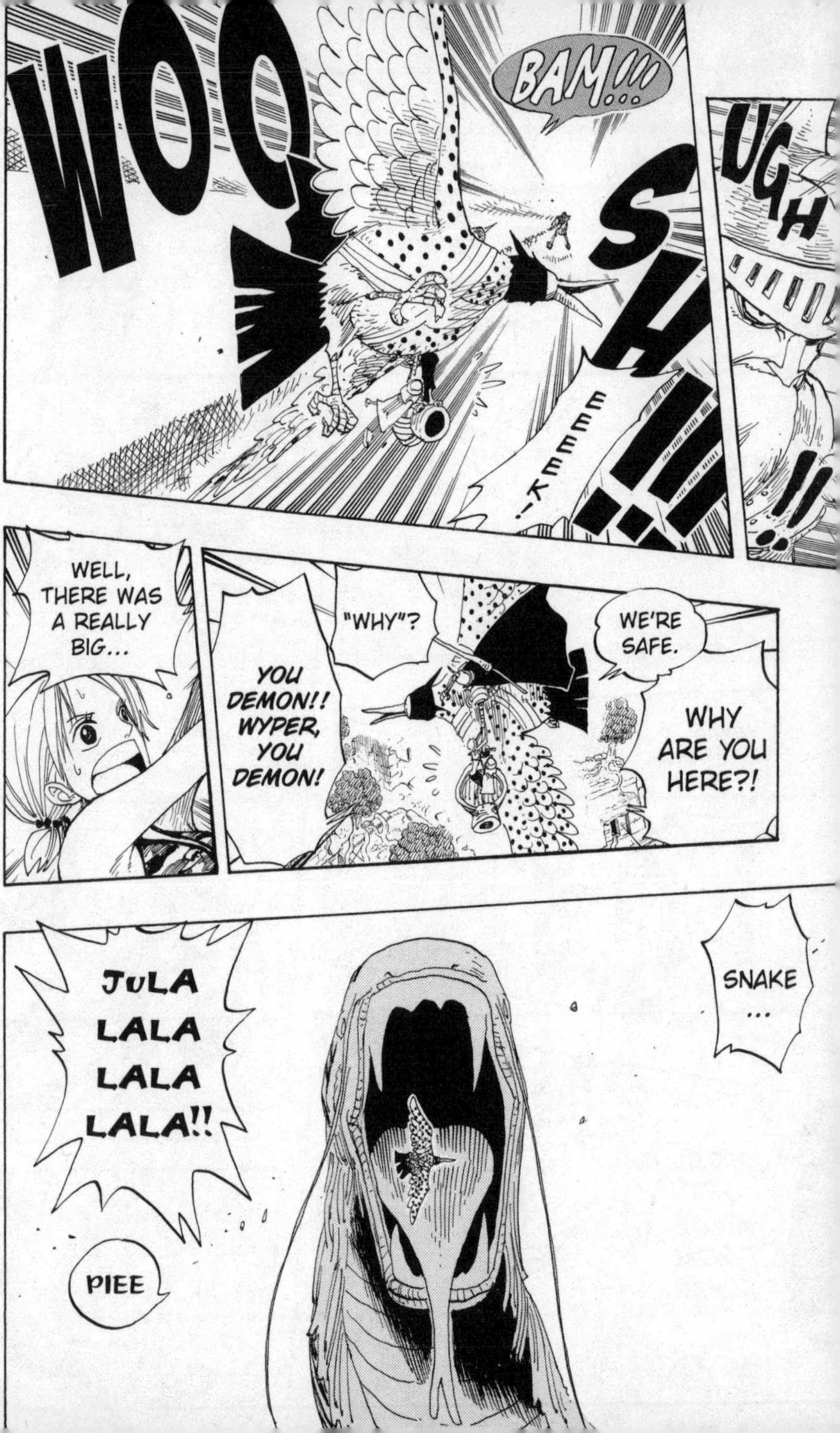
UGH!!
BAM!!!
WOOSH!!!
EEEEEEK!
WE'RE SAFE.
WHY ARE YOU HERE?!
"WHY"?
YOU DEMON!! WYPER, YOU DEMON!
WELL, THERE WAS A REALLY BIG...
SNAKE ...
JULA LALA LALA LALA!!
PIEE

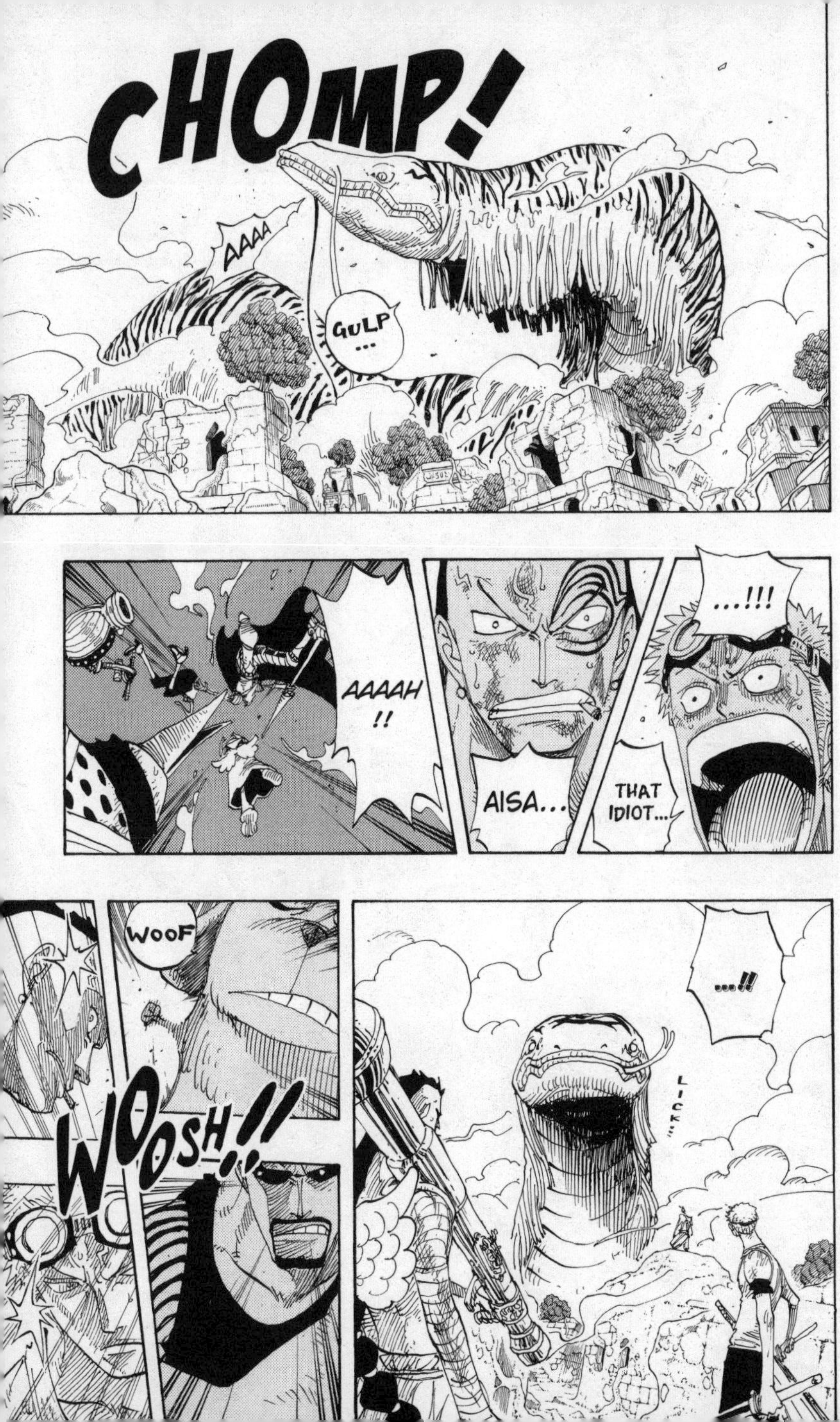
CHOMP!
AAAA
GULP ...
...!!!
THAT IDIOT...
AISA...
AAAAH !!
...!!
LICK...
WOOF
WOOSH!!

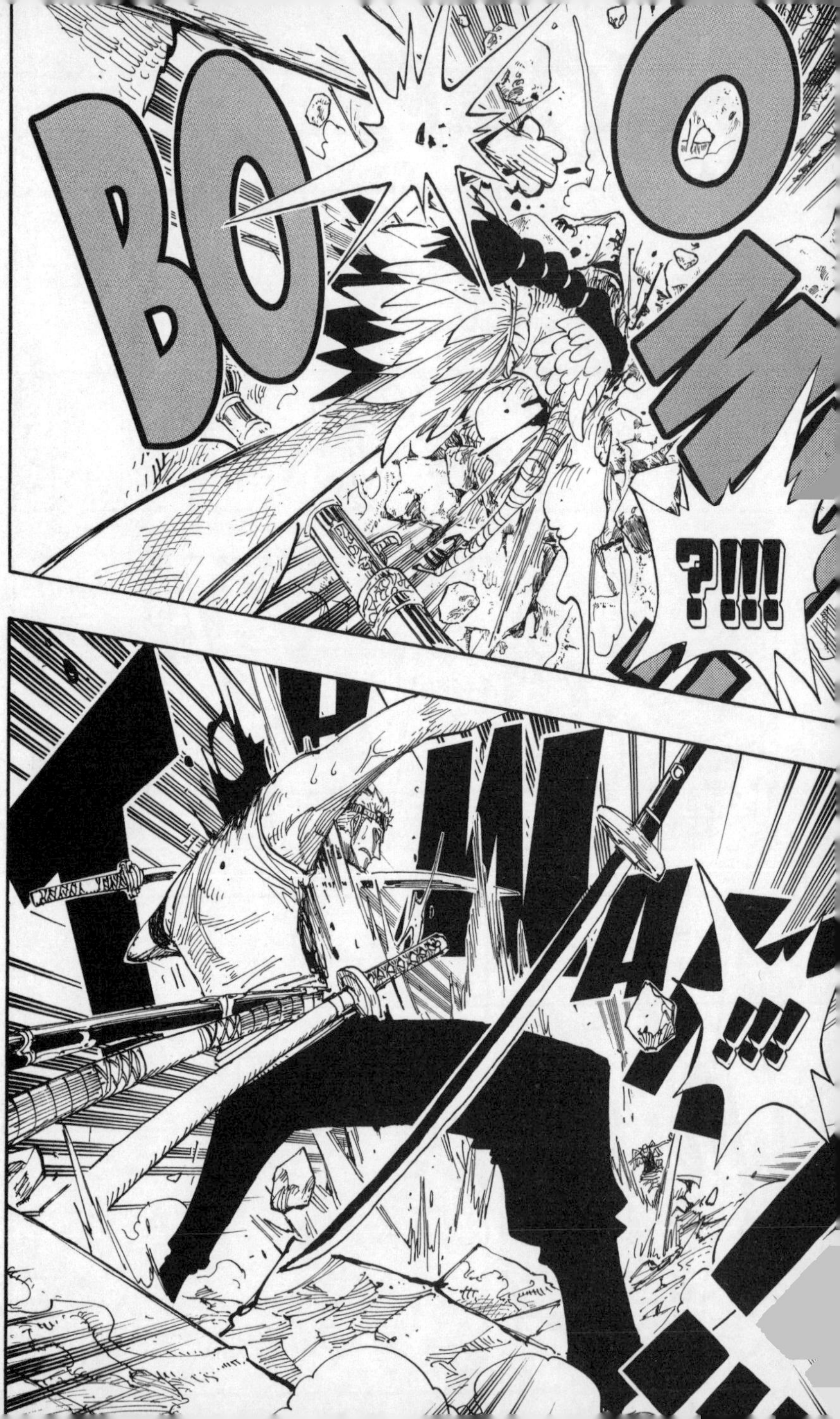
BOOM
?!!!

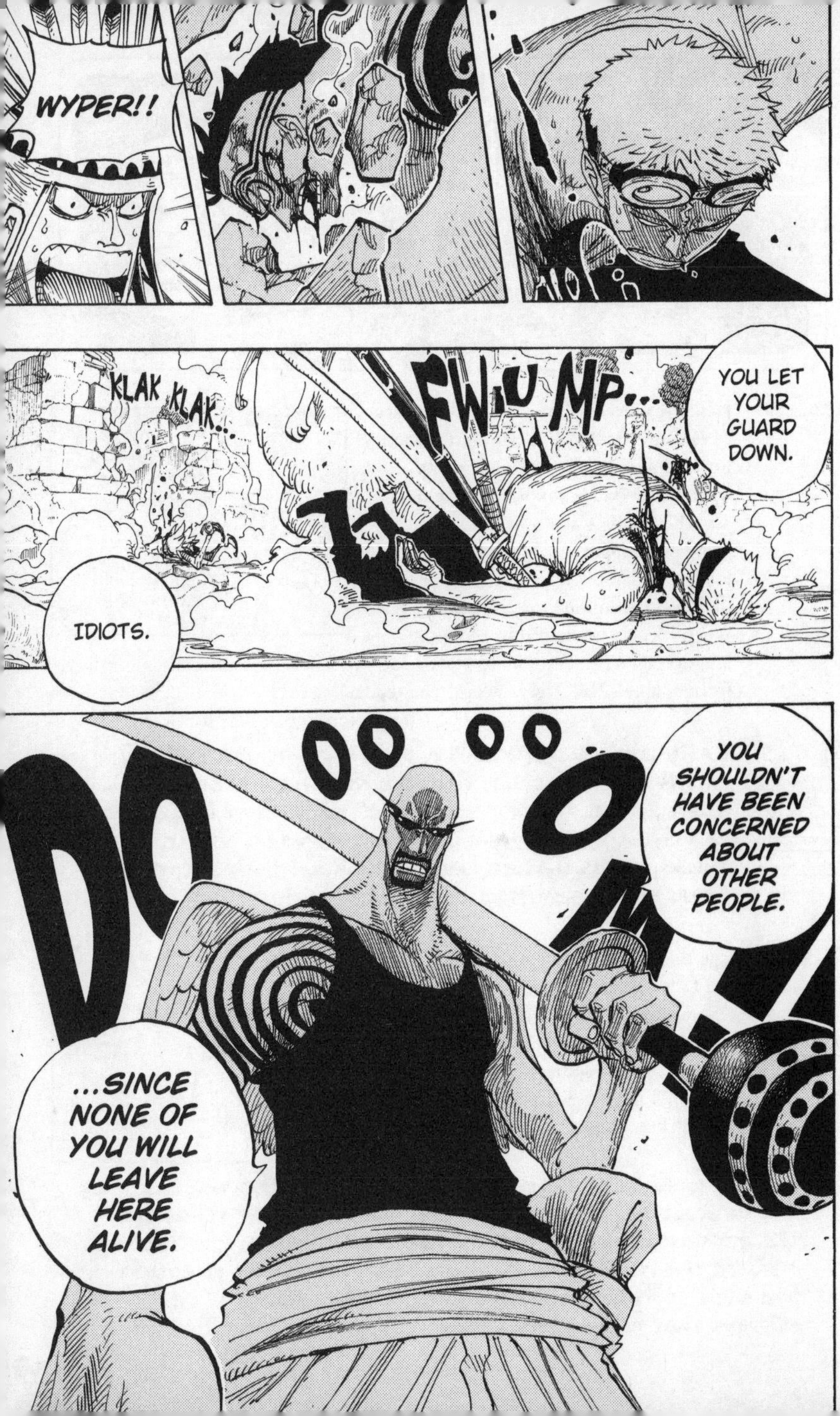
WYPER!!
YOU LET YOUR GUARD DOWN.
FWUMP...
KLAK KLAK...
IDIOTS.
YOU SHOULDN'T HAVE BEEN CONCERNED ABOUT OTHER PEOPLE.
...SINCE NONE OF YOU WILL LEAVE HERE ALIVE.

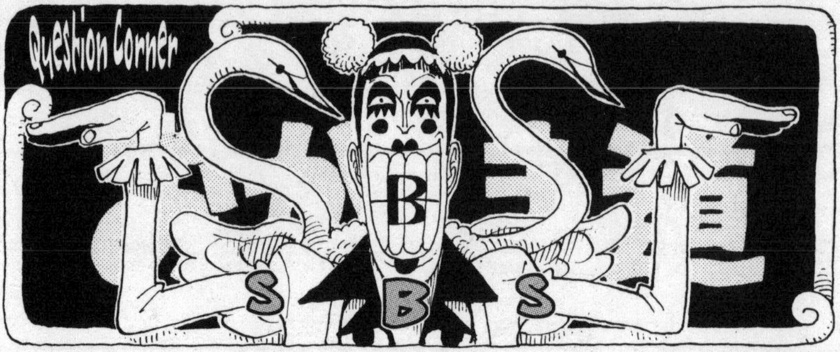
Question Corner
SBS

Reader: Hello. It's nice to meet you, Oda Sensei! There's something I've wondered about for a while. In chapter 198 of volume 22, when Crocodile grabs Vivi by the neck and she says, "I will save this…" I was wondering if the "…" part is connected to Vivi's line in volume 23, chapter 216: "I'd like to continue my adventures, but when it comes down to it, I love this kingdom!!!"? I was thinking, maybe the "..." in chapter 198 stands for "love" from chapter 216! That's what I wanted to know.

--It's Going to Be Okay for Sure

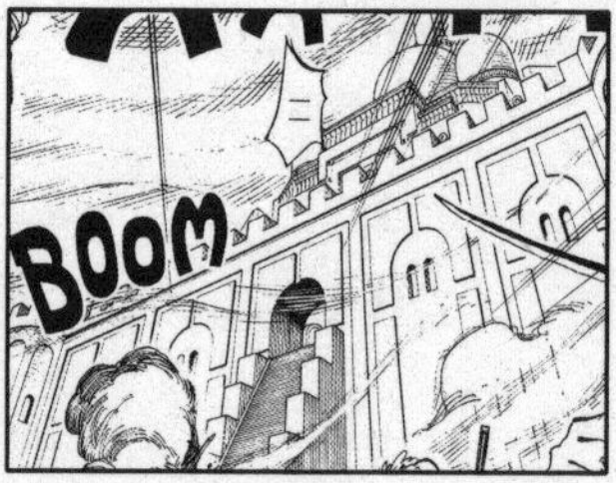
BOOM

Oda: Oh, thank you for reading into that. You're right, Vivi always feels that way. But the storm of rebellion stamped out the princess's feelings. In that last scene, the citizens must have been moved when Vivi uttered those words that echoed throughout the country (sniff). It's a beautiful story. Sob… Sob…

Q: Isn't it true that you can't tell your direction on the Grand Line? If that's the case, then why, in volume 24 (chapter 218), is Nami able to say, "Ahead west by northwest!" when she's asked, "What's your Log Pose course?" If you can't give me a straight answer, I request you go for an ice-cold dip at your local swimming pool.

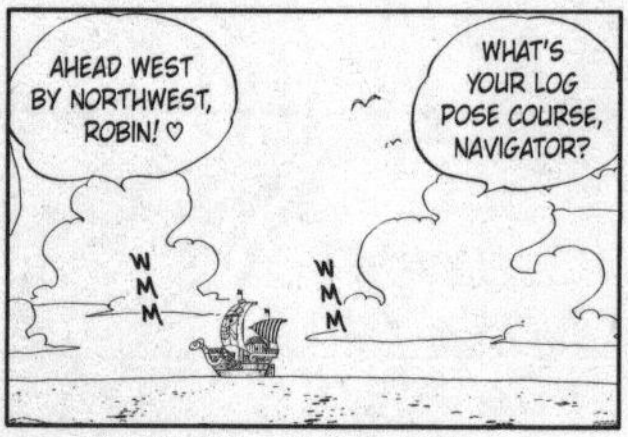
WHAT'S YOUR LOG POSE COURSE, NAVIGATOR?
AHEAD WEST BY NORTHWEST, ROBIN! ♡
WMM
WMM

A: Well, it is summer. Umm, it's all good. Even though it is the Grand Line, it's possible near the continent to gauge the correct direction. Nami knew that they were proceeding toward the next island in a west-by-northwest direction, and she's saying that they're on the right route. I'll be skipping that cold swim.

Chapter 270: SERENADE

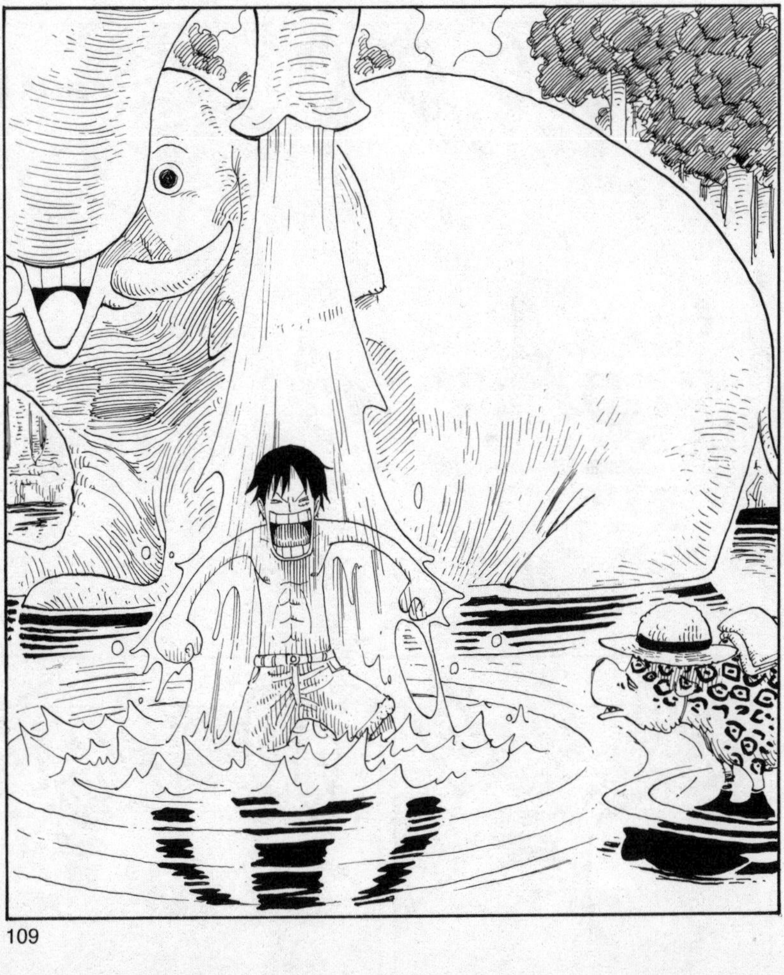

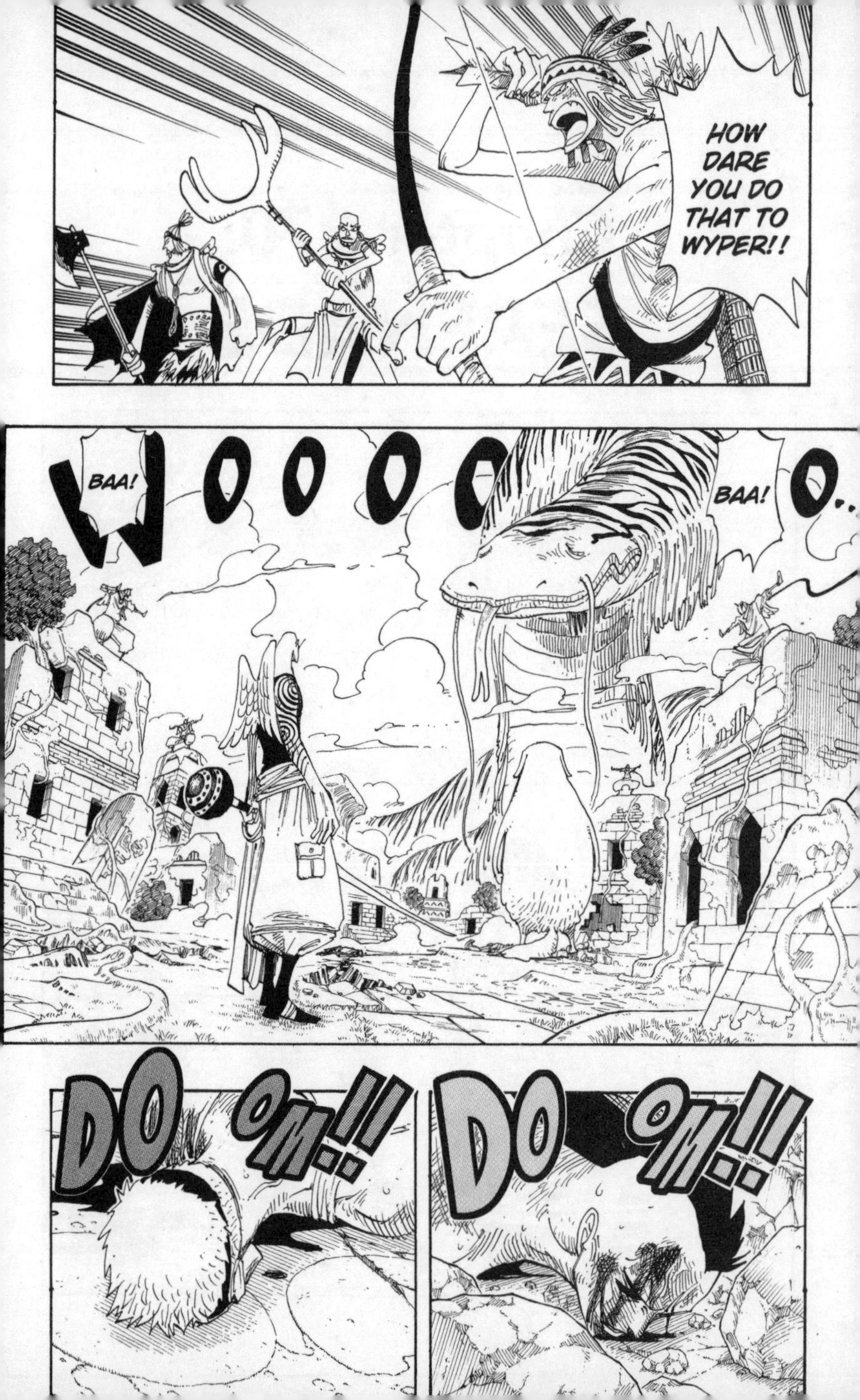
HOW DARE YOU DO THAT TO WYPER!!
BAA!
BAA!
WOOOOOO...
DOON!!
DOON!!

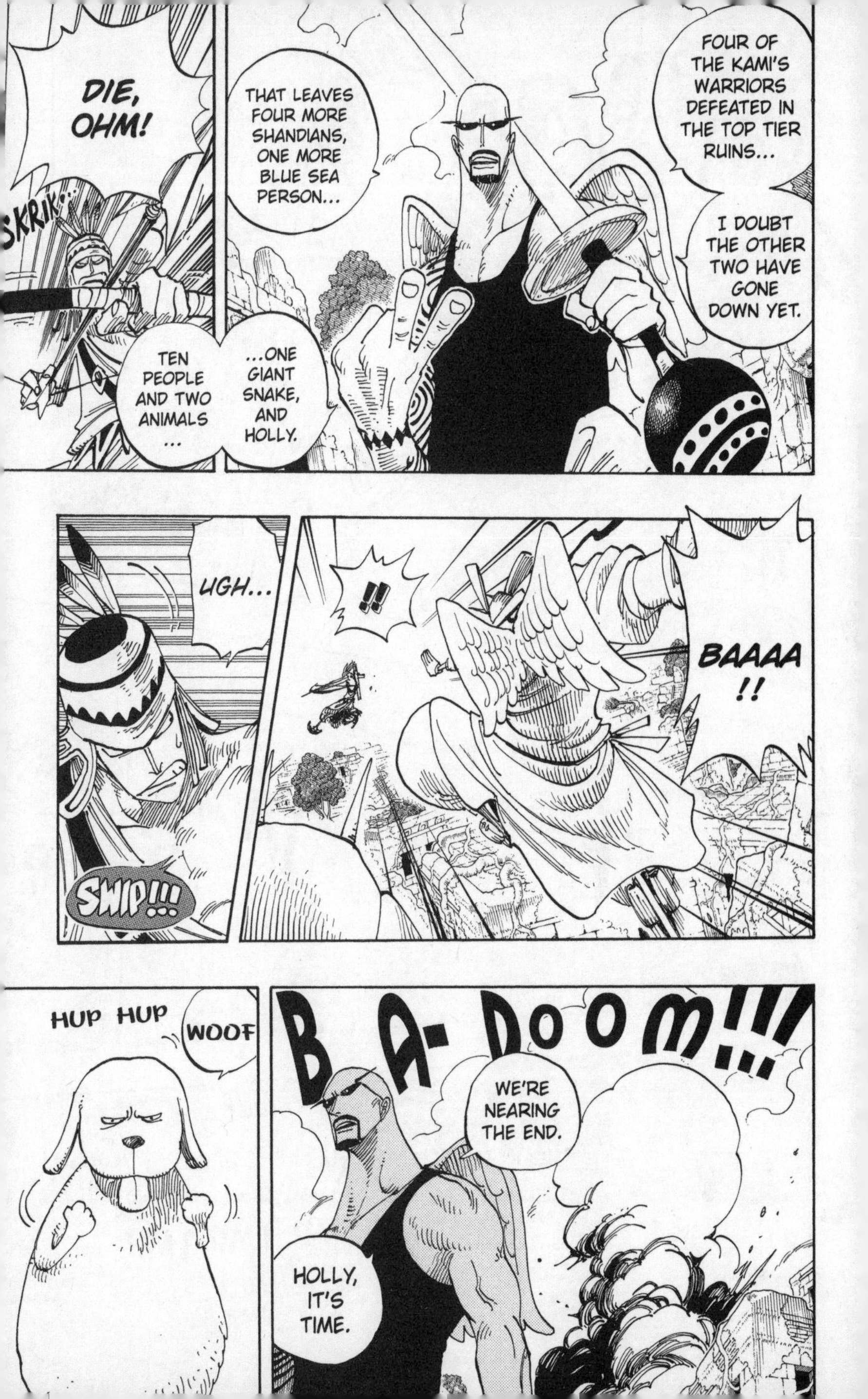
FOUR OF THE KAMI'S WARRIORS DEFEATED IN THE TOP TIER RUINS...
I DOUBT THE OTHER TWO HAVE GONE DOWN YET.
TEN PEOPLE AND TWO ANIMALS ...
THAT LEAVES FOUR MORE SHANDIANS, ONE MORE BLUE SEA PERSON...
...ONE GIANT SNAKE, AND HOLLY.
DIE, OHM!
SKRIK...
!!
BAAAA !!
UGH...
SWIP!!!
B A- DOOM!!!
WE'RE NEARING THE END.
HOLLY, IT'S TIME.
HUP HUP
WOOF

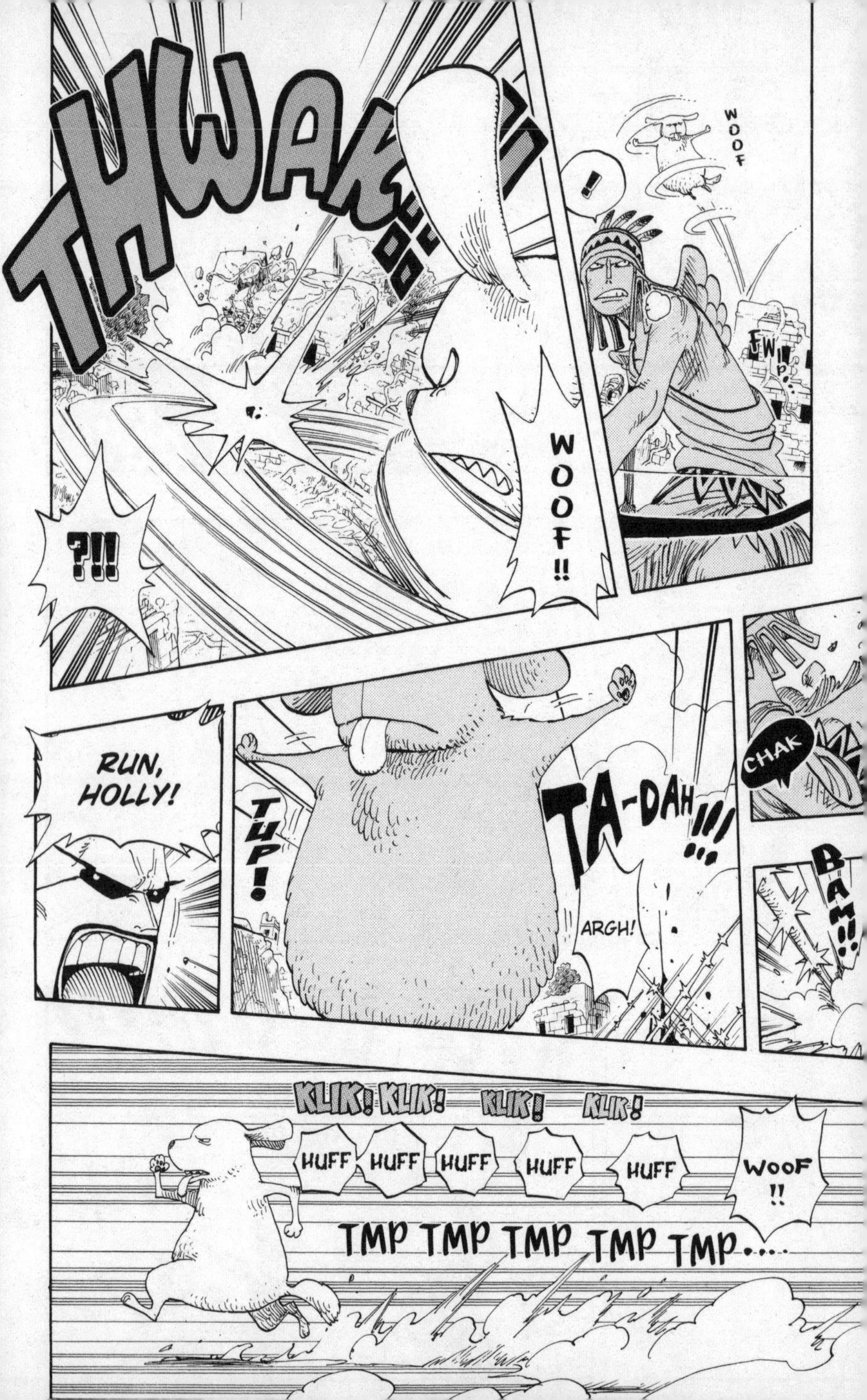
WOOF
!
FWIP...
THWAK!!
WOOF!!
?!!
CHAK
BAM!!
TA-DAH!!!
TUP!
ARGH!
RUN, HOLLY!
WOOF!!
KLIK! KLIK! KLIK! KLIK!
HUFF HUFF HUFF HUFF HUFF
TMP TMP TMP TMP TMP....

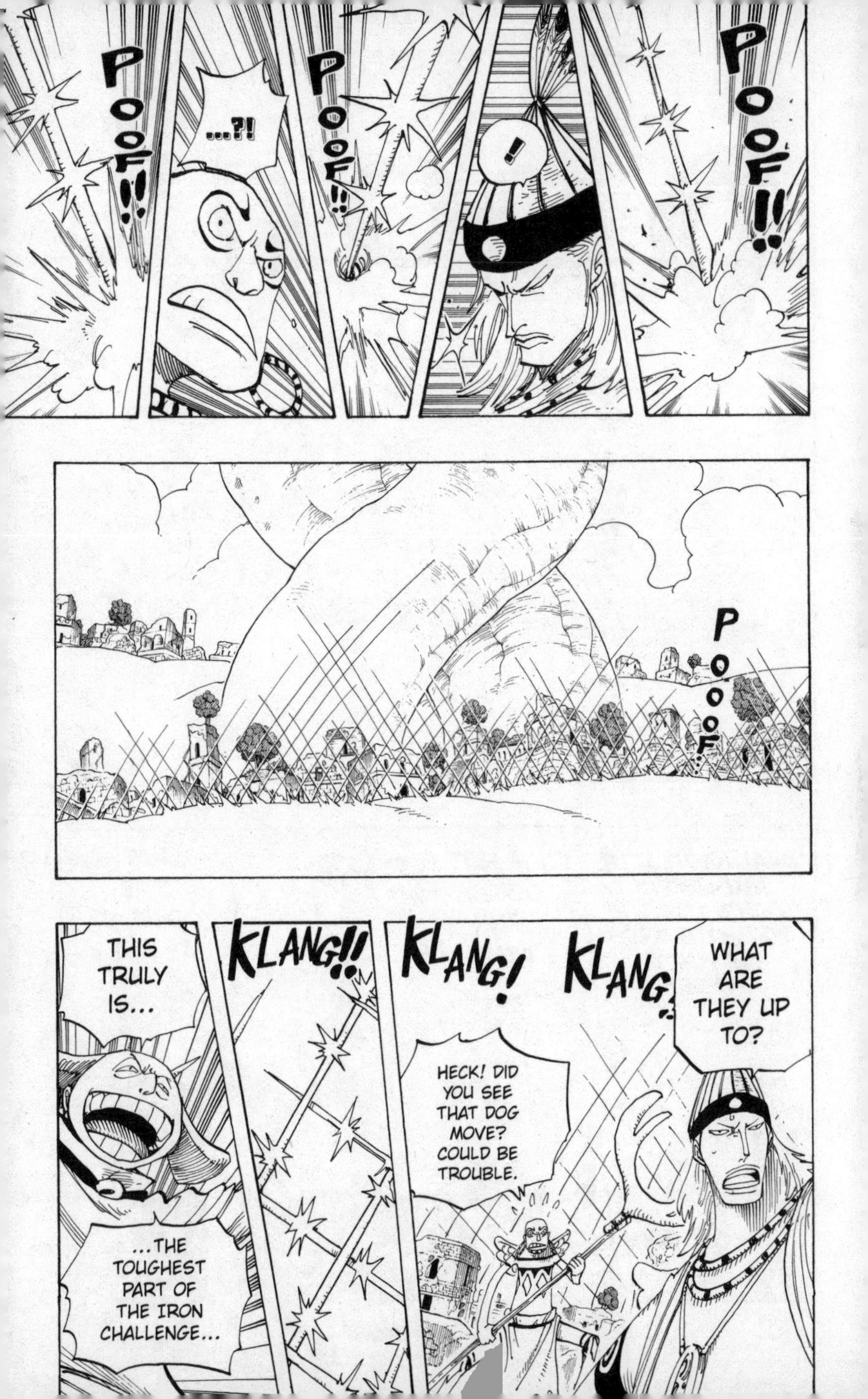

POOF!!
!
POOF!!
...?!
POOF!!
POOOOF...
WHAT ARE THEY UP TO?
KLANG...
KLANG!
HECK! DID YOU SEE THAT DOG MOVE? COULD BE TROUBLE.
KLANG!!
THIS TRULY IS...
...THE TOUGHEST PART OF THE IRON CHALLENGE...

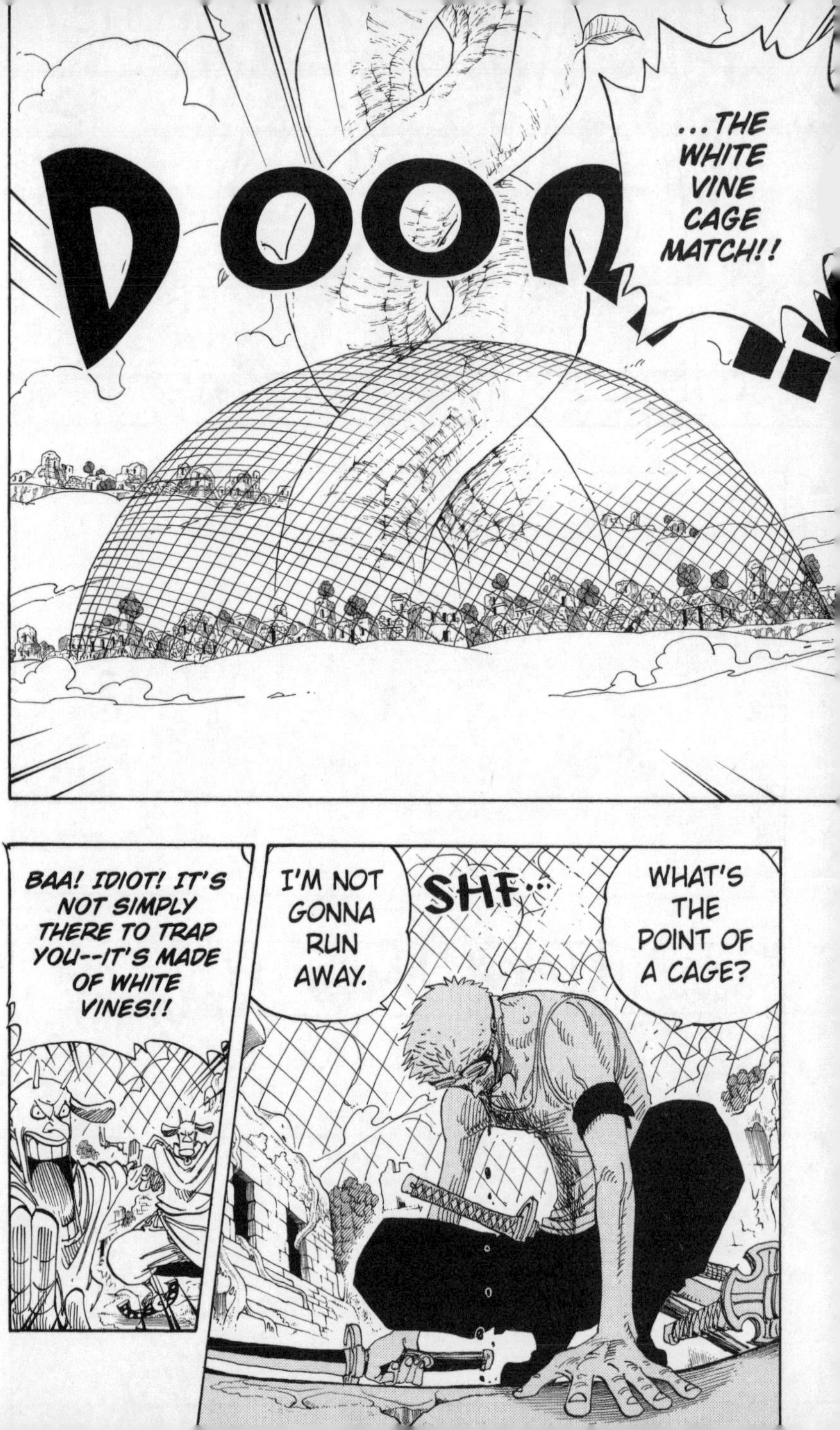
DOOON!!
...THE WHITE VINE CAGE MATCH!!
WHAT'S THE POINT OF A CAGE?
SHF...
I'M NOT GONNA RUN AWAY.
BAA! IDIOT! IT'S NOT SIMPLY THERE TO TRAP YOU--IT'S MADE OF WHITE VINES!!

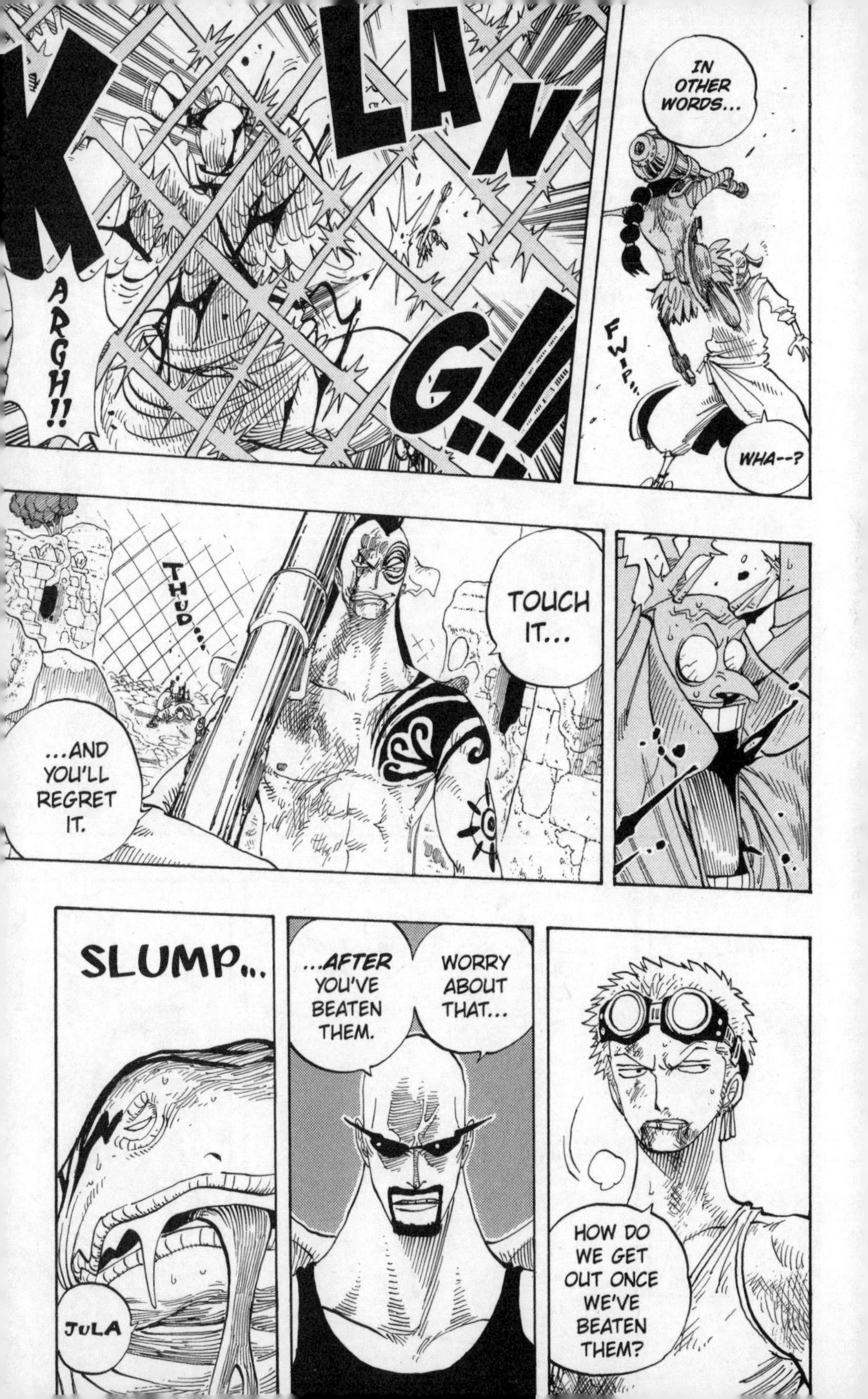
IN OTHER WORDS...
FWIP...
WHA--?
KLANG!!
ARGH!!
TOUCH IT...
THUD...
...AND YOU'LL REGRET IT.
HOW DO WE GET OUT ONCE WE'VE BEATEN THEM?
WORRY ABOUT THAT...
...AFTER YOU'VE BEATEN THEM.
SLUMP...
JULA

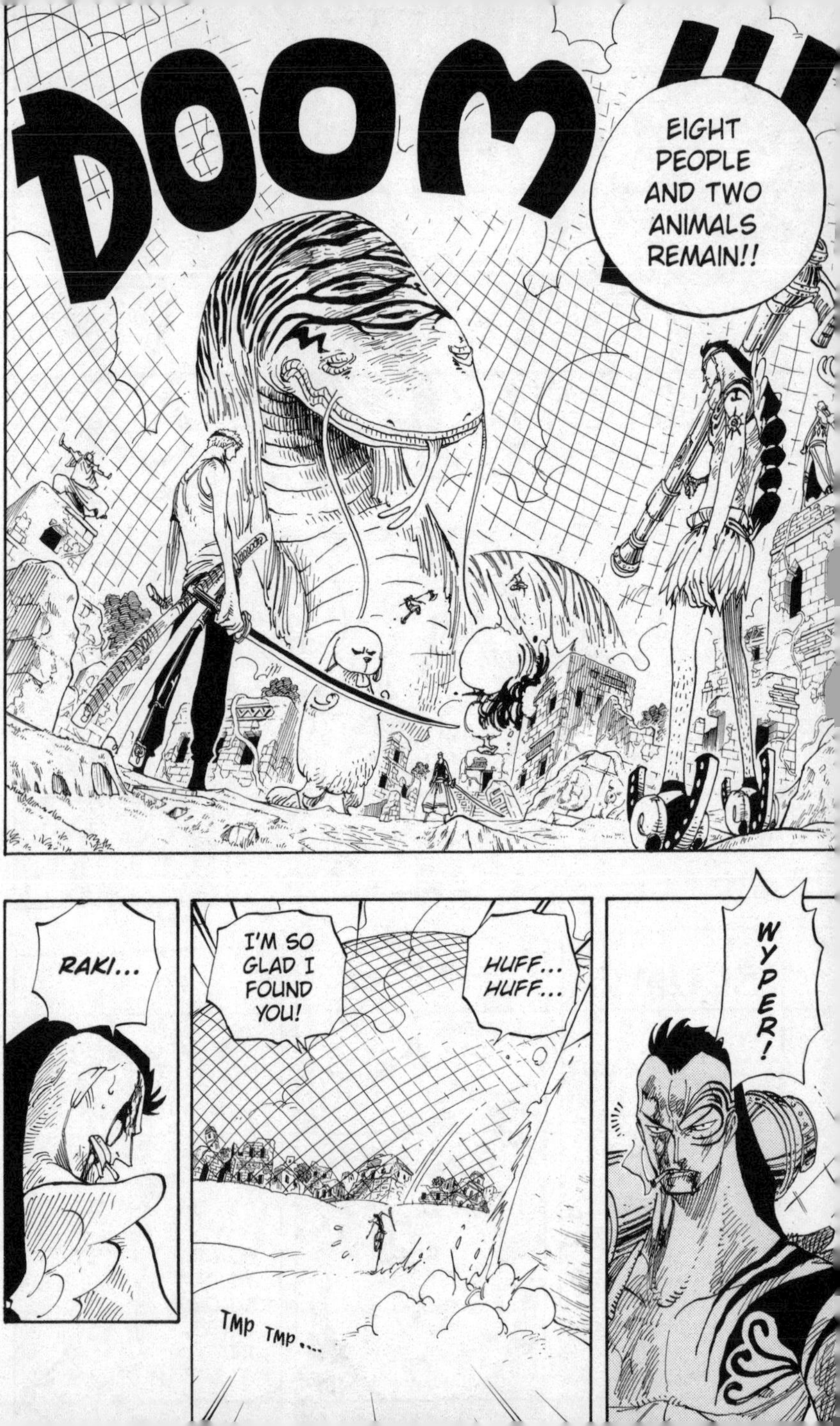

DOOM!!!
EIGHT PEOPLE AND TWO ANIMALS REMAIN!!
WYPER!
HUFF... HUFF...
I'M SO GLAD I FOUND YOU!
TMP TMP...
RAKI...

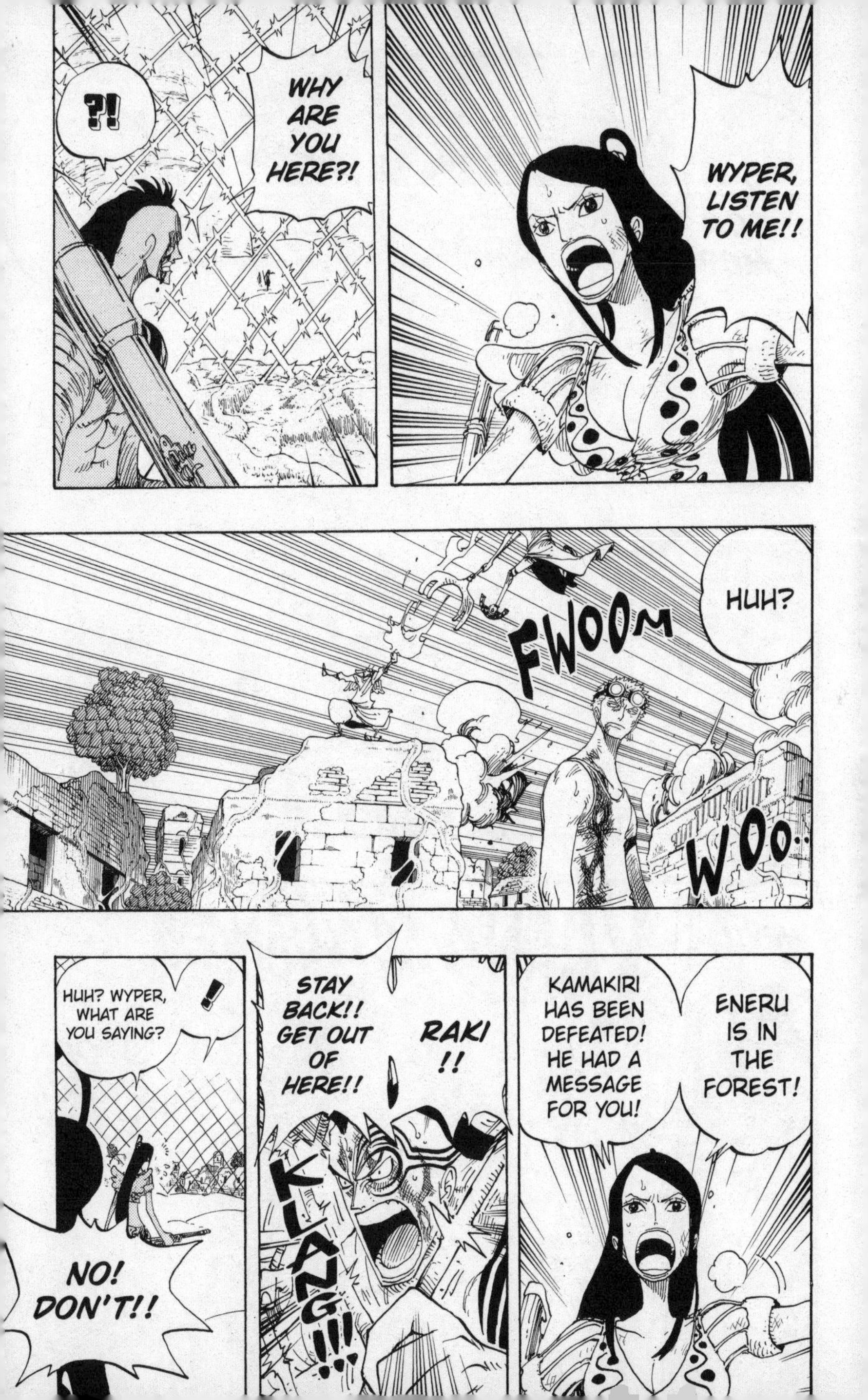
WYPER, LISTEN TO ME!!
WHY ARE YOU HERE?!
?!
HUH?
FWOOM
WOO...
ENERU IS IN THE FOREST!
KAMAKIRI HAS BEEN DEFEATED! HE HAD A MESSAGE FOR YOU!
RAKI!!
STAY BACK!! GET OUT OF HERE!!
KLANG!!!
!
HUH? WYPER, WHAT ARE YOU SAYING?
NO! DON'T!!

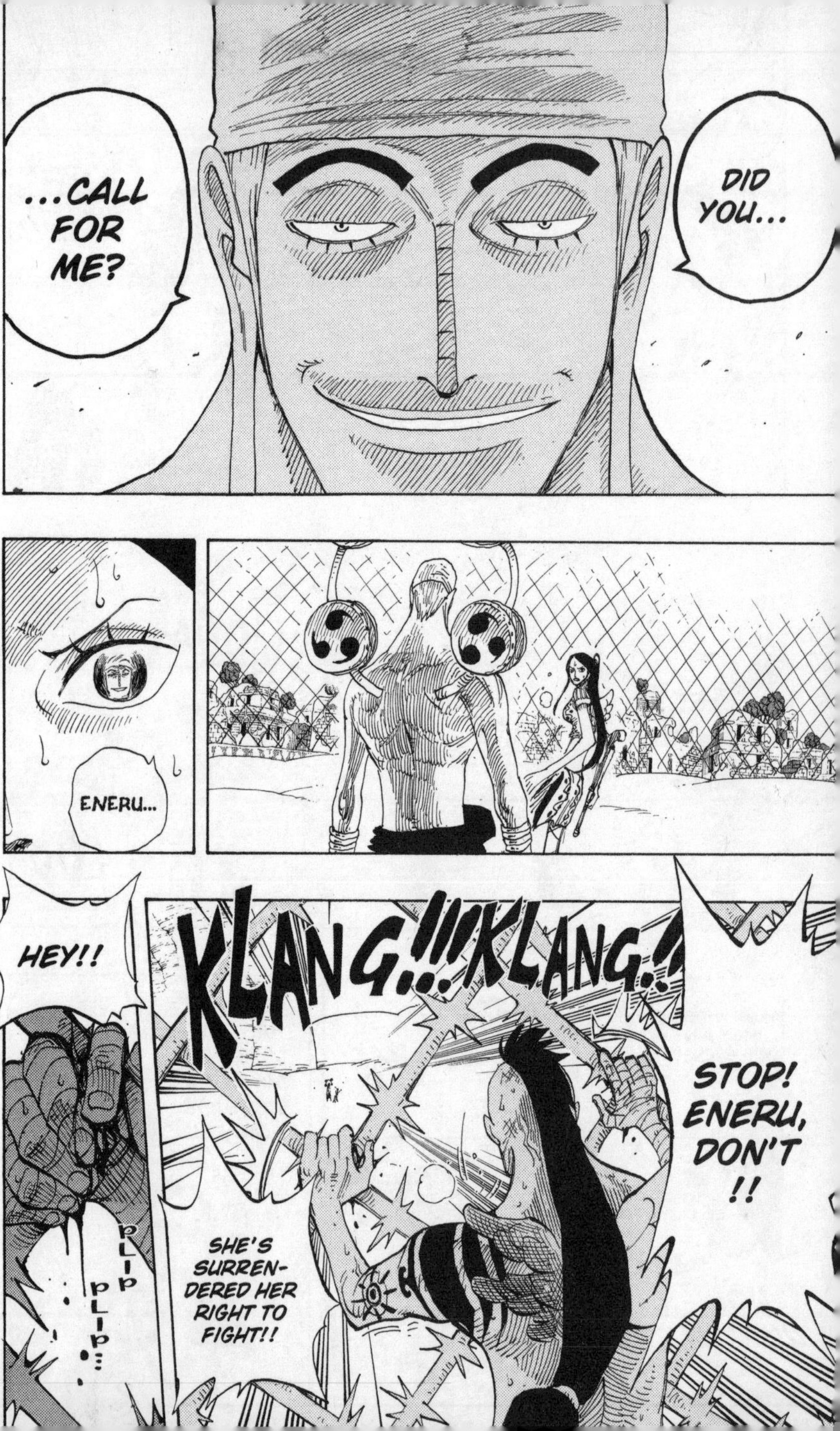
DID YOU...
...CALL FOR ME?
ENERU...
KLANG...!!! KLANG...!!
HEY!!
STOP! ENERU, DON'T!!
SHE'S SURREN-DERED HER RIGHT TO FIGHT!!
pLip pLip...

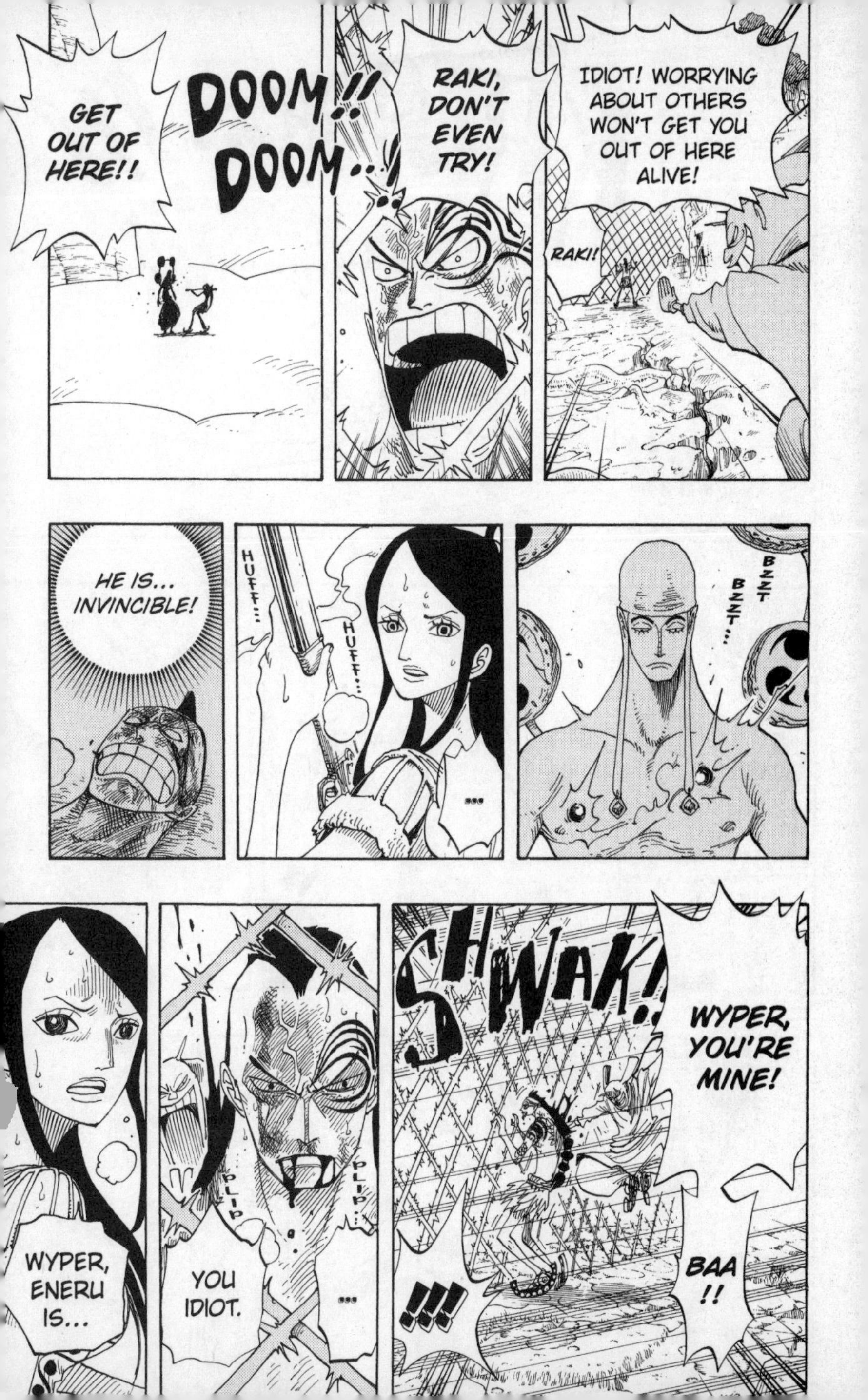
IDIOT! WORRYING ABOUT OTHERS WON'T GET YOU OUT OF HERE ALIVE!
RAKI!
RAKI, DON'T EVEN TRY!
DOOM!!
DOOM..!!
GET OUT OF HERE!!
BZZT
BZZT...
HUFF...
HUFF...
...
HE IS... INVINCIBLE!
WYPER, YOU'RE MINE!
SHWAK!!
BAA!!
!!!
PLIP
PLIP...
YOU IDIOT.
...
WYPER, ENERU IS...

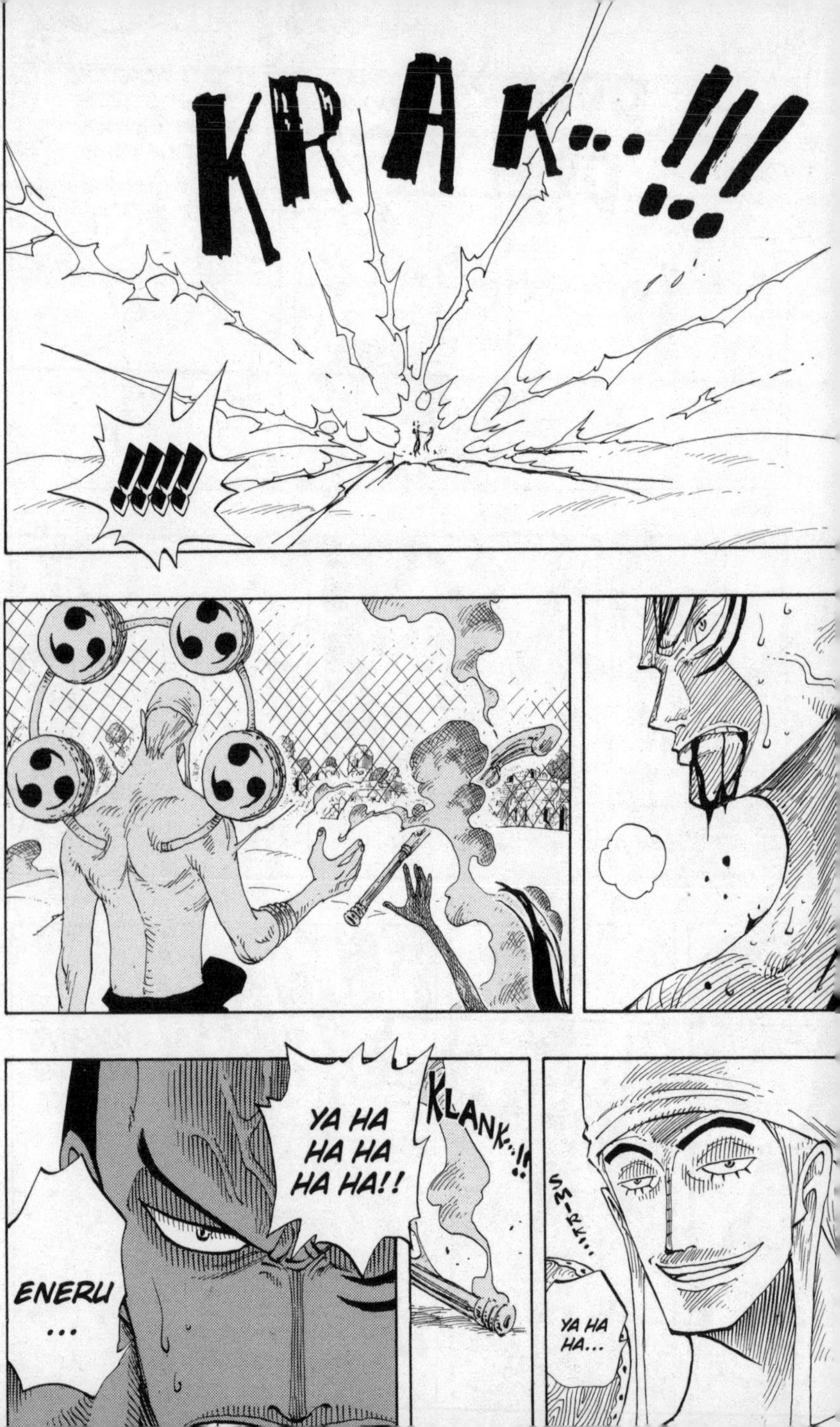
KRAK...!!!
!!!!
SMIRK...
YA HA HA...
KLANK..!!
YA HA HA HA HA HA!!
ENERU ...

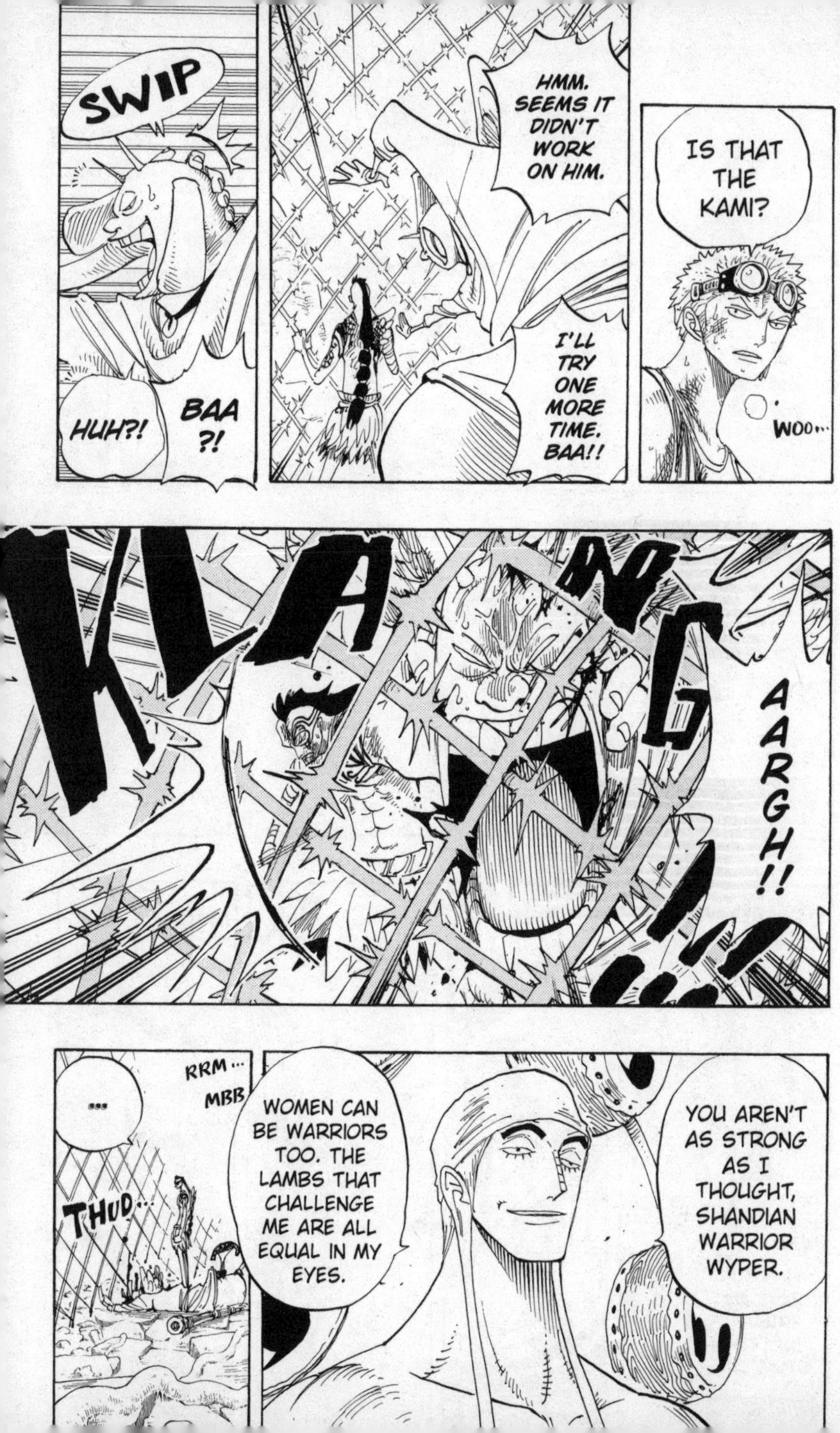
IS THAT THE KAMI?
WOO...
HMM. SEEMS IT DIDN'T WORK ON HIM.
I'LL TRY ONE MORE TIME. BAA!!
SWIP
BAA ?!
HUH?!
KLANG
AARGH!!
YOU AREN'T AS STRONG AS I THOUGHT, SHANDIAN WARRIOR WYPER.
WOMEN CAN BE WARRIORS TOO. THE LAMBS THAT CHALLENGE ME ARE ALL EQUAL IN MY EYES.
RRM... MBB
...
THUD...

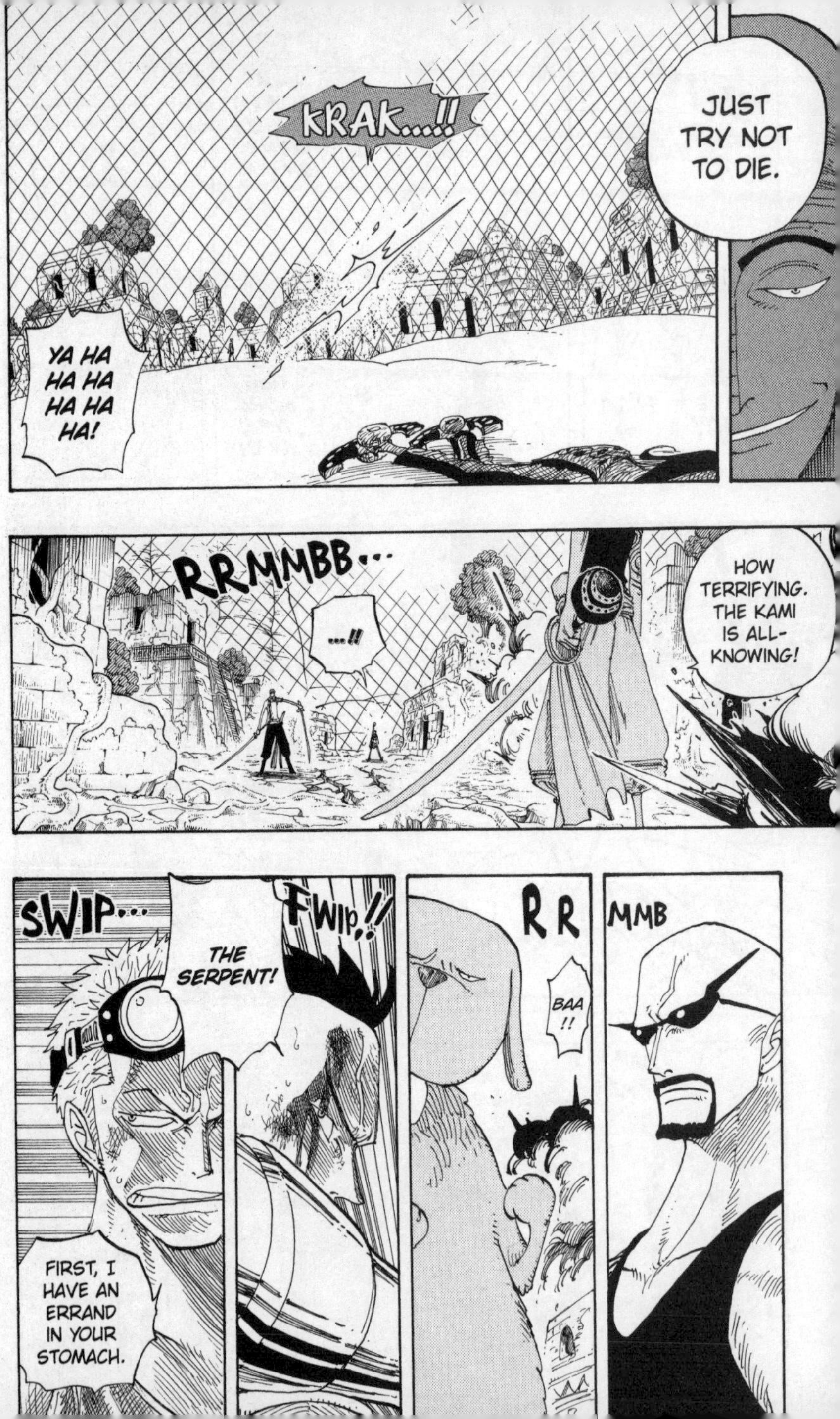
JUST TRY NOT TO DIE.
KRAK...!!
YA HA HA HA HA HA HA!
HOW TERRIFYING. THE KAMI IS ALL-KNOWING!
...!!
RRMMBB...
MMB
R R
BAA !!
FWIP!!
THE SERPENT!
SWIP...
FIRST, I HAVE AN ERRAND IN YOUR STOMACH.

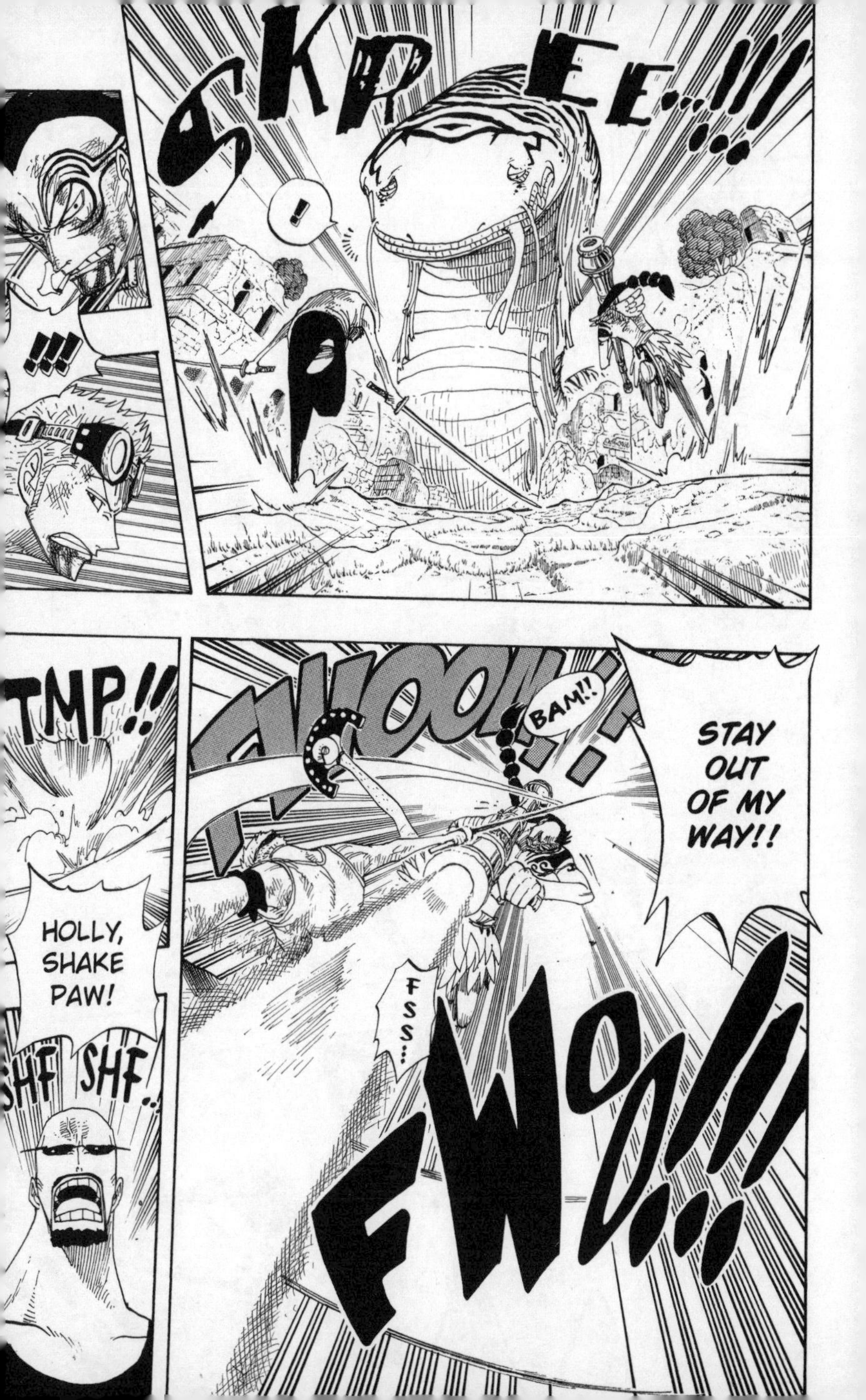
SKREE...!!!
!
!!!!
FWOOM!!
BAM!!
STAY OUT OF MY WAY!!
FSS...
FWO...!!
TMP!!
HOLLY, SHAKE PAW!
SHF SHF...

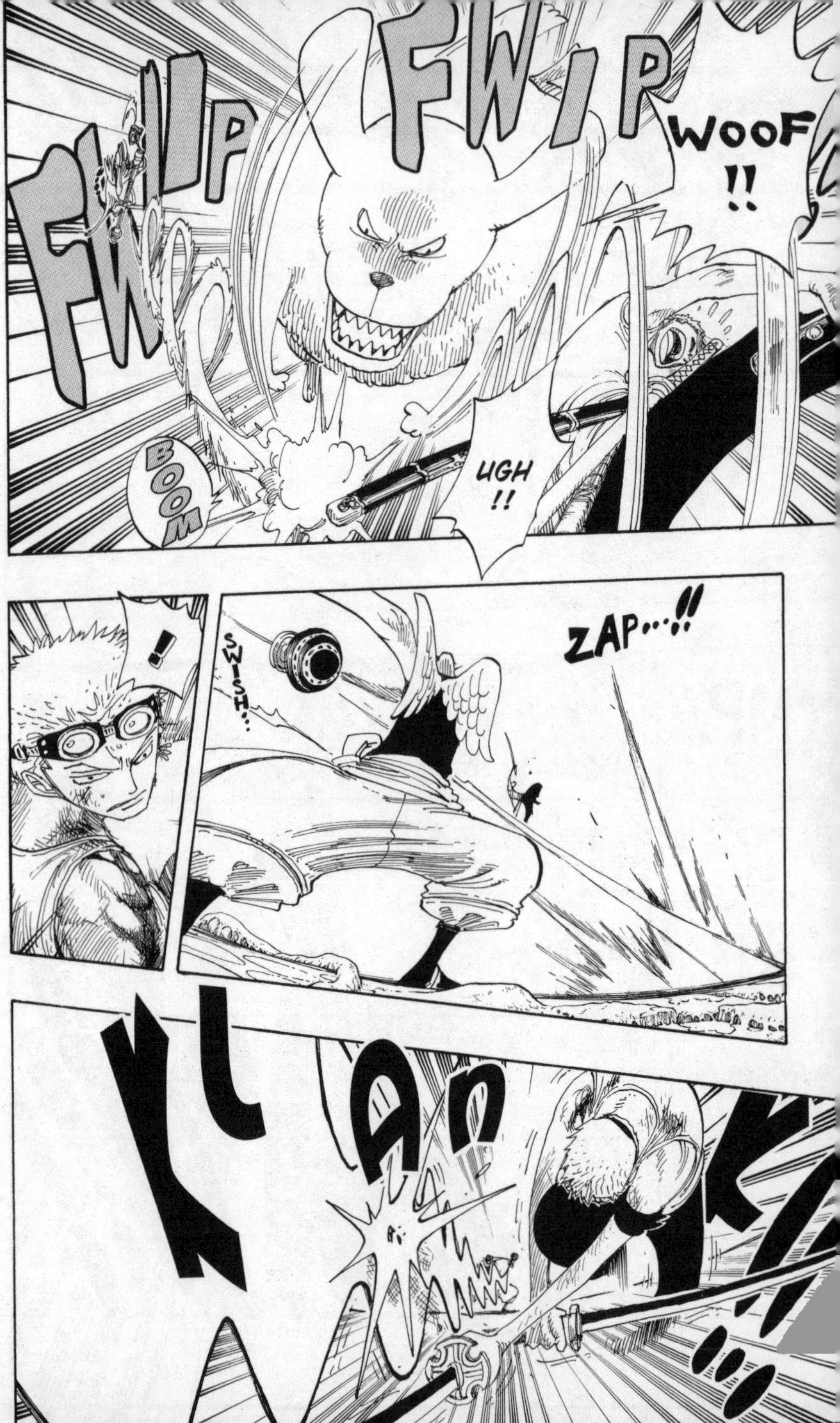
WOOF !!
FWIP
FWIP
UGH !!
BOOM
ZAP...!!
SWISH...
!
KLANK!!

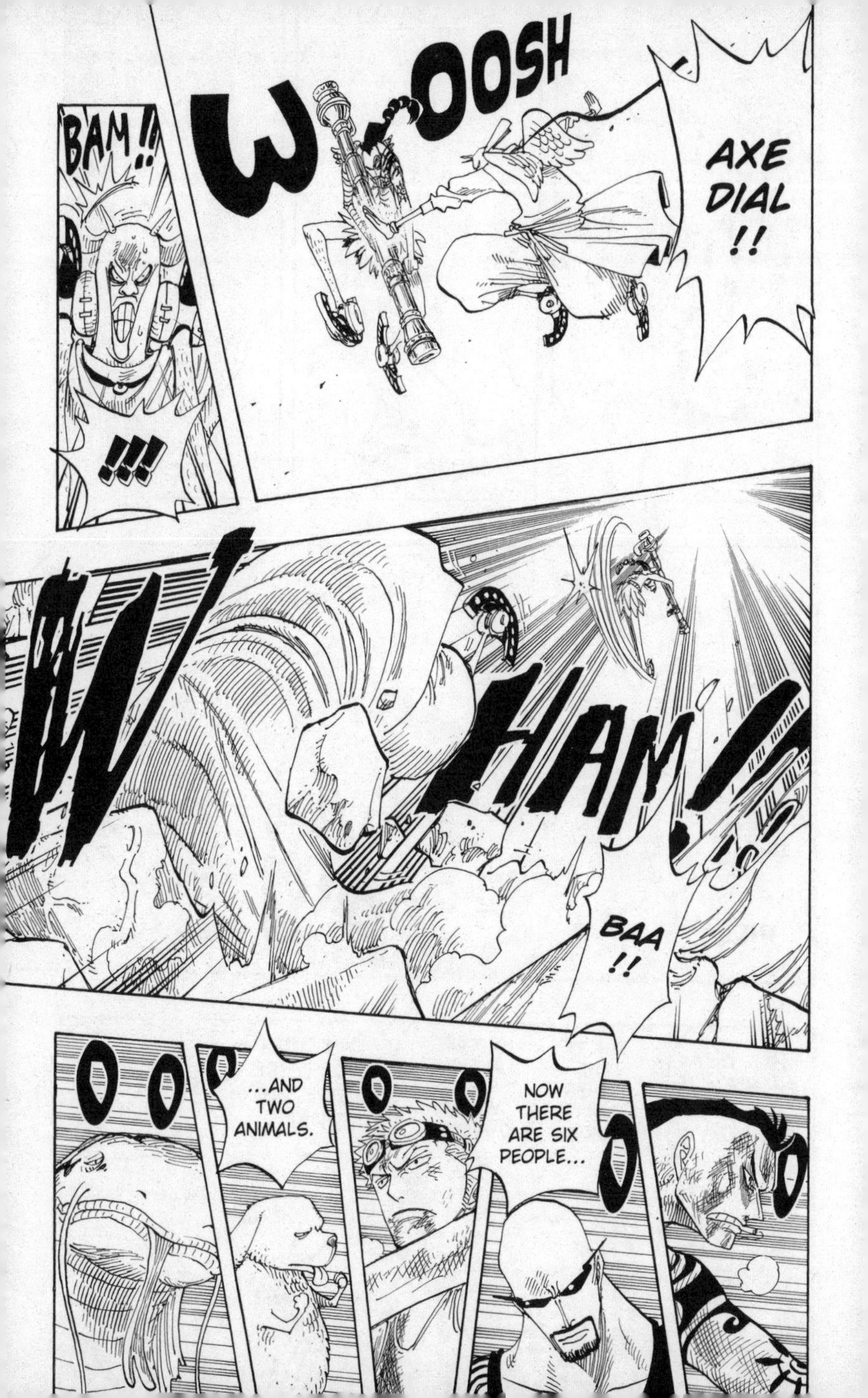
WOOSH
AXE DIAL!!
BAM!!
!!!
WHAM!!
BAA!!
NOW THERE ARE SIX PEOPLE...
...AND TWO ANIMALS.

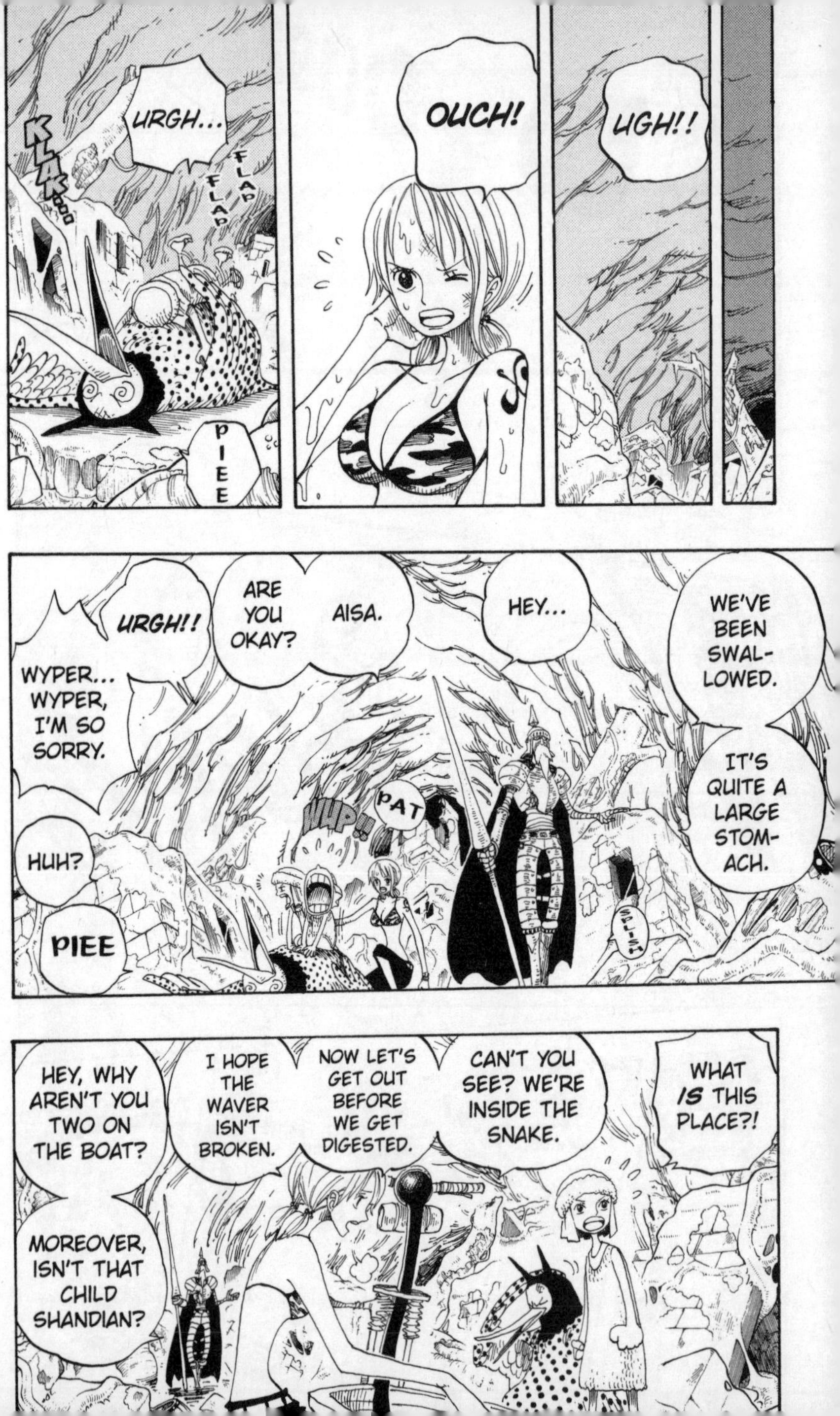
UGH!!
OUCH!
URGH...
KLAK
FLAP FLAP
PIEE
WE'VE BEEN SWAL-LOWED.
IT'S QUITE A LARGE STOM-ACH.
HEY...
AISA.
ARE YOU OKAY?
URGH!!
WYPER... WYPER, I'M SO SORRY.
PAT
WUP!!
SPLISH
HUH?
PIEE
WHAT *IS* THIS PLACE?!
CAN'T YOU SEE? WE'RE INSIDE THE SNAKE.
NOW LET'S GET OUT BEFORE WE GET DIGESTED.
I HOPE THE WAVER ISN'T BROKEN.
HEY, WHY AREN'T YOU TWO ON THE BOAT?
MOREOVER, ISN'T THAT CHILD SHANDIAN?

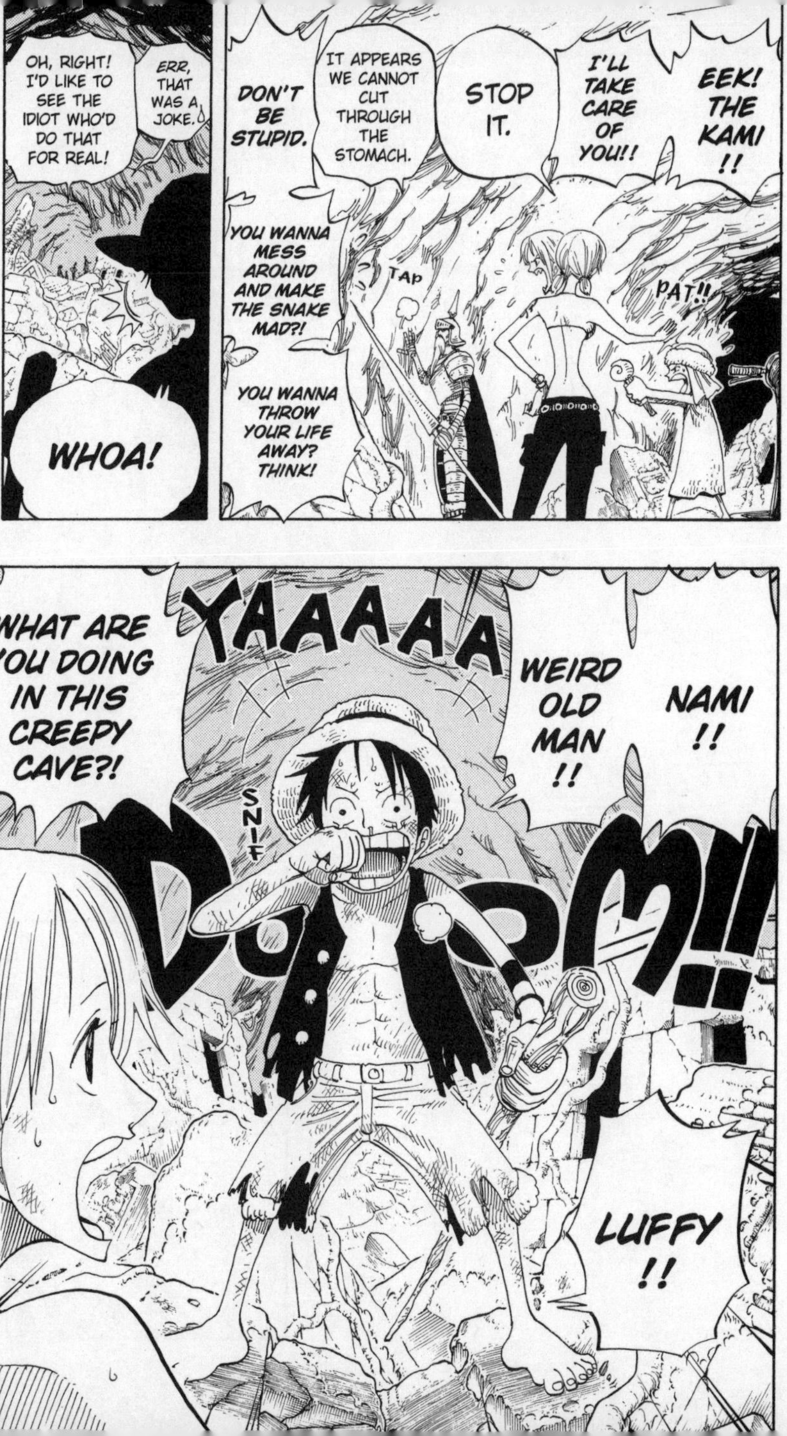
EEK! THE KAMI!!
I'LL TAKE CARE OF YOU!!
STOP IT.
IT APPEARS WE CANNOT CUT THROUGH THE STOMACH.
DON'T BE STUPID.
YOU WANNA MESS AROUND AND MAKE THE SNAKE MAD?!
PAT!!
TAP
YOU WANNA THROW YOUR LIFE AWAY? THINK!
ERR, THAT WAS A JOKE.
OH, RIGHT! I'D LIKE TO SEE THE IDIOT WHO'D DO THAT FOR REAL!
WHOA!
NAMI!!
WEIRD OLD MAN!!
YAAAAA
WHAT ARE YOU DOING IN THIS CREEPY CAVE?!
SNIF
LUFFY!!

Chapter 271:
PIRATE ZOLO VS. VASSAL OHM

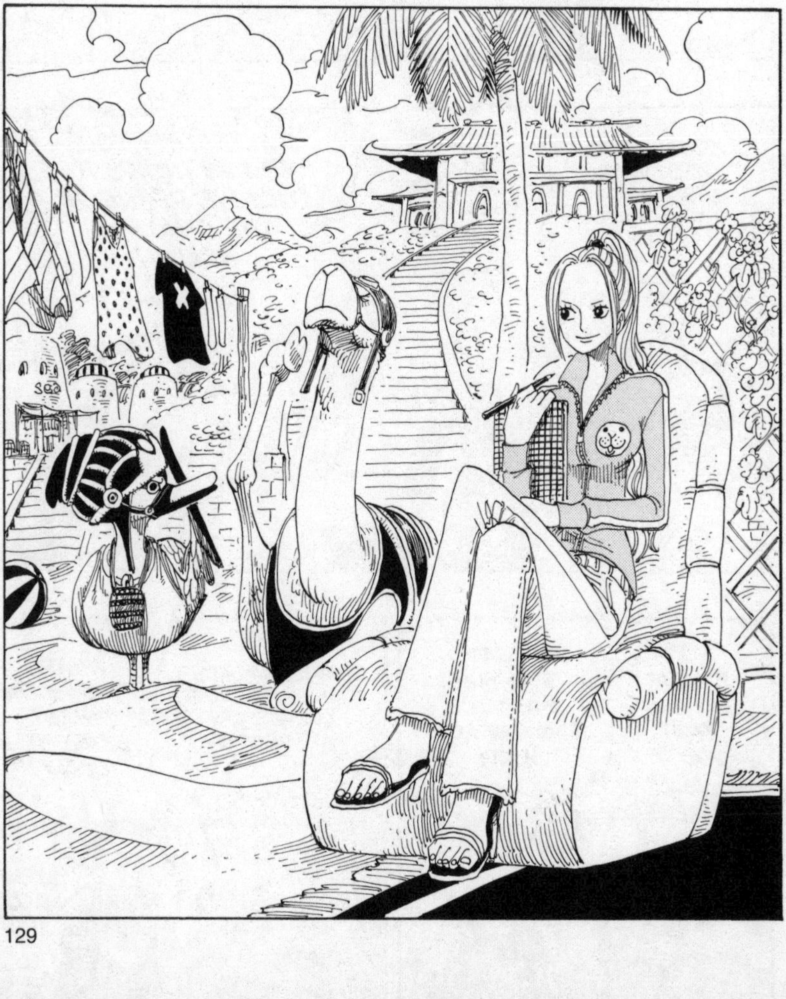

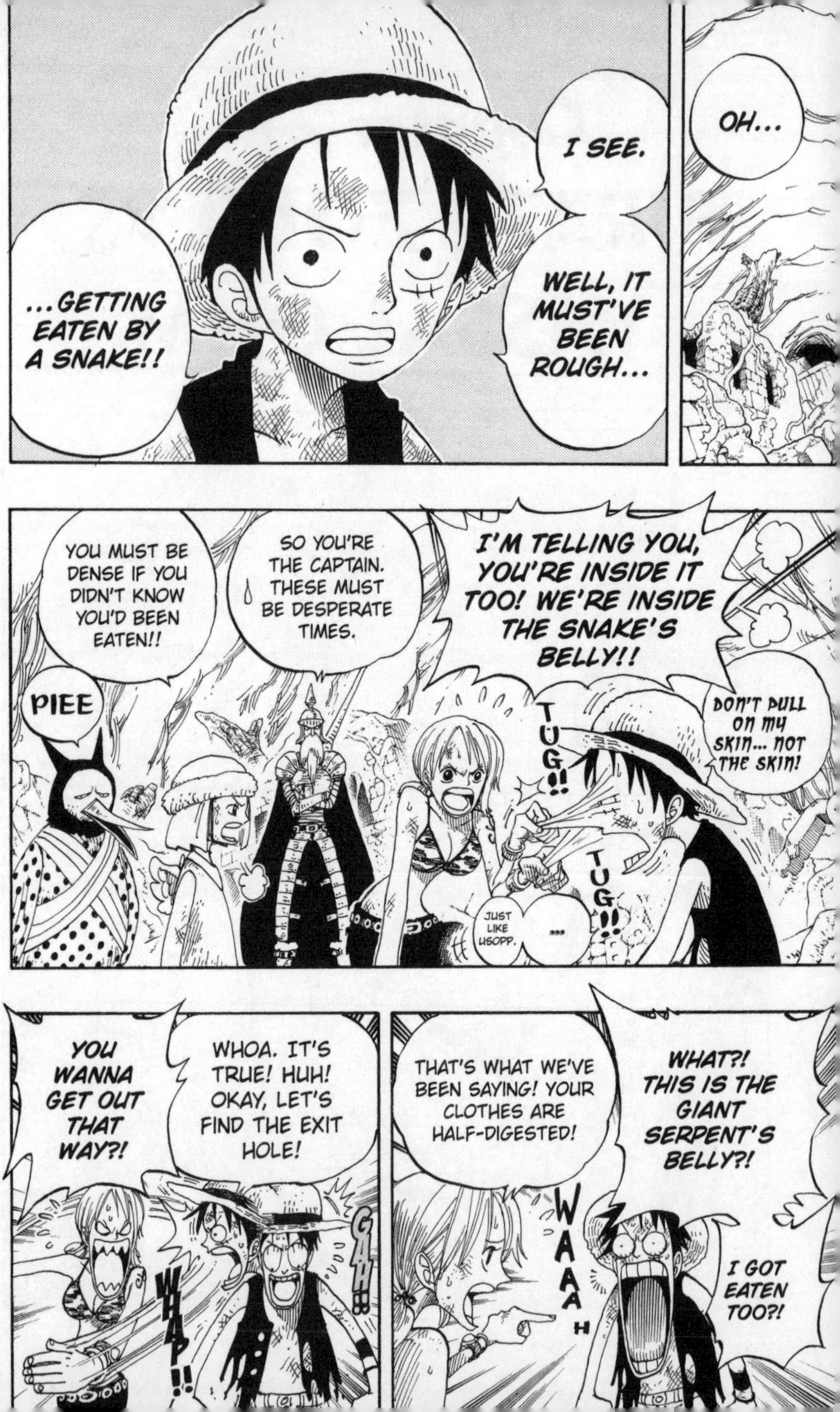
OH...
I SEE.
WELL, IT MUST'VE BEEN ROUGH...
...GETTING EATEN BY A SNAKE!!
I'M TELLING YOU, YOU'RE INSIDE IT TOO! WE'RE INSIDE THE SNAKE'S BELLY!!
DON'T PULL ON MY SKIN... NOT THE SKIN!
TUG!!
TUG!!
SO YOU'RE THE CAPTAIN. THESE MUST BE DESPERATE TIMES.
YOU MUST BE DENSE IF YOU DIDN'T KNOW YOU'D BEEN EATEN!!
...
JUST LIKE USOPP.
PIEE
WHAT?! THIS IS THE GIANT SERPENT'S BELLY?!
THAT'S WHAT WE'VE BEEN SAYING! YOUR CLOTHES ARE HALF-DIGESTED!
WAAAH
I GOT EATEN TOO?!
WHOA. IT'S TRUE! HUH! OKAY, LET'S FIND THE EXIT HOLE!
YOU WANNA GET OUT THAT WAY?!
GAH!!
WHAP!!

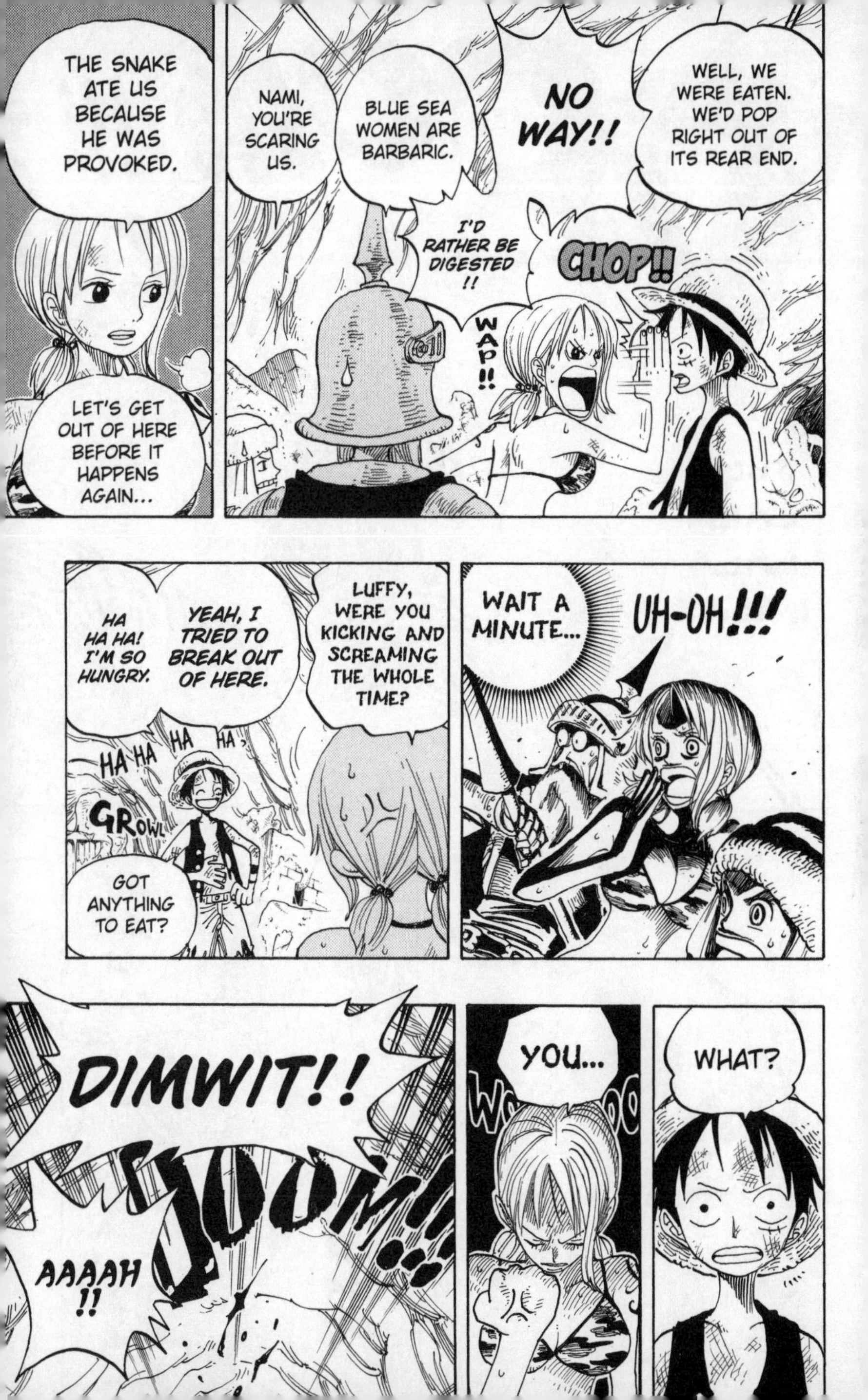
WELL, WE WERE EATEN. WE'D POP RIGHT OUT OF ITS REAR END.
NO WAY!!
BLUE SEA WOMEN ARE BARBARIC.
NAMI, YOU'RE SCARING US.
CHOP!!
I'D RATHER BE DIGESTED!!
WAP!!
THE SNAKE ATE US BECAUSE HE WAS PROVOKED.
LET'S GET OUT OF HERE BEFORE IT HAPPENS AGAIN...
UH-OH!!!
WAIT A MINUTE...
LUFFY, WERE YOU KICKING AND SCREAMING THE WHOLE TIME?
YEAH, I TRIED TO BREAK OUT OF HERE.
HA HA HA! I'M SO HUNGRY.
HA HA HA HA,
GROWL
GOT ANYTHING TO EAT?
WHAT?
YOU...
DIMWIT!!
AAAAH!!

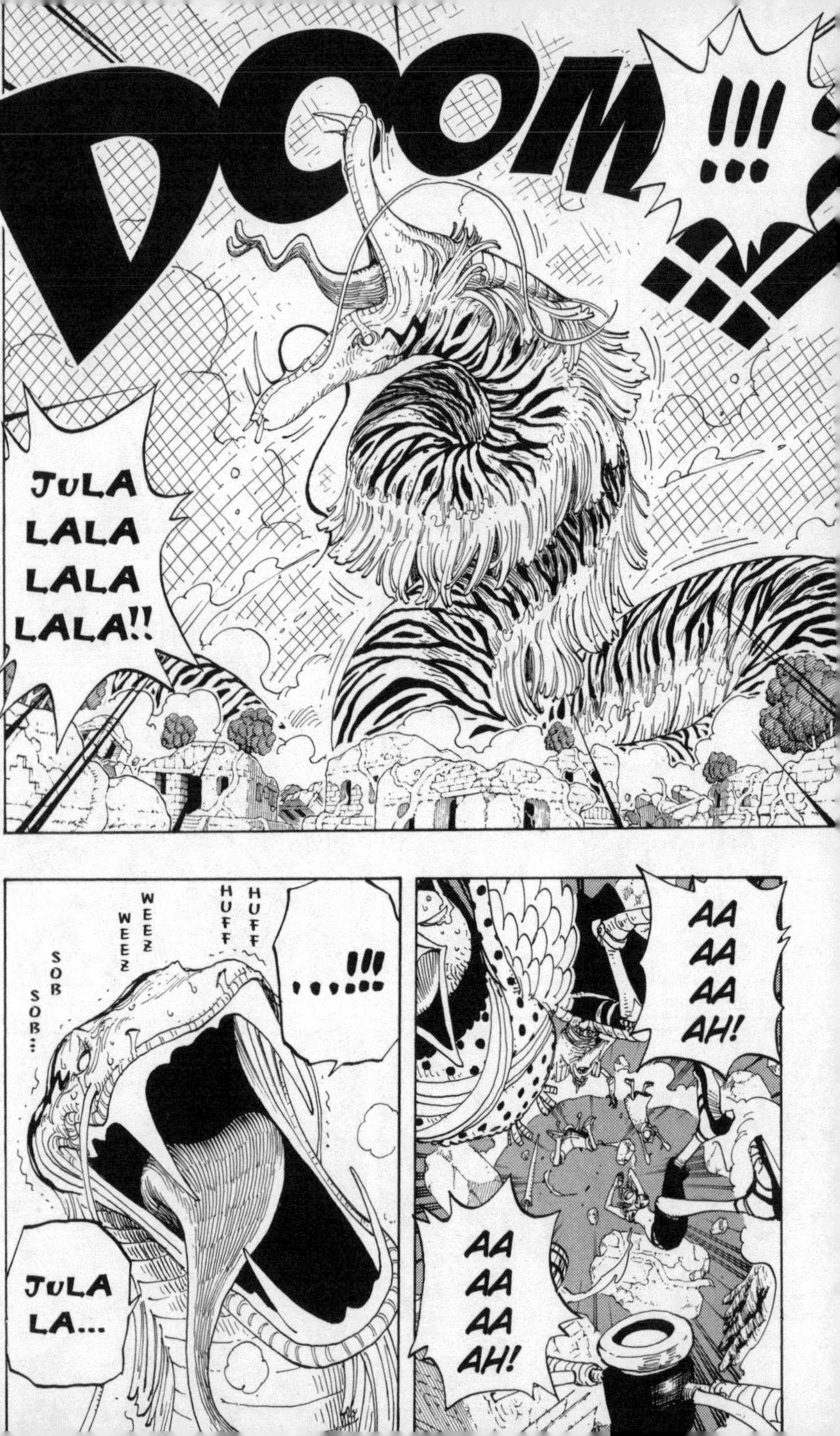
DOOM!!!
JULA LALA LALA LALA!!
AA AA AA AH!
AA AA AA AH!
...!!!
HUFF HUFF
WEEZ WEEZ
SOB SOB...
JULA LA...

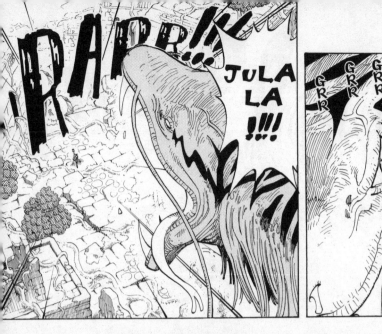

GRR GRR GRR GRR
RARRK...!!
JULA LA!!!!
IT'S MOANING LIKE MAD, JUST AS I HOPED!!
DON'T FALL INTO THE STOMACH ACID, AISA!!
WOOSH!
I'LL CUT ITS BELLY OPEN RIGHT NOW!
FWOOO!!!

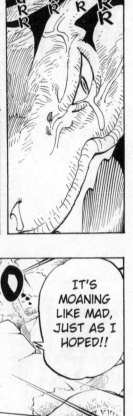

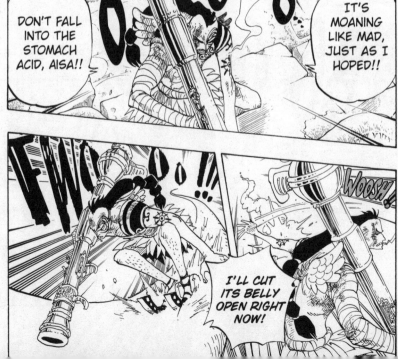

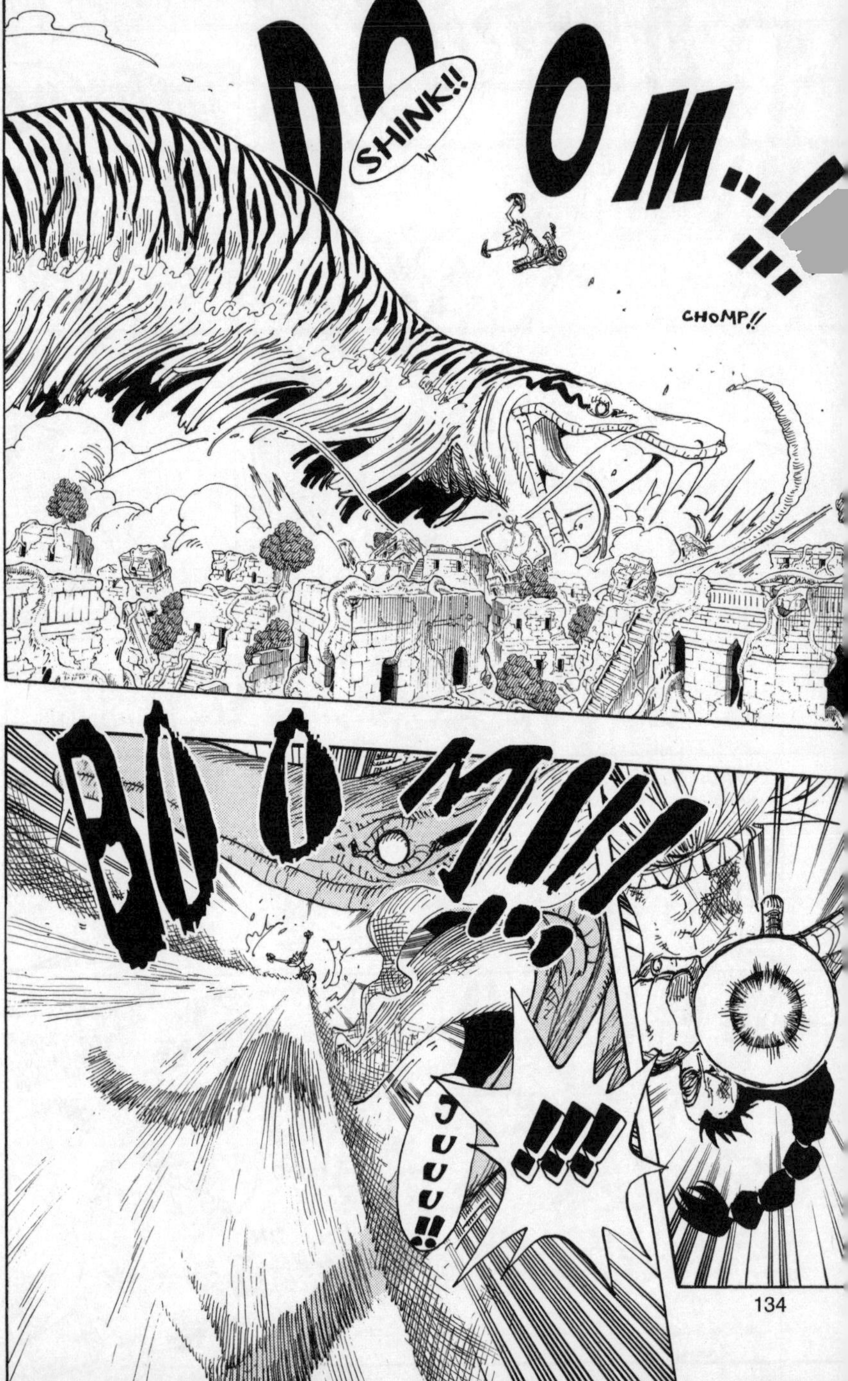
DOOM..!!
SHINK!!
CHOMP!!
BOOM!!
!!!
JUUUU!!

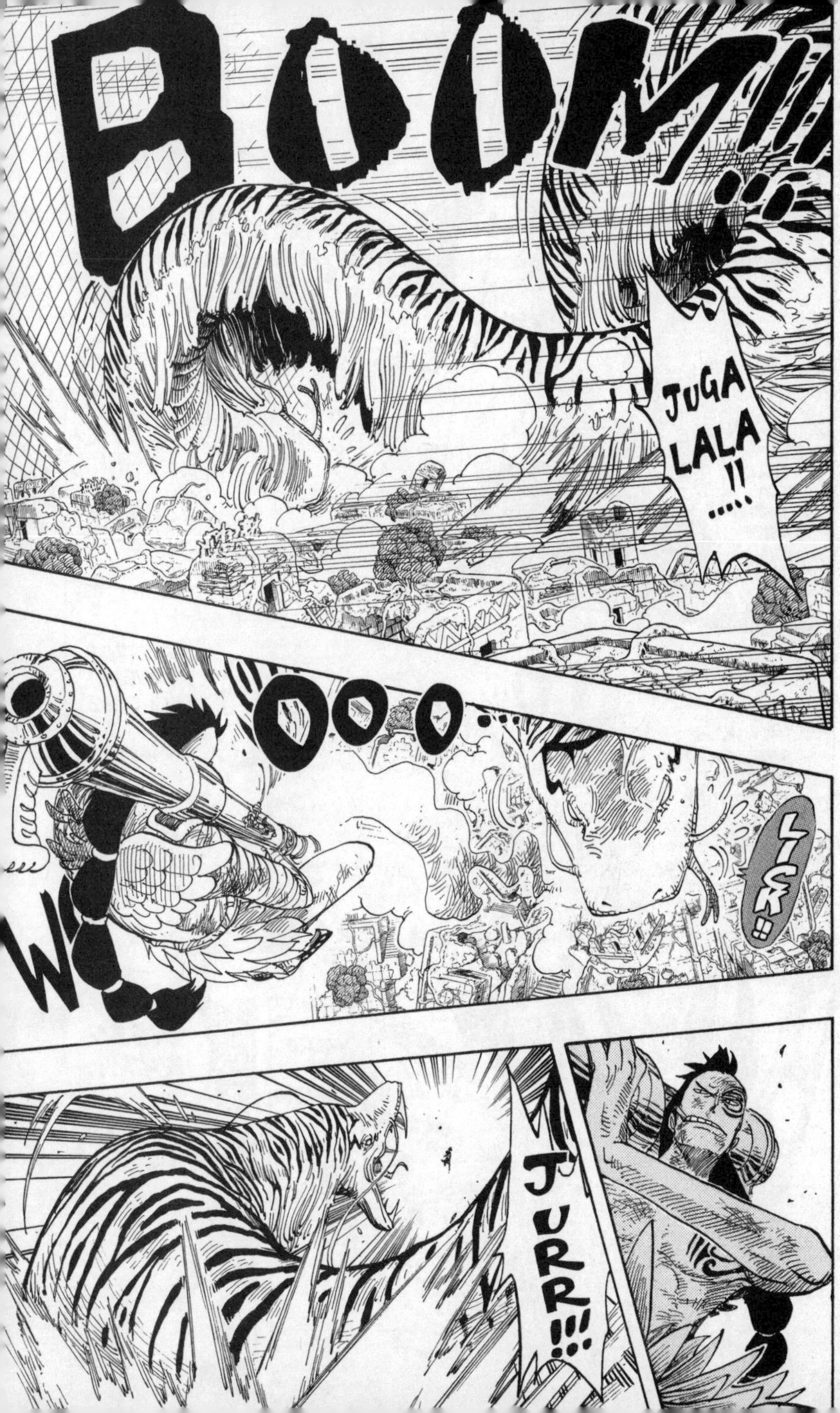
BOOOM!!
JUGA LALA !! .....
LICK!!
WOOOO...
JURR!!!

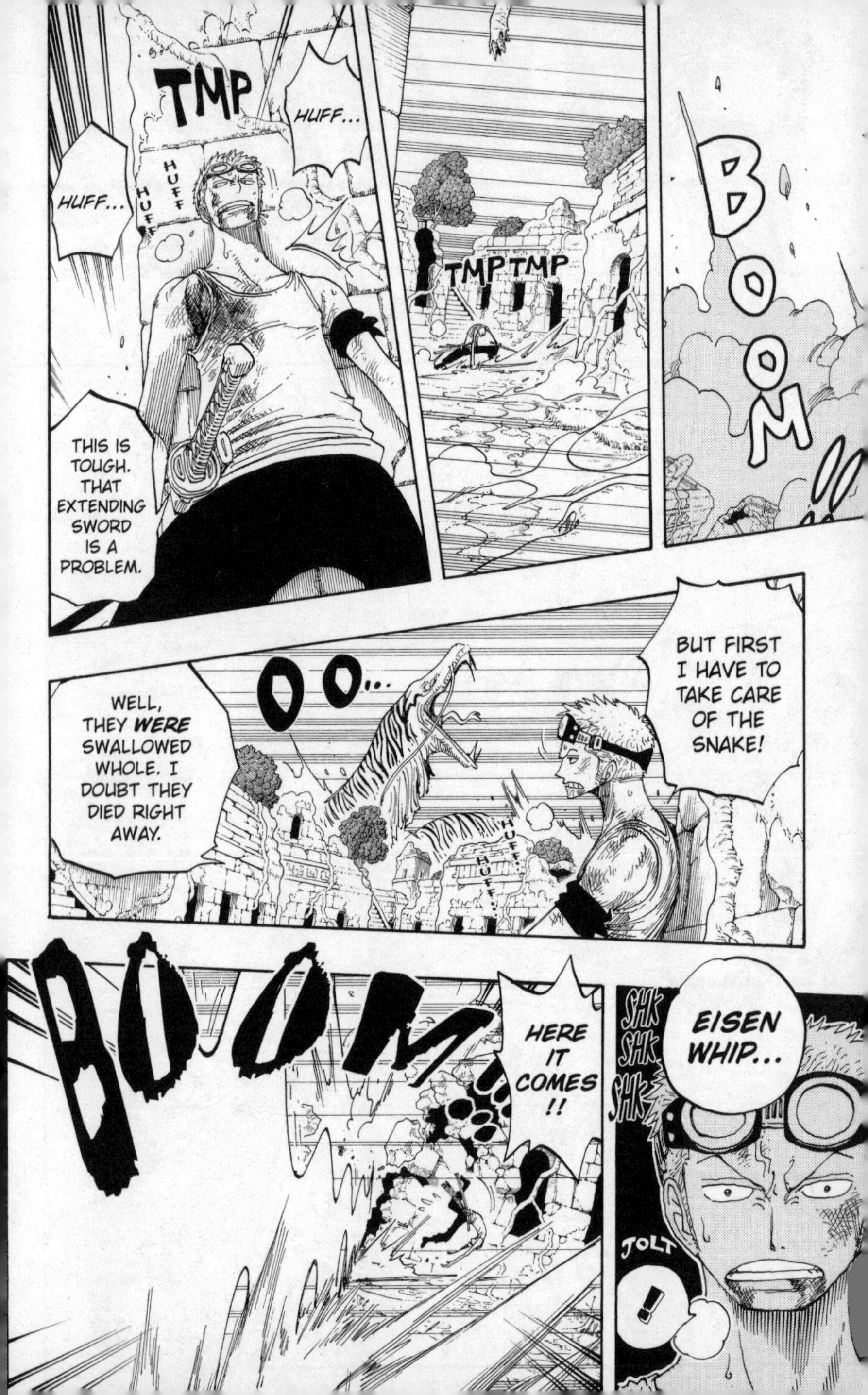
BOOM!!
TMP TMP
HUFF...
TMP
HUFF HUFF
HUFF...
THIS IS TOUGH. THAT EXTENDING SWORD IS A PROBLEM.
BUT FIRST I HAVE TO TAKE CARE OF THE SNAKE!
OO...
WELL, THEY *WERE* SWALLOWED WHOLE. I DOUBT THEY DIED RIGHT AWAY.
HUFF... HUFF...
EISEN WHIP...
SHK SHK SHK
JOLT
!
HERE IT COMES!!
BOOM

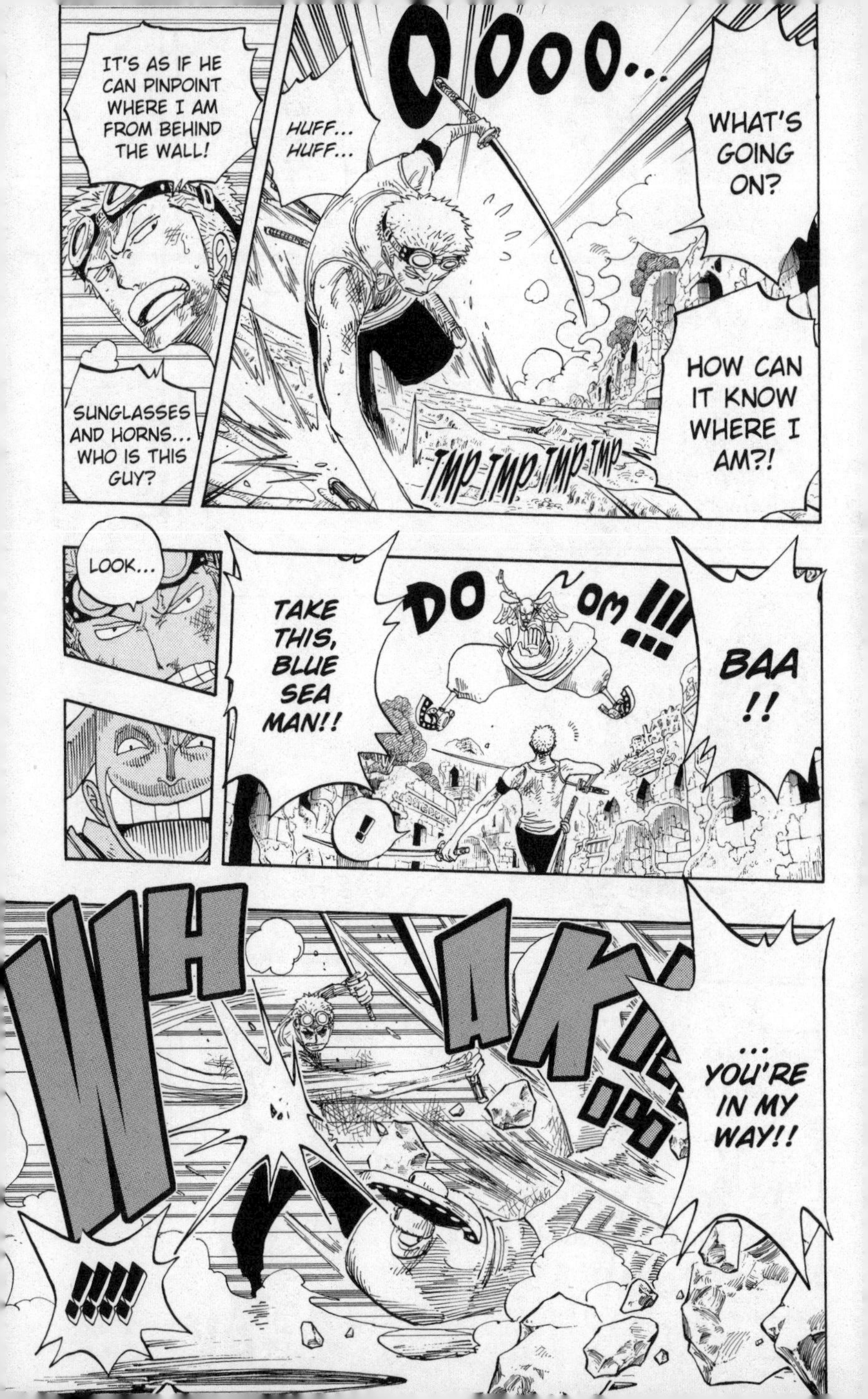
WHAT'S GOING ON?
OOOO...
HUFF... HUFF...
HOW CAN IT KNOW WHERE I AM?!
TMP TMP TMP TMP
IT'S AS IF HE CAN PINPOINT WHERE I AM FROM BEHIND THE WALL!
SUNGLASSES AND HORNS... WHO IS THIS GUY?
BAA!!
DOom!!!
TAKE THIS, BLUE SEA MAN!!
!
LOOK...
...YOU'RE IN MY WAY!!
WHAK
!!!!

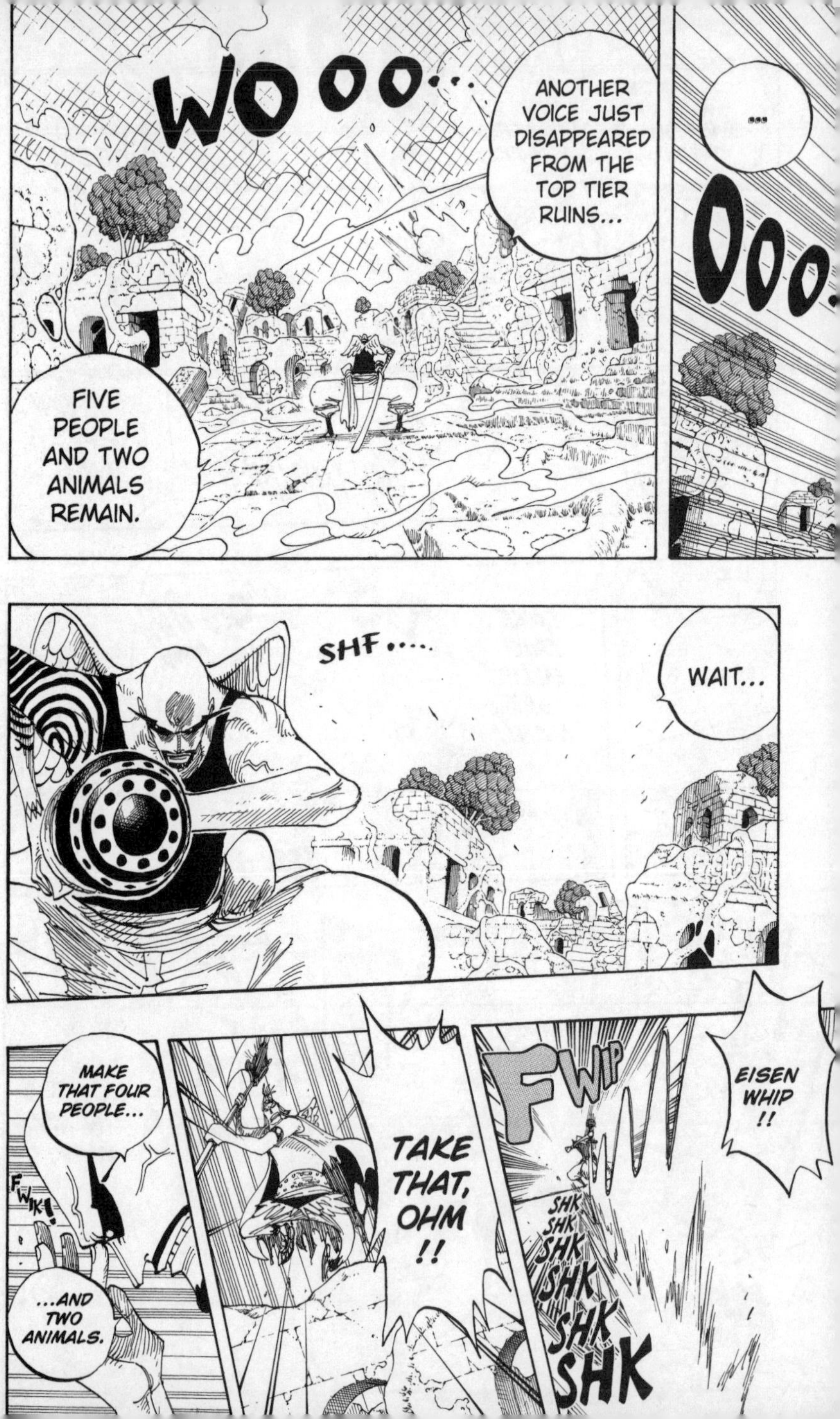
...
OOO...
WOOO...
ANOTHER VOICE JUST DISAPPEARED FROM THE TOP TIER RUINS...
FIVE PEOPLE AND TWO ANIMALS REMAIN.
WAIT...
SHF....
EISEN WHIP !!
FWIP
SHK SHK SHK SHK SHK SHK SHK
TAKE THAT, OHM !!
MAKE THAT FOUR PEOPLE...
FWIK!
...AND TWO ANIMALS.

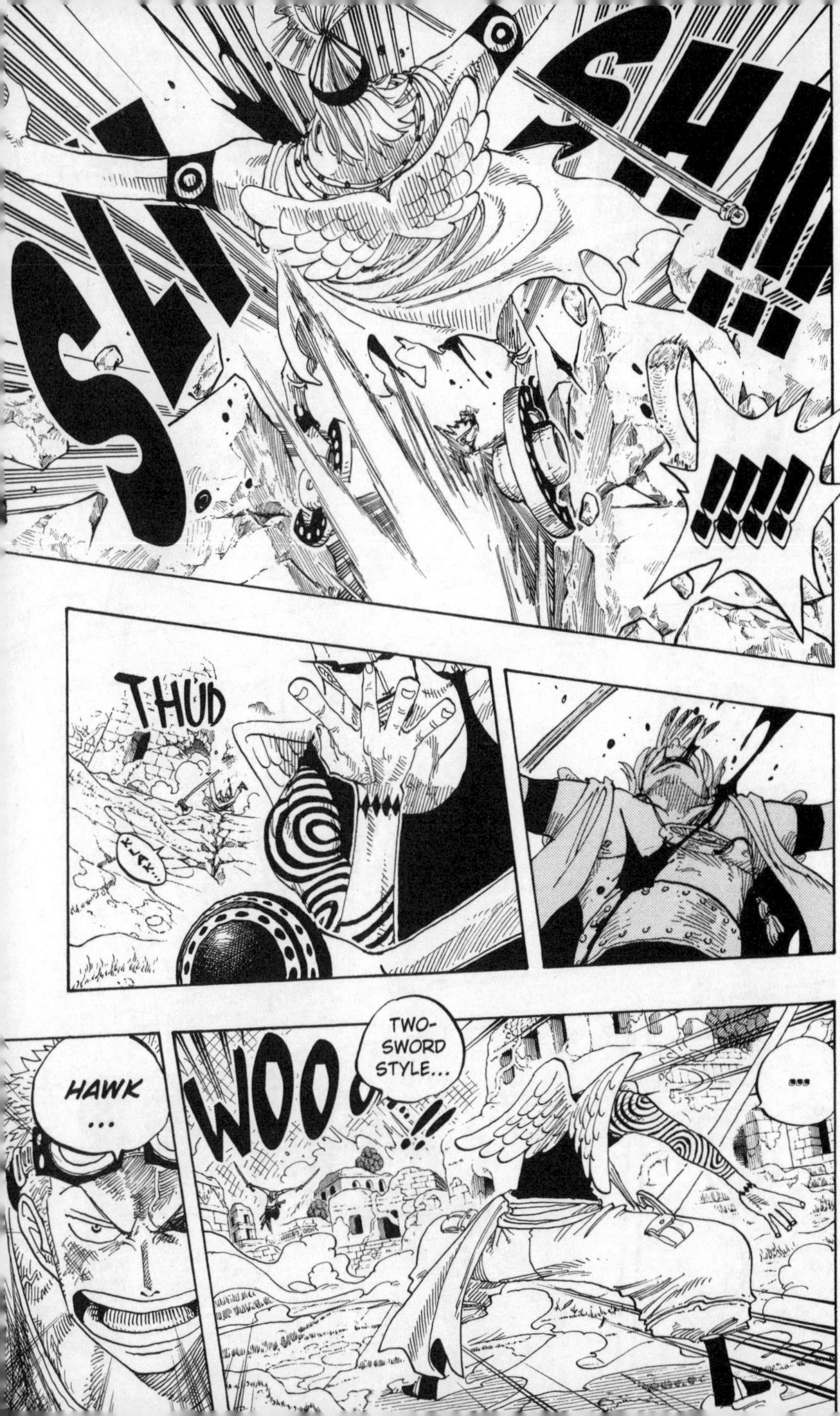
SH!!!
!!!!
SHI
THUD
...
TWO-SWORD STYLE...
WOO!!
HAWK ...

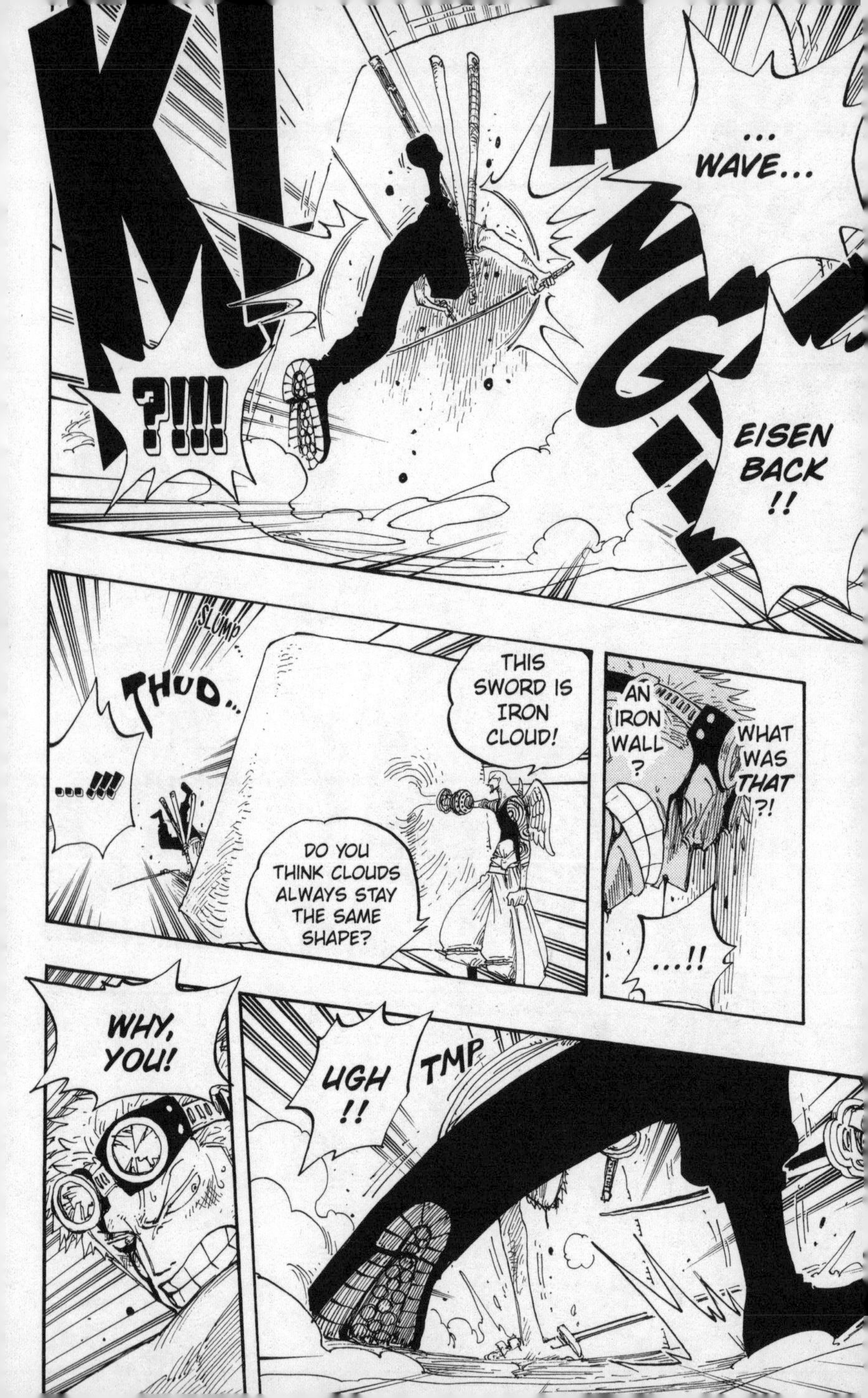
...WAVE...
EISEN BACK!!
KLANG
?!!!
AN IRON WALL?
WHAT WAS THAT?!
...!!
THIS SWORD IS IRON CLOUD!
SLUMP
THUD...
DO YOU THINK CLOUDS ALWAYS STAY THE SAME SHAPE?
...!!!
TMP
UGH!!
WHY, YOU!

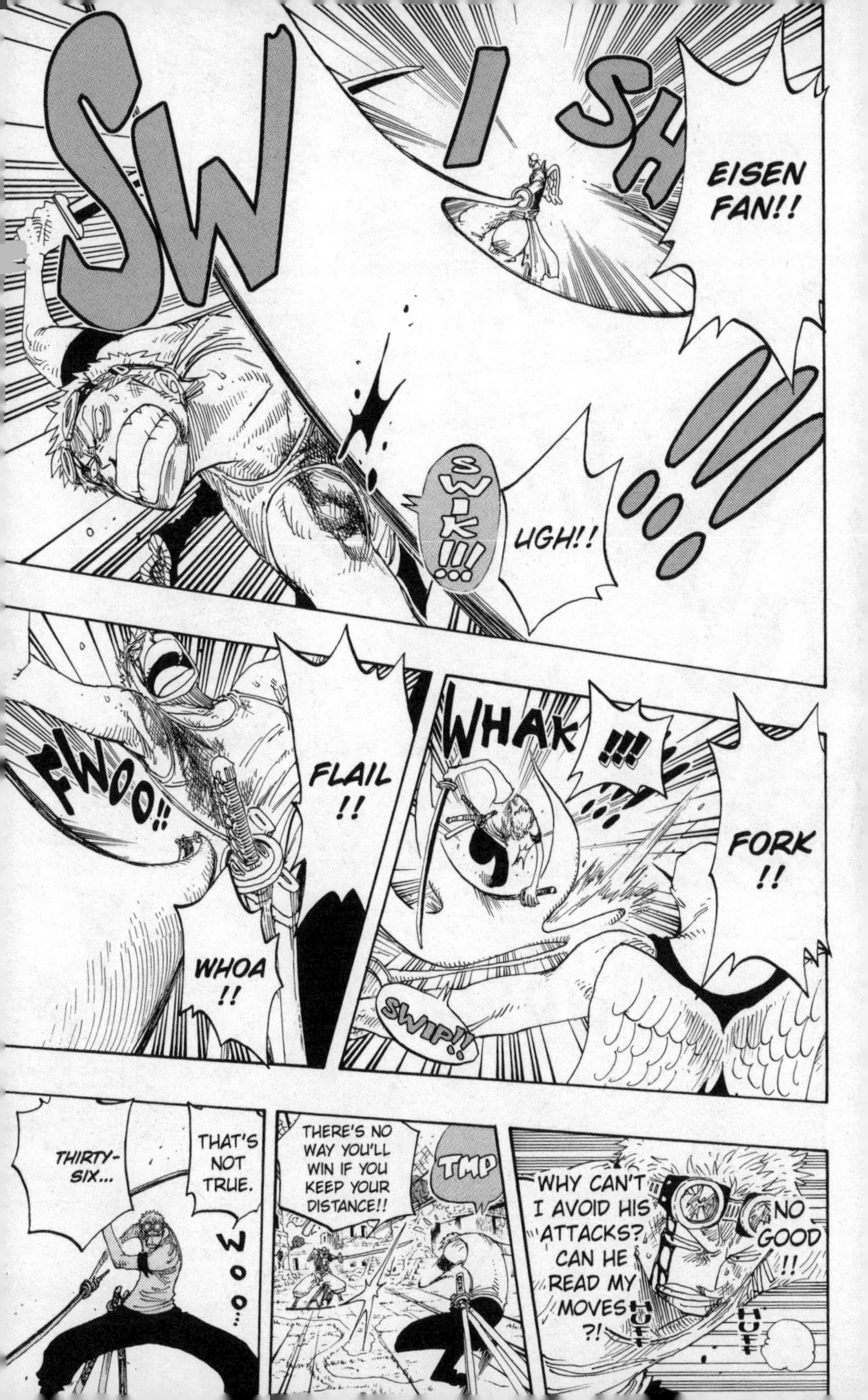
SWISH
EISEN FAN!!
UGH!!
SWIK!!!
WHAK!!!
FORK!!
SWIP!!
FLAIL!!
FWOO!!
WHOA!!
NO GOOD!!
WHY CAN'T I AVOID HIS ATTACKS? CAN HE READ MY MOVES?!
HUFF
HUFF
TMP
THERE'S NO WAY YOU'LL WIN IF YOU KEEP YOUR DISTANCE!!
THAT'S NOT TRUE.
THIRTY-SIX...
WOO...

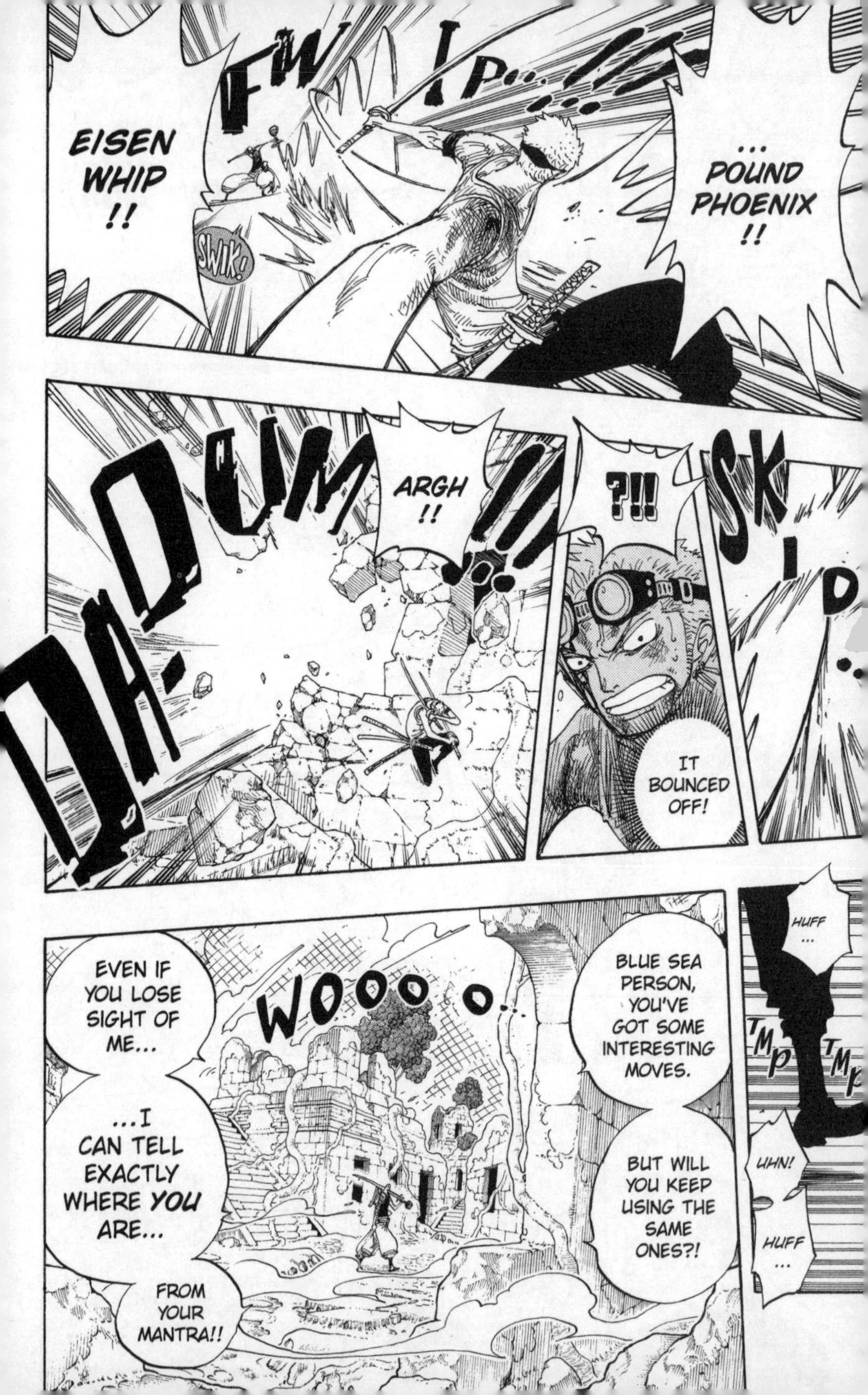
...POUND PHOENIX!!
FWIP...!!!
EISEN WHIP!!
SWIK!
SKID...
?!!
IT BOUNCED OFF!
ARGH!!
DADUM...!!
HUFF...
TMP TMP
UHN!
HUFF...
BLUE SEA PERSON, YOU'VE GOT SOME INTERESTING MOVES.
BUT WILL YOU KEEP USING THE SAME ONES?!
WOOOO...
EVEN IF YOU LOSE SIGHT OF ME...
...I CAN TELL EXACTLY WHERE YOU ARE...
FROM YOUR MANTRA!!

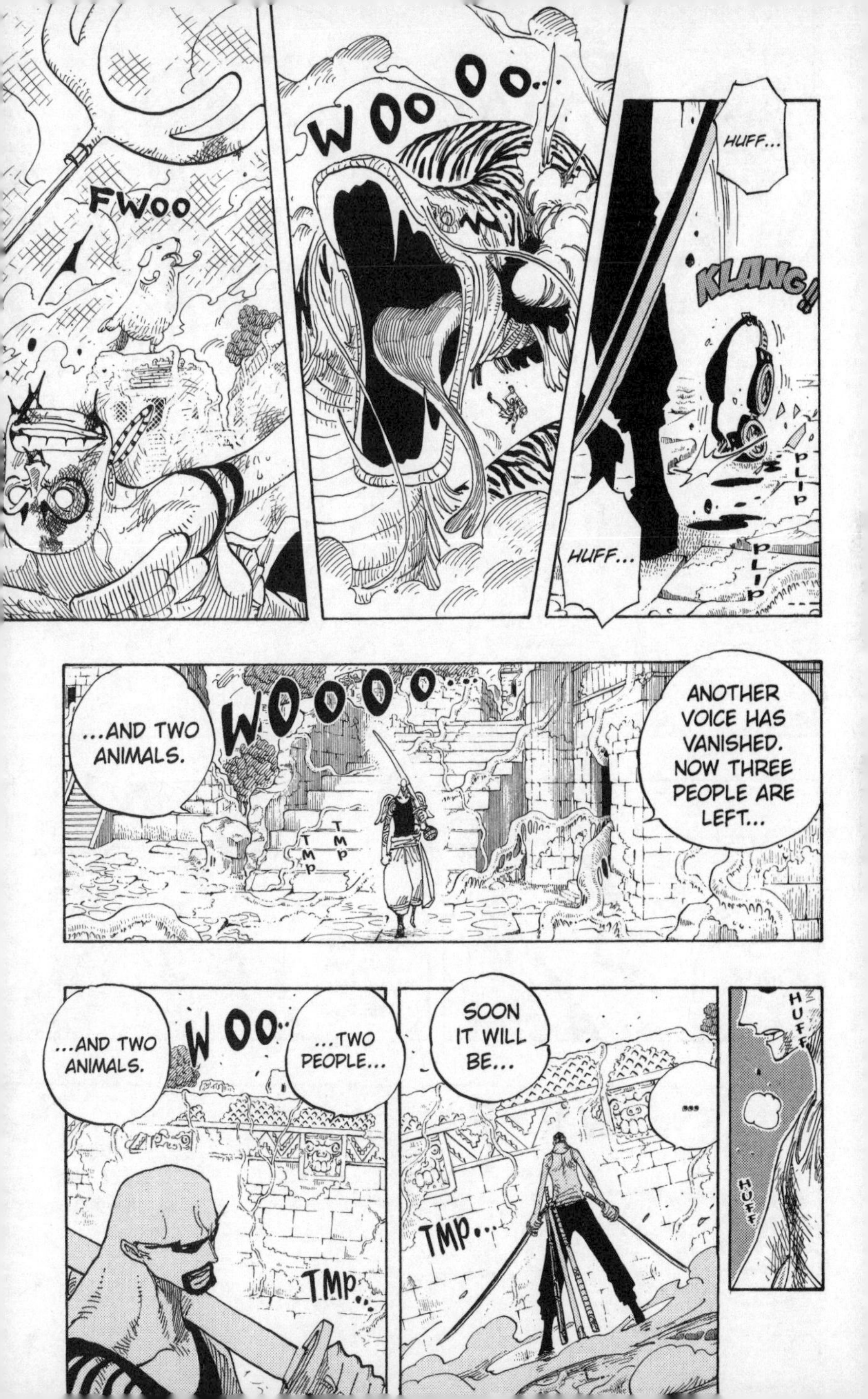
HUFF...
KLANG!!
PLIP
PLIP
HUFF...
WOO OO...
FWOO
ANOTHER VOICE HAS VANISHED. NOW THREE PEOPLE ARE LEFT...
WOOOO...
TMP
TMP
...AND TWO ANIMALS.
HUFF
HUFF
SOON IT WILL BE...
...
TMP...
...TWO PEOPLE...
WOO...
...AND TWO ANIMALS.
TMP...

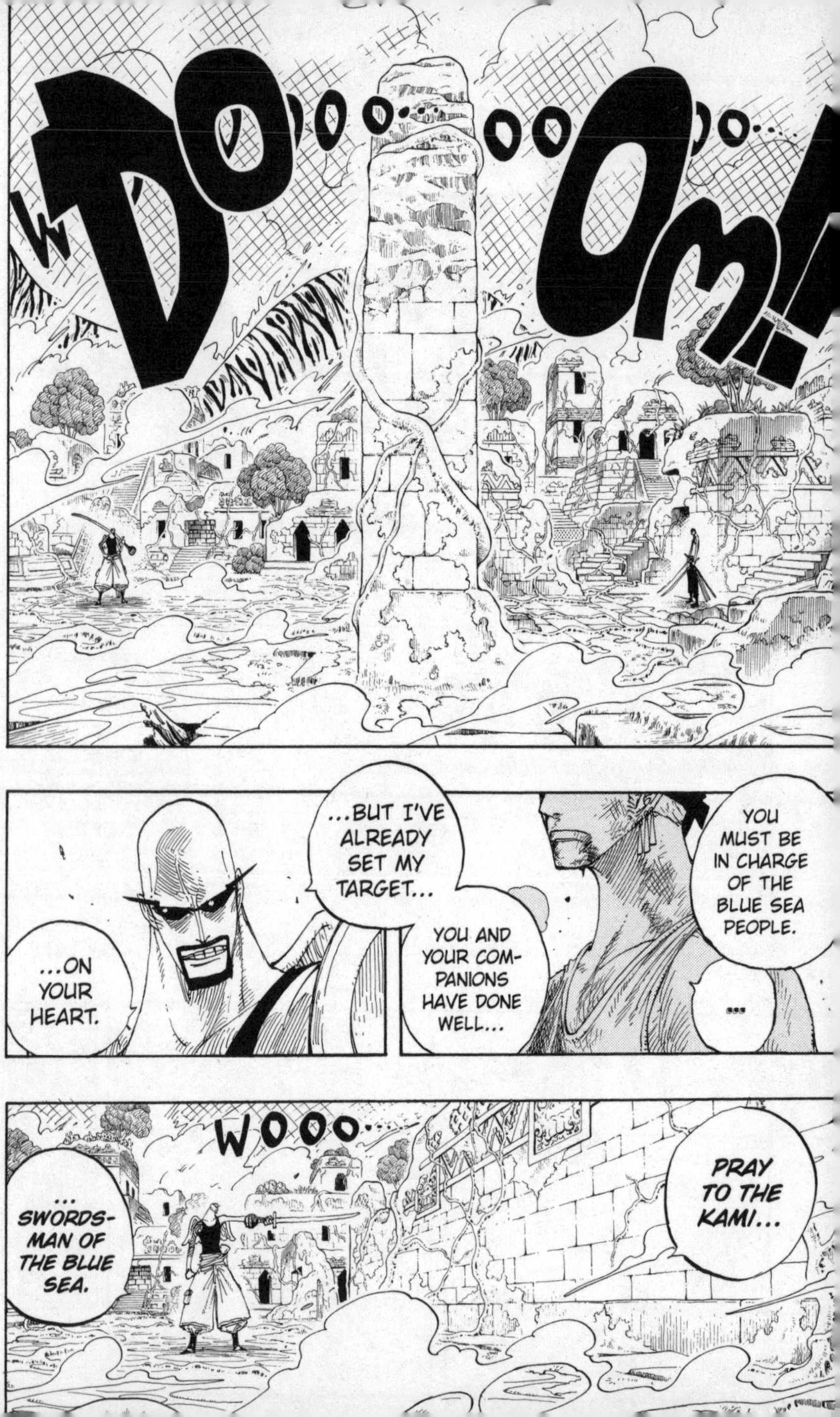
DOOOOOOOOM!!
YOU MUST BE IN CHARGE OF THE BLUE SEA PEOPLE.
...
YOU AND YOUR COMPANIONS HAVE DONE WELL...
...BUT I'VE ALREADY SET MY TARGET...
...ON YOUR HEART.
PRAY TO THE KAMI...
WOOO...
...SWORDSMAN OF THE BLUE SEA.

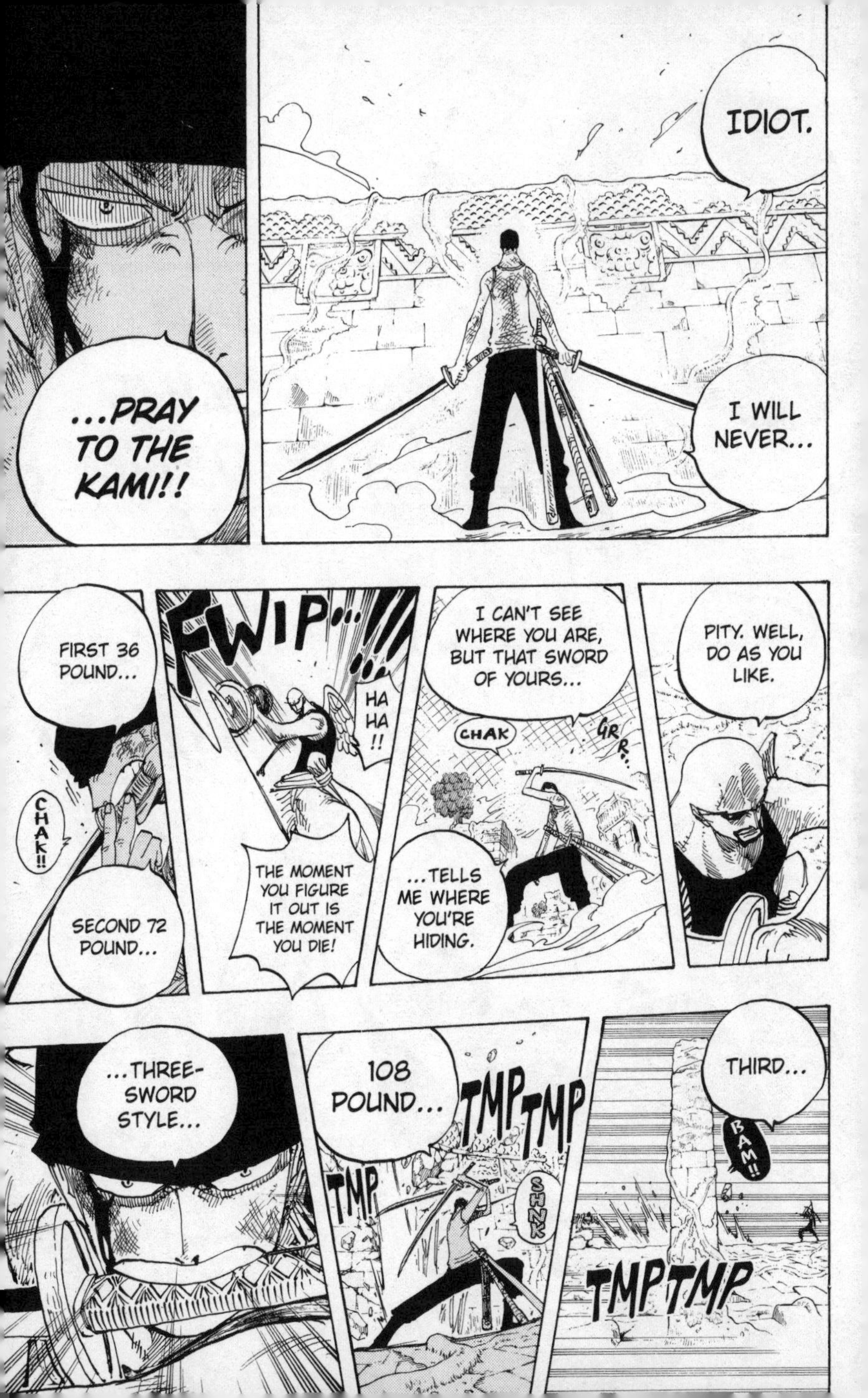
IDIOT.
I WILL NEVER...
...PRAY TO THE KAMI!!
PITY. WELL, DO AS YOU LIKE.
I CAN'T SEE WHERE YOU ARE, BUT THAT SWORD OF YOURS...
CHAK
GRR...
...TELLS ME WHERE YOU'RE HIDING.
FWIP...!!
HA HA!!
THE MOMENT YOU FIGURE IT OUT IS THE MOMENT YOU DIE!
FIRST 36 POUND...
CHAK!!
SECOND 72 POUND...
THIRD...
BAM!!
TMP TMP
108 POUND...
TMP TMP
TMP
SHNK
...THREE-SWORD STYLE...

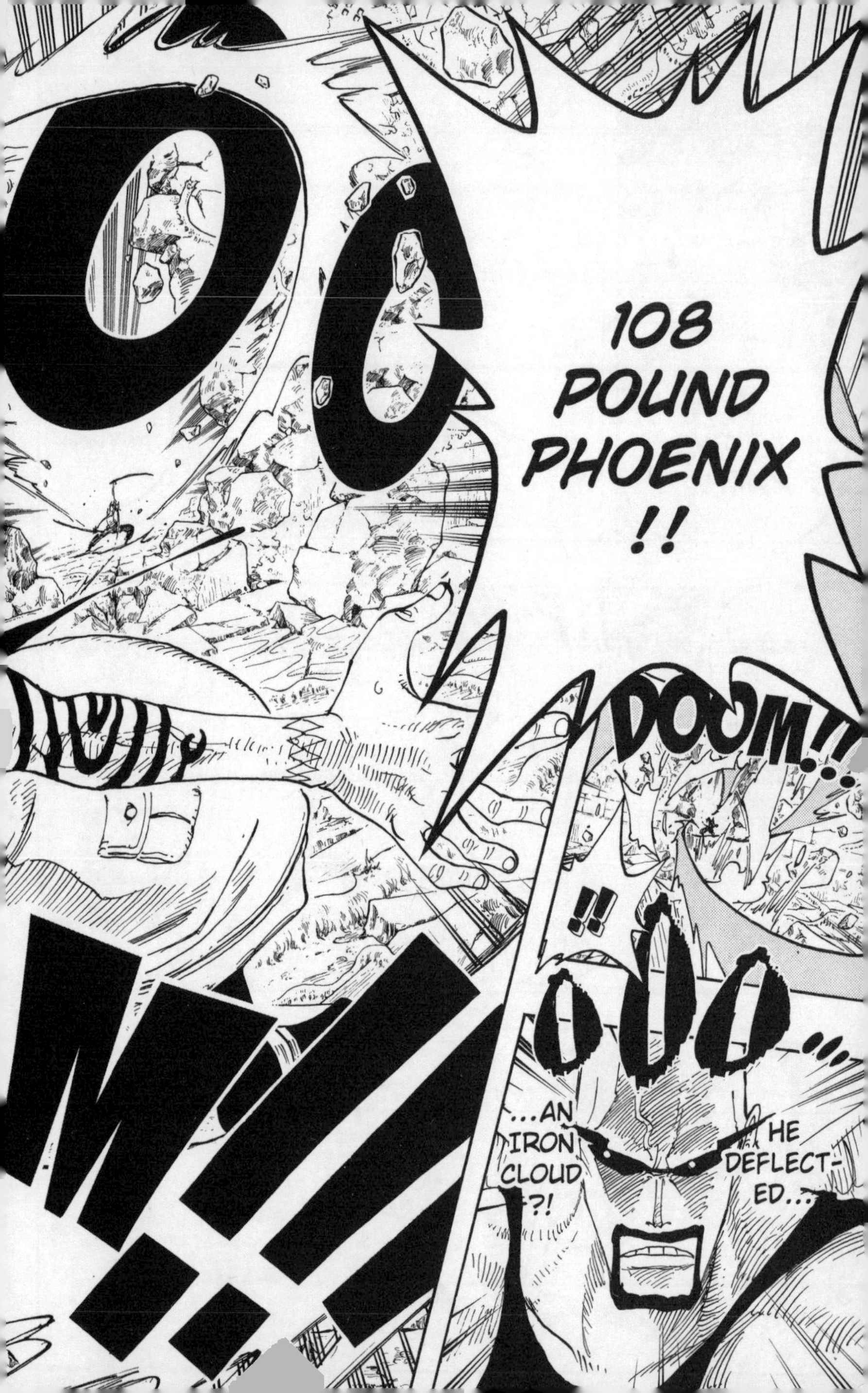
108 POUND PHOENIX !!
DOOM!!
!!
HE DEFLECT-ED...
...AN IRON CLOUD?!

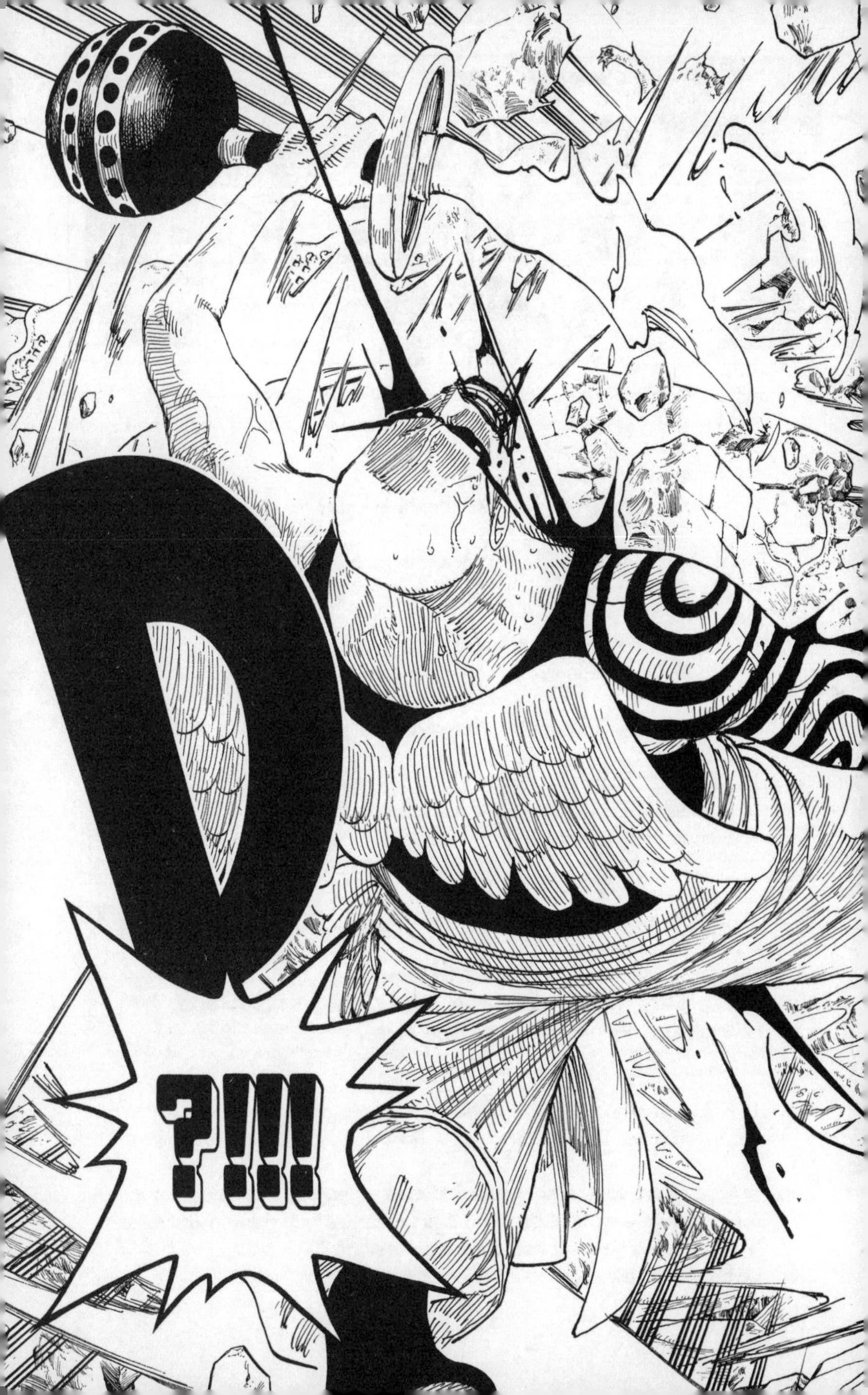
D
?!!!

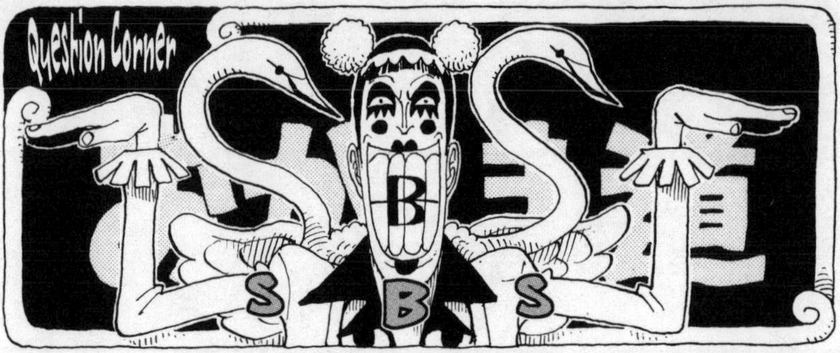
Question Corner
S B S

Reader: Using the pronunciation that Sanji uses to say "Nami-san ♡" in the *One Piece* anime series, try saying "nomison." They should sound exactly the same.
● Try this with your friends!
Me: "Nomiso-o-o-n!" What did I just say?
Friend: "Nami-san."
Me: Nope. The correct answer is "nomison."
● One person says either "Nami-san" or "nomison" to the other person.
● The other person guesses which it was.
● This continues forever (just kidding).
--Sasuke

Oda: Okaaay. Thank you, Sasuke. You keep that up forever.

Q: In volume 27, chapter 251, page 91, when Usopp says "Ka-ching," doesn't he pose like Kamen Rider? How much do you like Kamen Rider, Oda Sensei?
--Pen name: Yo'chan Takoyaki.

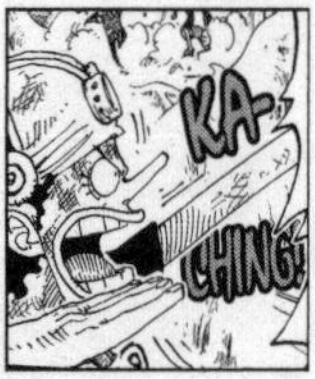
KA-
CHING!

A: Have you seen this?
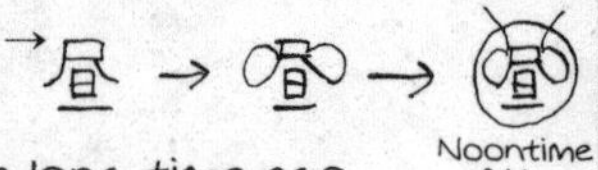
Noontime Rider
I used to watch Kamen Rider on TV a long time ago.
The original story was based on a manga by Shotaro Ishinomori. He has since passed away.

(The sketch shows a simplified way of drawing the face of the Japanese superhero Kamen Rider. First, start with the symbol for "noon" (昼) and add other elements to create the face.--Ed.)

Q: If Zolo and Sanji went head-to-head in all seriousness, who would be strongest? Since Zolo defeated Mr. 1, does that mean Zolo's stronger?

A: Whoa, that was a surprise. I thought you were asking me who would win if Zolo and Sanji compared their manliness. Watch how you phrase your sentences.
Let's meet again in the next volume!!

Chapter 272: PLAY

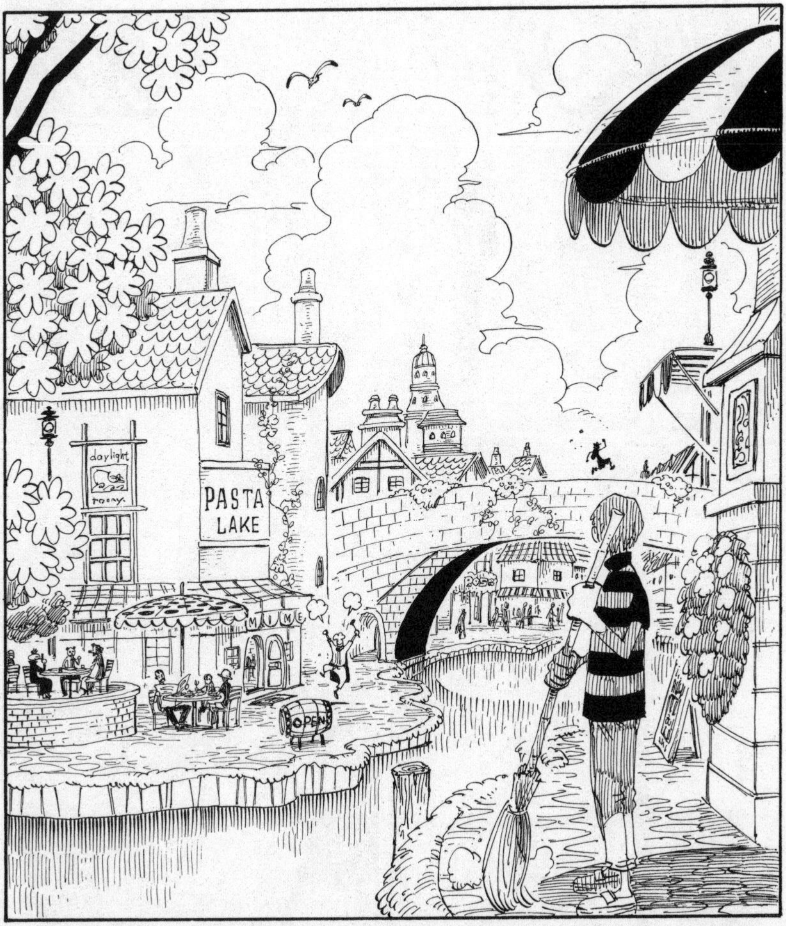
daylight
PASTA LAKE
MIME
OPEN

CHAPTER TITLE PAGE SERIES #6:
"CATCH THE THIEF THAT DIDN'T PAY THE TAB"

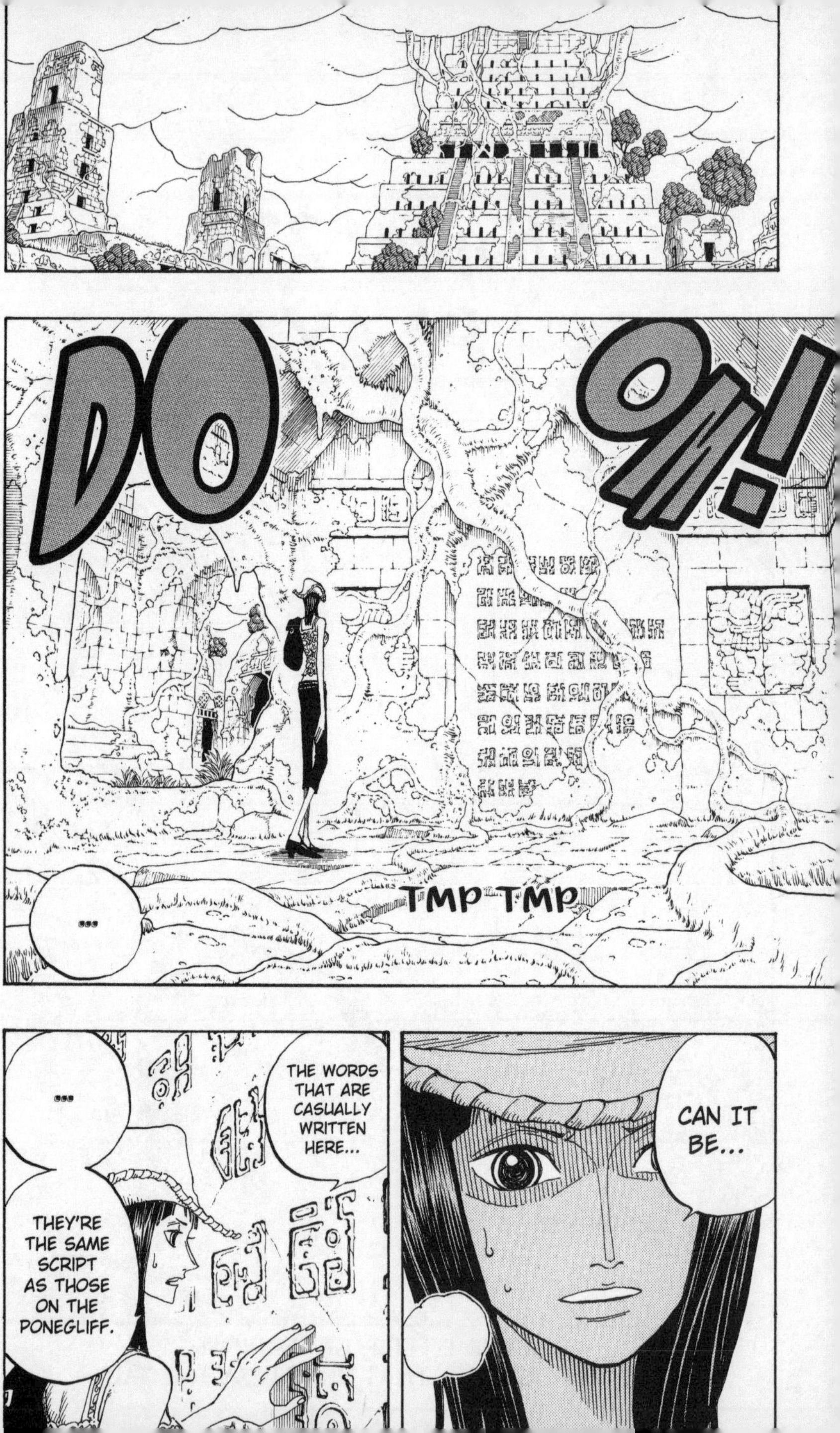
DOON!
TMP TMP
...
CAN IT BE...
THE WORDS THAT ARE CASUALLY WRITTEN HERE...
...
THEY'RE THE SAME SCRIPT AS THOSE ON THE PONEGLIFF.

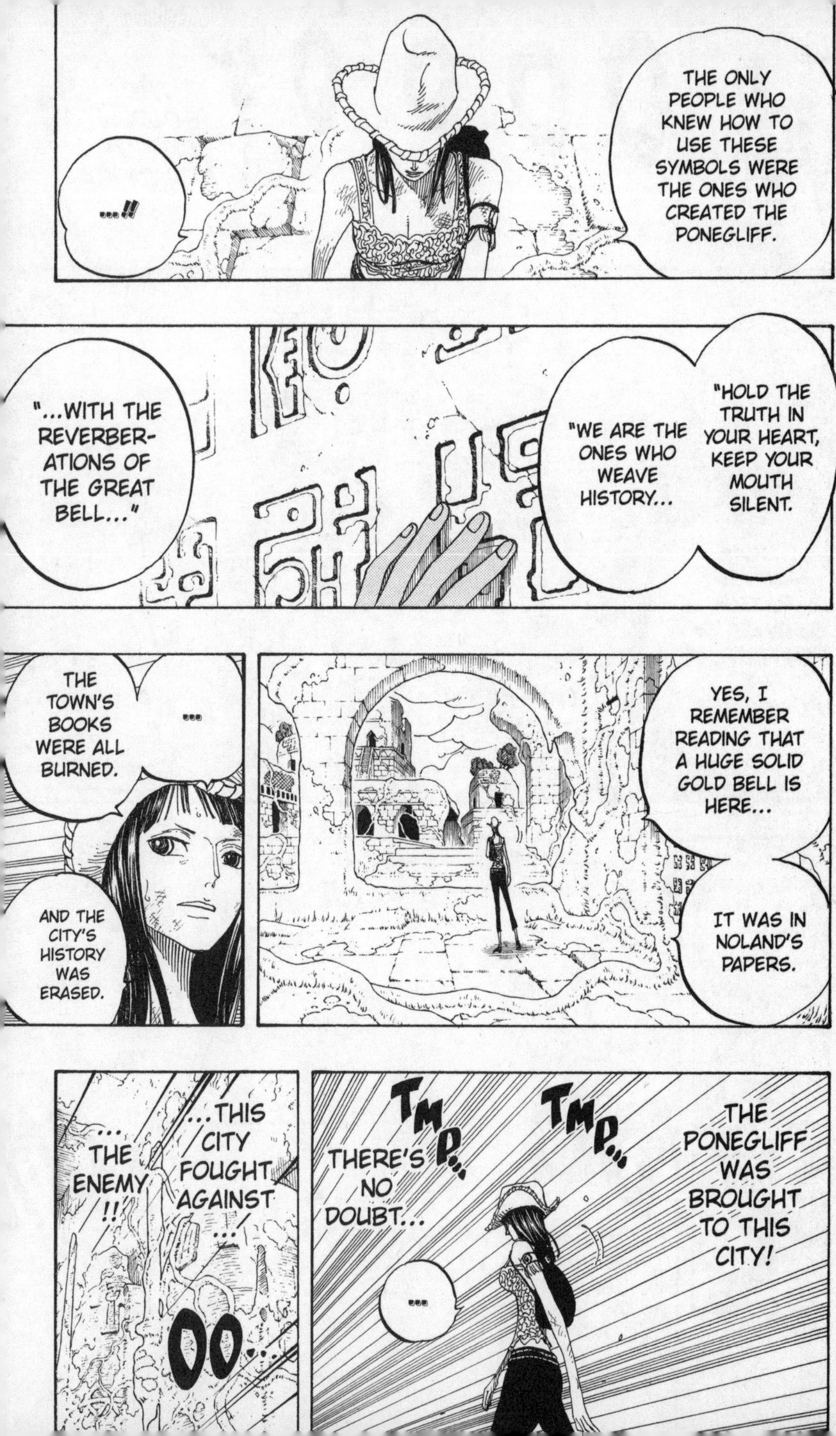
THE ONLY PEOPLE WHO KNEW HOW TO USE THESE SYMBOLS WERE THE ONES WHO CREATED THE PONEGLIFF.
...!!
"HOLD THE TRUTH IN YOUR HEART, KEEP YOUR MOUTH SILENT.
"WE ARE THE ONES WHO WEAVE HISTORY...
"...WITH THE REVERBER-ATIONS OF THE GREAT BELL..."
YES, I REMEMBER READING THAT A HUGE SOLID GOLD BELL IS HERE...
IT WAS IN NOLAND'S PAPERS.
...
THE TOWN'S BOOKS WERE ALL BURNED.
AND THE CITY'S HISTORY WAS ERASED.
THE PONEGLIFF WAS BROUGHT TO THIS CITY!
TMP...
TMP...
THERE'S NO DOUBT...
...
...THIS CITY FOUGHT AGAINST
...THE ENEMY!!
...

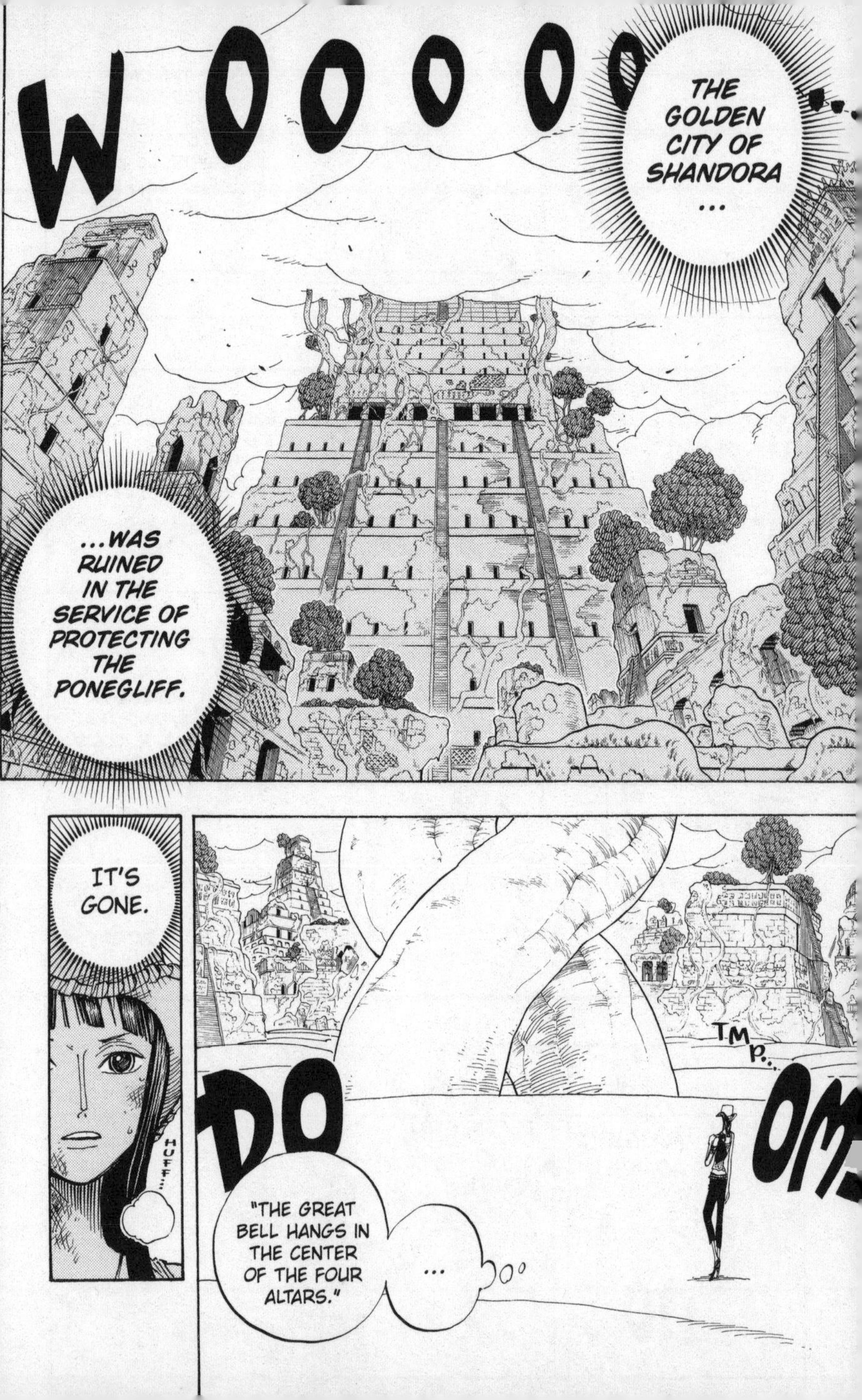
WOOOOO...
THE GOLDEN CITY OF SHANDORA...
...WAS RUINED IN THE SERVICE OF PROTECTING THE PONEGLIFF.
TMP...
DOOM
"THE GREAT BELL HANGS IN THE CENTER OF THE FOUR ALTARS."
...
IT'S GONE.
HUFF...

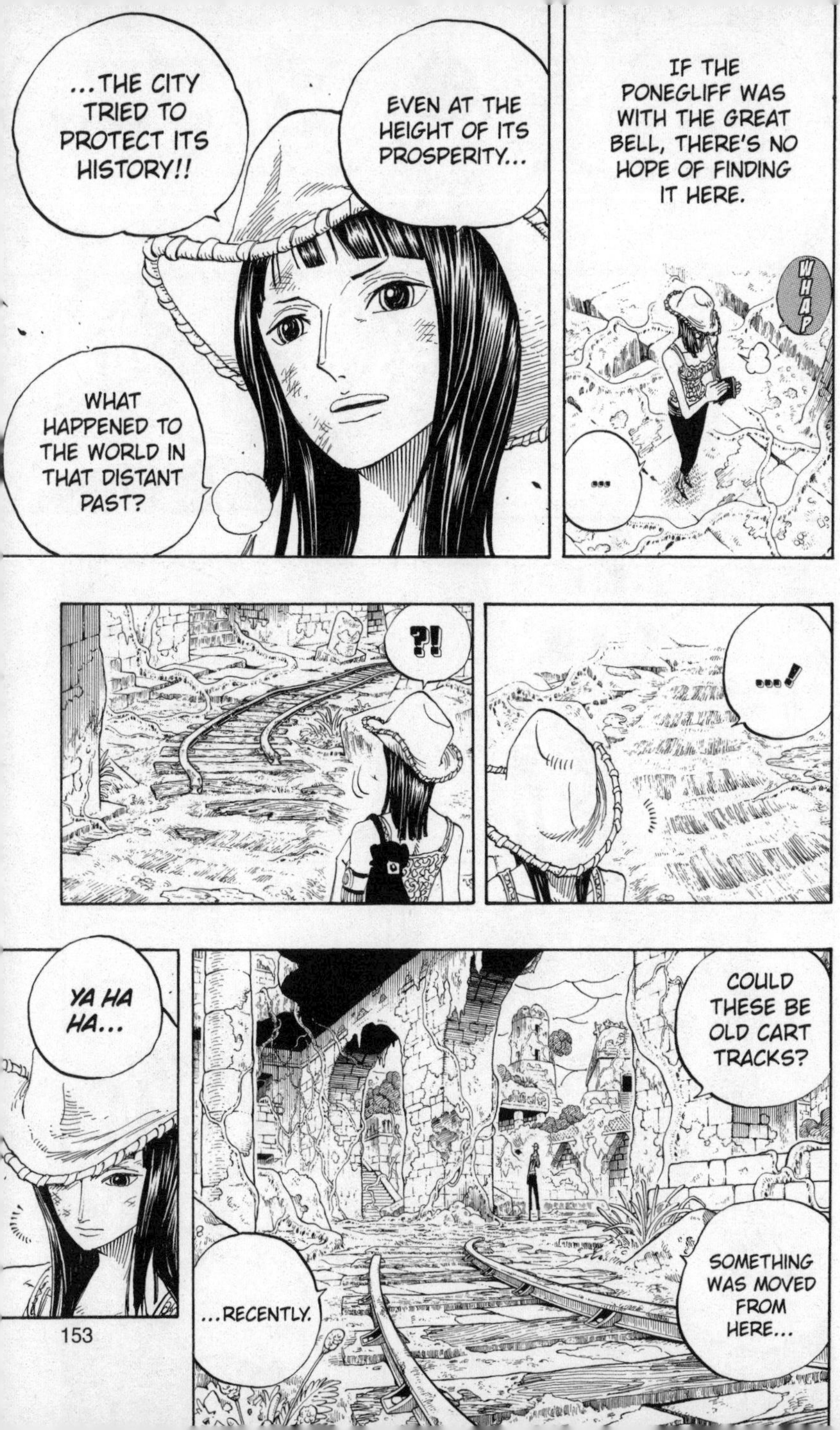
IF THE PONEGLIFF WAS WITH THE GREAT BELL, THERE'S NO HOPE OF FINDING IT HERE.
WHAP
...
EVEN AT THE HEIGHT OF ITS PROSPERITY...
...THE CITY TRIED TO PROTECT ITS HISTORY!!
WHAT HAPPENED TO THE WORLD IN THAT DISTANT PAST?
...!
?!
COULD THESE BE OLD CART TRACKS?
SOMETHING WAS MOVED FROM HERE...
...RECENTLY.
YA HA HA...

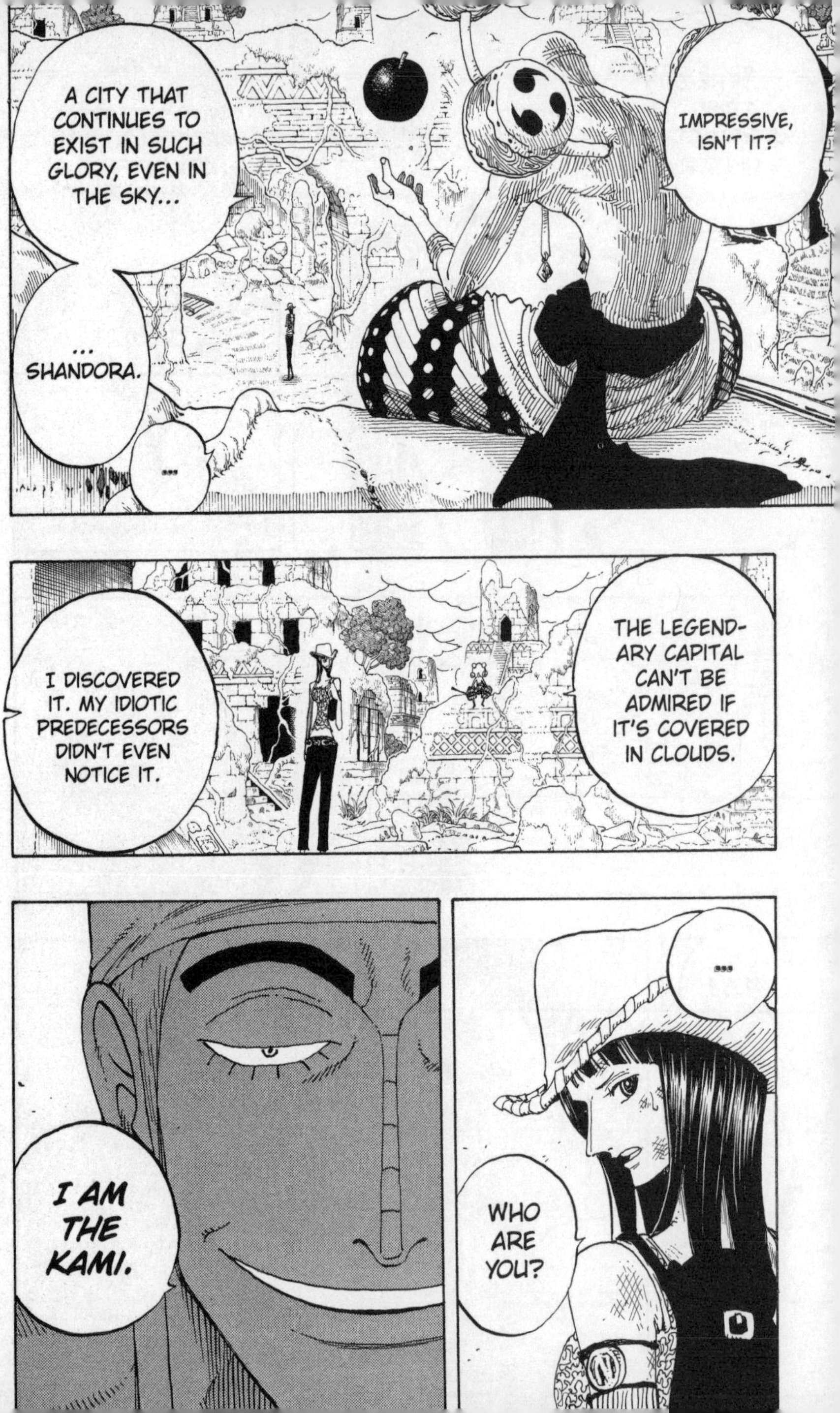
IMPRESSIVE, ISN'T IT?
A CITY THAT CONTINUES TO EXIST IN SUCH GLORY, EVEN IN THE SKY...
... SHANDORA.
...
THE LEGEND-ARY CAPITAL CAN'T BE ADMIRED IF IT'S COVERED IN CLOUDS.
I DISCOVERED IT. MY IDIOTIC PREDECESSORS DIDN'T EVEN NOTICE IT.
...
WHO ARE YOU?
I AM THE KAMI.

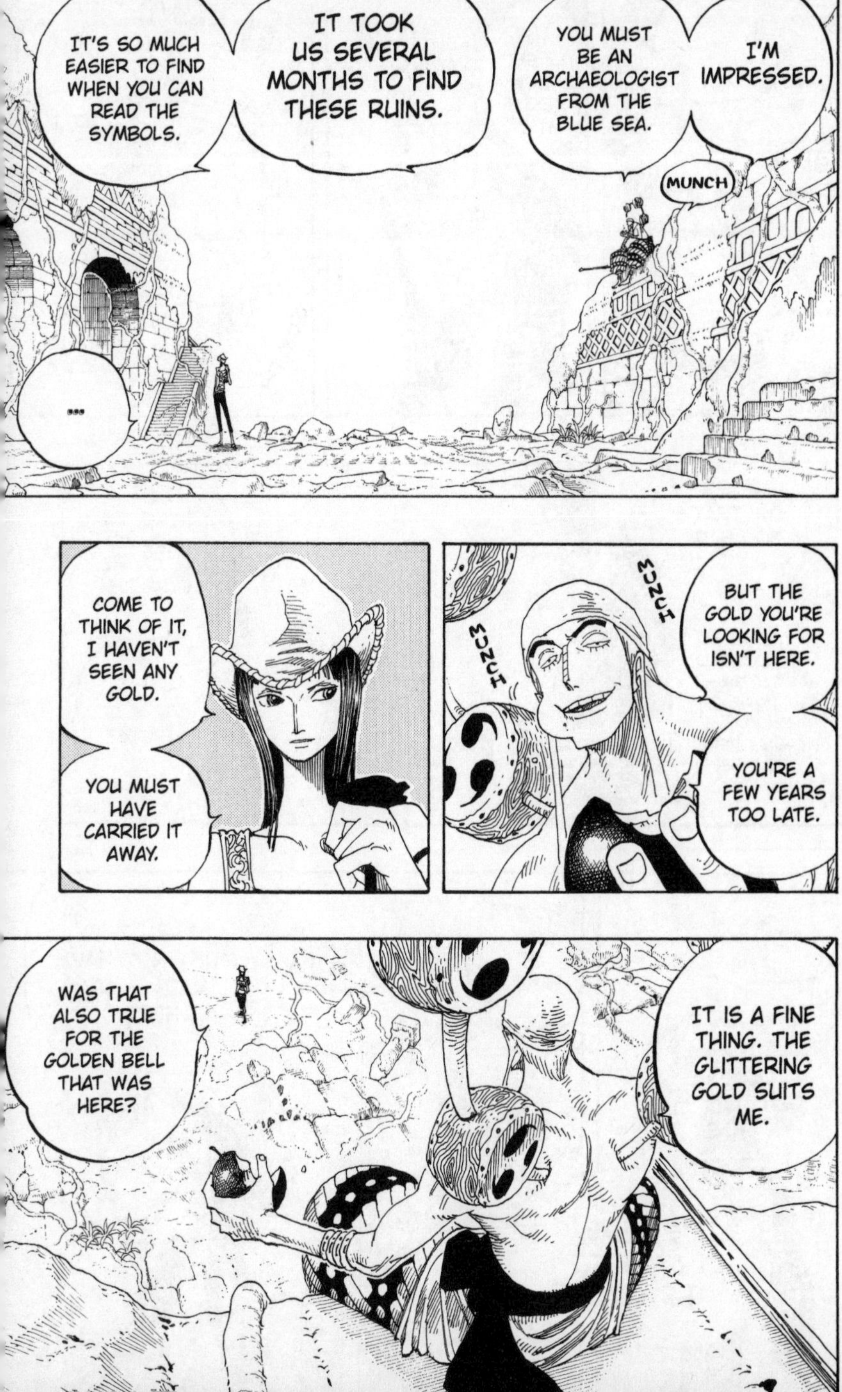
I'M IMPRESSED.
YOU MUST BE AN ARCHAEOLOGIST FROM THE BLUE SEA.
MUNCH
IT TOOK US SEVERAL MONTHS TO FIND THESE RUINS.
IT'S SO MUCH EASIER TO FIND WHEN YOU CAN READ THE SYMBOLS.
...
MUNCH
MUNCH
BUT THE GOLD YOU'RE LOOKING FOR ISN'T HERE.
YOU'RE A FEW YEARS TOO LATE.
COME TO THINK OF IT, I HAVEN'T SEEN ANY GOLD.
YOU MUST HAVE CARRIED IT AWAY.
IT IS A FINE THING. THE GLITTERING GOLD SUITS ME.
WAS THAT ALSO TRUE FOR THE GOLDEN BELL THAT WAS HERE?

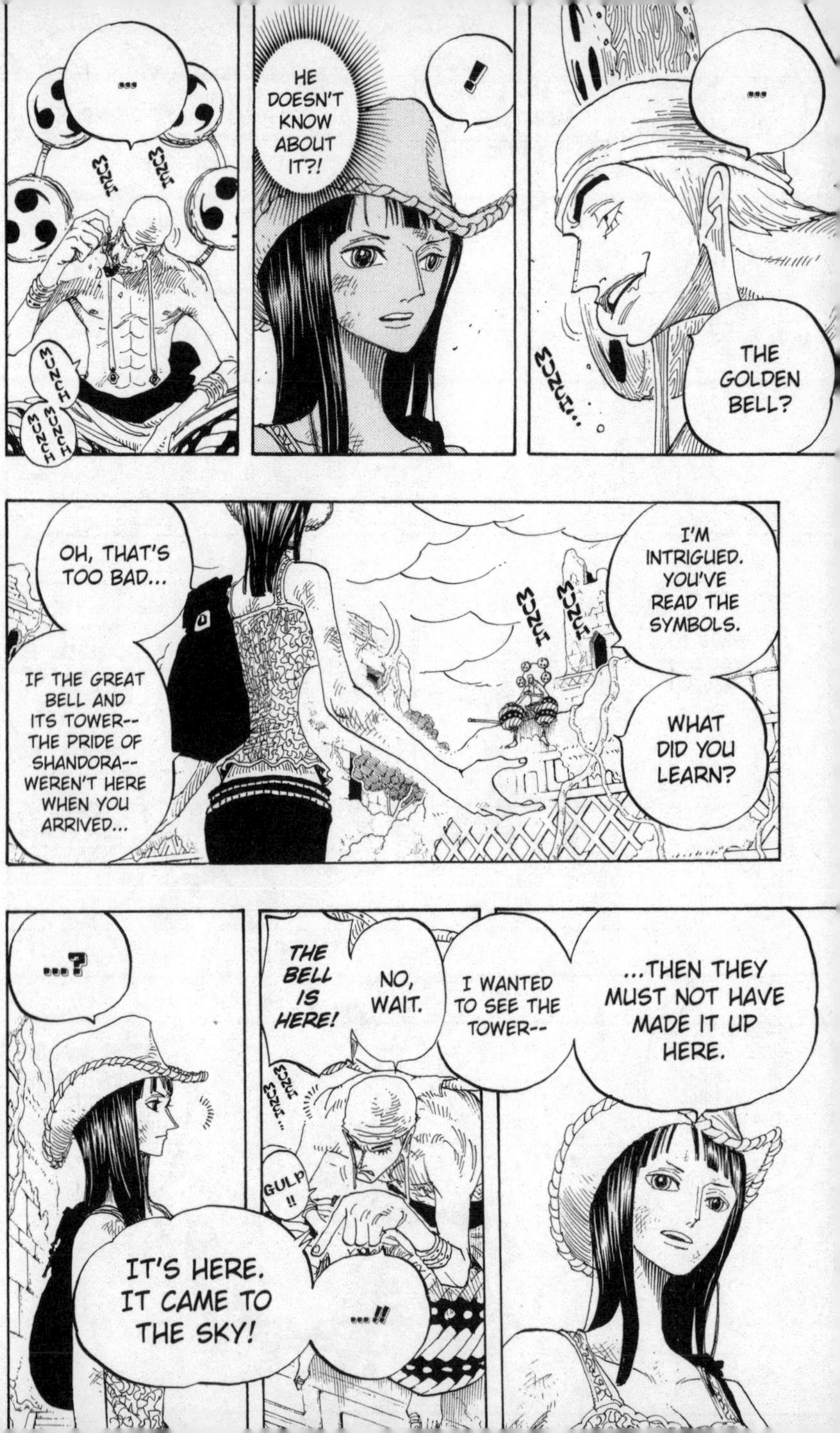
...
THE GOLDEN BELL?
MUNCH...
!
HE DOESN'T KNOW ABOUT IT?!
...
MUNCH MUNCH
MUNCH MUNCH MUNCH
I'M INTRIGUED. YOU'VE READ THE SYMBOLS.
WHAT DID YOU LEARN?
MUNCH MUNCH
OH, THAT'S TOO BAD...
IF THE GREAT BELL AND ITS TOWER-- THE PRIDE OF SHANDORA-- WEREN'T HERE WHEN YOU ARRIVED...
...THEN THEY MUST NOT HAVE MADE IT UP HERE.
I WANTED TO SEE THE TOWER--
NO, WAIT.
THE BELL IS HERE!
MUNCH MUNCH...
GULP!!
IT'S HERE. IT CAME TO THE SKY!
...!!
...?

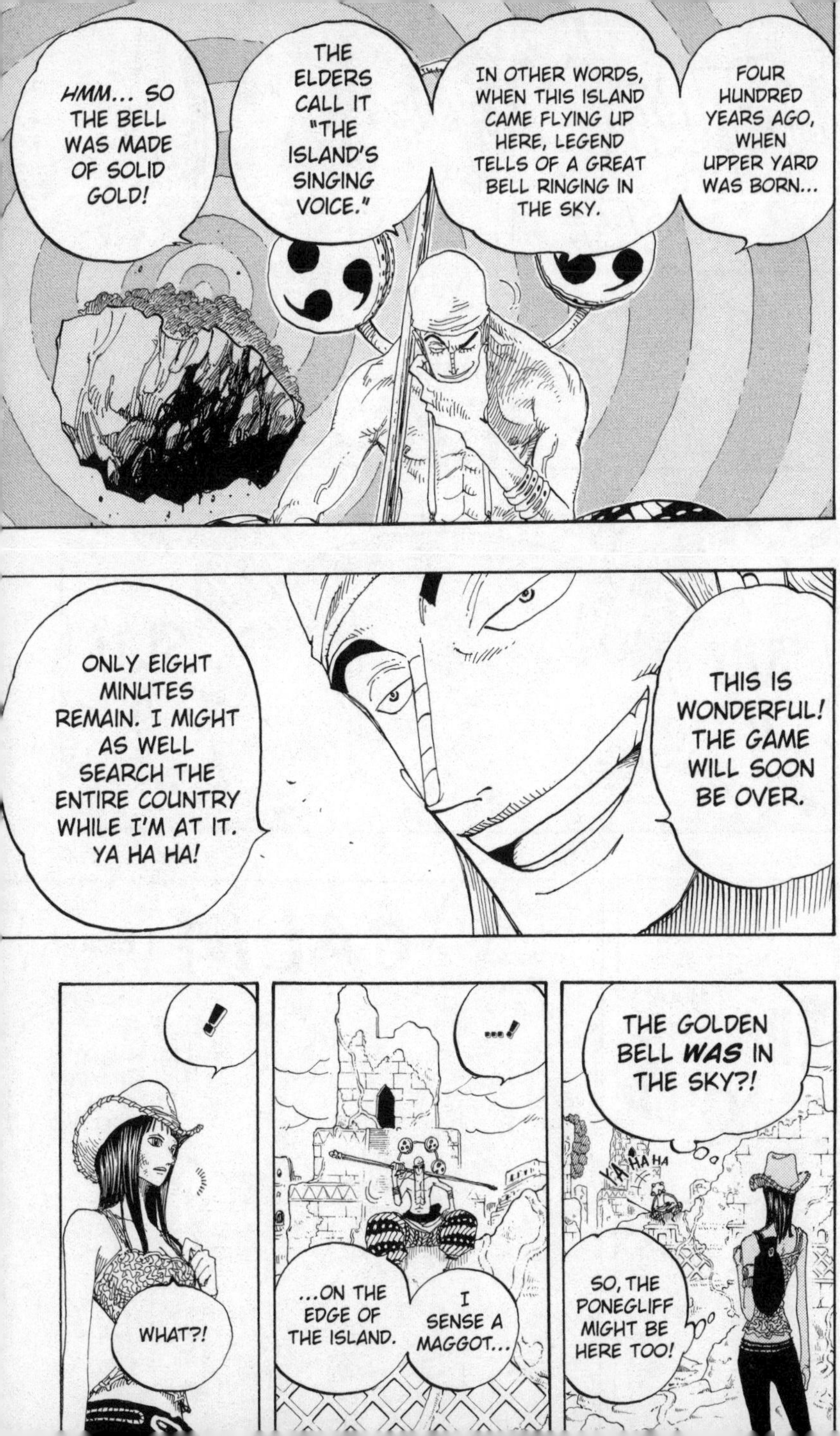
FOUR HUNDRED YEARS AGO, WHEN UPPER YARD WAS BORN...
IN OTHER WORDS, WHEN THIS ISLAND CAME FLYING UP HERE, LEGEND TELLS OF A GREAT BELL RINGING IN THE SKY.
THE ELDERS CALL IT "THE ISLAND'S SINGING VOICE."
HMM... SO THE BELL WAS MADE OF SOLID GOLD!
THIS IS WONDERFUL! THE GAME WILL SOON BE OVER.
ONLY EIGHT MINUTES REMAIN. I MIGHT AS WELL SEARCH THE ENTIRE COUNTRY WHILE I'M AT IT. YA HA HA!
THE GOLDEN BELL *WAS* IN THE SKY?!
YA HA HA
SO, THE PONEGLIFF MIGHT BE HERE TOO!
...!
I SENSE A MAGGOT...
...ON THE EDGE OF THE ISLAND.
!
WHAT?!

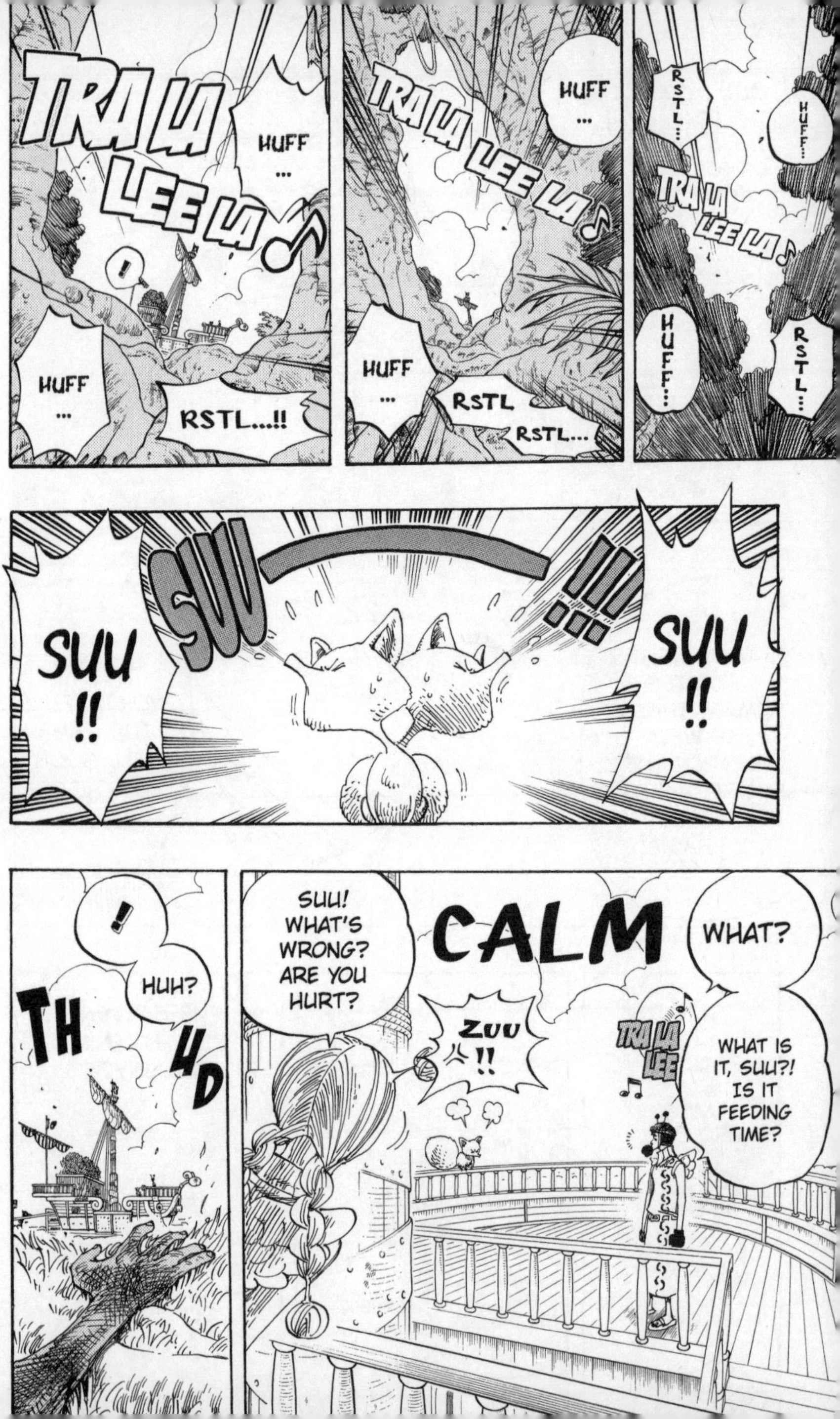
HUFF...
RSTL...
TRA LA LEE LA ♪
RSTL...
HUFF...
HUFF ...
TRA LA LEE LA ♪
HUFF ...
RSTL
RSTL...
HUFF ...
TRA LA LEE LA ♪
!
HUFF ...
RSTL...!!
SUU !!
SUU——!!!!!
SUU !!
WHAT?
WHAT IS IT, SUU?! IS IT FEEDING TIME?
TRA LA LEE ♪
CALM
ZUU !!
SUU! WHAT'S WRONG? ARE YOU HURT?
!
HUH?
THUD

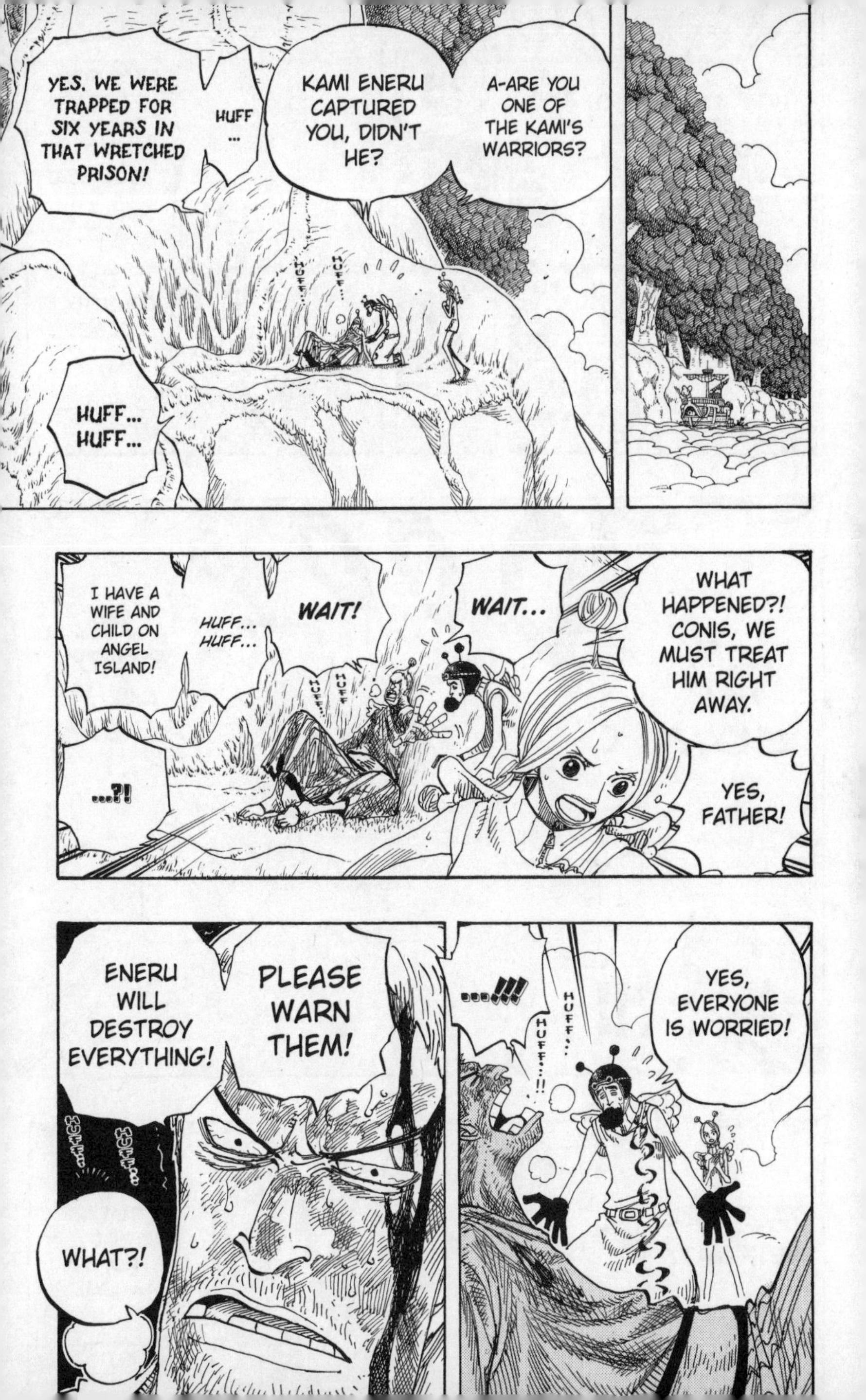
A-ARE YOU ONE OF THE KAMI'S WARRIORS?
KAMI ENERU CAPTURED YOU, DIDN'T HE?
HUFF ...
YES. WE WERE TRAPPED FOR SIX YEARS IN THAT WRETCHED PRISON!
HUFF... HUFF...
HUFF... HUFF...
WHAT HAPPENED?! CONIS, WE MUST TREAT HIM RIGHT AWAY.
YES, FATHER!
WAIT...
WAIT!
HUFF... HUFF...
HUFF HUFF...
I HAVE A WIFE AND CHILD ON ANGEL ISLAND!
...?!
YES, EVERYONE IS WORRIED!
HUFF... HUFF...!!
...!!!
PLEASE WARN THEM!
ENERU WILL DESTROY EVERYTHING!
HUFF... HUFF...
WHAT?!

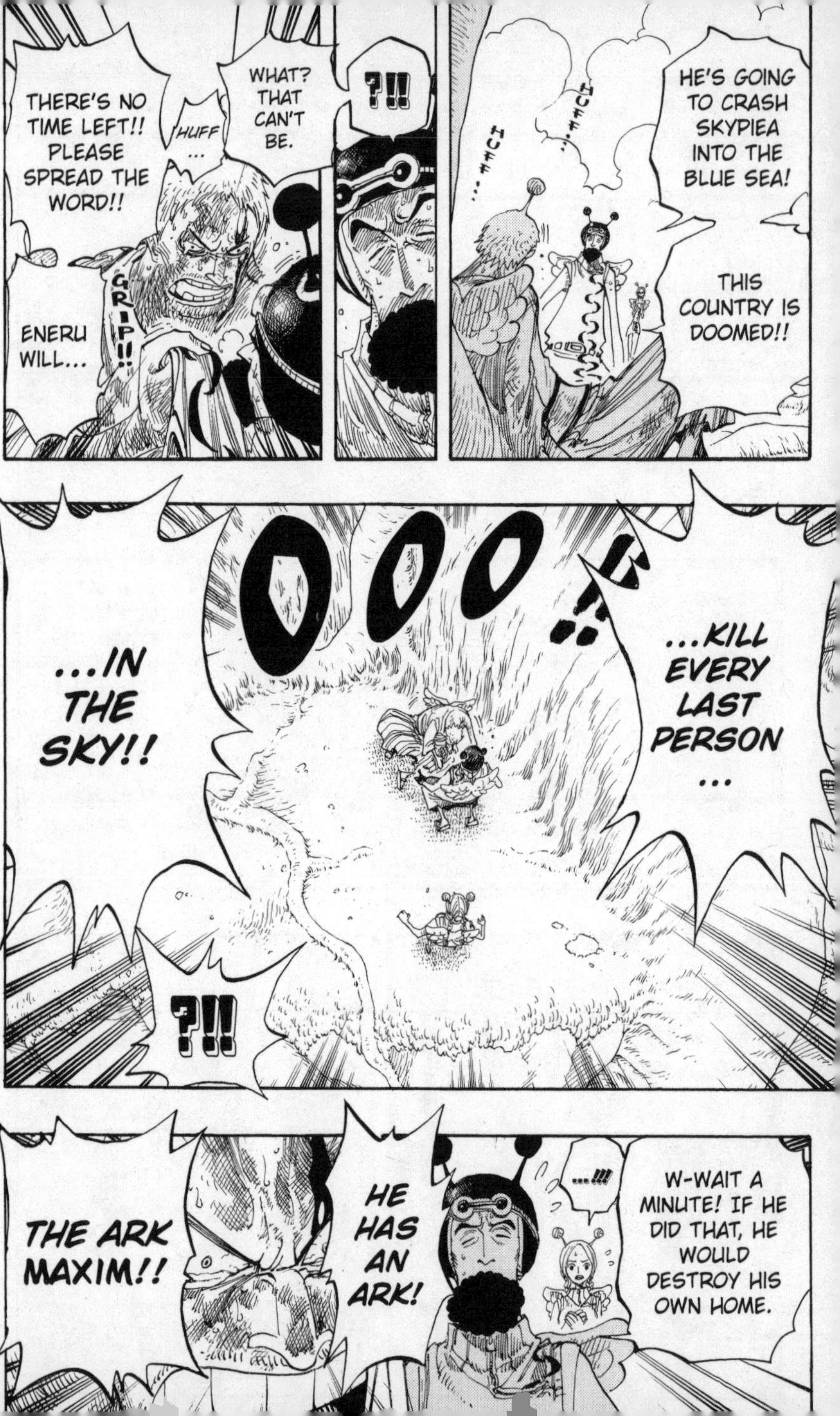
HE'S GOING TO CRASH SKYPIEA INTO THE BLUE SEA!
THIS COUNTRY IS DOOMED!!
HUFF...
HUFF...
?!!
WHAT? THAT CAN'T BE.
THERE'S NO TIME LEFT!! PLEASE SPREAD THE WORD!!
HUFF...
ENERU WILL...
GRIP!!
...KILL EVERY LAST PERSON...
OOO!!
...IN THE SKY!!
?!!
W-WAIT A MINUTE! IF HE DID THAT, HE WOULD DESTROY HIS OWN HOME.
...!!!
HE HAS AN ARK!
THE ARK MAXIM!!

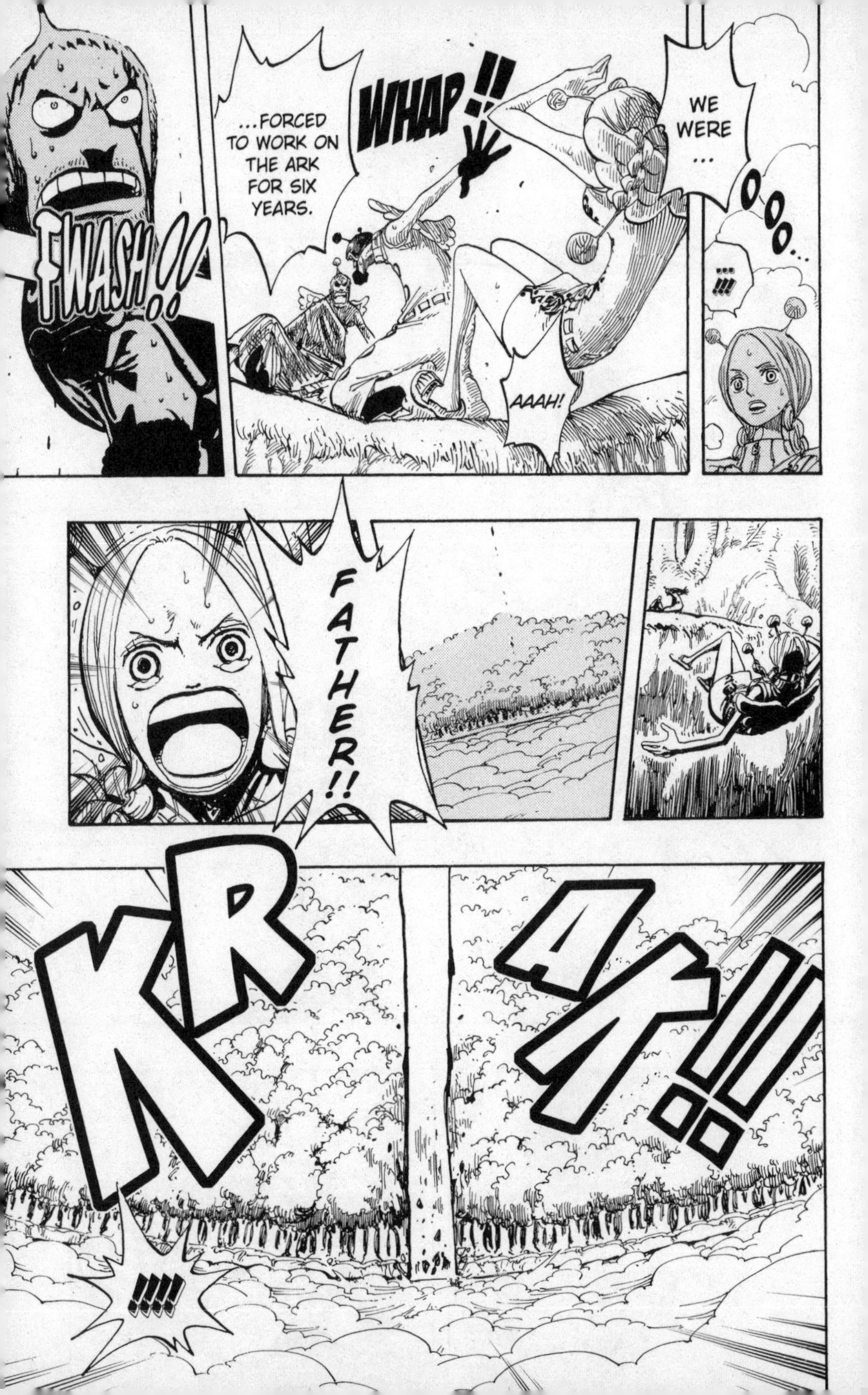

WE WERE ...
OOO...
...!!!
...FORCED TO WORK ON THE ARK FOR SIX YEARS.
WHAP!!
AAAH!
FWASH!!
FATHER!!
KRAK!!
!!!!

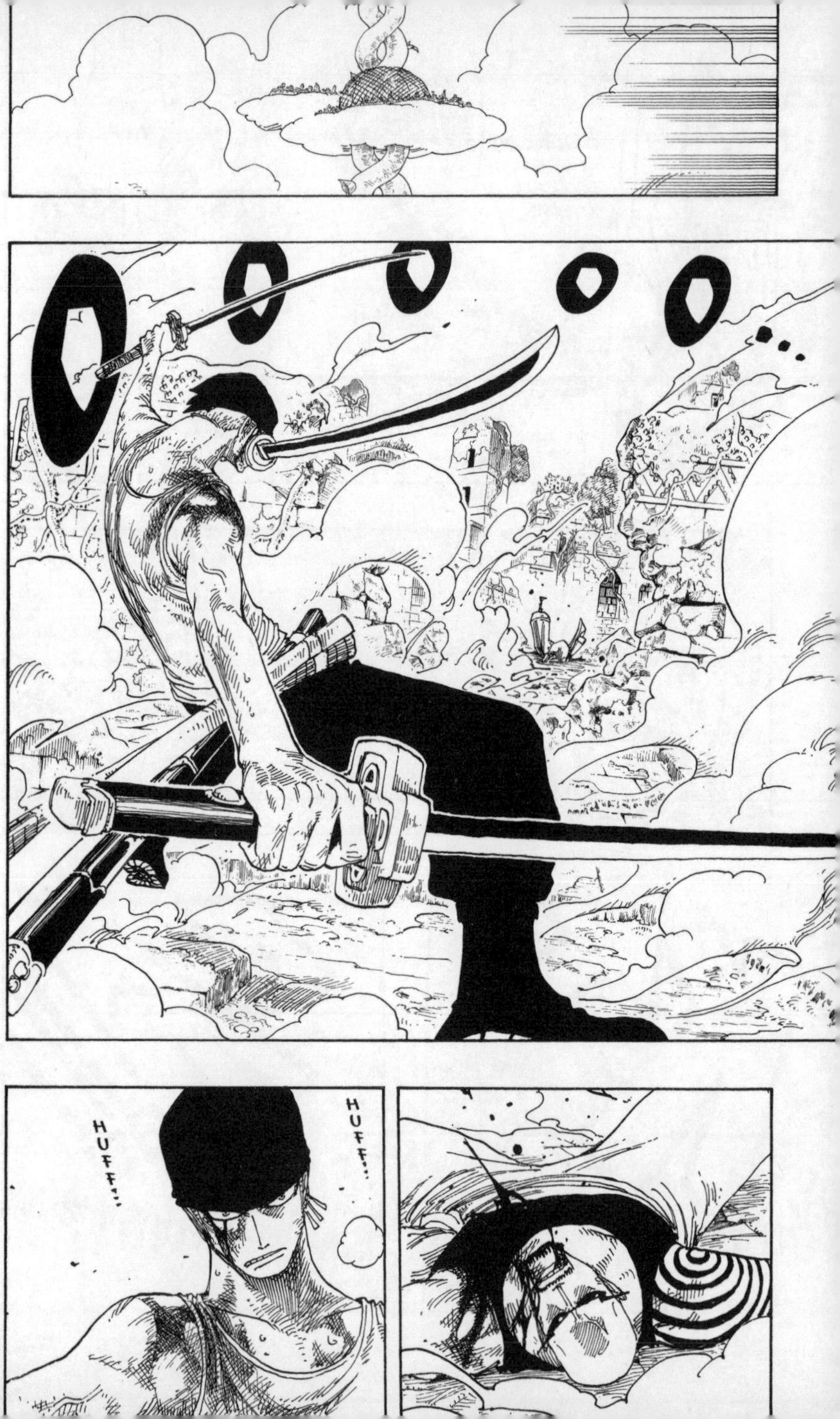
OOOOOO...
HUFF...
HUFF...

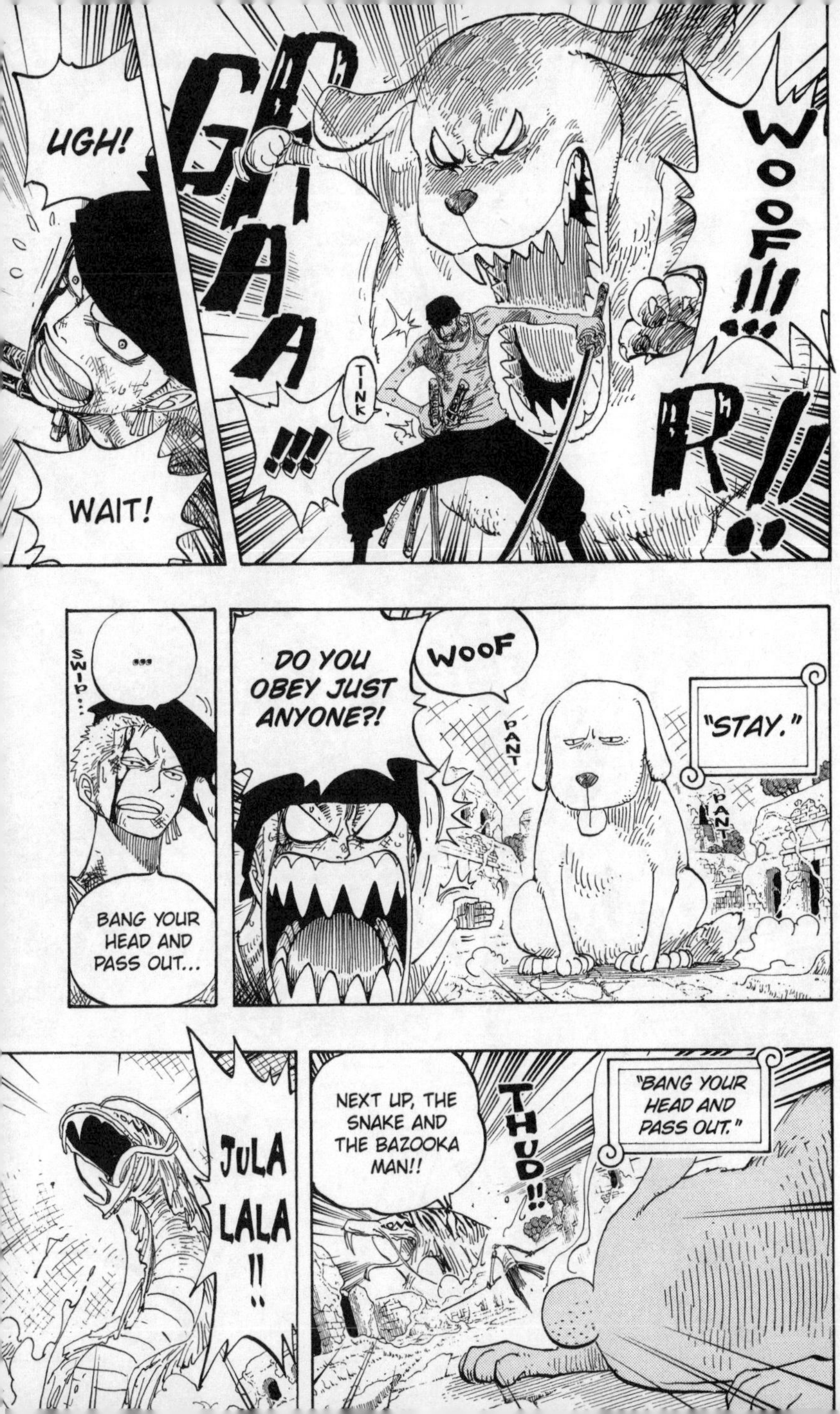
WOOF!!!...
R!!..
GAAA!!!!
TINK
UGH!
WAIT!
"STAY."
PANT
PANT
WOOF
DO YOU OBEY JUST ANYONE?!
...
SWIP...
BANG YOUR HEAD AND PASS OUT...
"BANG YOUR HEAD AND PASS OUT."
THUD!!
NEXT UP, THE SNAKE AND THE BAZOOKA MAN!!
JULA LALA!!

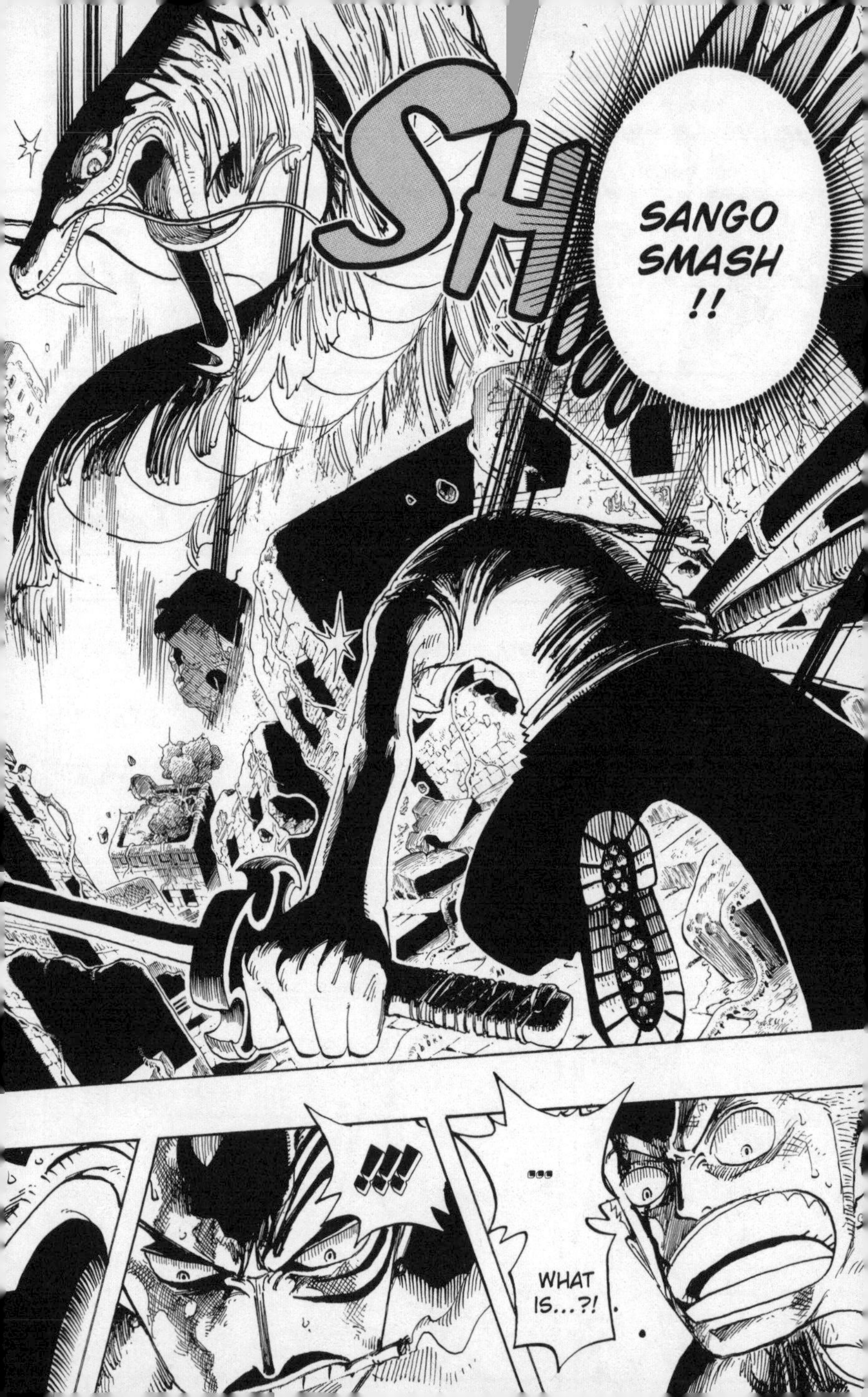
SH
SANGO SMASH !!
...
WHAT IS...?!
!!!

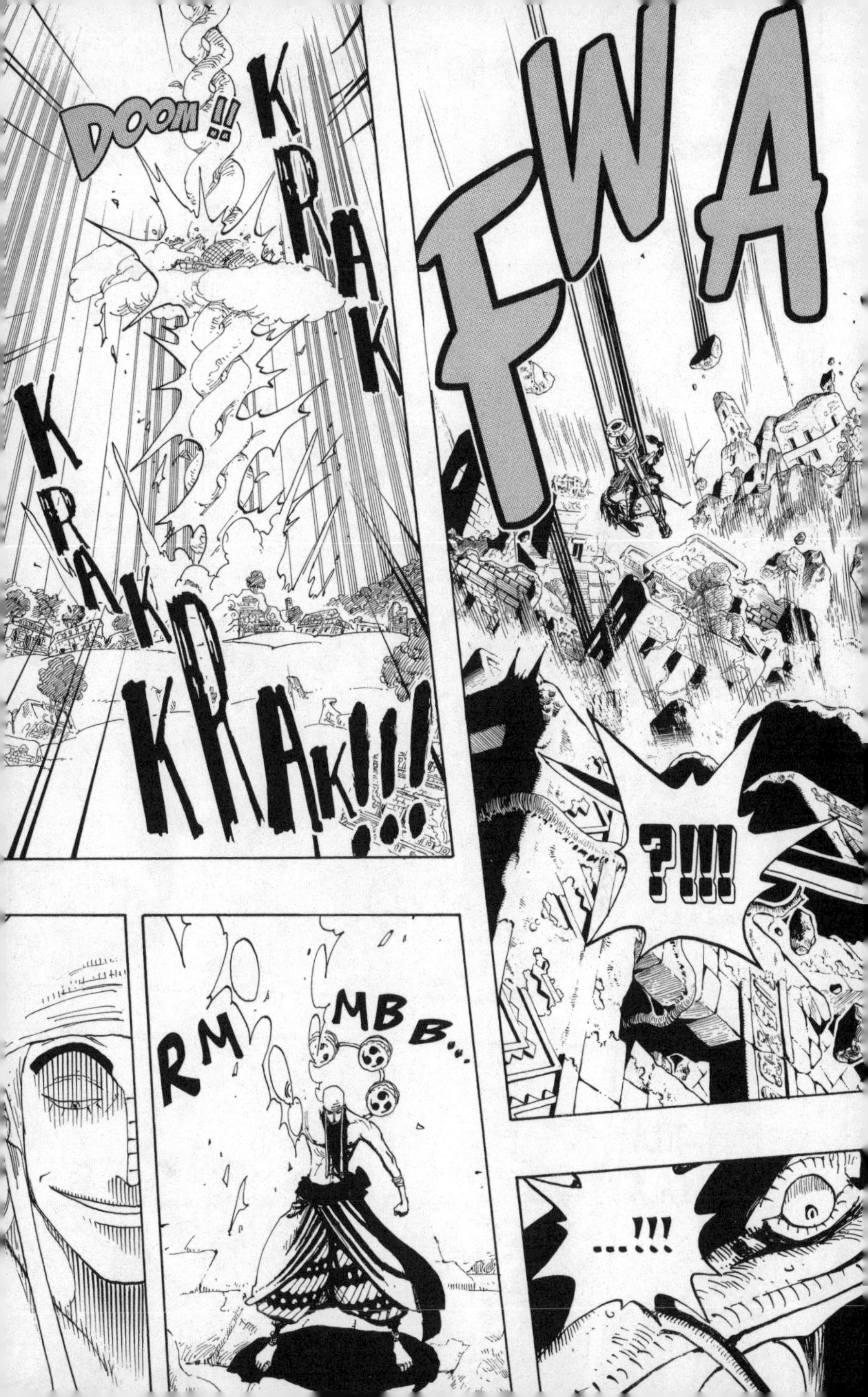
FWA
?!!!
...!!!
DOOM!!
KRAK
KRAK
KRAK!!!
RMMBB...

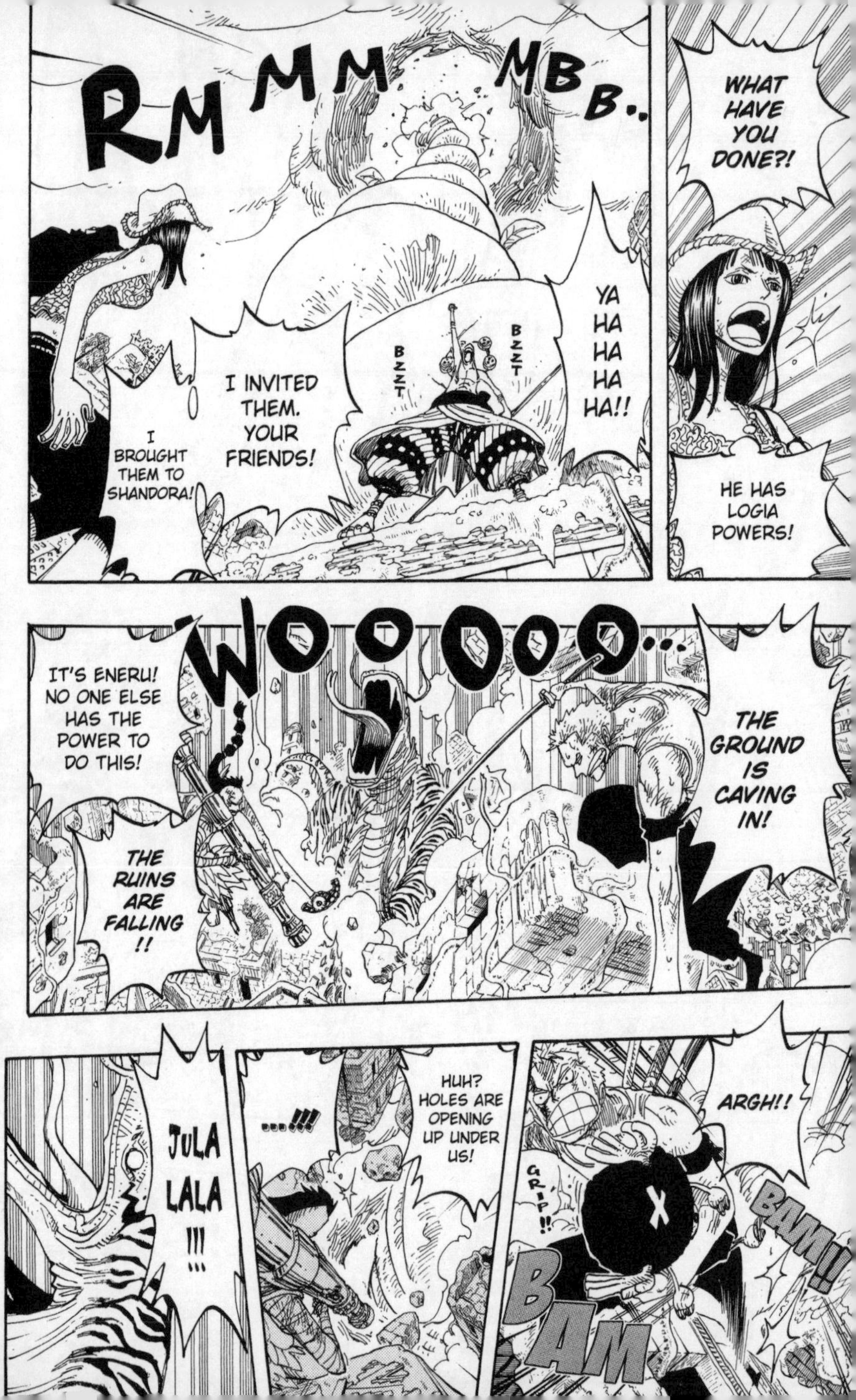
WHAT HAVE YOU DONE?!
HE HAS LOGIA POWERS!
RMMMMBB..
YA HA HA HA HA!!
BZZT
BZZT
I INVITED THEM. YOUR FRIENDS!
I BROUGHT THEM TO SHANDORA!
WOOOOO...
THE GROUND IS CAVING IN!
IT'S ENERU! NO ONE ELSE HAS THE POWER TO DO THIS!
THE RUINS ARE FALLING!!
ARGH!!
GRIP!!
BAM!!
BAM
HUH? HOLES ARE OPENING UP UNDER US!
...!!!
JULA LALA!!!

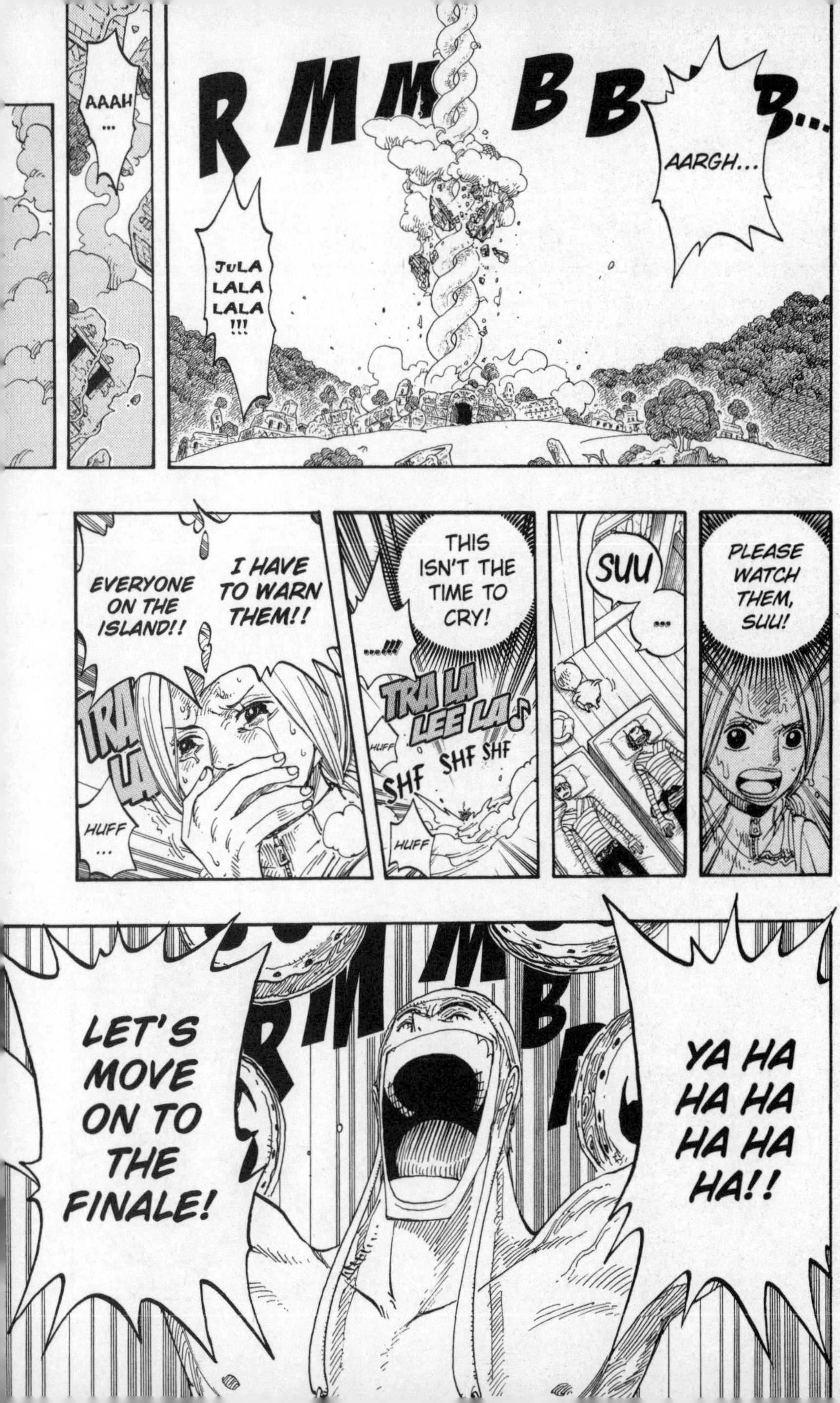
RMMBBB...
AARGH...
JULA LALA LALA!!!
AAAH...
PLEASE WATCH THEM, SUU!
...
SUU
THIS ISN'T THE TIME TO CRY!
...!!!
TRA LA LEE LA♪
SHF SHF
SHF
HUFF
HUFF
I HAVE TO WARN THEM!!
EVERYONE ON THE ISLAND!!
TRA LA
HUFF...
YA HA HA HA HA HA HA HA!!
RMMB
LET'S MOVE ON TO THE FINALE!

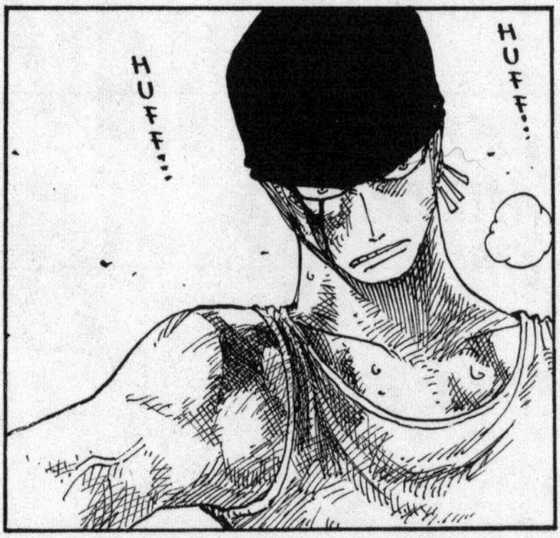
HUFF...
HUFF...

Chapter 273:
QUINTET

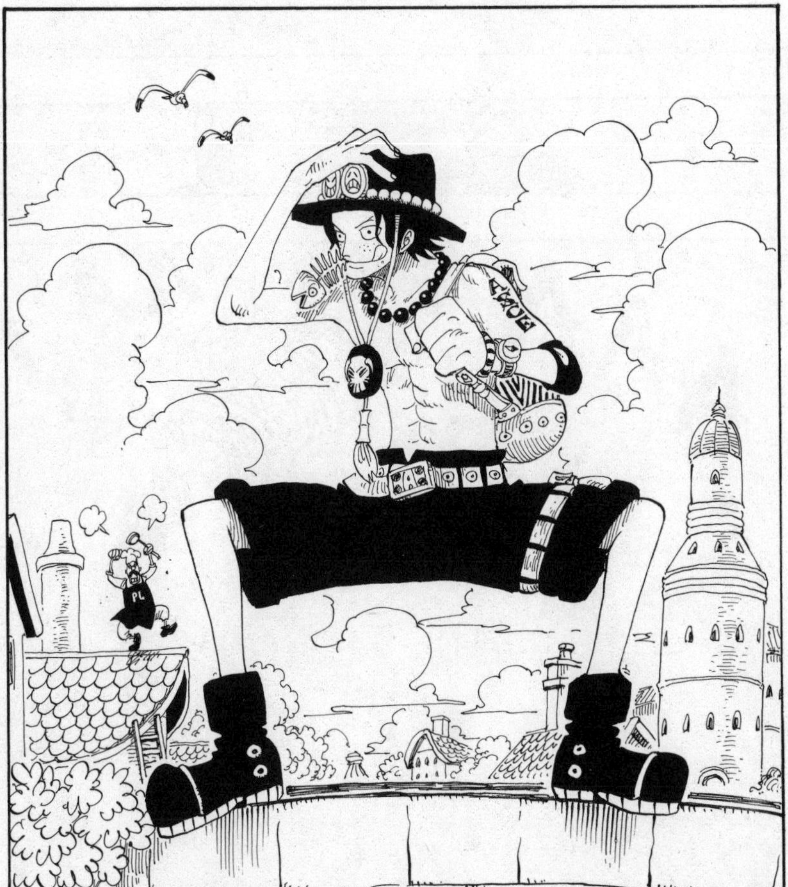
ACE
PL

ACE'S GREAT SEARCH FOR BLACKBEARD, VOL. 2:
"SORRY ABOUT THE DINE AND DASH!"

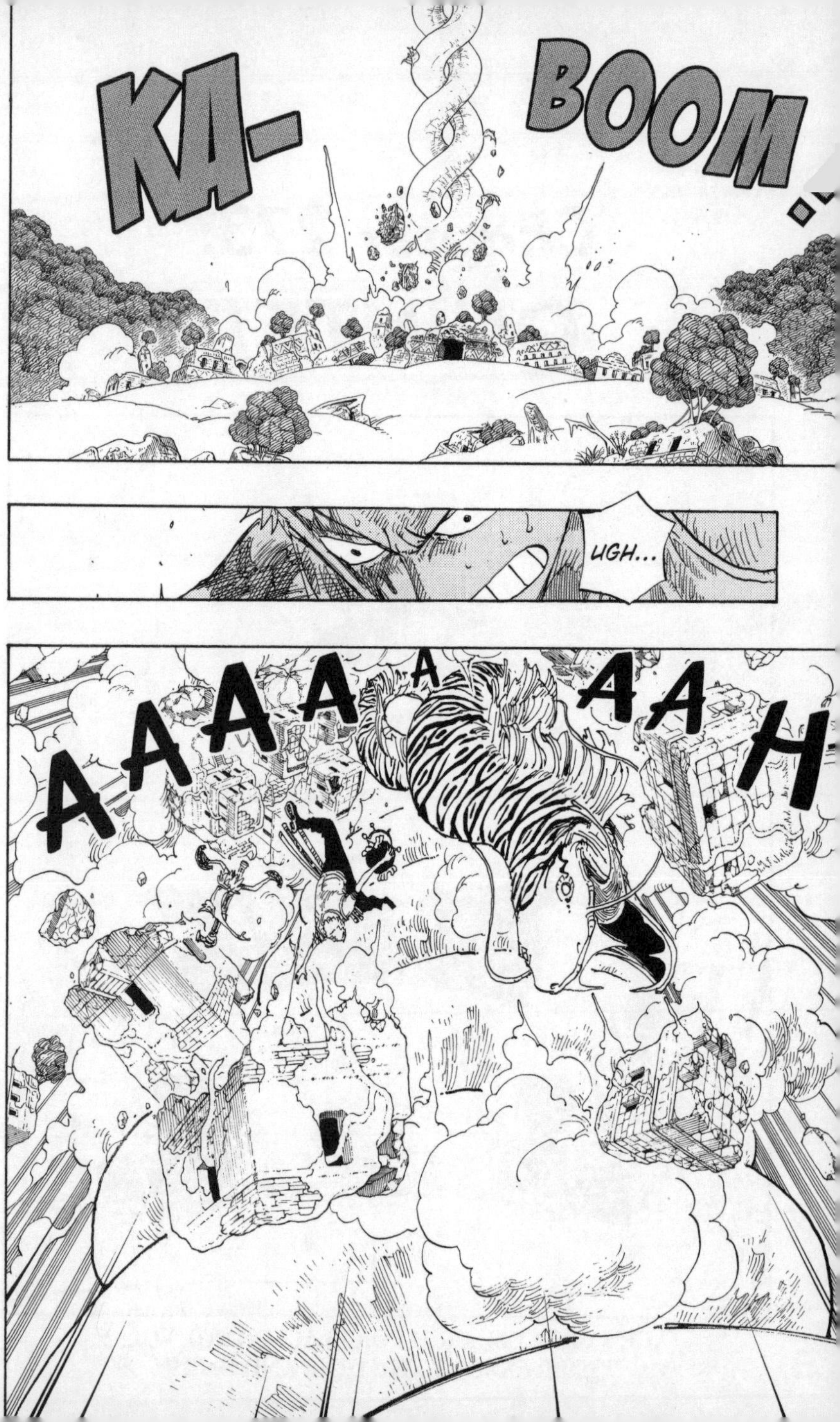
KA-
BOOM
UGH...
AAAAAAAAH

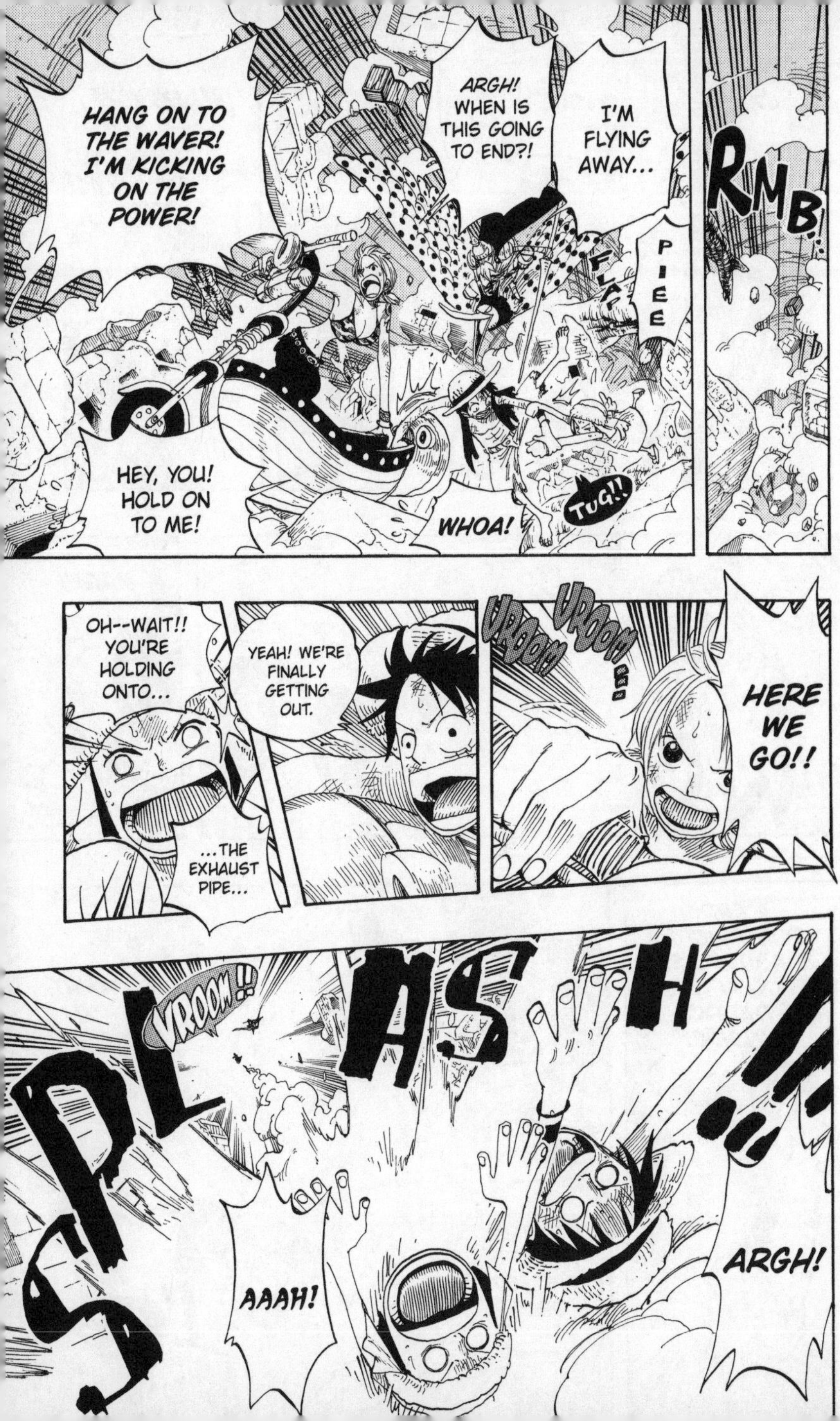
RMB..
PIEE
FLAP
I'M FLYING AWAY...
ARGH! WHEN IS THIS GOING TO END?!
HANG ON TO THE WAVER! I'M KICKING ON THE POWER!
TUG!!
WHOA!
HEY, YOU! HOLD ON TO ME!
HERE WE GO!!
VROOM
VROOM
YEAH! WE'RE FINALLY GETTING OUT.
OH--WAIT!! YOU'RE HOLDING ONTO...
...THE EXHAUST PIPE...
SPLASH!!
VROOM!!
ARGH!
AAAH!

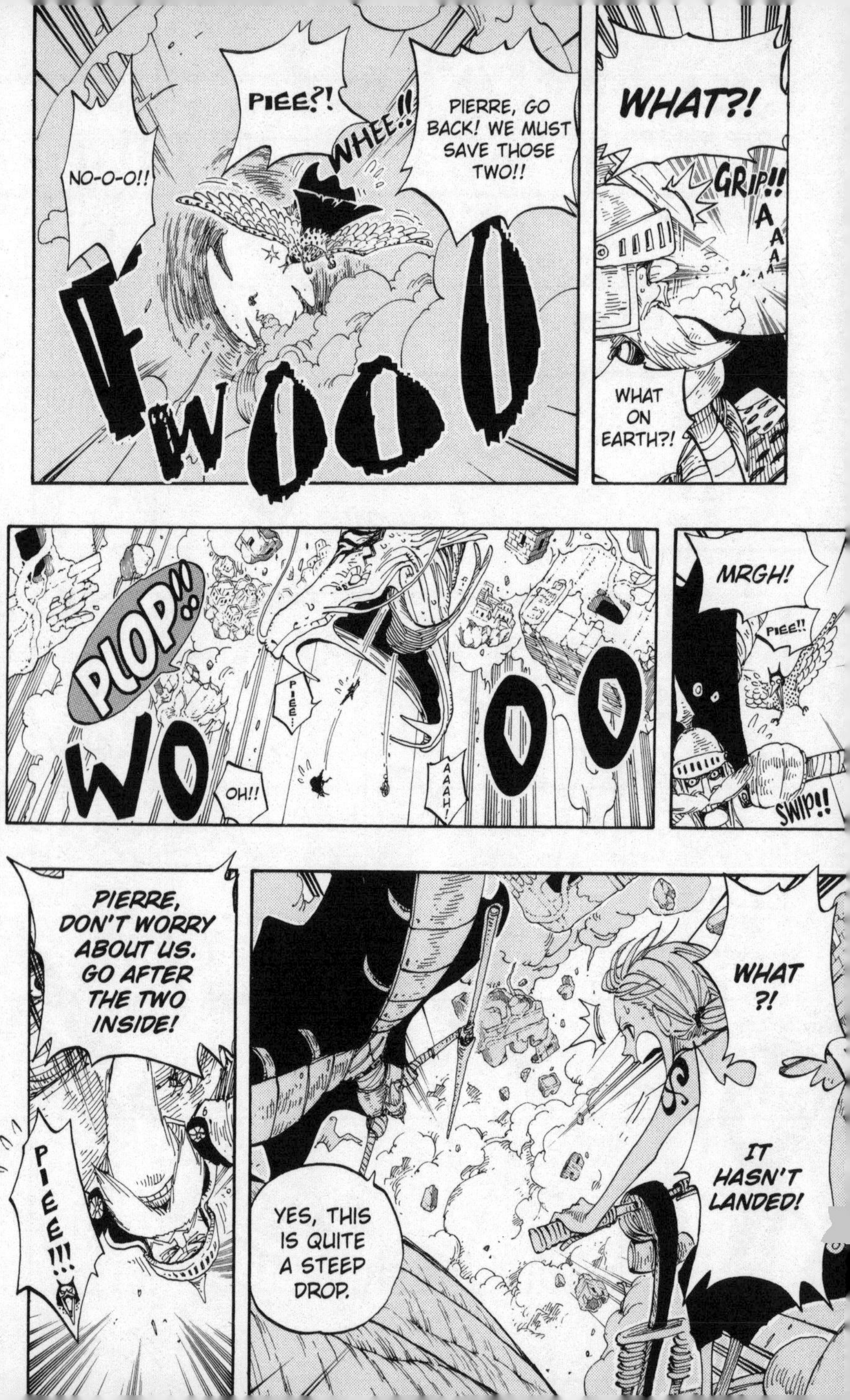
WHAT?!
GRIP!!
AAAAA
WHAT ON EARTH?!
PIERRE, GO BACK! WE MUST SAVE THOSE TWO!!
WHEE!!
PIEE?!
NO-O-O!!
FWOOOO
MRGH!
PIEE!!
SWIP!!
PLOP!!
PIEE...
AAAH!
OH!!
WOOOO
WHAT?!
IT HASN'T LANDED!
YES, THIS IS QUITE A STEEP DROP.
PIERRE, DON'T WORRY ABOUT US. GO AFTER THE TWO INSIDE!
PIEE!!!

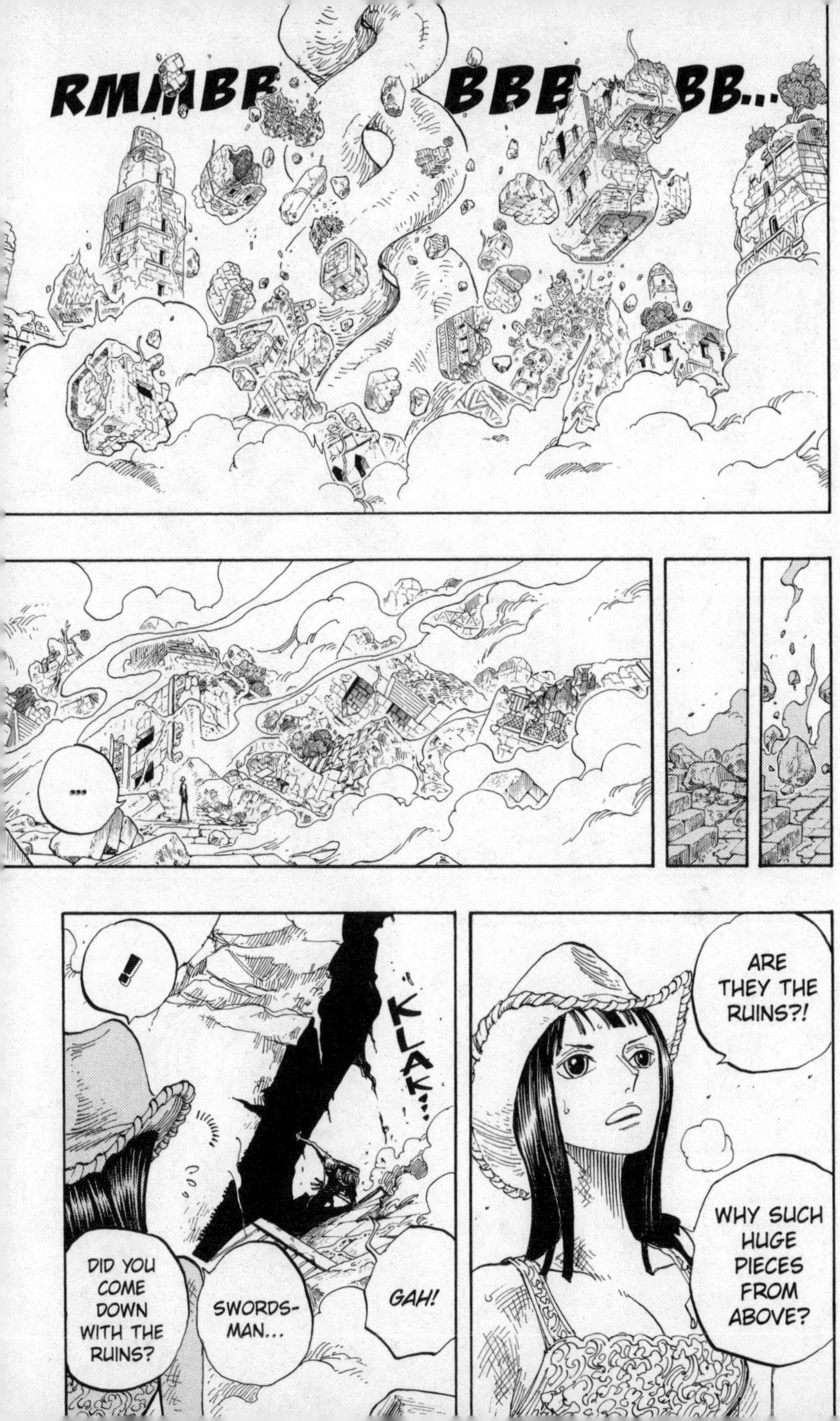
RMMBB BBB BB...
...
ARE THEY THE RUINS?!
WHY SUCH HUGE PIECES FROM ABOVE?
KLAK!!
!
GAH!
SWORDS-MAN...
DID YOU COME DOWN WITH THE RUINS?

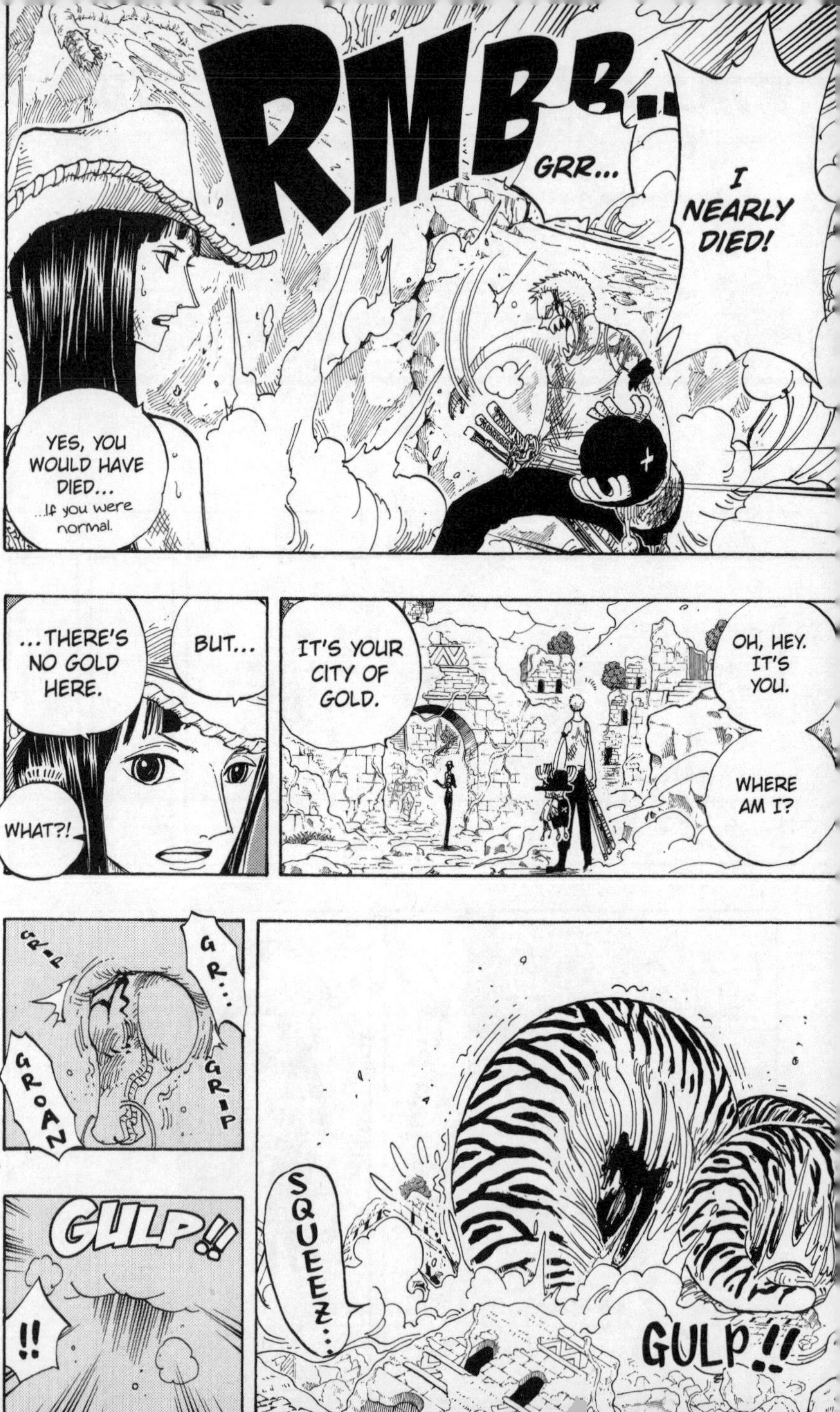
RMBB..
I NEARLY DIED!
GRR...
YES, YOU WOULD HAVE DIED...
...If you were normal.
OH, HEY. IT'S YOU.
WHERE AM I?
IT'S YOUR CITY OF GOLD.
BUT...
...THERE'S NO GOLD HERE.
WHAT?!
SQUEEZ...
GULP!!
GR...
GROAN
GRIP
GULP!!
!!

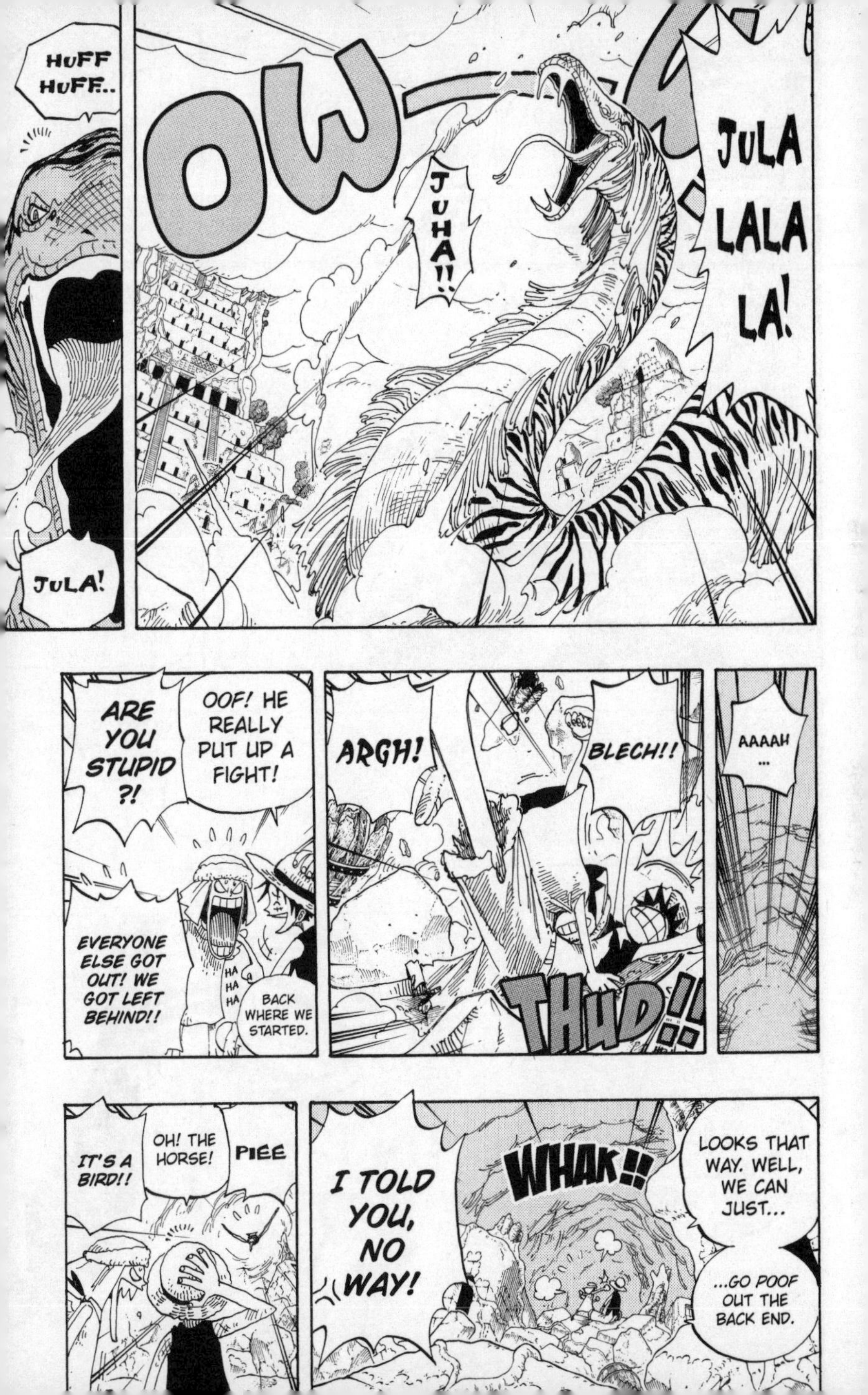
JULA LALA LA!
OW—
JUHA!!
HUFF HUFF...
JULA!
AAAAH ...
BLECH!!
ARGH!
THUD!!
OOF! HE REALLY PUT UP A FIGHT!
ARE YOU STUPID?!
BACK WHERE WE STARTED.
HA HA HA
EVERYONE ELSE GOT OUT! WE GOT LEFT BEHIND!!
LOOKS THAT WAY. WELL, WE CAN JUST...
WHAK!!
...GO POOF OUT THE BACK END.
I TOLD YOU, NO WAY!
PIEE
OH! THE HORSE!
IT'S A BIRD!!

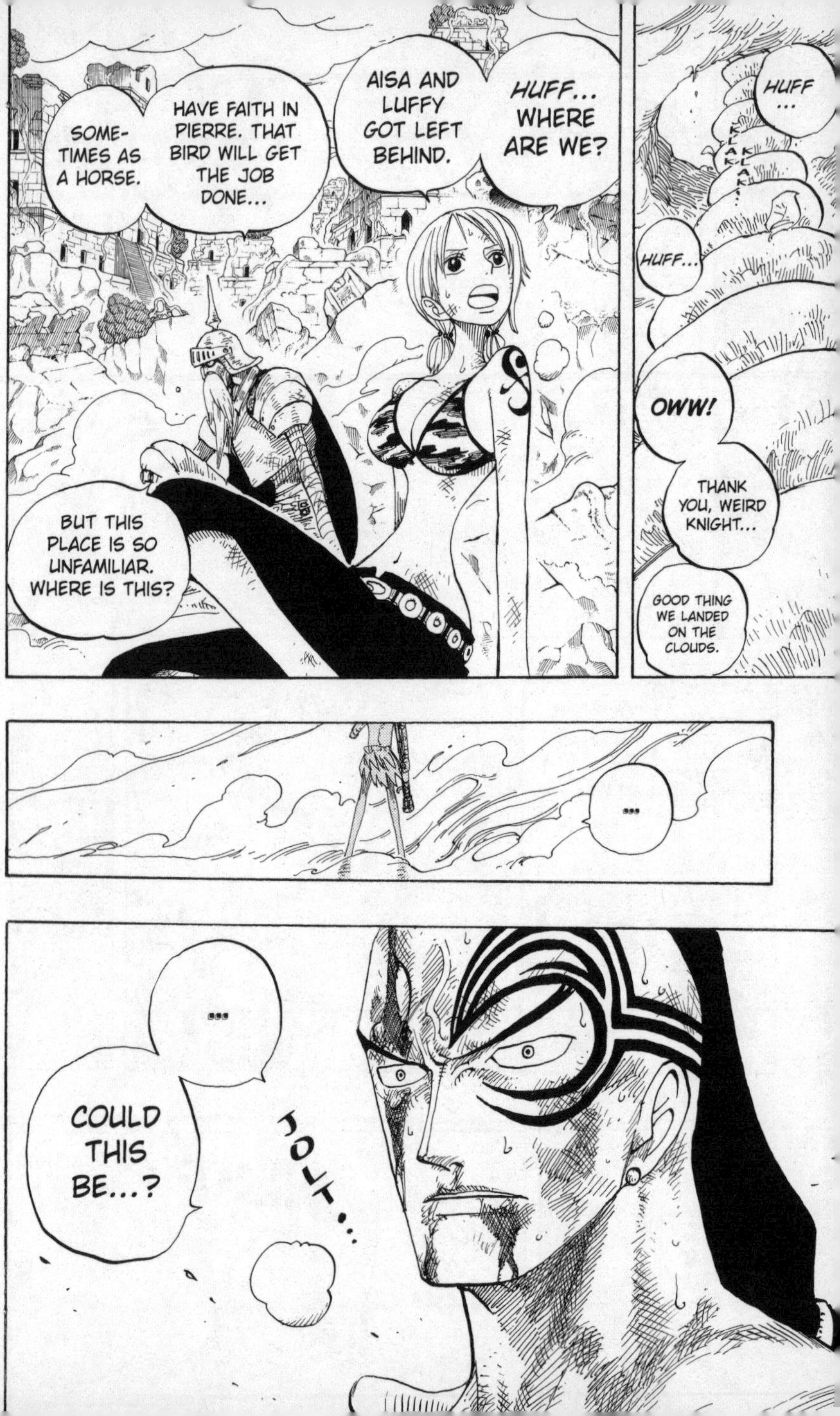
HUFF...
KLAK KLAK...
HUFF...
OWW!
THANK YOU, WEIRD KNIGHT...
GOOD THING WE LANDED ON THE CLOUDS.
HUFF... WHERE ARE WE?
AISA AND LUFFY GOT LEFT BEHIND.
HAVE FAITH IN PIERRE. THAT BIRD WILL GET THE JOB DONE...
SOME-TIMES AS A HORSE.
BUT THIS PLACE IS SO UNFAMILIAR. WHERE IS THIS?
...
...
COULD THIS BE...?
JOLT...

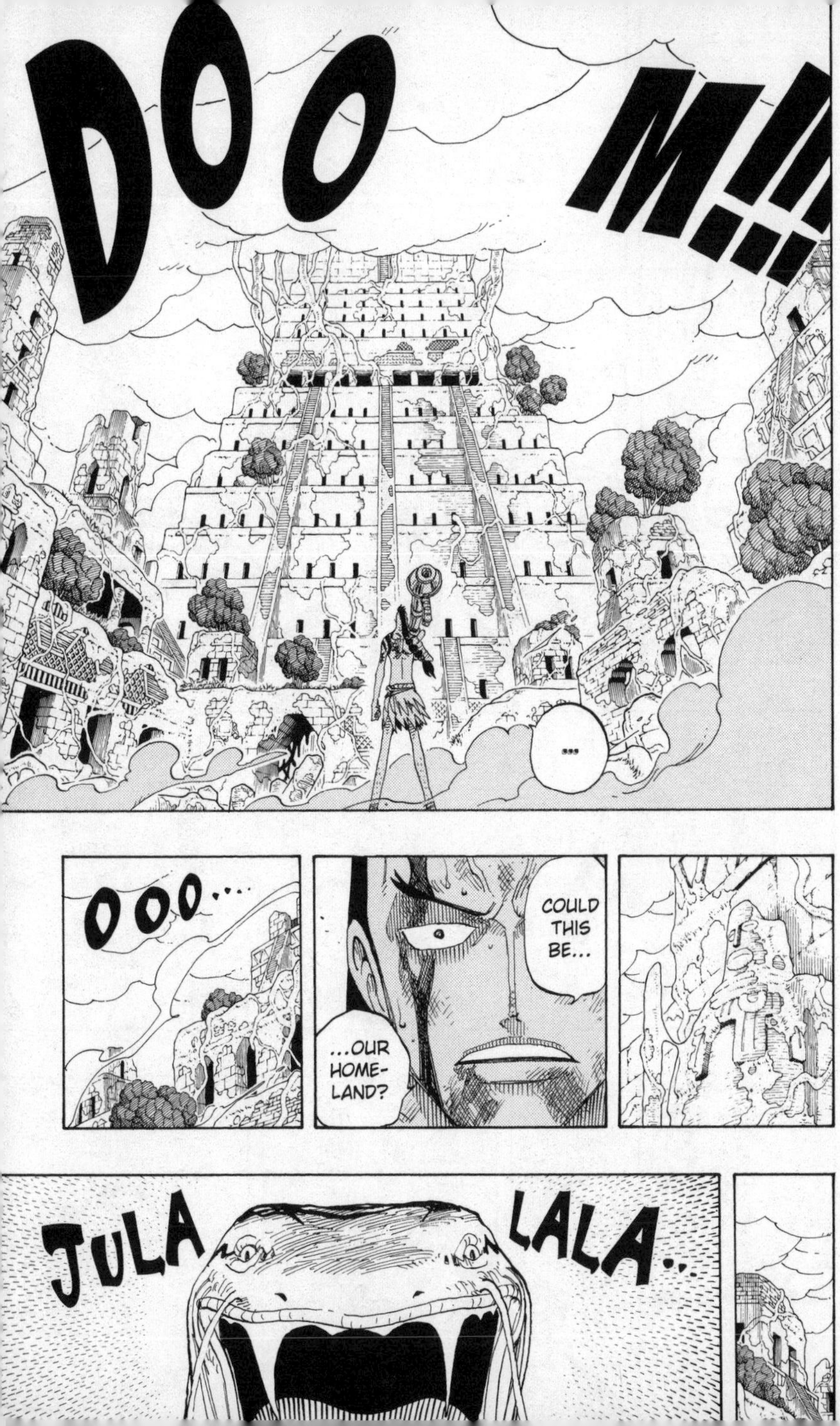
DOOM!!!
...
COULD THIS BE...
...OUR HOMELAND?
OOO....
JULA LALA..

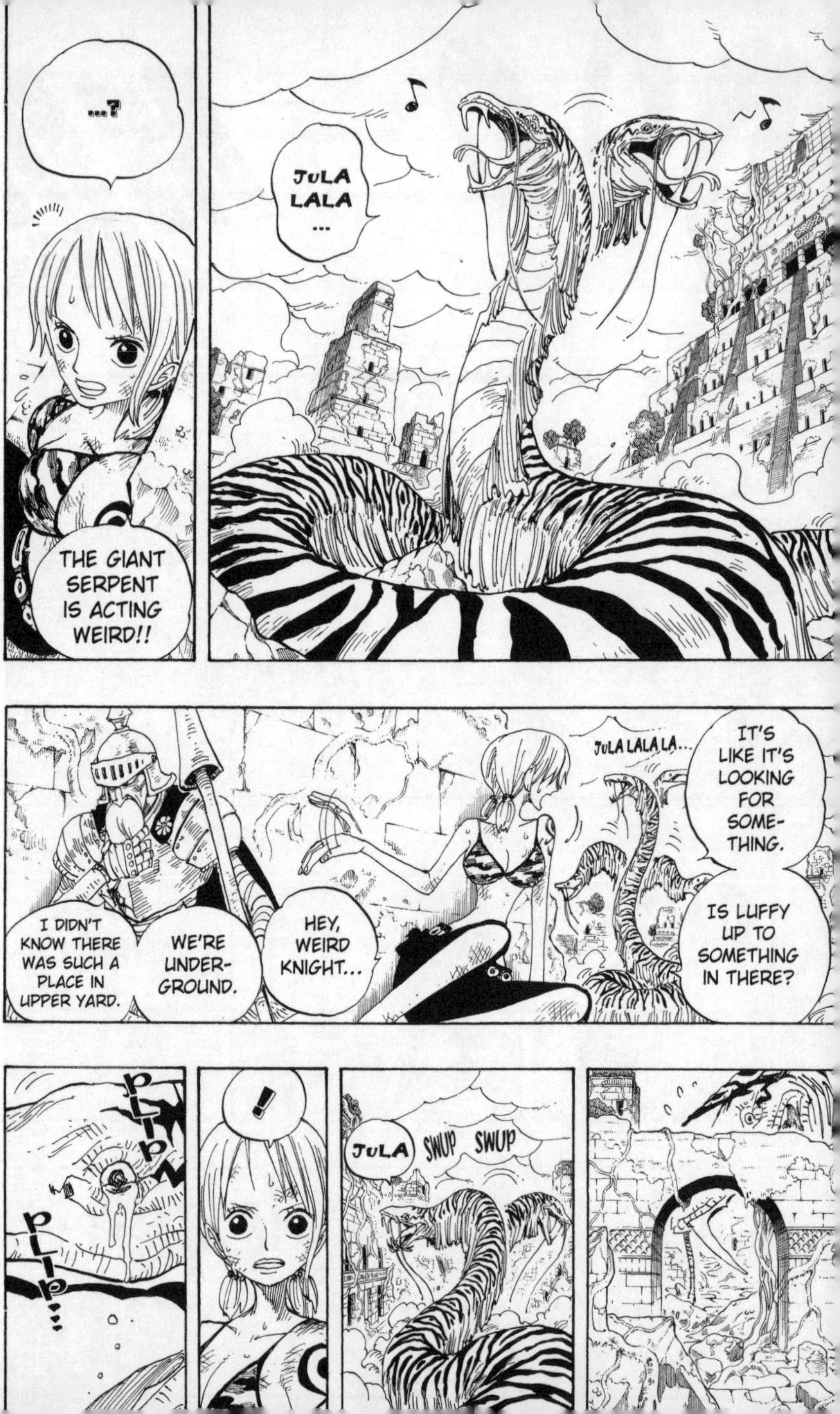
JULA LALA ...
...?
THE GIANT SERPENT IS ACTING WEIRD!!
JULA LALA LA...
IT'S LIKE IT'S LOOKING FOR SOMETHING.
IS LUFFY UP TO SOMETHING IN THERE?
HEY, WEIRD KNIGHT...
WE'RE UNDER-GROUND.
I DIDN'T KNOW THERE WAS SUCH A PLACE IN UPPER YARD.
SWUP SWUP
JULA
!
PLIP
PLIP...

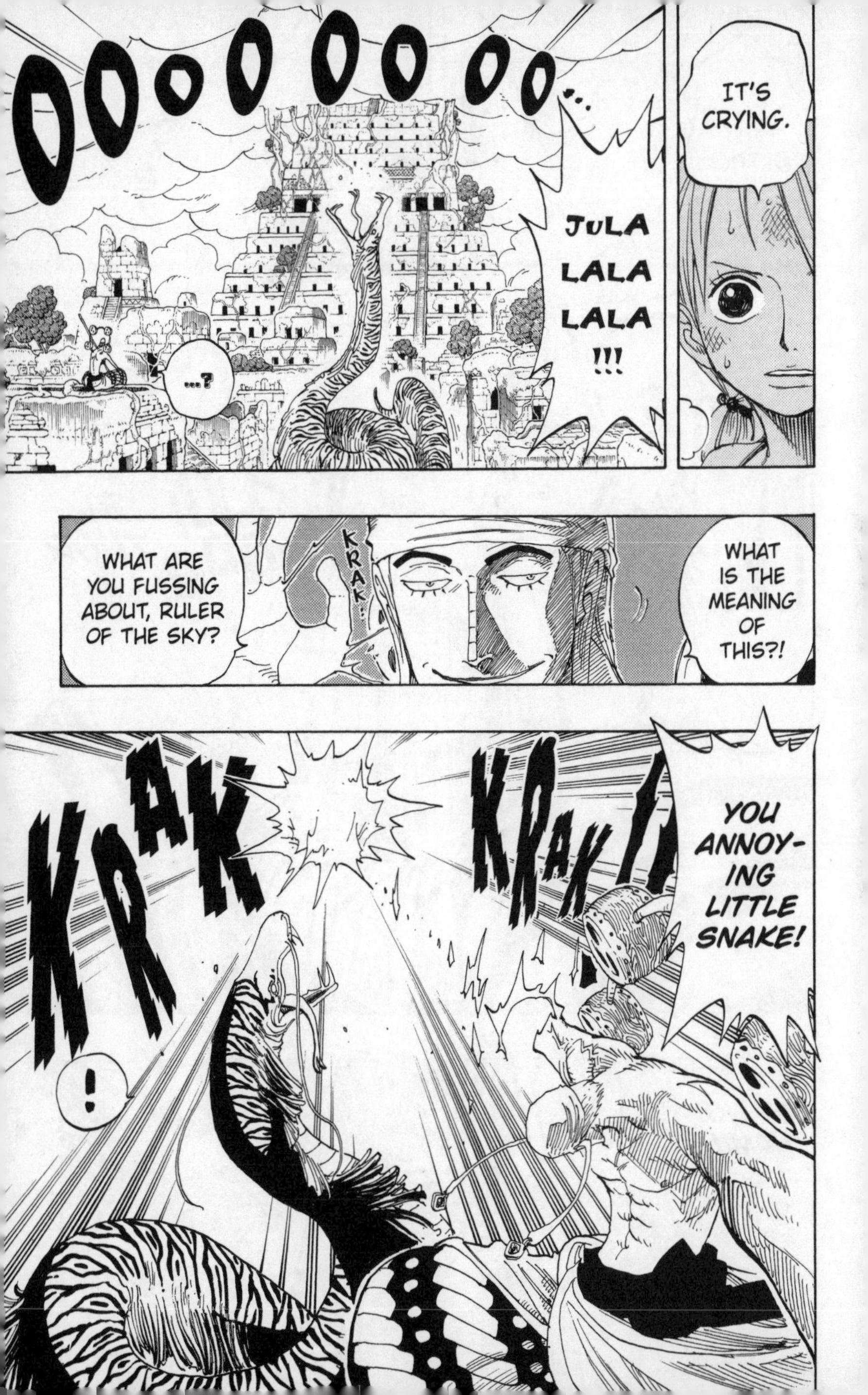
IT'S CRYING.
OOOOOOO...
JULA LALA LALA!!!
...?
WHAT IS THE MEANING OF THIS?!
KRAK
WHAT ARE YOU FUSSING ABOUT, RULER OF THE SKY?
YOU ANNOY-ING LITTLE SNAKE!
KRAK!
KRAK
!

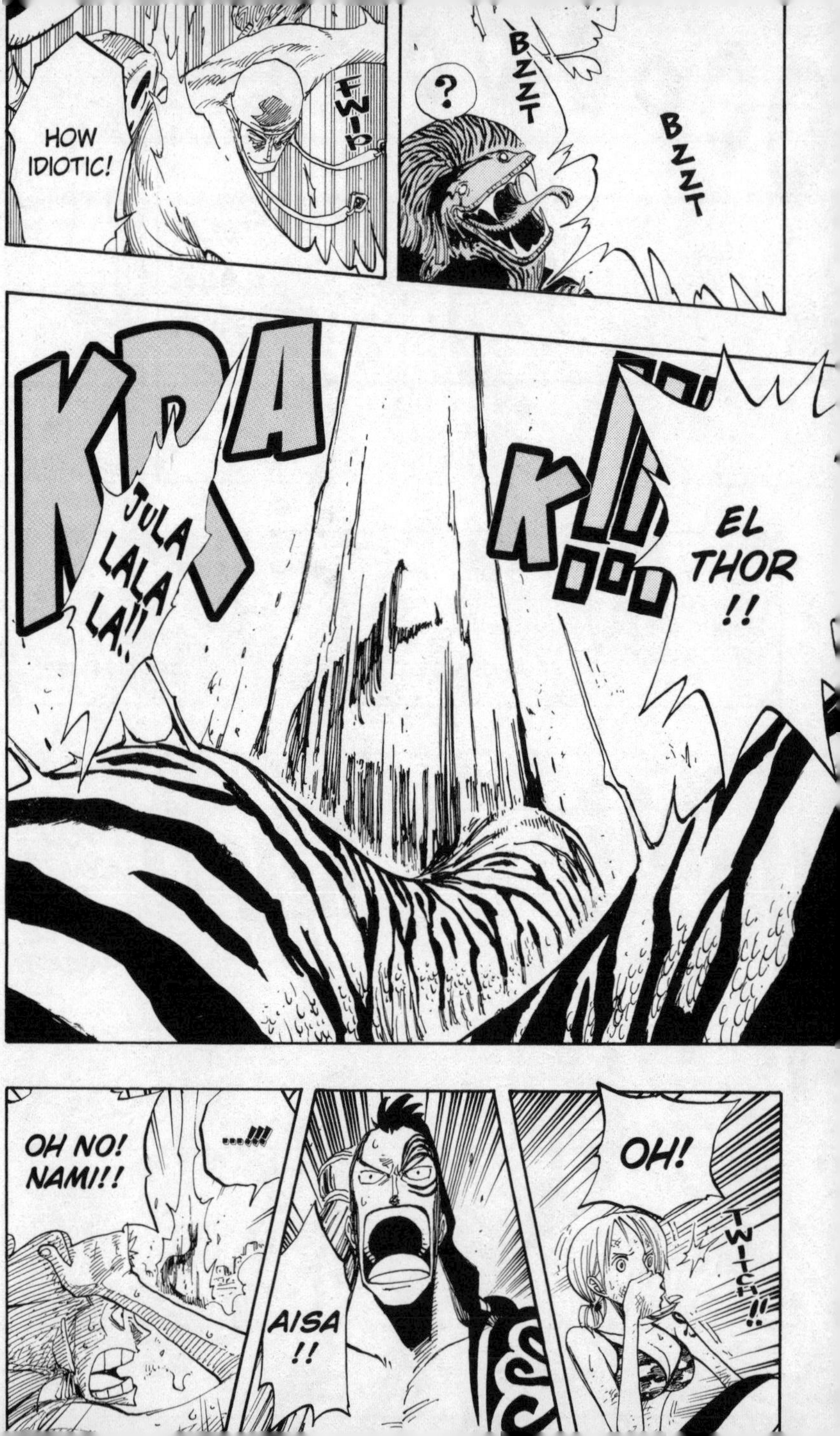
?
BZZT
BZZT
FWIP
HOW IDIOTIC!
EL THOR!!
KRA
JULA LALALA LA!!
OH!
TWITCH!!
AISA!!
OH NO! NAMI!!
...!!!

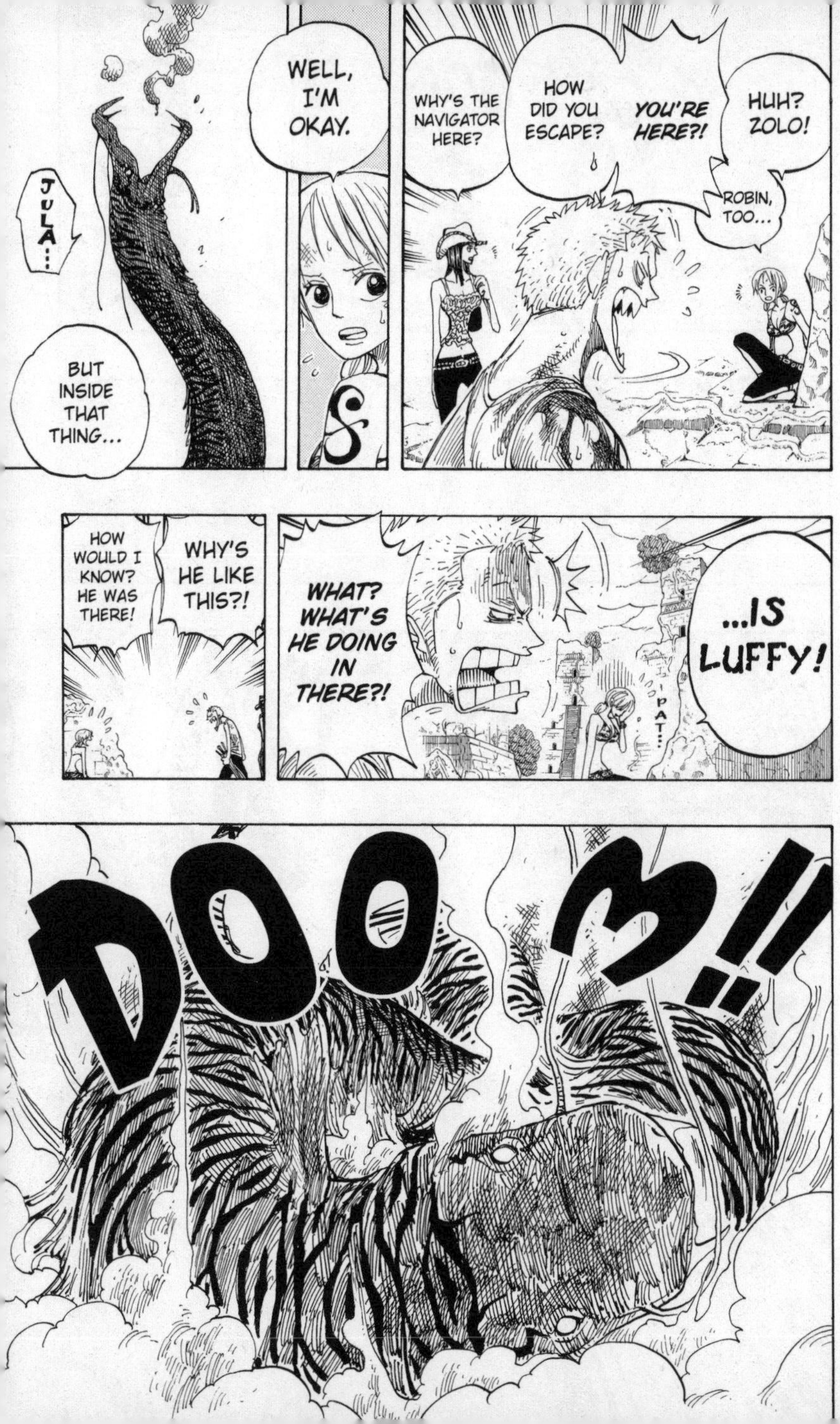
HUH? ZOLO!
ROBIN, TOO...
YOU'RE HERE?!
HOW DID YOU ESCAPE?
WHY'S THE NAVIGATOR HERE?
WELL, I'M OKAY.
JULA...
BUT INSIDE THAT THING...
...IS LUFFY!
PAT...
WHAT? WHAT'S HE DOING IN THERE?!
WHY'S HE LIKE THIS?!
HOW WOULD I KNOW? HE WAS THERE!
DOOM!!

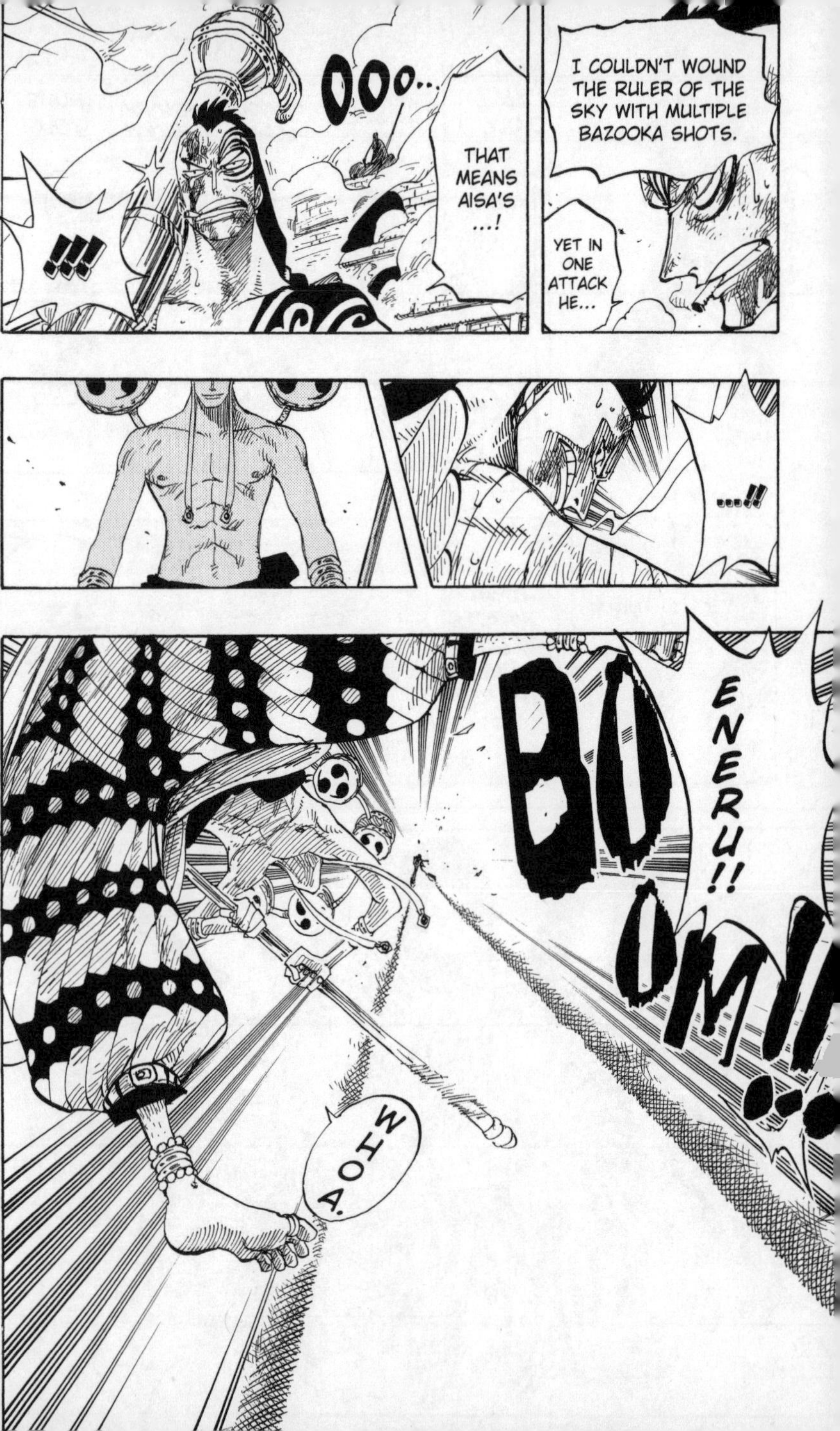
I COULDN'T WOUND THE RULER OF THE SKY WITH MULTIPLE BAZOOKA SHOTS.
YET IN ONE ATTACK HE...
OOO...
THAT MEANS AISA'S ...!
!!!!
...!!
ENERU!!
BOOM!!
WHOA.

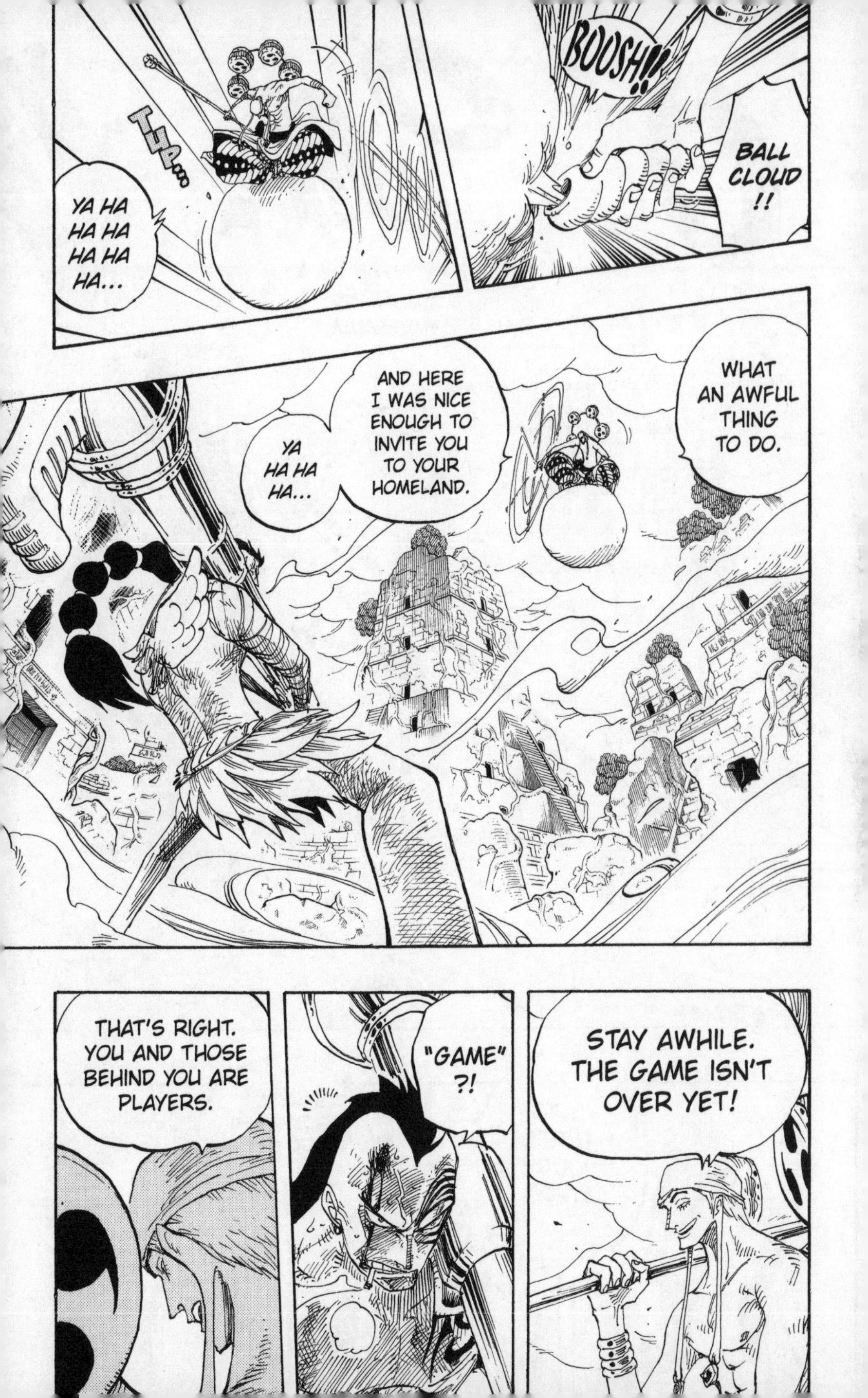
BOOSH!!
BALL CLOUD !!
TUP...
YA HA HA HA HA HA HA...
WHAT AN AWFUL THING TO DO.
AND HERE I WAS NICE ENOUGH TO INVITE YOU TO YOUR HOMELAND.
YA HA HA HA...
STAY AWHILE. THE GAME ISN'T OVER YET!
"GAME" ?!
THAT'S RIGHT. YOU AND THOSE BEHIND YOU ARE PLAYERS.

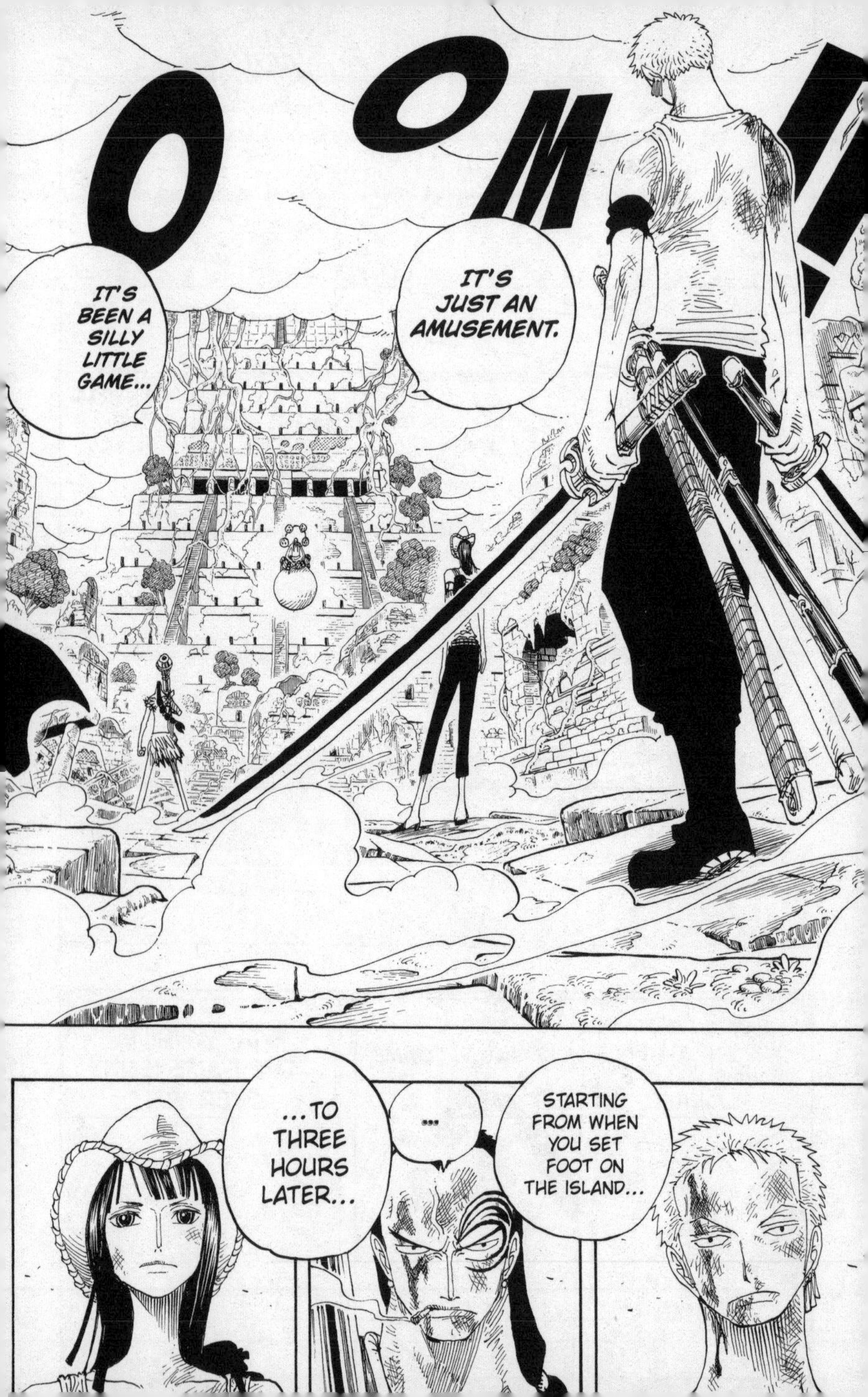
OOM
IT'S JUST AN AMUSEMENT.
IT'S BEEN A SILLY LITTLE GAME...
STARTING FROM WHEN YOU SET FOOT ON THE ISLAND...
...
...TO THREE HOURS LATER...

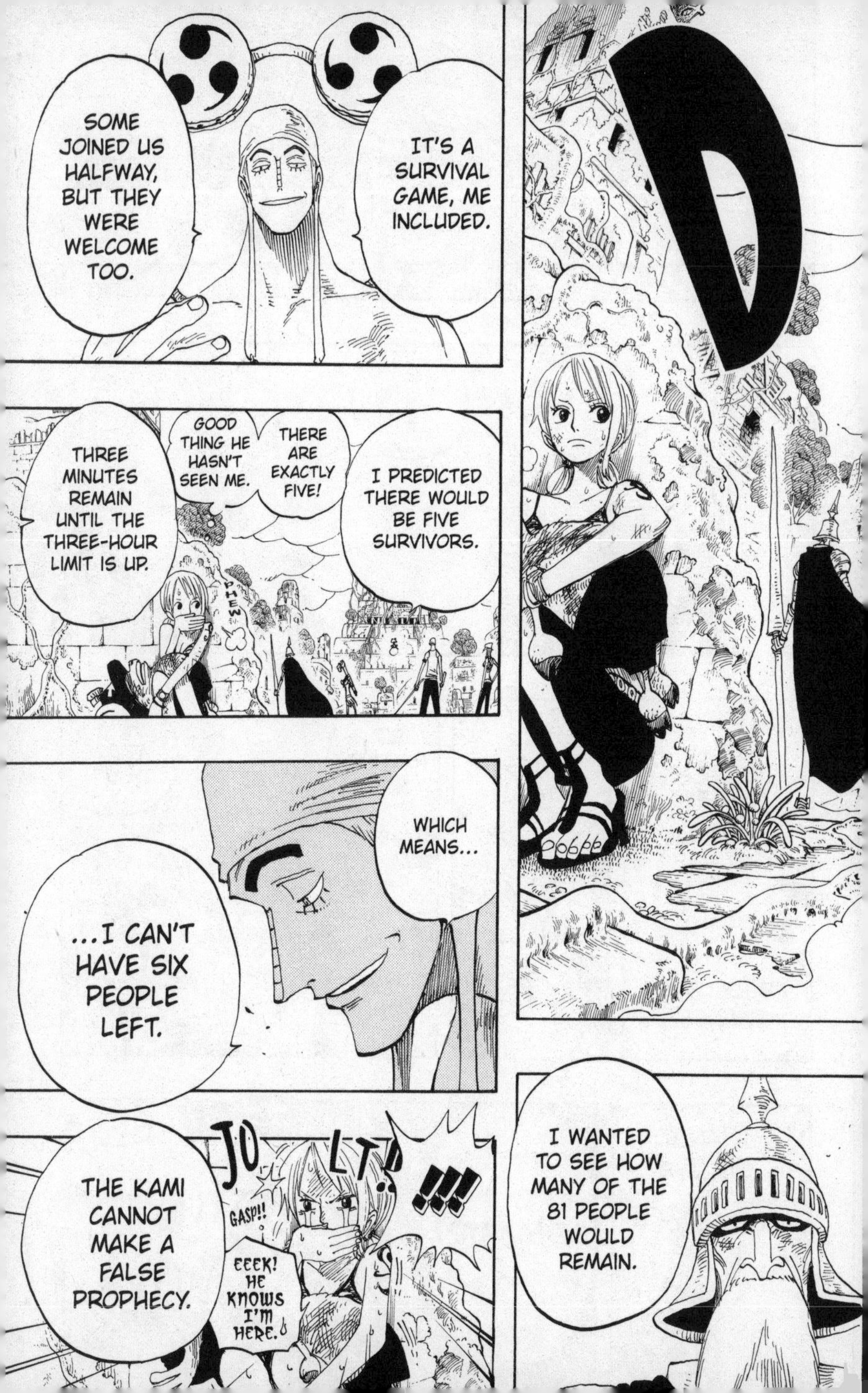
D
IT'S A SURVIVAL GAME, ME INCLUDED.
SOME JOINED US HALFWAY, BUT THEY WERE WELCOME TOO.
I PREDICTED THERE WOULD BE FIVE SURVIVORS.
THERE ARE EXACTLY FIVE!
GOOD THING HE HASN'T SEEN ME.
THREE MINUTES REMAIN UNTIL THE THREE-HOUR LIMIT IS UP.
PHEW
WHICH MEANS...
...I CAN'T HAVE SIX PEOPLE LEFT.
I WANTED TO SEE HOW MANY OF THE 81 PEOPLE WOULD REMAIN.
JOLT!!!
GASP!!
EEEK! HE KNOWS I'M HERE.
THE KAMI CANNOT MAKE A FALSE PROPHECY.

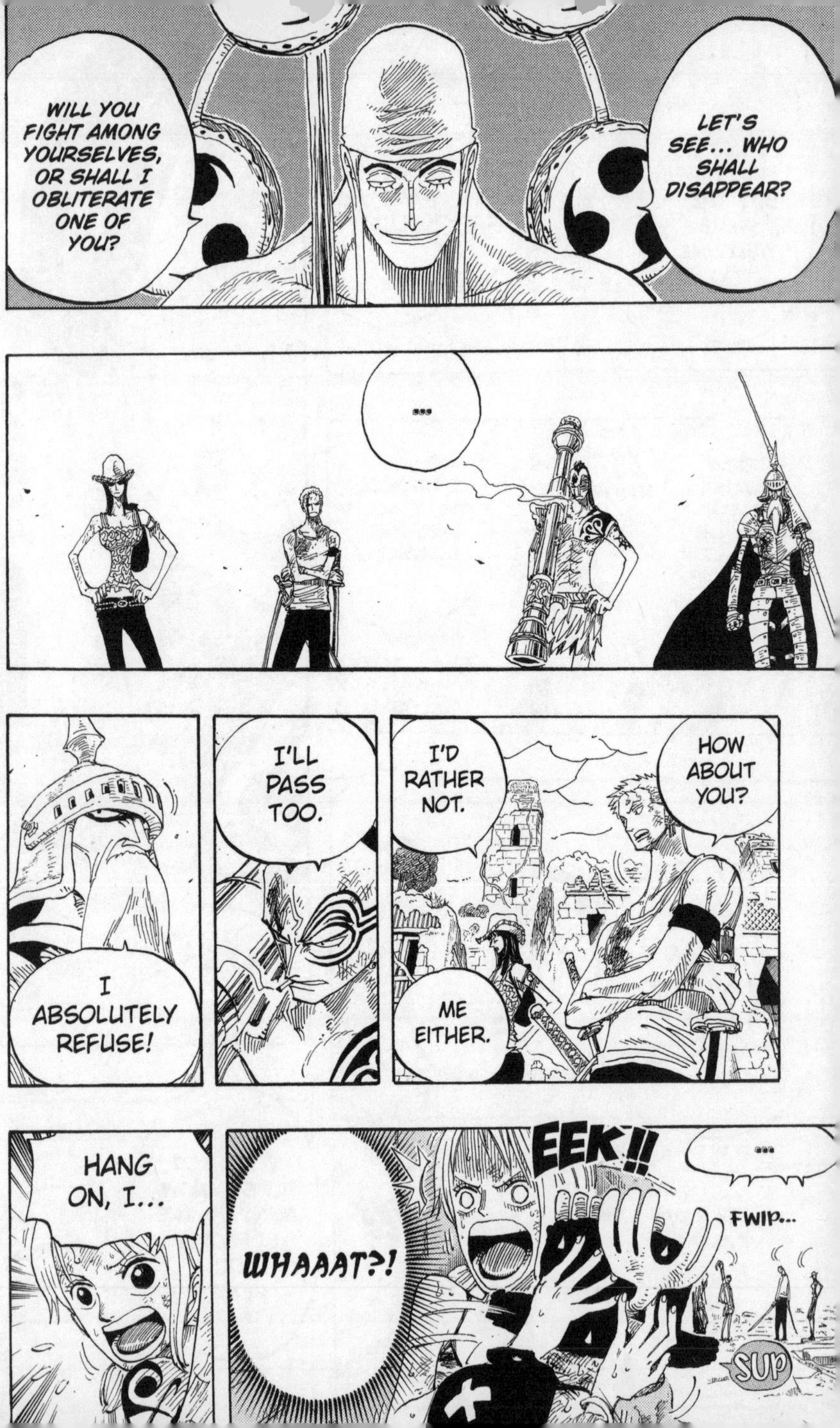
LET'S SEE... WHO SHALL DISAPPEAR?
WILL YOU FIGHT AMONG YOURSELVES, OR SHALL I OBLITERATE ONE OF YOU?
...
HOW ABOUT YOU?
I'D RATHER NOT.
ME EITHER.
I'LL PASS TOO.
I ABSOLUTELY REFUSE!
...
EEK!!
FWIP...
WHAAAT?!
SUP
HANG ON, I...

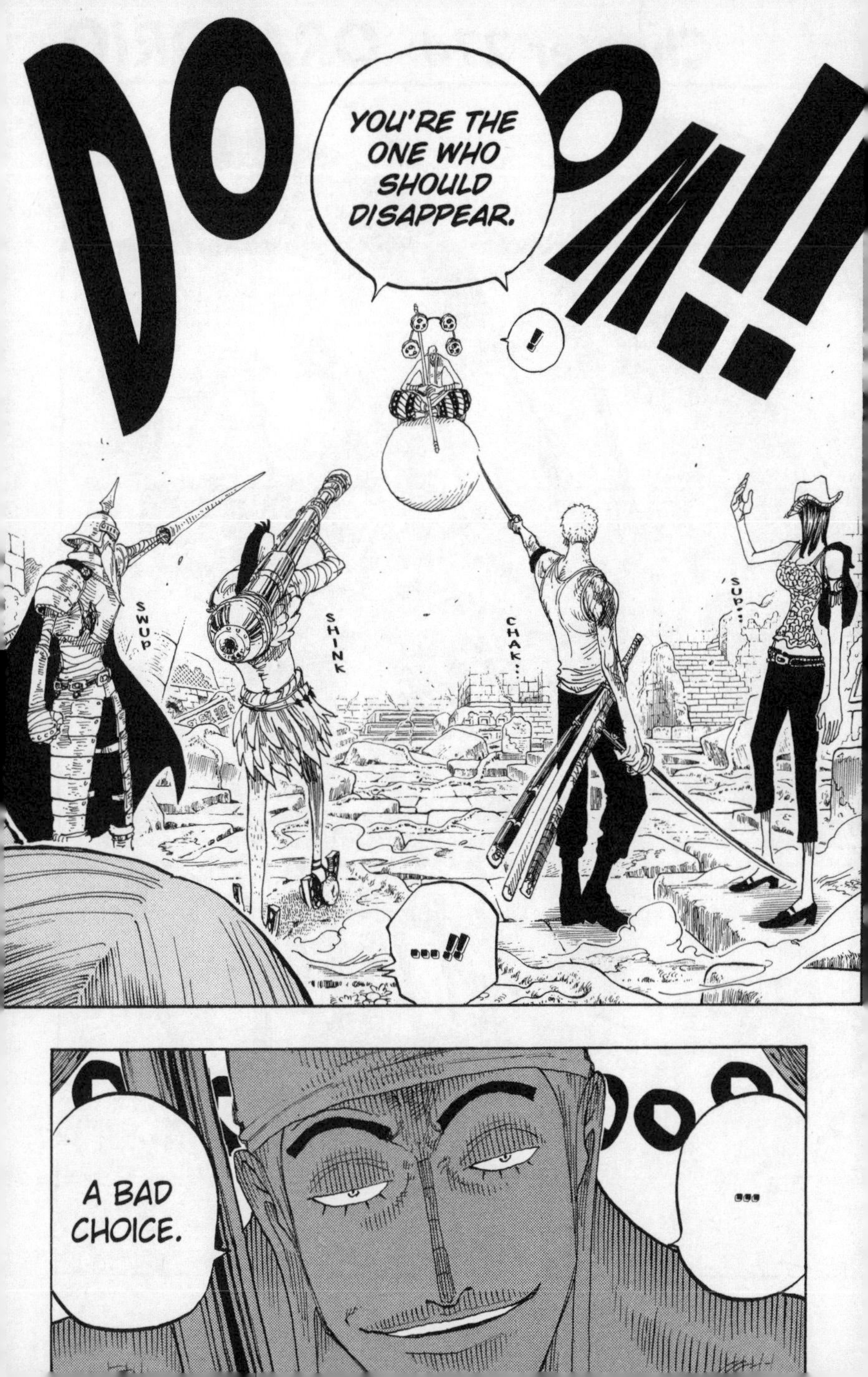
DOOM!!
YOU'RE THE ONE WHO SHOULD DISAPPEAR.
!
SUP...
CHAK...
SHINK
SWUP
...!!
...
A BAD CHOICE.

Chapter 274: ORATORIO

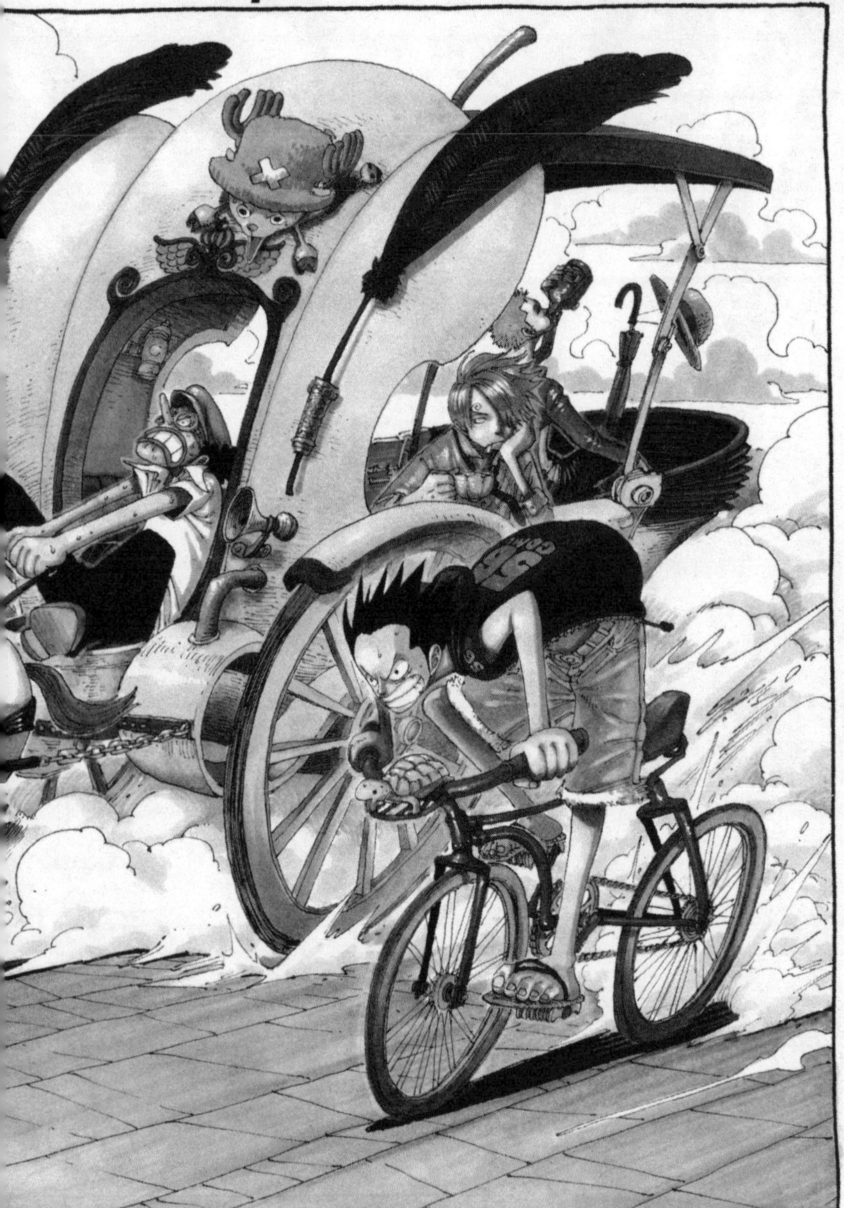

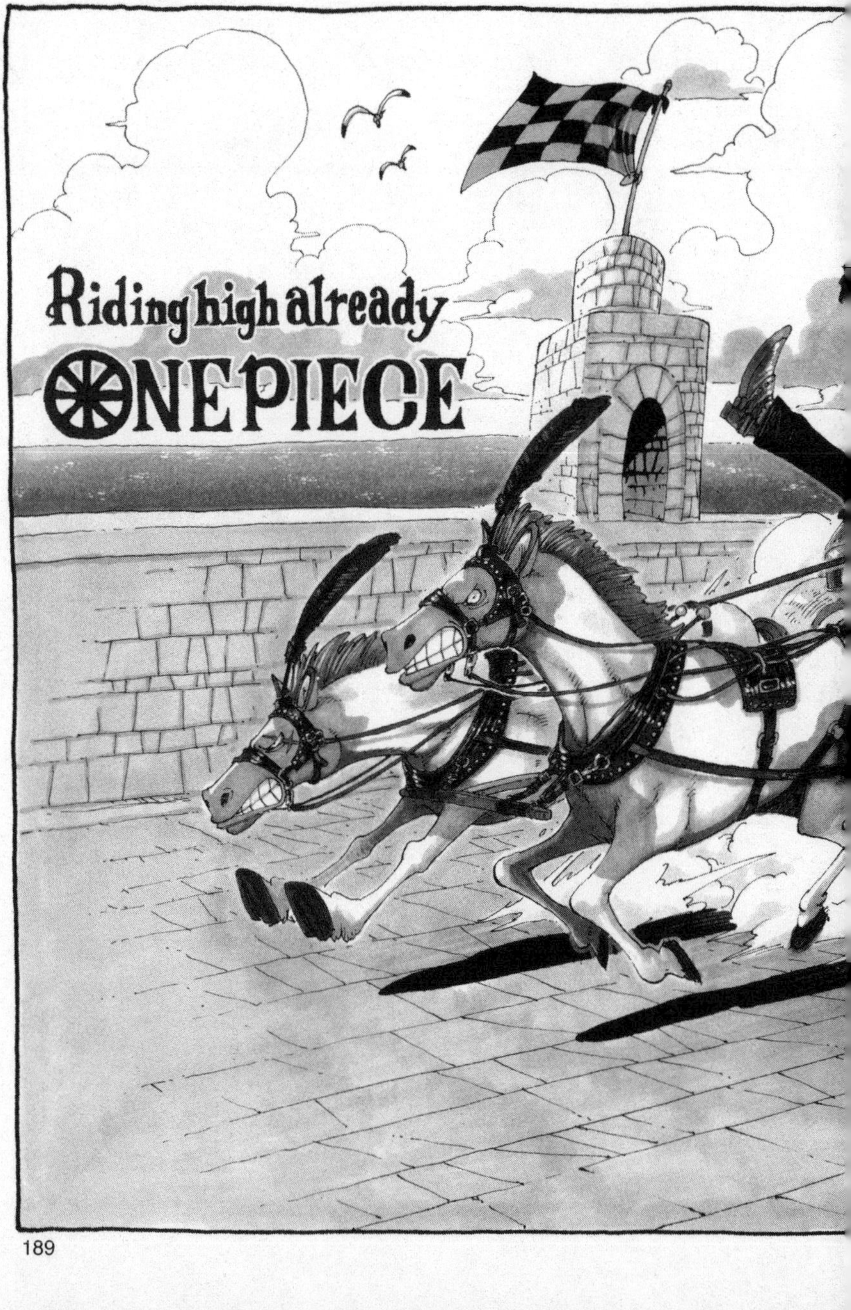
Riding high already
ONE PIECE

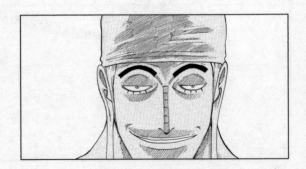

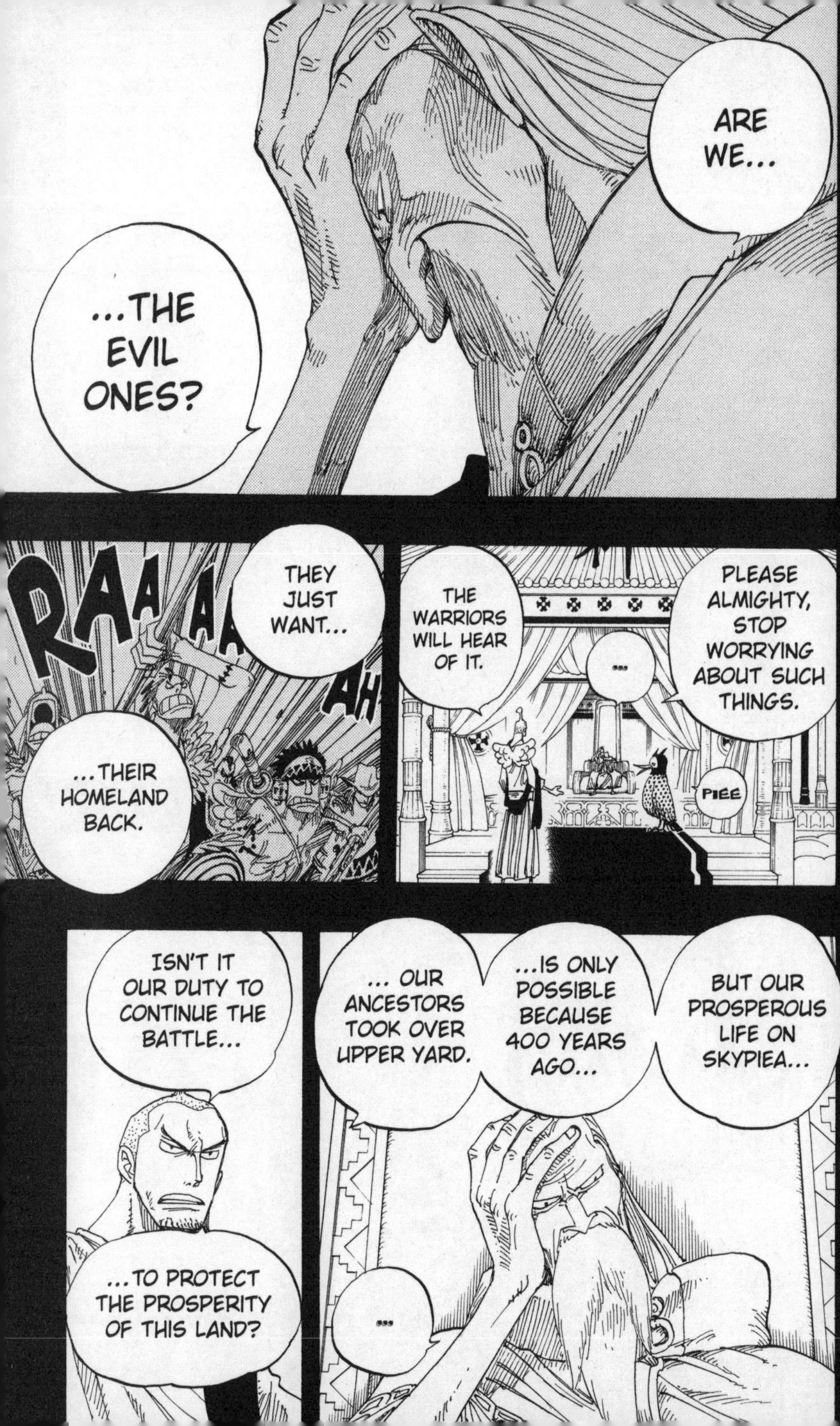
ARE WE...
...THE EVIL ONES?
PLEASE ALMIGHTY, STOP WORRYING ABOUT SUCH THINGS.
THE WARRIORS WILL HEAR OF IT.
...
PIEE
RAAAAH
THEY JUST WANT...
...THEIR HOMELAND BACK.
BUT OUR PROSPEROUS LIFE ON SKYPIEA...
...IS ONLY POSSIBLE BECAUSE 400 YEARS AGO...
... OUR ANCESTORS TOOK OVER UPPER YARD.
...
ISN'T IT OUR DUTY TO CONTINUE THE BATTLE...
...TO PROTECT THE PROSPERITY OF THIS LAND?

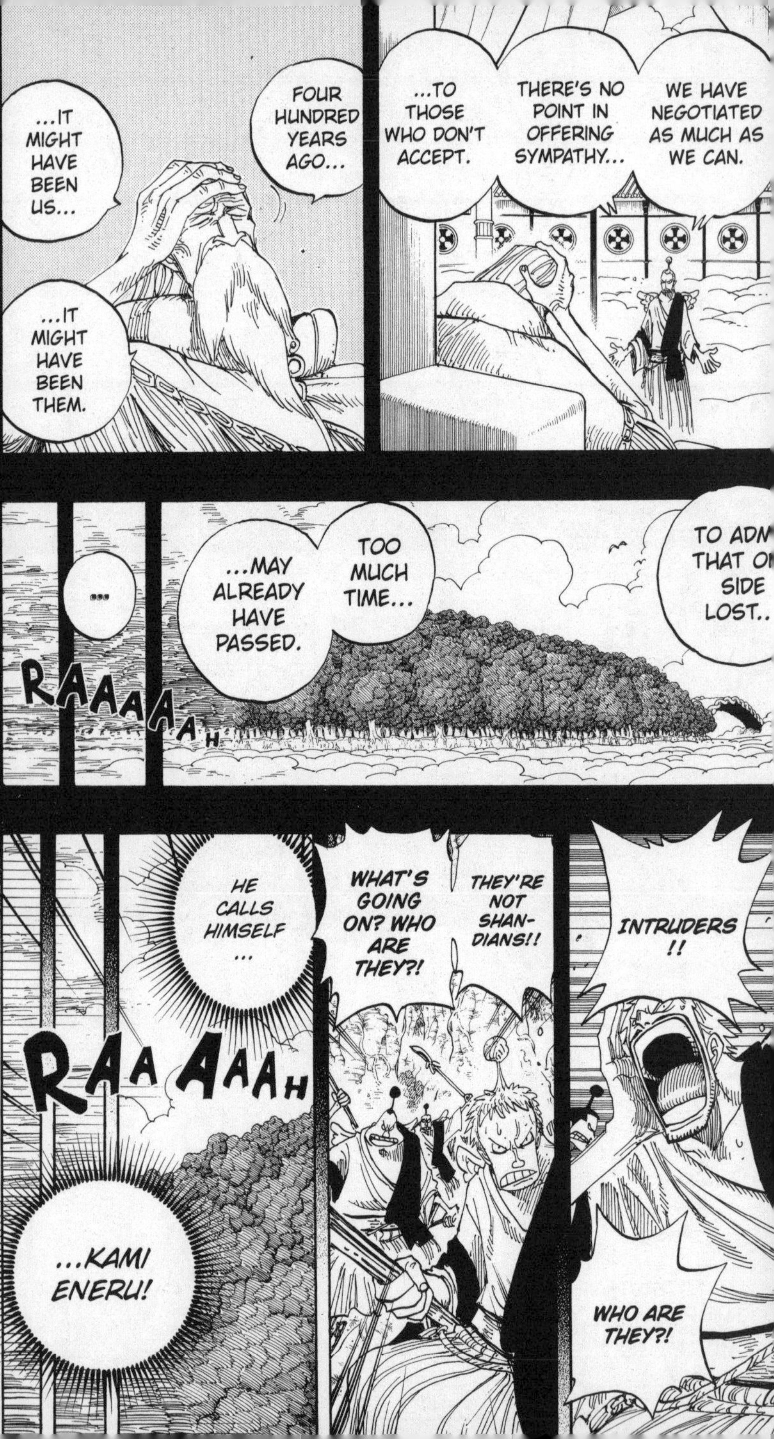
WE HAVE NEGOTIATED AS MUCH AS WE CAN.
THERE'S NO POINT IN OFFERING SYMPATHY...
...TO THOSE WHO DON'T ACCEPT.
FOUR HUNDRED YEARS AGO...
...IT MIGHT HAVE BEEN US...
...IT MIGHT HAVE BEEN THEM.
TO ADM THAT O SIDE LOST..
TOO MUCH TIME...
...MAY ALREADY HAVE PASSED.
...
RAAAAAAH
INTRUDERS!!
WHO ARE THEY?!
THEY'RE NOT SHAN-DIANS!!
WHAT'S GOING ON? WHO ARE THEY?!
HE CALLS HIMSELF ...
RAAAAAAH
...KAMI ENERU!

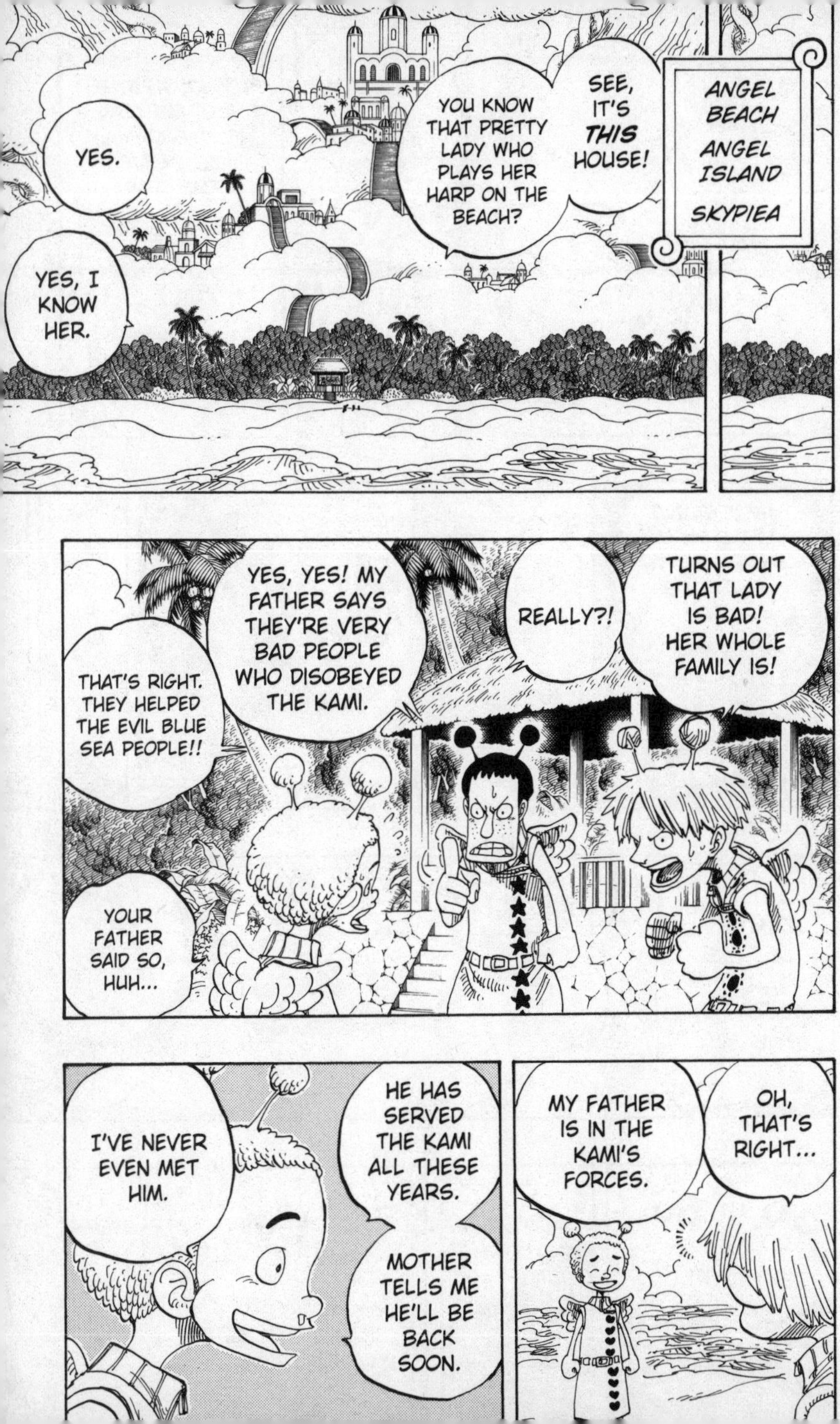
ANGEL BEACH
ANGEL ISLAND
SKYPIEA
SEE, IT'S THIS HOUSE!
YOU KNOW THAT PRETTY LADY WHO PLAYS HER HARP ON THE BEACH?
YES.
YES, I KNOW HER.
TURNS OUT THAT LADY IS BAD! HER WHOLE FAMILY IS!
REALLY?!
YES, YES! MY FATHER SAYS THEY'RE VERY BAD PEOPLE WHO DISOBEYED THE KAMI.
THAT'S RIGHT. THEY HELPED THE EVIL BLUE SEA PEOPLE!!
YOUR FATHER SAID SO, HUH...
OH, THAT'S RIGHT...
MY FATHER IS IN THE KAMI'S FORCES.
HE HAS SERVED THE KAMI ALL THESE YEARS.
MOTHER TELLS ME HE'LL BE BACK SOON.
I'VE NEVER EVEN MET HIM.

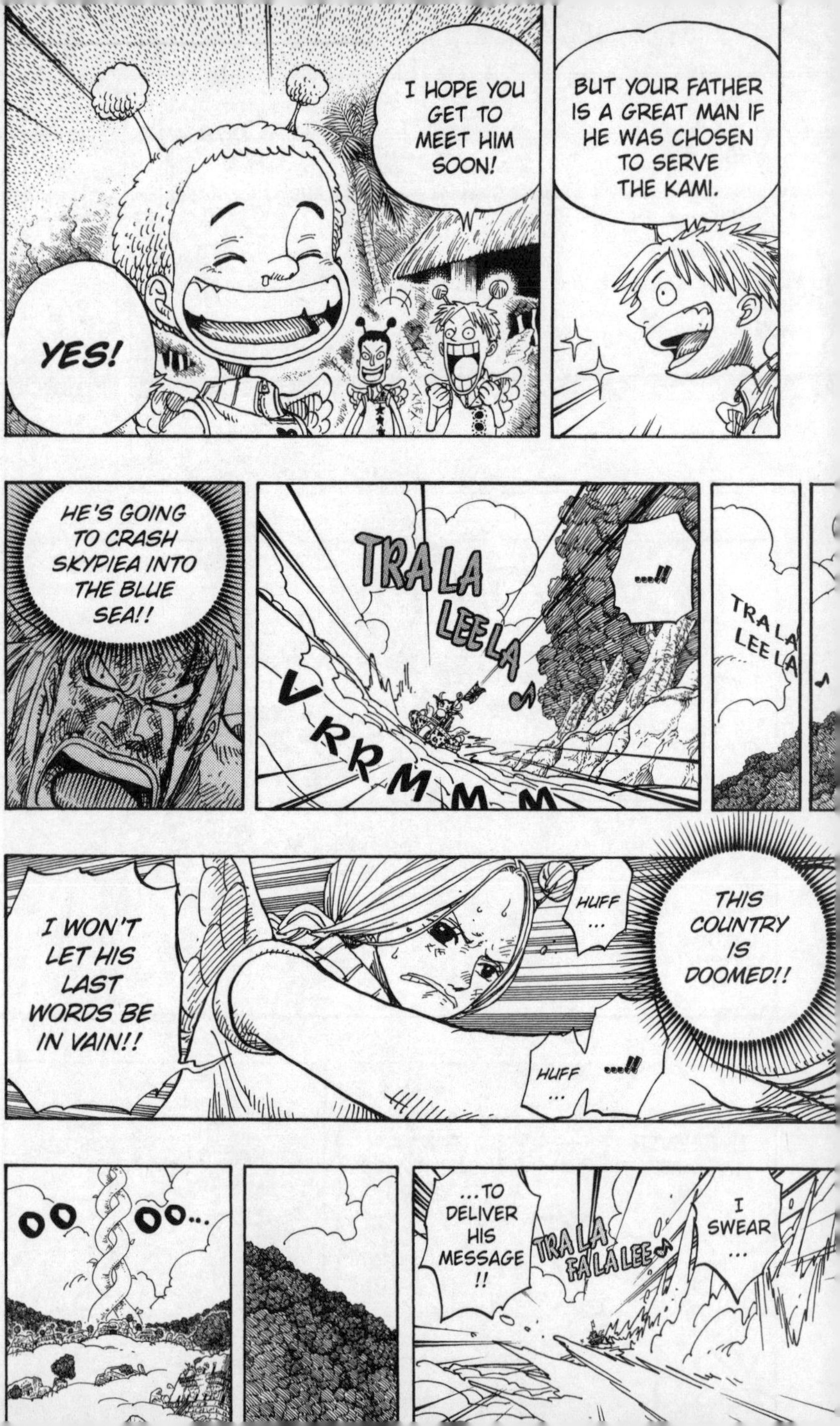
BUT YOUR FATHER IS A GREAT MAN IF HE WAS CHOSEN TO SERVE THE KAMI.
I HOPE YOU GET TO MEET HIM SOON!
YES!
TRA LA LEE LA
...!!
TRA LA LEE LA
VRRMMMM
HE'S GOING TO CRASH SKYPIEA INTO THE BLUE SEA!!
THIS COUNTRY IS DOOMED!!
HUFF ...
...!!
HUFF ...
I WON'T LET HIS LAST WORDS BE IN VAIN!!
I SWEAR ...
TRA LA FA LA LEE
...TO DELIVER HIS MESSAGE !!
OO OO...

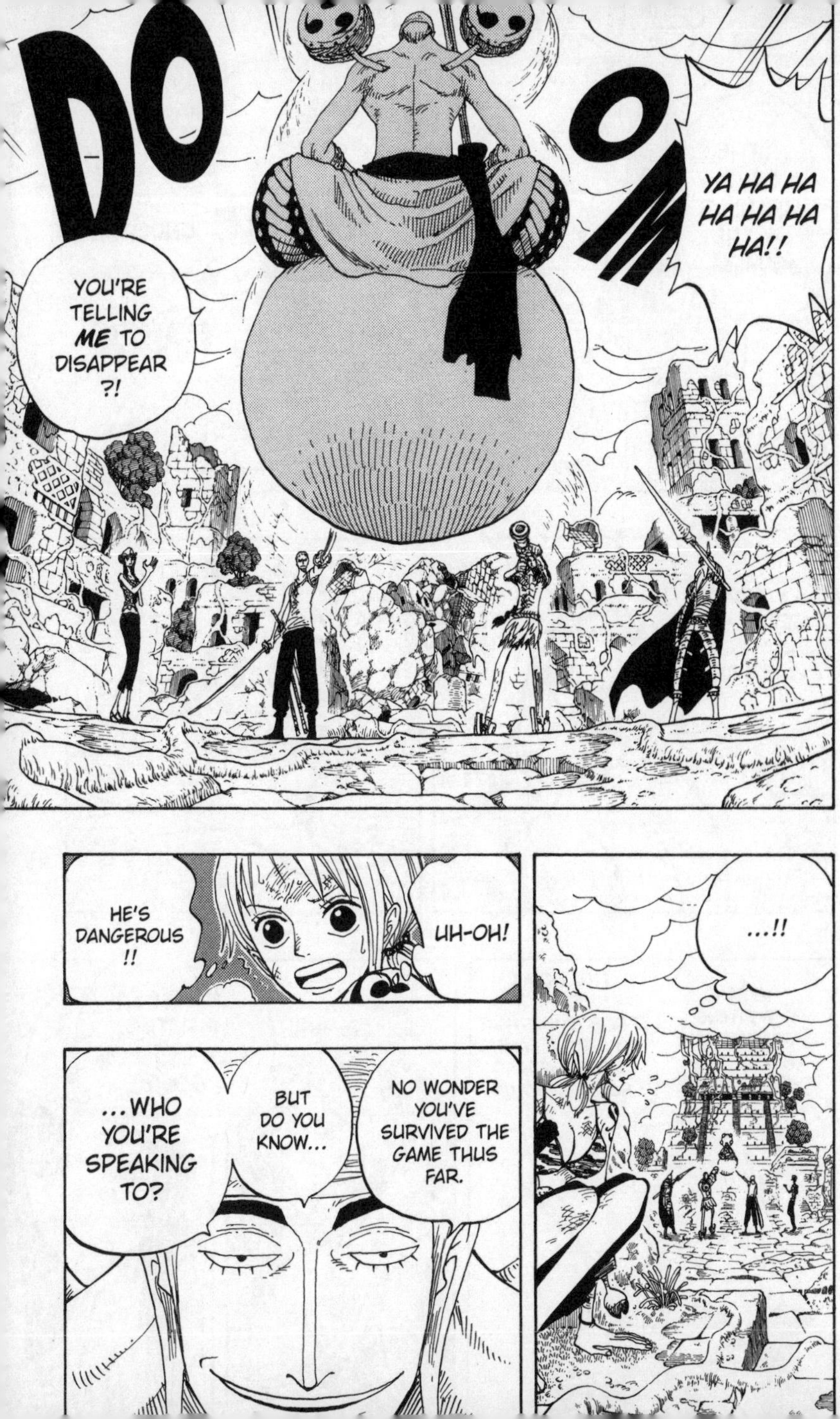
DOOM
YA HA HA HA HA HA HA!!
YOU'RE TELLING *ME* TO DISAPPEAR?!
...!!
UH-OH!
HE'S DANGEROUS!!
NO WONDER YOU'VE SURVIVED THE GAME THUS FAR.
BUT DO YOU KNOW...
...WHO YOU'RE SPEAKING TO?

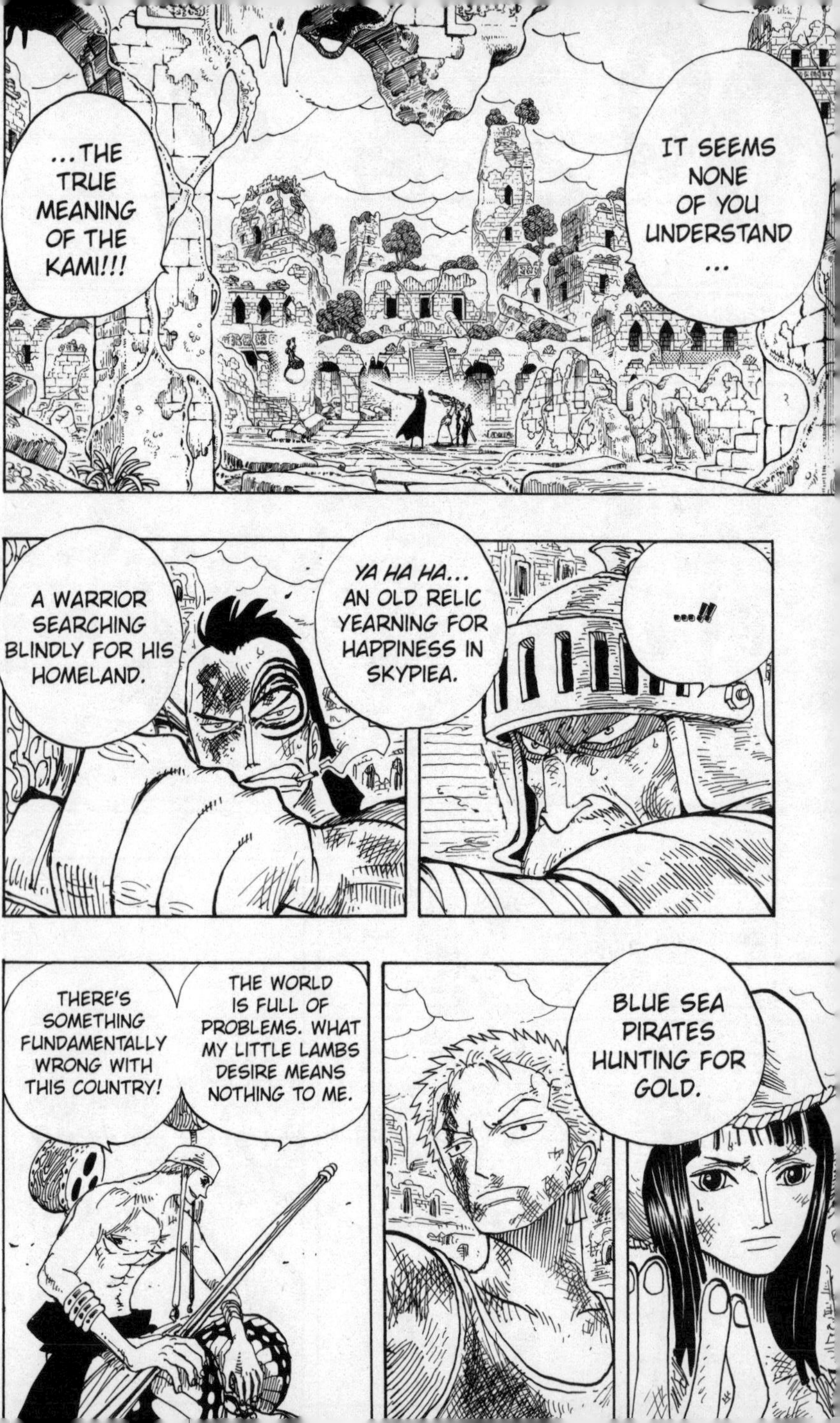
IT SEEMS NONE OF YOU UNDERSTAND ...
...THE TRUE MEANING OF THE KAMI!!!
YA HA HA... AN OLD RELIC YEARNING FOR HAPPINESS IN SKYPIEA.
...!!
A WARRIOR SEARCHING BLINDLY FOR HIS HOMELAND.
BLUE SEA PIRATES HUNTING FOR GOLD.
THE WORLD IS FULL OF PROBLEMS. WHAT MY LITTLE LAMBS DESIRE MEANS NOTHING TO ME.
THERE'S SOMETHING FUNDAMENTALLY WRONG WITH THIS COUNTRY!

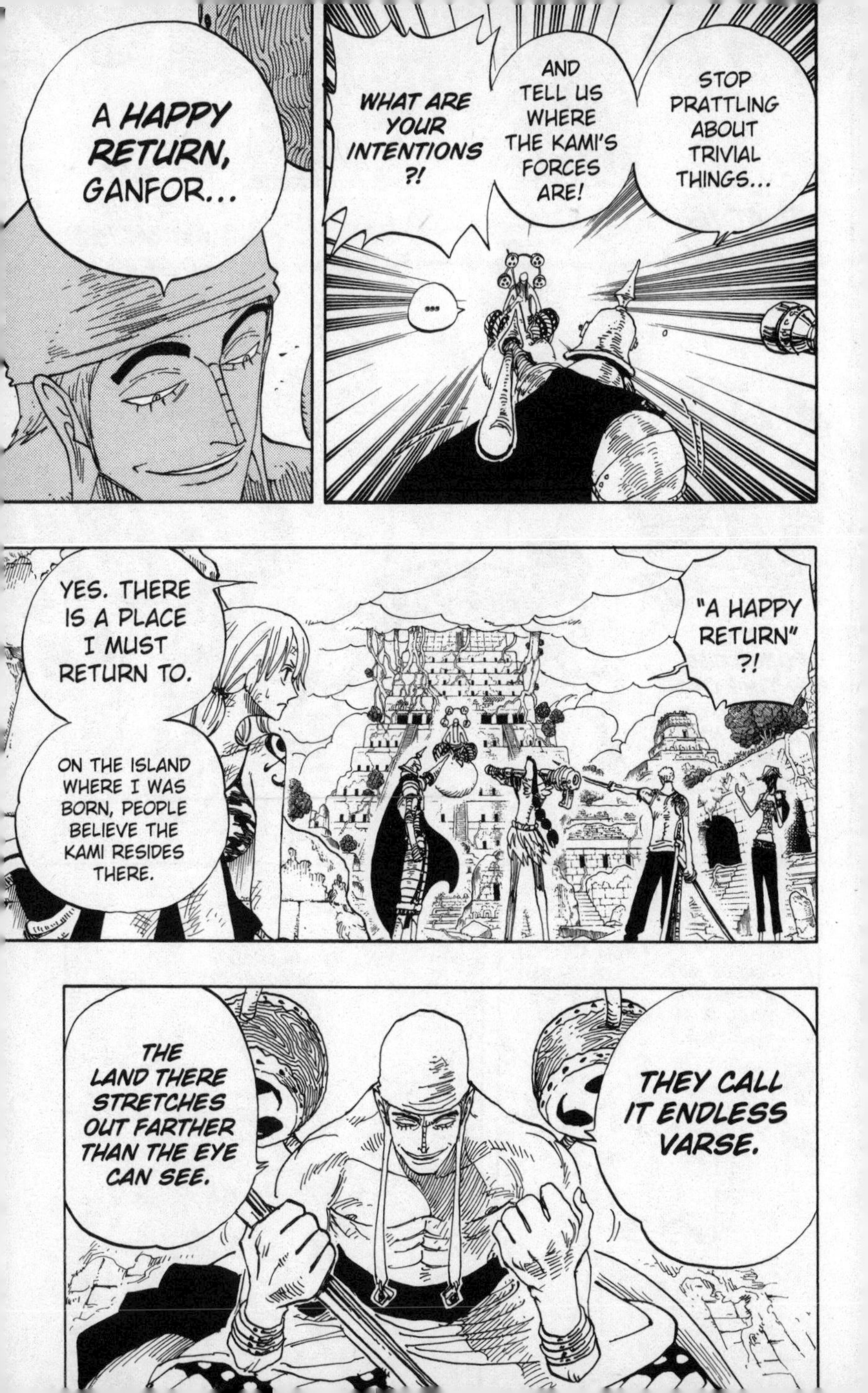
STOP PRATTLING ABOUT TRIVIAL THINGS...
AND TELL US WHERE THE KAMI'S FORCES ARE!
WHAT ARE YOUR INTENTIONS ?!
...
A HAPPY RETURN, GANFOR...
"A HAPPY RETURN" ?!
YES. THERE IS A PLACE I MUST RETURN TO.
ON THE ISLAND WHERE I WAS BORN, PEOPLE BELIEVE THE KAMI RESIDES THERE.
THEY CALL IT ENDLESS VARSE.
THE LAND THERE STRETCHES OUT FARTHER THAN THE EYE CAN SEE.

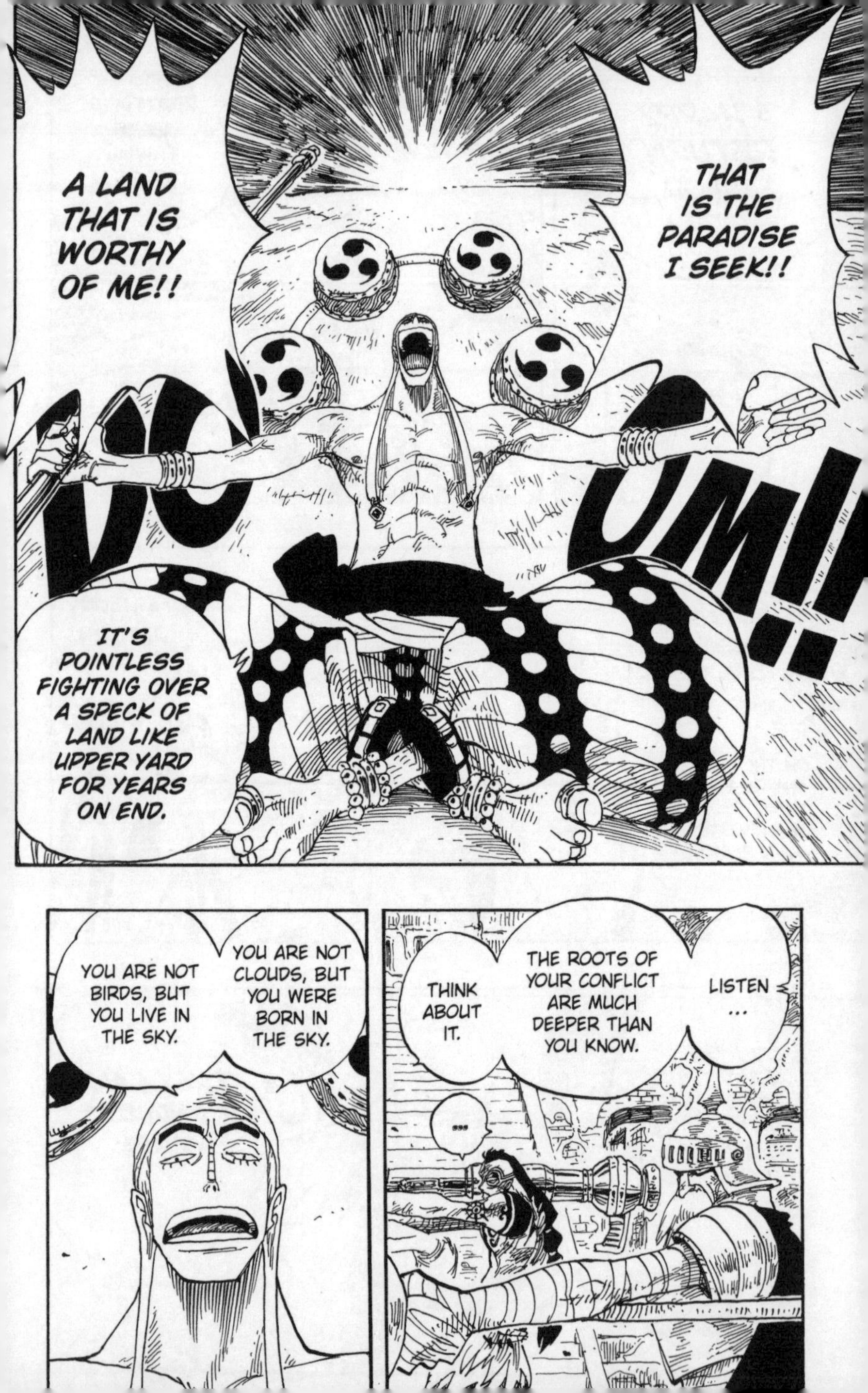
THAT IS THE PARADISE I SEEK!!
A LAND THAT IS WORTHY OF ME!!
VOOM!!
IT'S POINTLESS FIGHTING OVER A SPECK OF LAND LIKE UPPER YARD FOR YEARS ON END.
LISTEN...
THE ROOTS OF YOUR CONFLICT ARE MUCH DEEPER THAN YOU KNOW.
THINK ABOUT IT.
...
YOU ARE NOT CLOUDS, BUT YOU WERE BORN IN THE SKY.
YOU ARE NOT BIRDS, BUT YOU LIVE IN THE SKY.

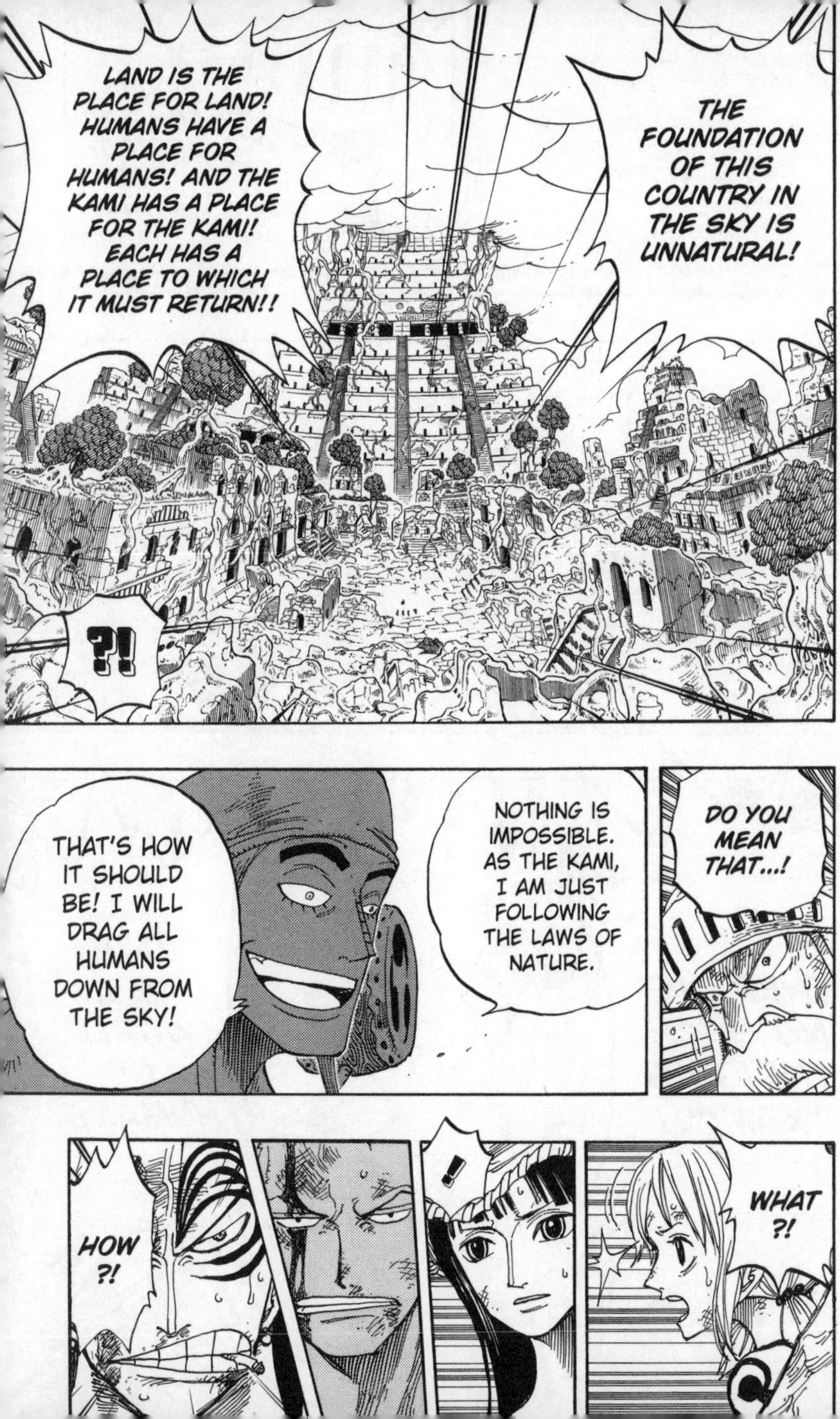
THE FOUNDATION OF THIS COUNTRY IN THE SKY IS UNNATURAL!
LAND IS THE PLACE FOR LAND! HUMANS HAVE A PLACE FOR HUMANS! AND THE KAMI HAS A PLACE FOR THE KAMI! EACH HAS A PLACE TO WHICH IT MUST RETURN!!
?!
DO YOU MEAN THAT...!
NOTHING IS IMPOSSIBLE. AS THE KAMI, I AM JUST FOLLOWING THE LAWS OF NATURE.
THAT'S HOW IT SHOULD BE! I WILL DRAG ALL HUMANS DOWN FROM THE SKY!
WHAT ?!
!
HOW ?!

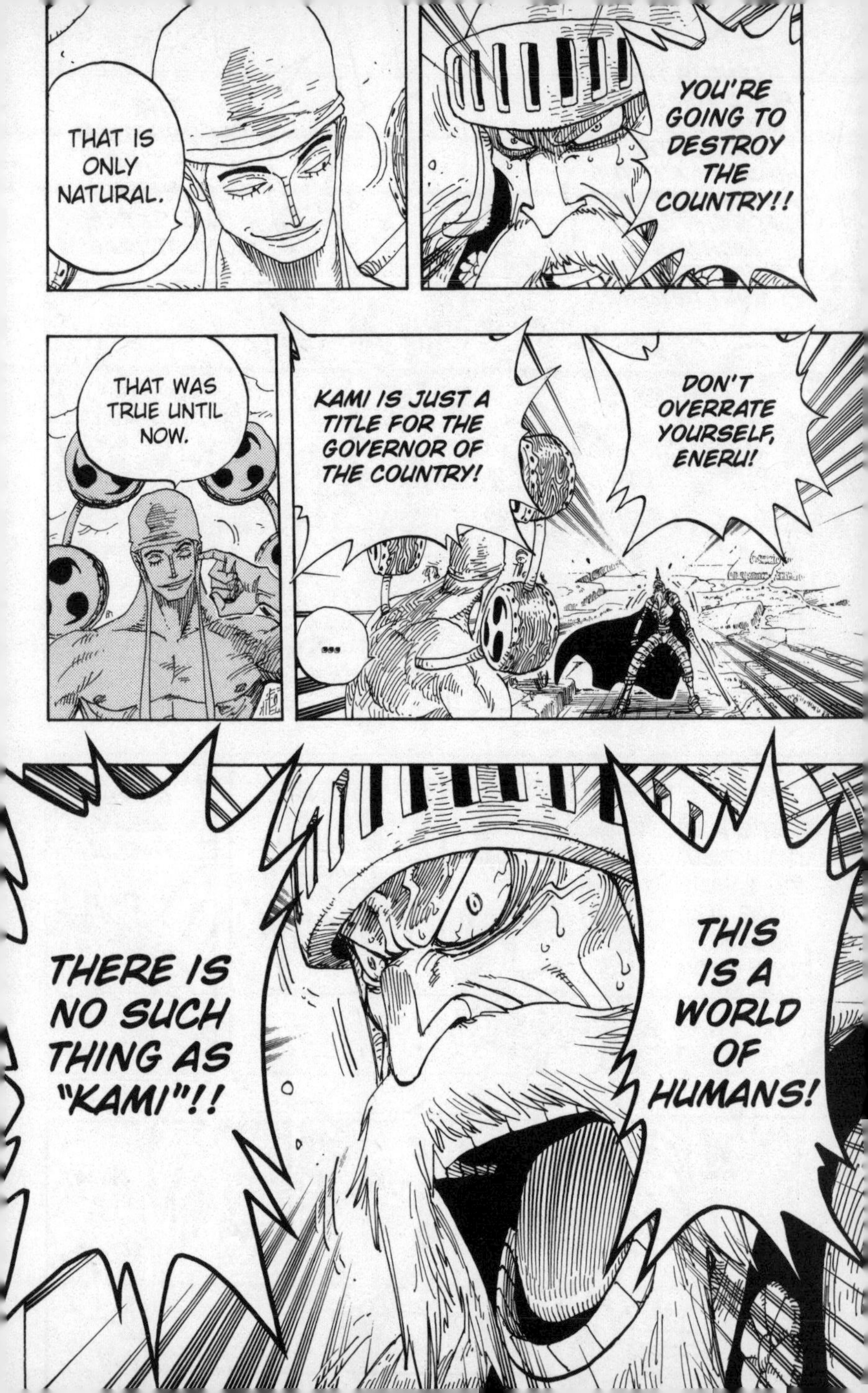
YOU'RE GOING TO DESTROY THE COUNTRY!!
THAT IS ONLY NATURAL.
DON'T OVERRATE YOURSELF, ENERU!
KAMI IS JUST A TITLE FOR THE GOVERNOR OF THE COUNTRY!
...
THAT WAS TRUE UNTIL NOW.
THIS IS A WORLD OF HUMANS!
THERE IS NO SUCH THING AS "KAMI"!!

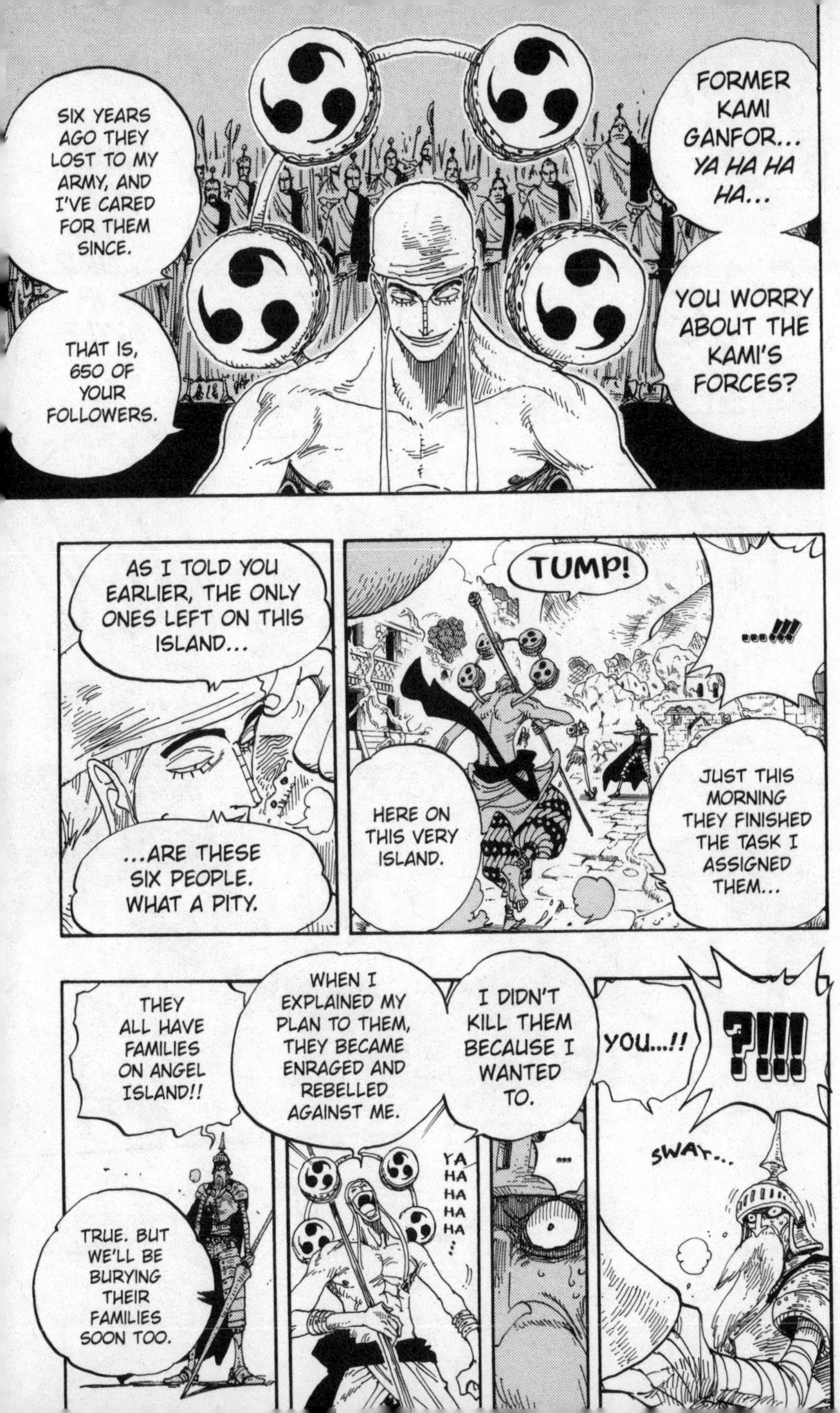
FORMER KAMI GANFOR... YA HA HA HA...
YOU WORRY ABOUT THE KAMI'S FORCES?
SIX YEARS AGO THEY LOST TO MY ARMY, AND I'VE CARED FOR THEM SINCE.
THAT IS, 650 OF YOUR FOLLOWERS.
TUMP!
...!!!
JUST THIS MORNING THEY FINISHED THE TASK I ASSIGNED THEM...
HERE ON THIS VERY ISLAND.
AS I TOLD YOU EARLIER, THE ONLY ONES LEFT ON THIS ISLAND...
...ARE THESE SIX PEOPLE. WHAT A PITY.
?!!!
YOU...!!
SWAY...
I DIDN'T KILL THEM BECAUSE I WANTED TO.
...
WHEN I EXPLAINED MY PLAN TO THEM, THEY BECAME ENRAGED AND REBELLED AGAINST ME.
YA HA HA HA HA HA...
THEY ALL HAVE FAMILIES ON ANGEL ISLAND!!
TRUE. BUT WE'LL BE BURYING THEIR FAMILIES SOON TOO.

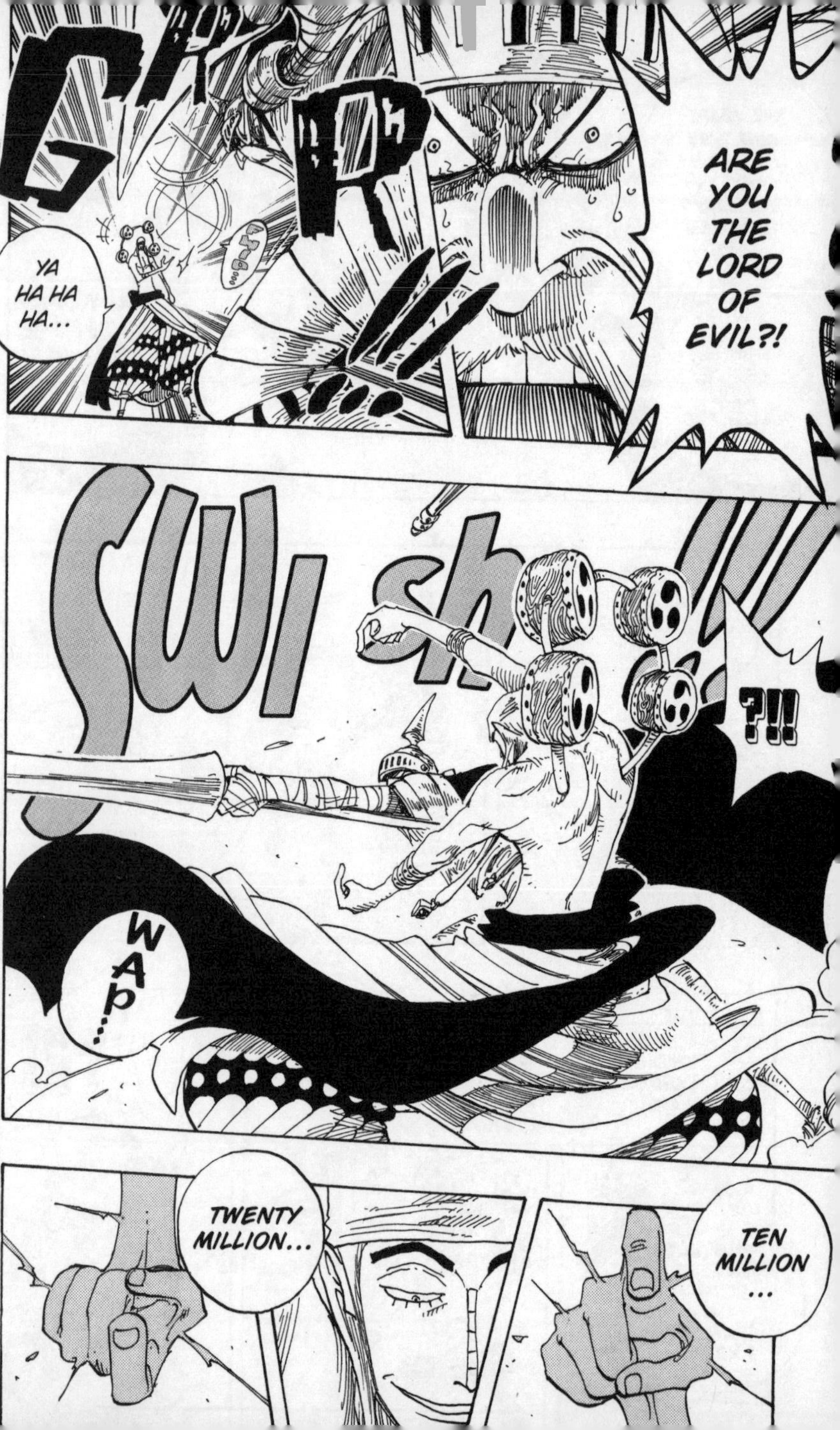
ARE YOU THE LORD OF EVIL?!
GRR
YA HA HA HA...
SWISH
?!!
WAP...
TEN MILLION ...
TWENTY MILLION...

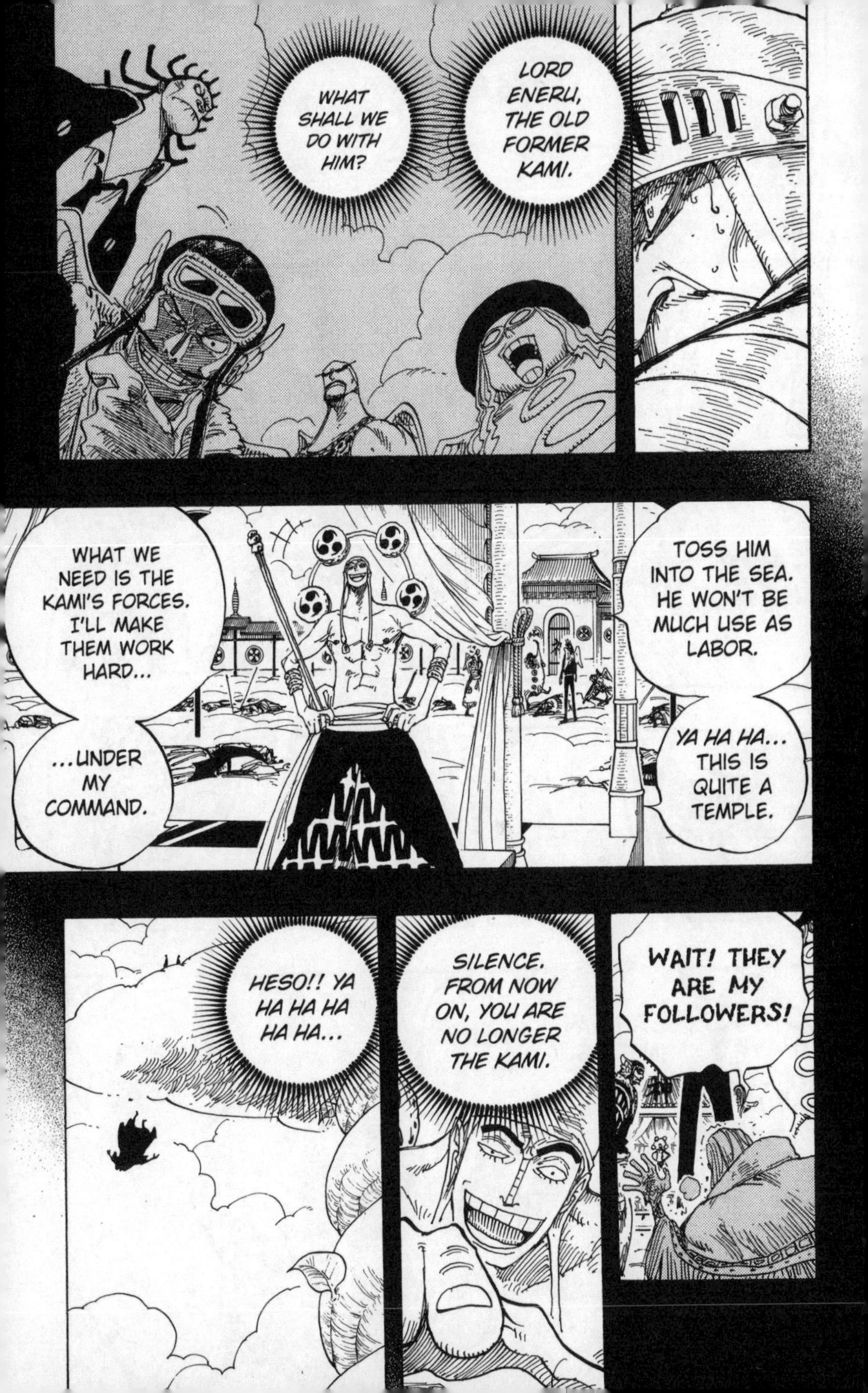
LORD ENERU, THE OLD FORMER KAMI.
WHAT SHALL WE DO WITH HIM?
TOSS HIM INTO THE SEA. HE WON'T BE MUCH USE AS LABOR.
YA HA HA... THIS IS QUITE A TEMPLE.
WHAT WE NEED IS THE KAMI'S FORCES. I'LL MAKE THEM WORK HARD...
...UNDER MY COMMAND.
WAIT! THEY ARE MY FOLLOWERS!
SILENCE. FROM NOW ON, YOU ARE NO LONGER THE KAMI.
HESO!! YA HA HA HA HA HA...

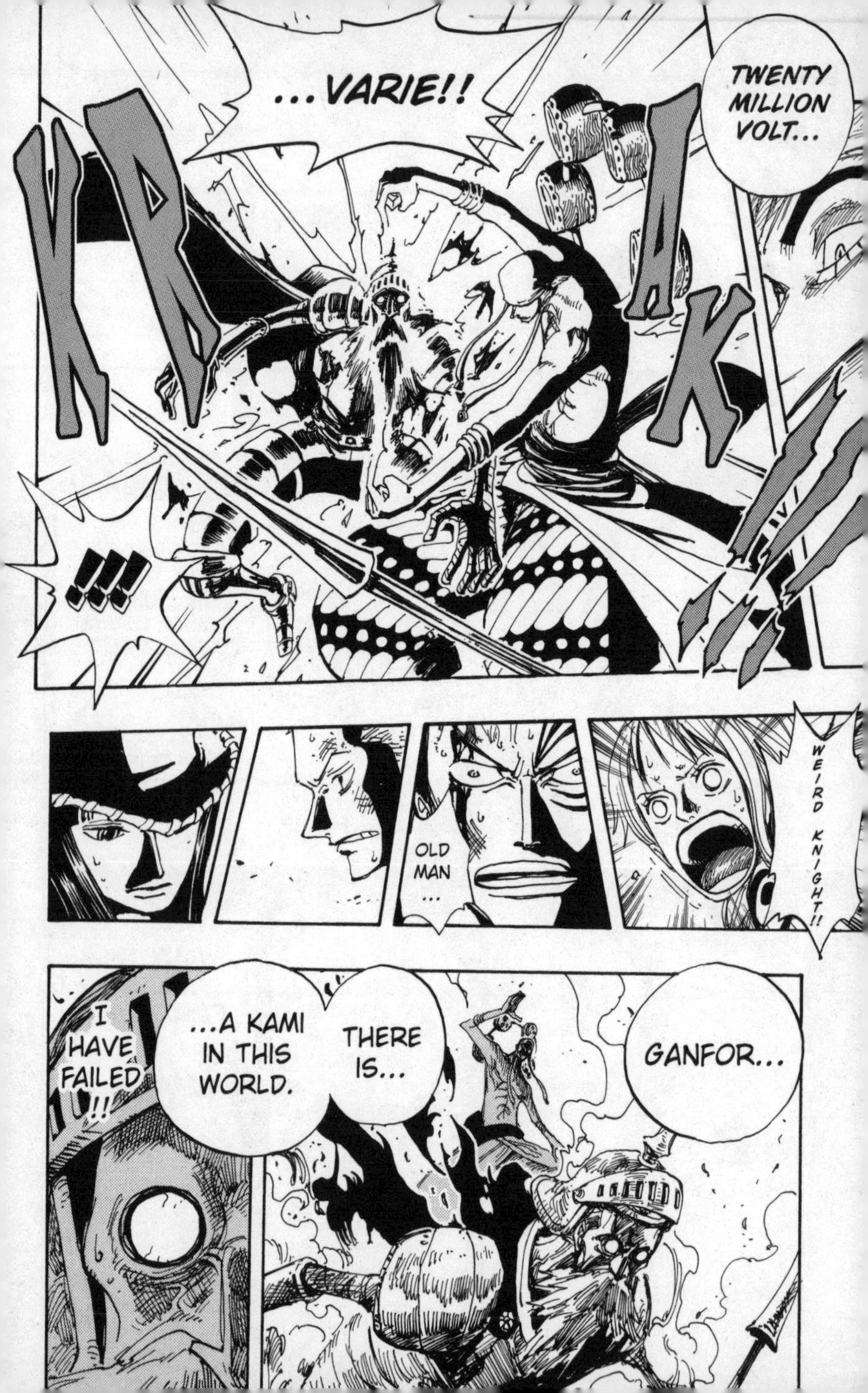
TWENTY MILLION VOLT...
...VARIE!!
KRAK
!!!
WEIRD KNIGHT!!
OLD MAN...
GANFOR...
THERE IS...
...A KAMI IN THIS WORLD.
I HAVE FAILED!!

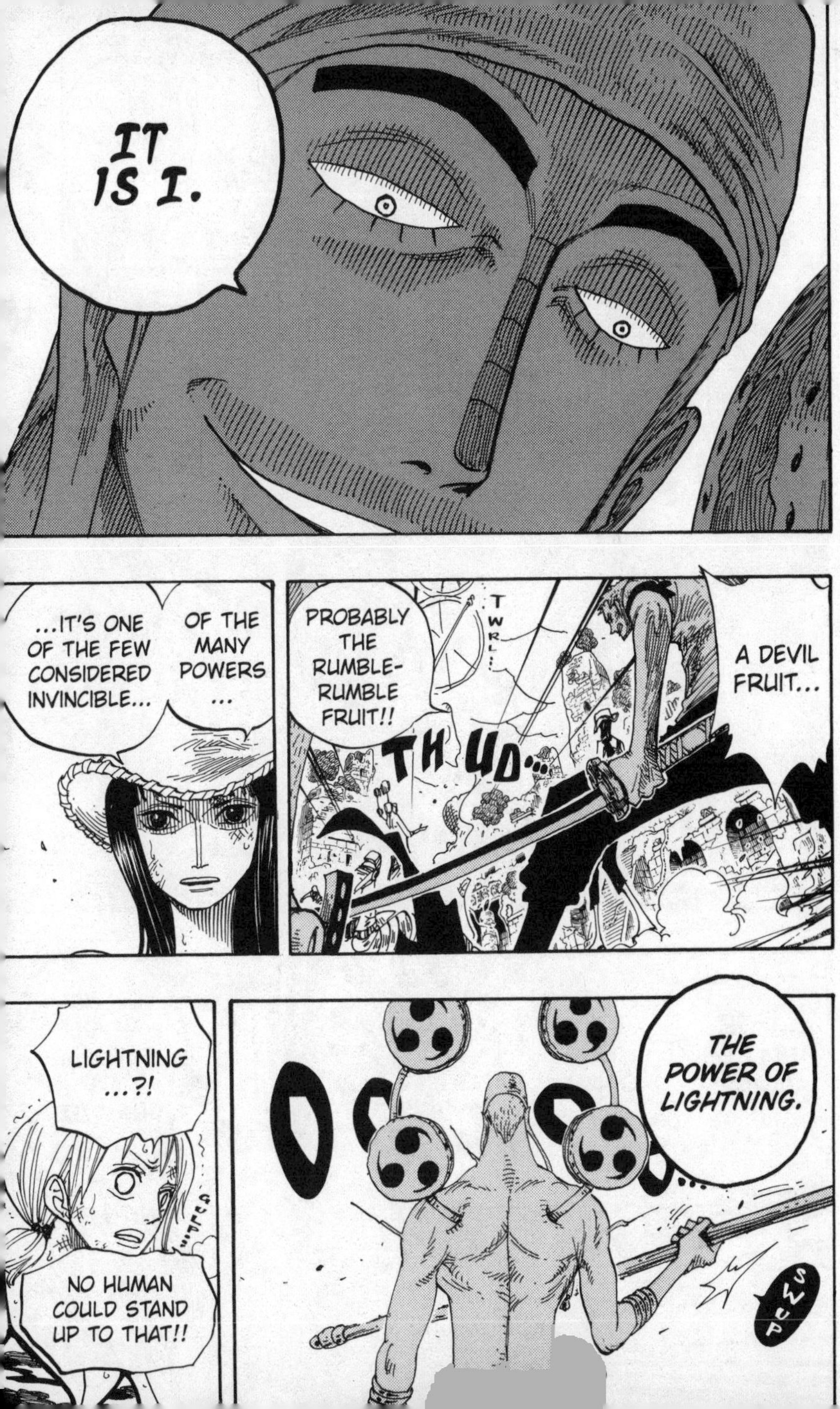
IT IS I.
A DEVIL FRUIT...
PROBABLY THE RUMBLE-RUMBLE FRUIT!!
TWRL...
THUD...
OF THE MANY POWERS...
...IT'S ONE OF THE FEW CONSIDERED INVINCIBLE...
THE POWER OF LIGHTNING.
SWUP
LIGHTNING...?!
GULP...
NO HUMAN COULD STAND UP TO THAT!!

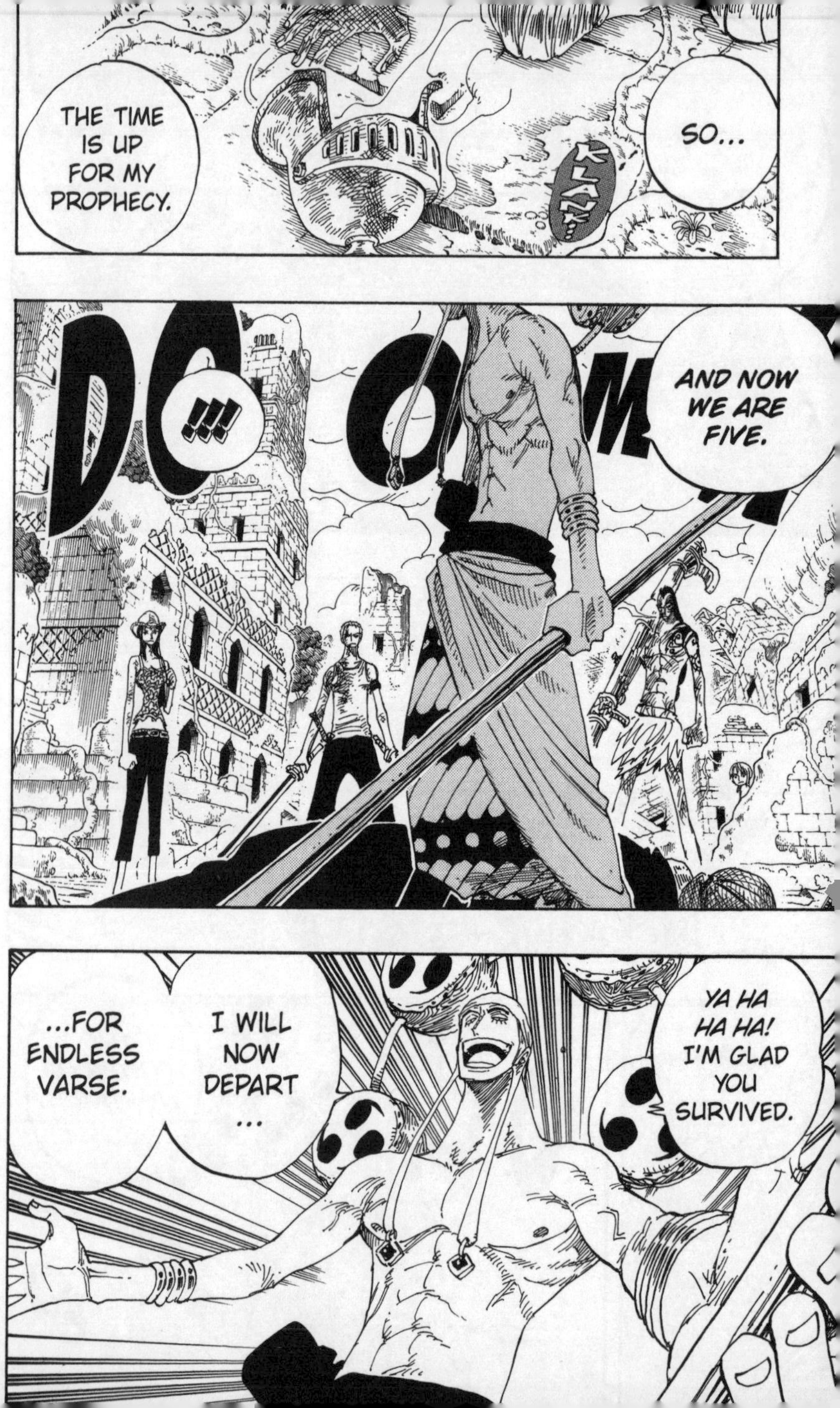
SO...
KLANK...
THE TIME IS UP FOR MY PROPHECY.
AND NOW WE ARE FIVE.
DOOM
!!!
YA HA HA HA! I'M GLAD YOU SURVIVED.
I WILL NOW DEPART...
...FOR ENDLESS VARSE.

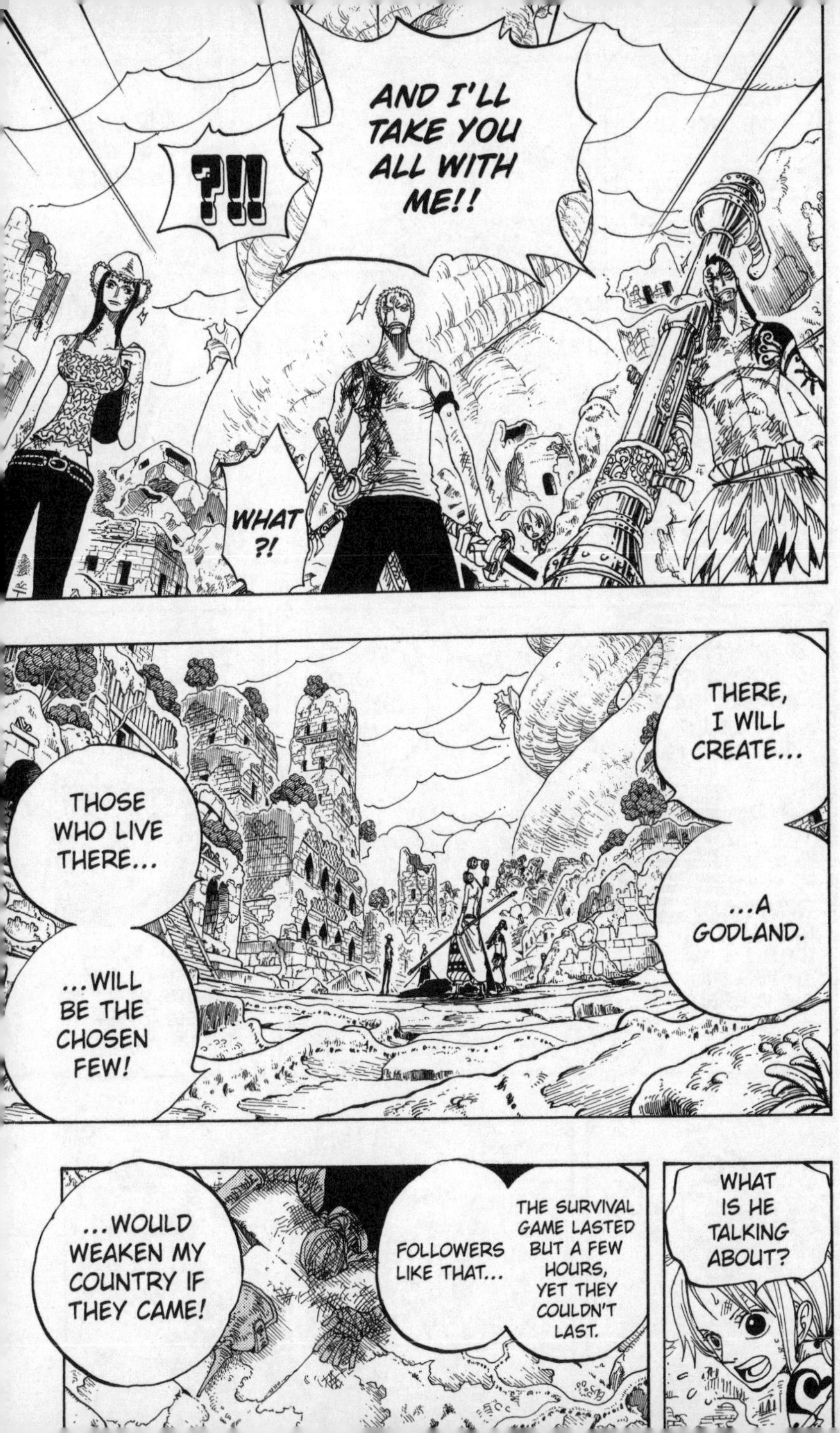
AND I'LL TAKE YOU ALL WITH ME!!
?!!
WHAT ?!
THERE, I WILL CREATE...
...A GODLAND.
THOSE WHO LIVE THERE...
...WILL BE THE CHOSEN FEW!
WHAT IS HE TALKING ABOUT?
THE SURVIVAL GAME LASTED BUT A FEW HOURS, YET THEY COULDN'T LAST.
FOLLOWERS LIKE THAT...
...WOULD WEAKEN MY COUNTRY IF THEY CAME!

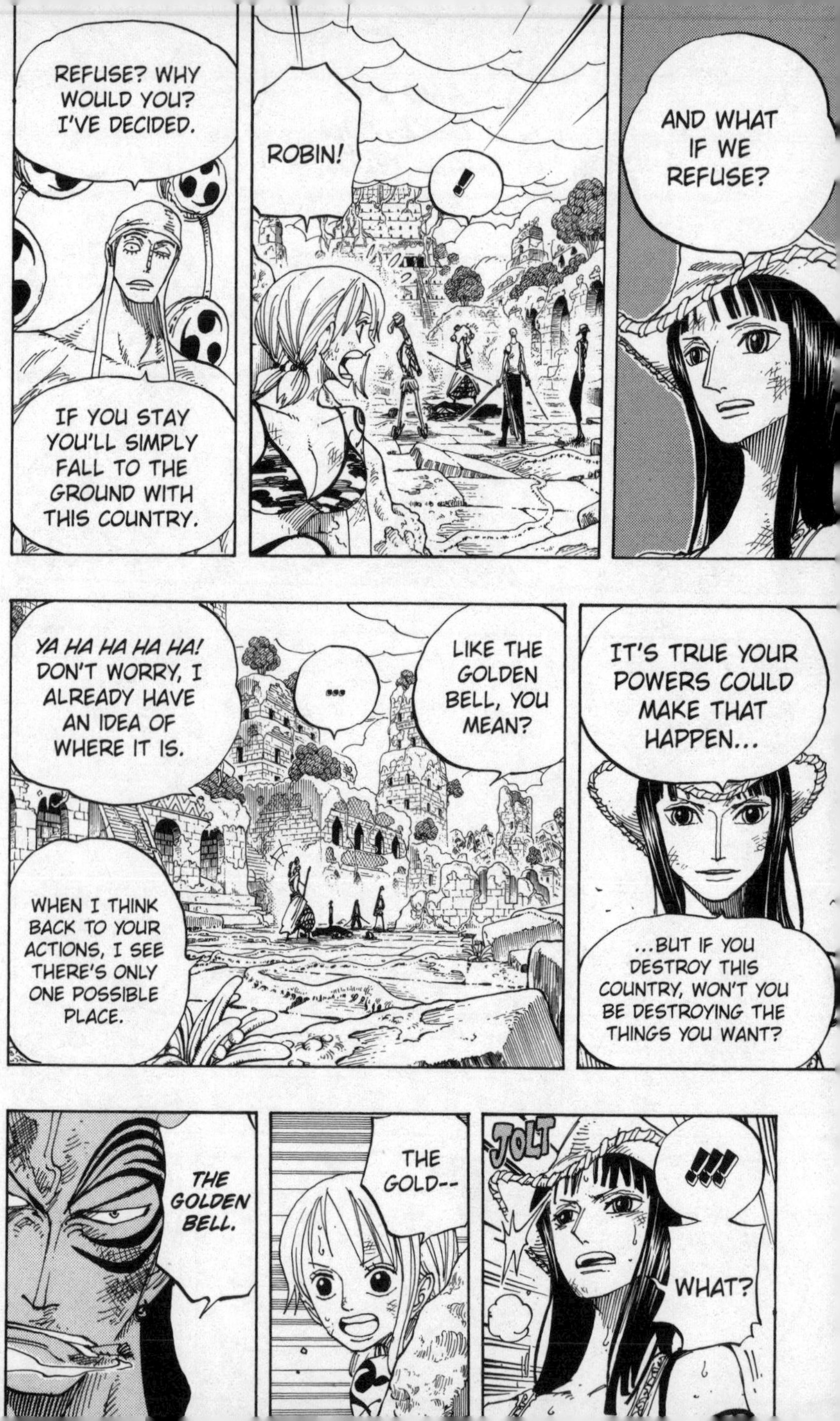
AND WHAT IF WE REFUSE?
ROBIN!
!
REFUSE? WHY WOULD YOU? I'VE DECIDED.
IF YOU STAY YOU'LL SIMPLY FALL TO THE GROUND WITH THIS COUNTRY.
IT'S TRUE YOUR POWERS COULD MAKE THAT HAPPEN...
...BUT IF YOU DESTROY THIS COUNTRY, WON'T YOU BE DESTROYING THE THINGS YOU WANT?
LIKE THE GOLDEN BELL, YOU MEAN?
...
YA HA HA HA HA! DON'T WORRY, I ALREADY HAVE AN IDEA OF WHERE IT IS.
WHEN I THINK BACK TO YOUR ACTIONS, I SEE THERE'S ONLY ONE POSSIBLE PLACE.
JOLT
!!!
WHAT?
THE GOLD--
THE GOLDEN BELL.

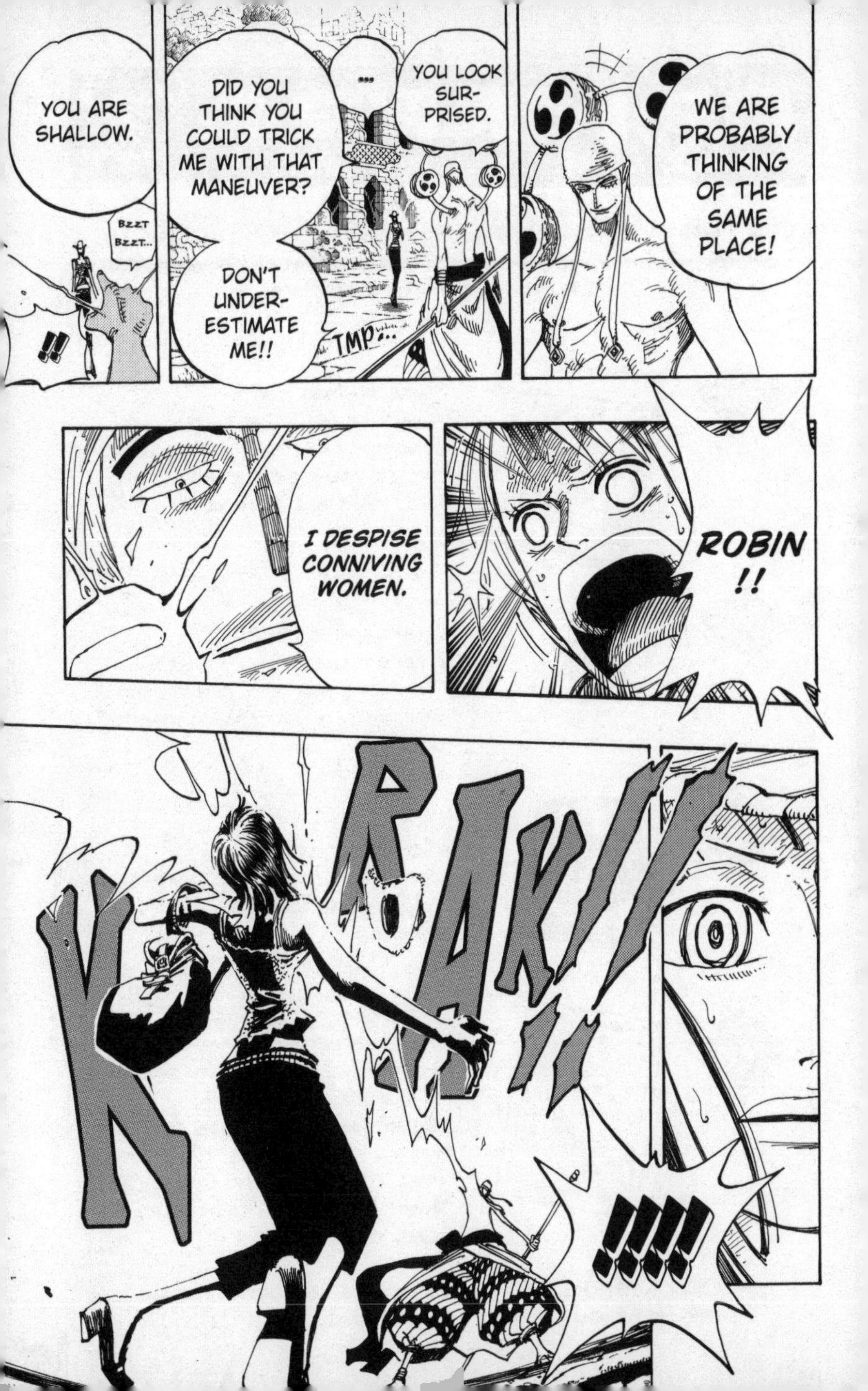
WE ARE PROBABLY THINKING OF THE SAME PLACE!
YOU LOOK SUR- PRISED.
...
DID YOU THINK YOU COULD TRICK ME WITH THAT MANEUVER?
DON'T UNDER- ESTIMATE ME!!
TMP...
YOU ARE SHALLOW.
BZZT BZZT...
!!
ROBIN !!
I DESPISE CONNIVING WOMEN.
!!!!
KRAK!!

GO MANGA
CORNER (SHORTENED TO "GOMA")

Oda: I get a lot of questions about the materials I use for my manga. I'm no specialist (hey!), so I'll just present what I tend to use. To be honest, you can use anything.

Paper

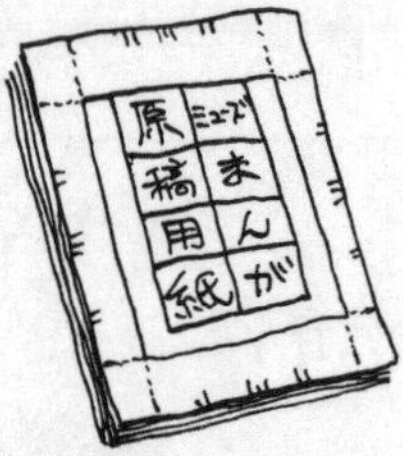
原稿用紙
ミューズ まんが

Muse Manga Paper
A pack has 40 sheets. It's completely white. If you're starting out, it might be better to use paper that has gridlines.

Pen

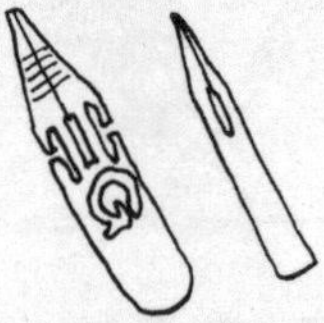

Zebra G Pen (left)
Zebra Round Pen (right)
These are pen nibs. Buy readily available pen holders and insert the nibs.

Ink

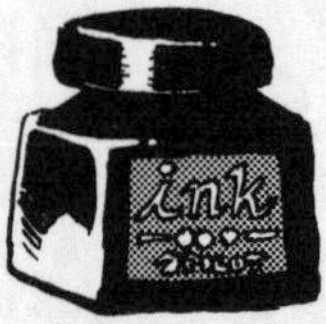
ink

Pilot Business Ink
Opinions seem divided on this. Most people use drafting ink instead.

Tone

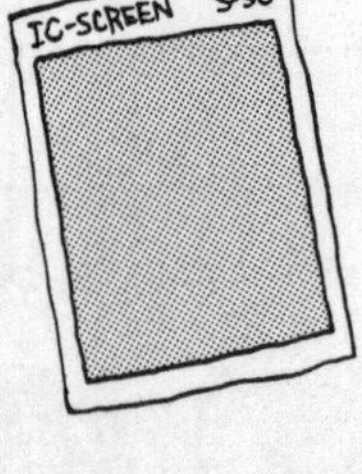
IC-SCREEN
S-50

IC-Screen
This is screen tone. When you read manga and see panels with a light shade, there's a thin sticker-like sheet that's been cut out and pasted there. It's a lot of work for those who use it often. There are lots of techniques for using it, too.

Okay, with this information you can become a manga artist. All you need is the technique.

Chapter 275:
DIVINA COMMEDIA

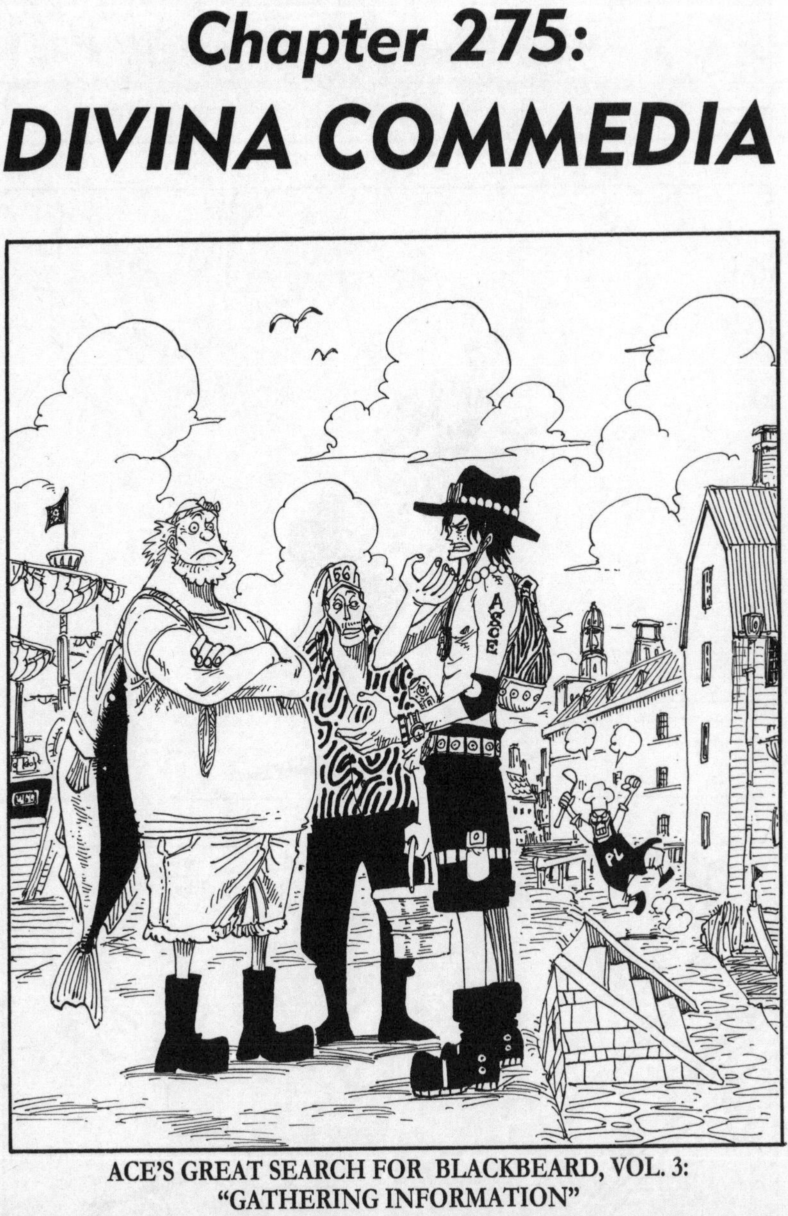
ACE

ACE'S GREAT SEARCH FOR BLACKBEARD, VOL. 3:
"GATHERING INFORMATION"

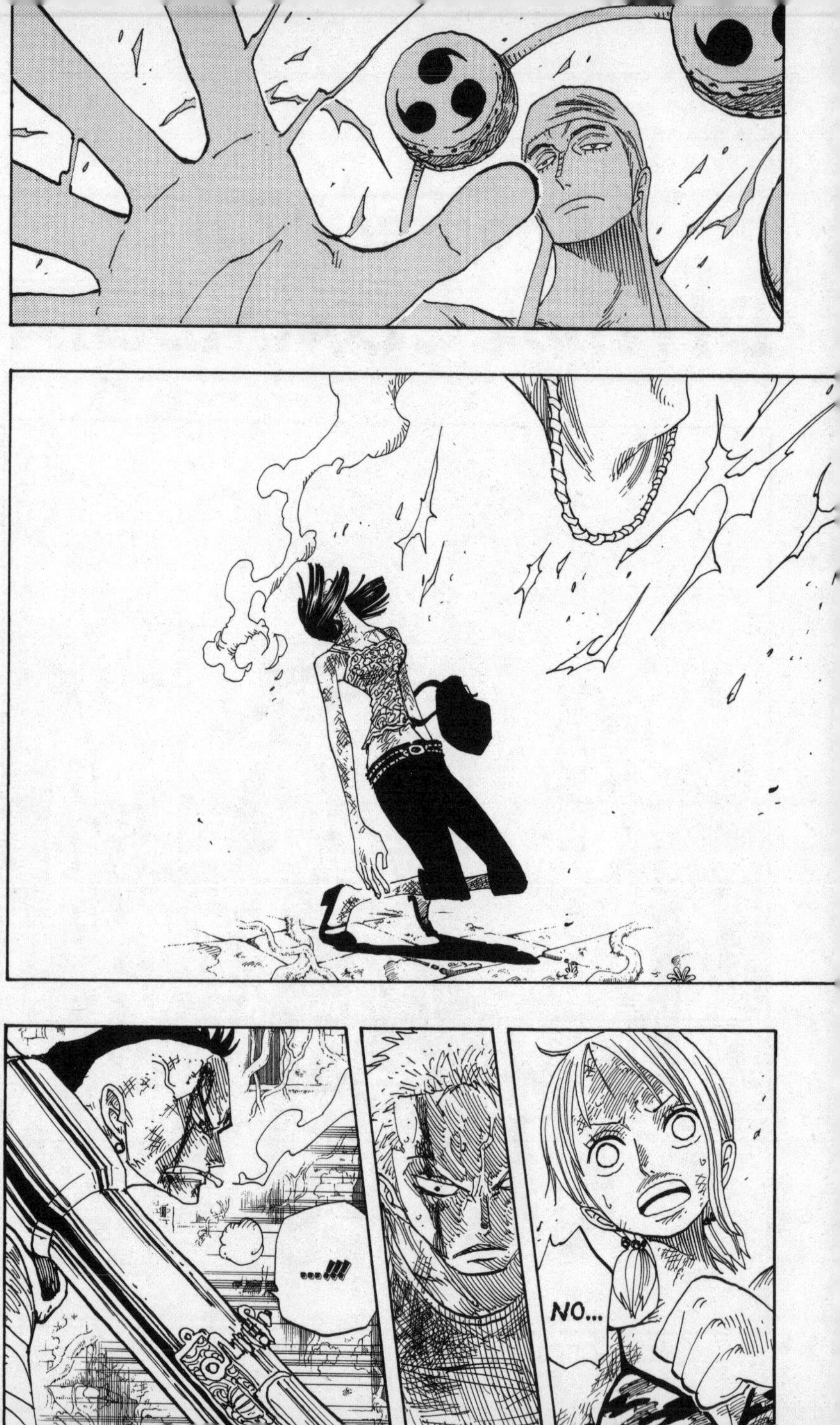
NO...
...!!!

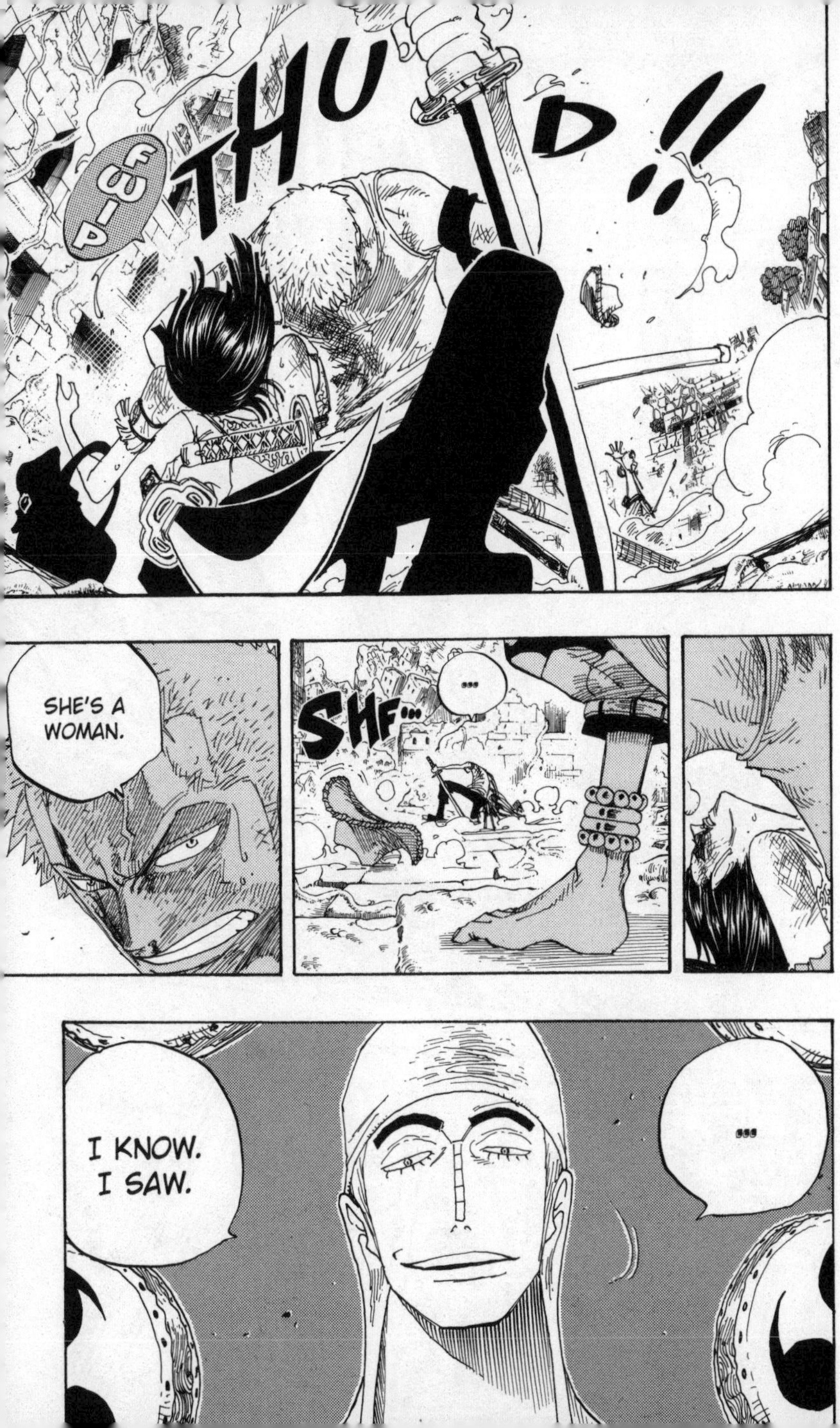
THUD!!
FWIP
...
SHF...
SHE'S A WOMAN.
...
I KNOW. I SAW.

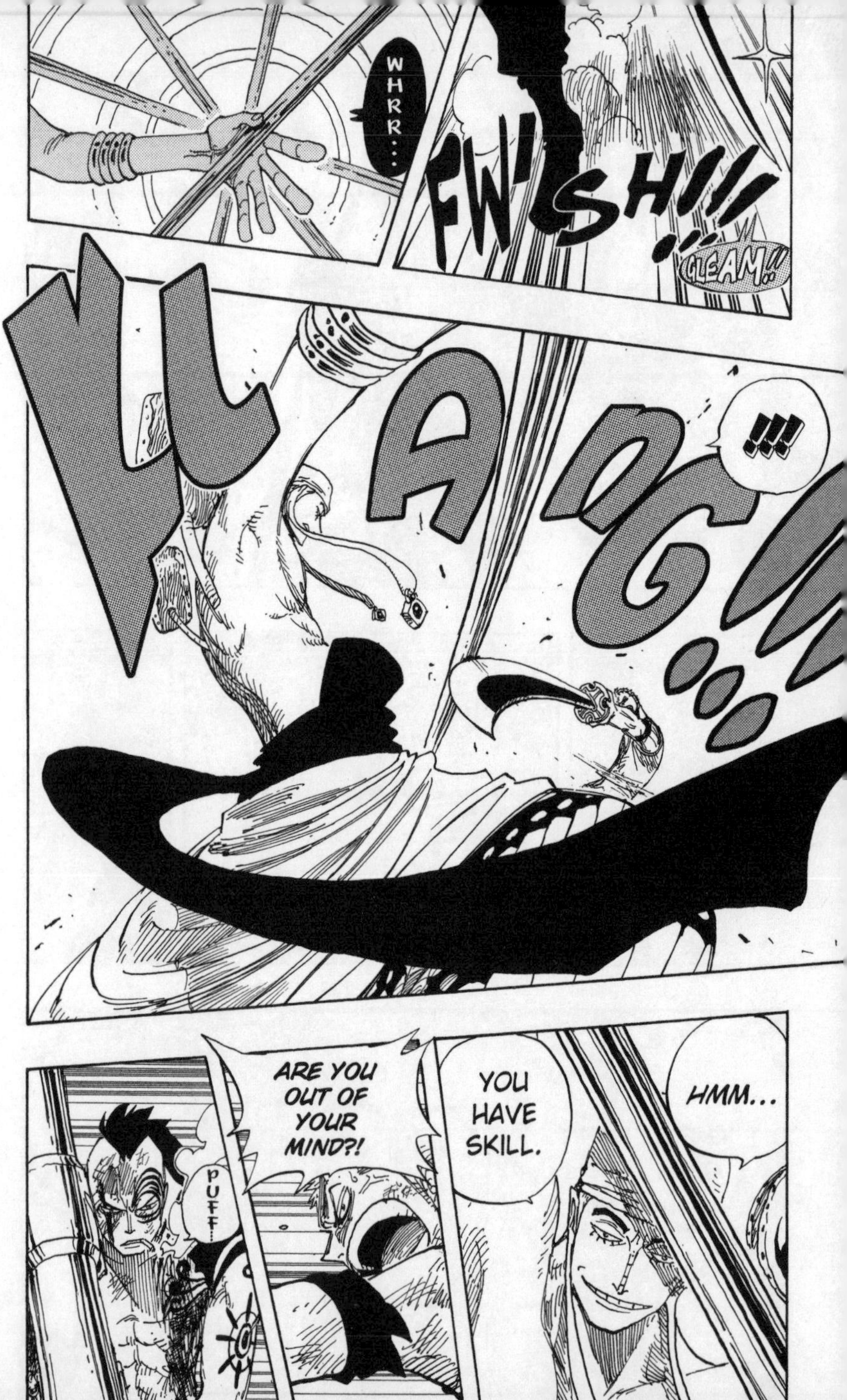
FW'SH!!
GLEAM!!
WHRR...
KLANG!!
!!!
HMM...
YOU HAVE SKILL.
ARE YOU OUT OF YOUR MIND?!
PUFF...

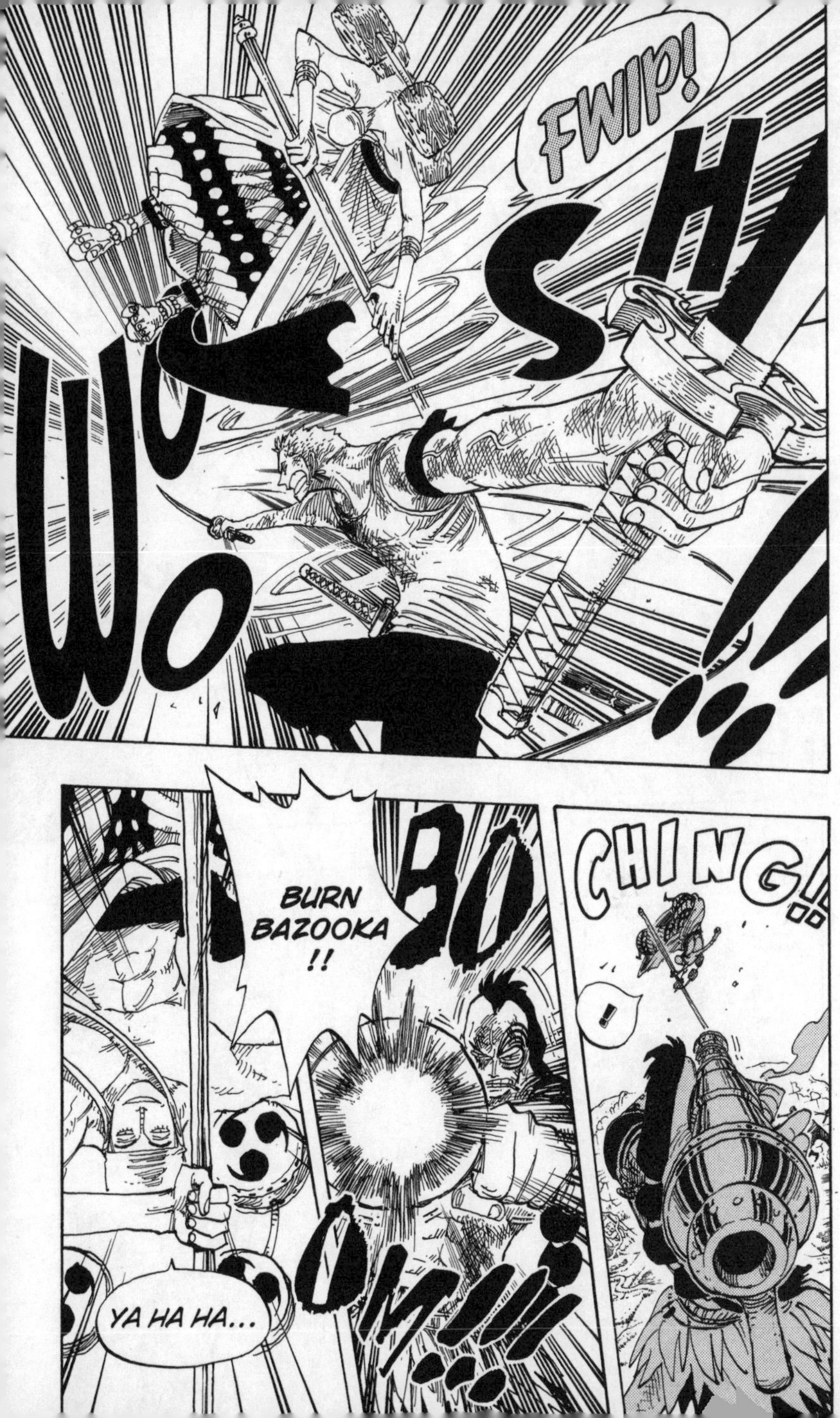
FWIP!
WOOSH!!
CHING!!
!
BURN BAZOOKA!!
BOOM!!!
YA HA HA...

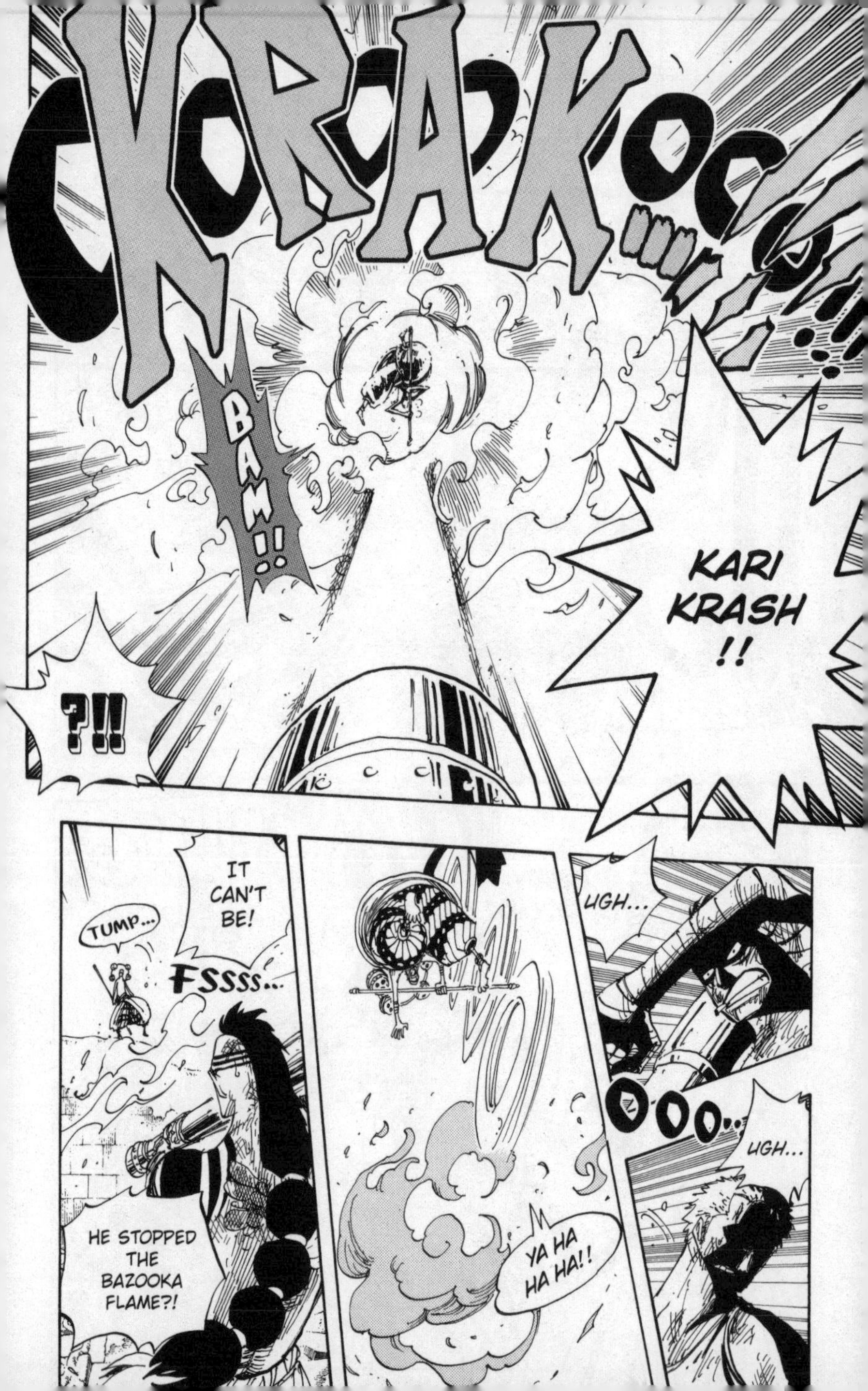
KRAKOO!!!
KARI KRASH !!
BAM!!
?!!
UGH...
OOO...
UGH...
YA HA HA HA!!
IT CAN'T BE!
TUMP...
FSSSS...
HE STOPPED THE BAZOOKA FLAME?!

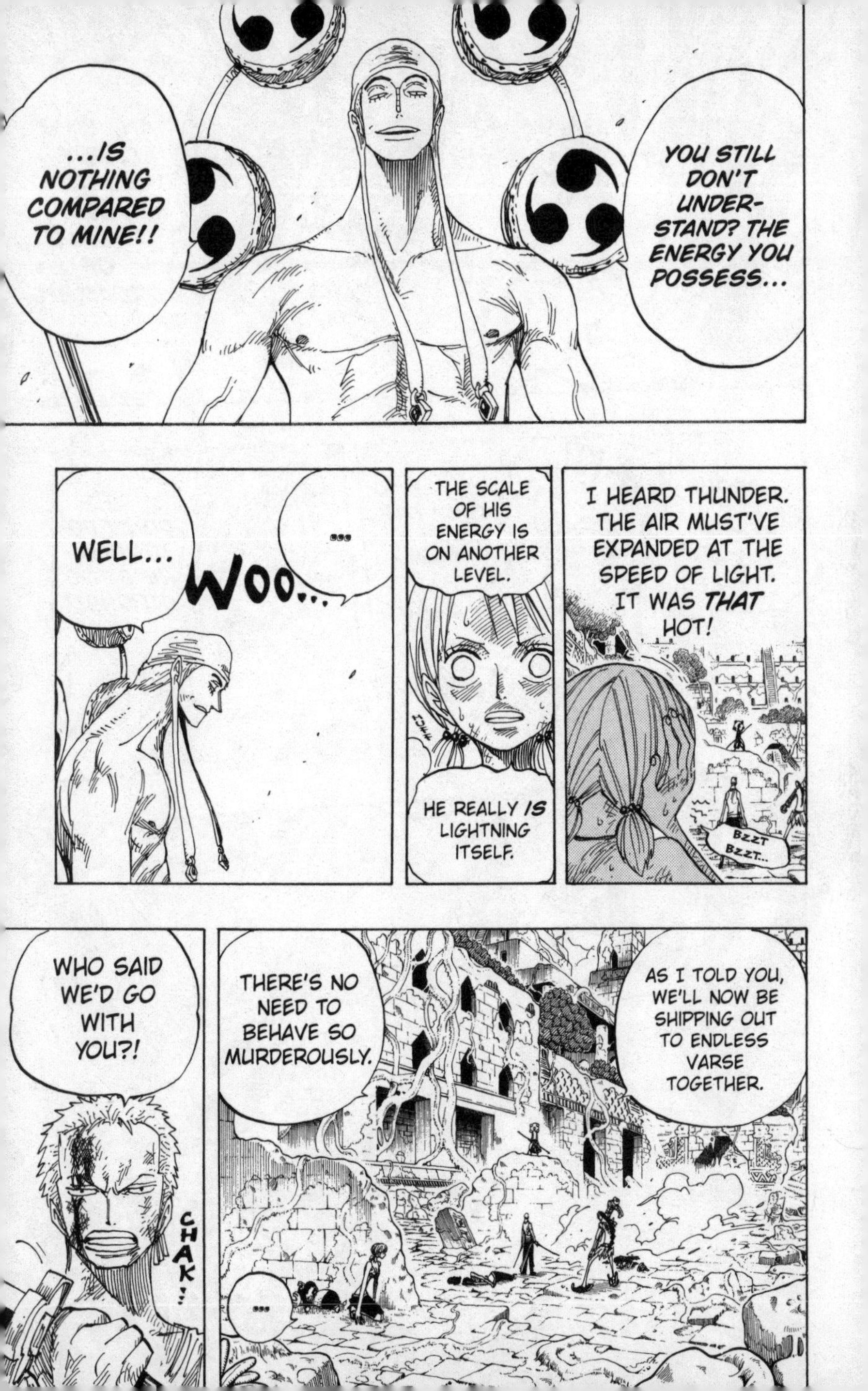
YOU STILL DON'T UNDER-STAND? THE ENERGY YOU POSSESS...
...IS NOTHING COMPARED TO MINE!!
I HEARD THUNDER. THE AIR MUST'VE EXPANDED AT THE SPEED OF LIGHT. IT WAS *THAT* HOT!
BZZT BZZT...
THE SCALE OF HIS ENERGY IS ON ANOTHER LEVEL.
HE REALLY *IS* LIGHTNING ITSELF.
...
WELL...
WOO...
AS I TOLD YOU, WE'LL NOW BE SHIPPING OUT TO ENDLESS VARSE TOGETHER.
THERE'S NO NEED TO BEHAVE SO MURDEROUSLY.
...
WHO SAID WE'D GO WITH YOU?!
CHAK!!

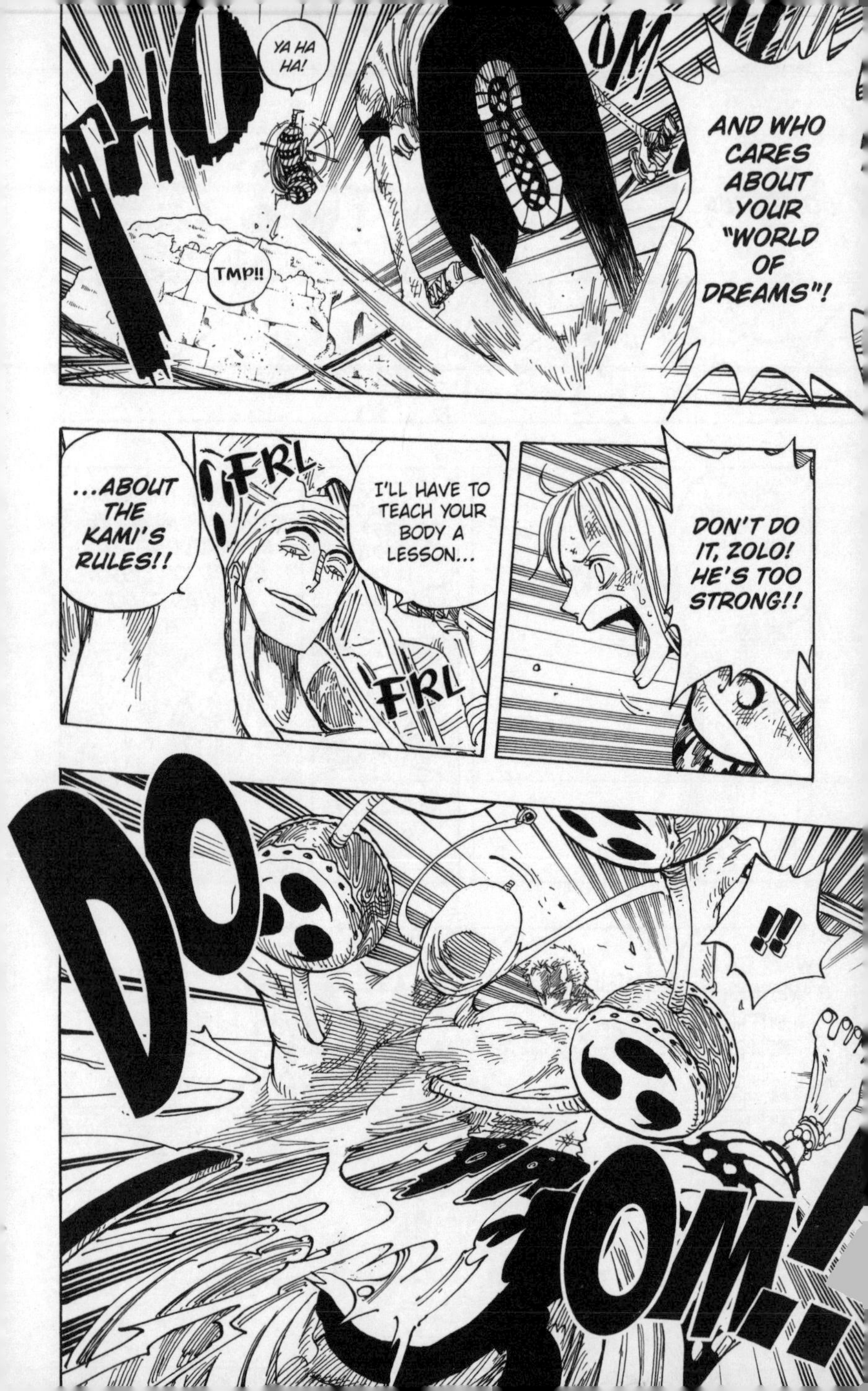
AND WHO CARES ABOUT YOUR "WORLD OF DREAMS"!
YA HA HA!
THOOOM
TMP!!
DON'T DO IT, ZOLO! HE'S TOO STRONG!!
I'LL HAVE TO TEACH YOUR BODY A LESSON...
FRL
...ABOUT THE KAMI'S RULES!!
FRL
!!
DOOOM!!

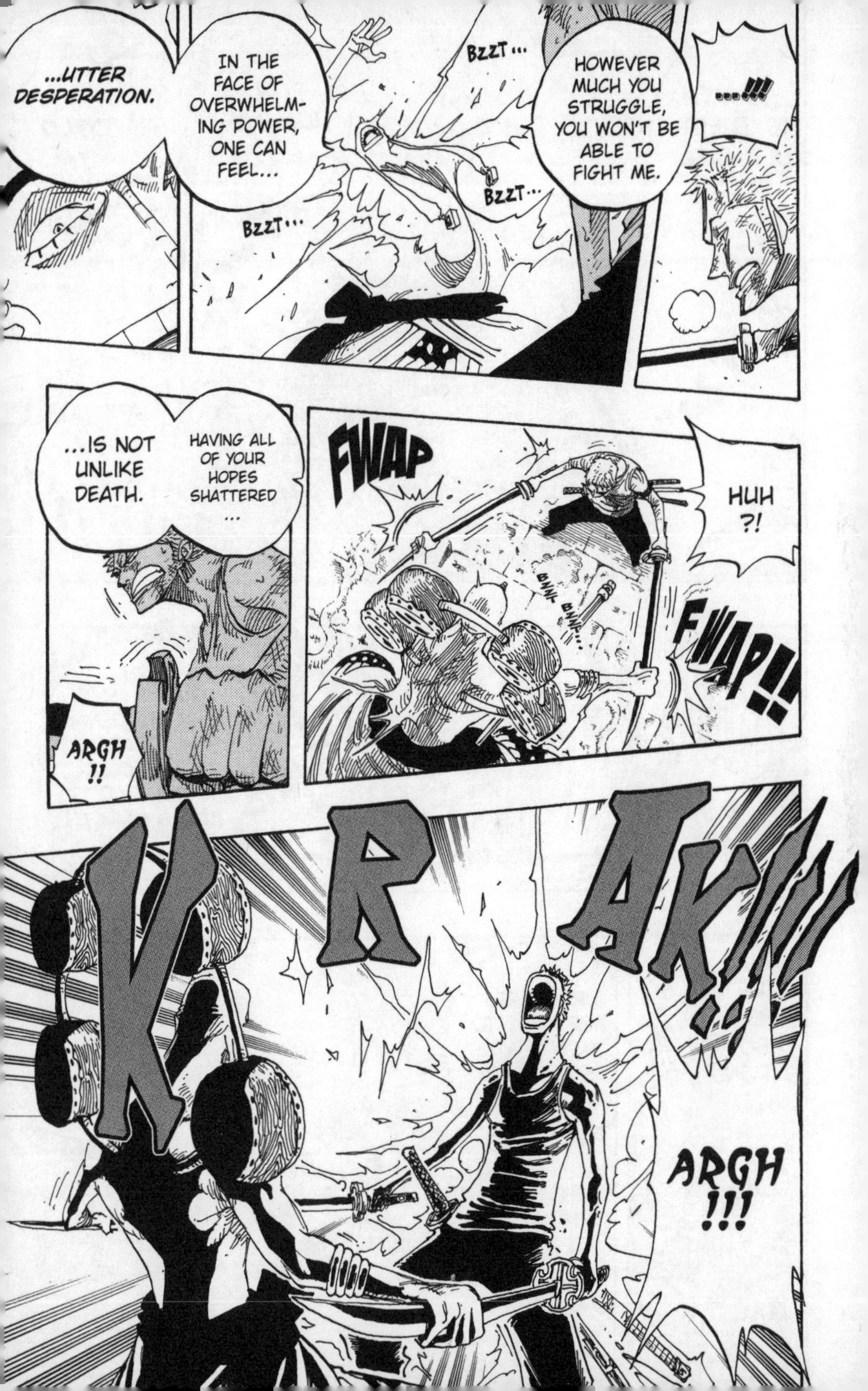
...!!!
HOWEVER MUCH YOU STRUGGLE, YOU WON'T BE ABLE TO FIGHT ME.
BZZT...
IN THE FACE OF OVERWHELMING POWER, ONE CAN FEEL...
BZZT...
BZZT...
...UTTER DESPERATION.
HUH ?!
FWAP
BZZT
BZZT...
FWAP!!
HAVING ALL OF YOUR HOPES SHATTERED ...
...IS NOT UNLIKE DEATH.
ARGH !!
KRAK!!!
ARGH !!!

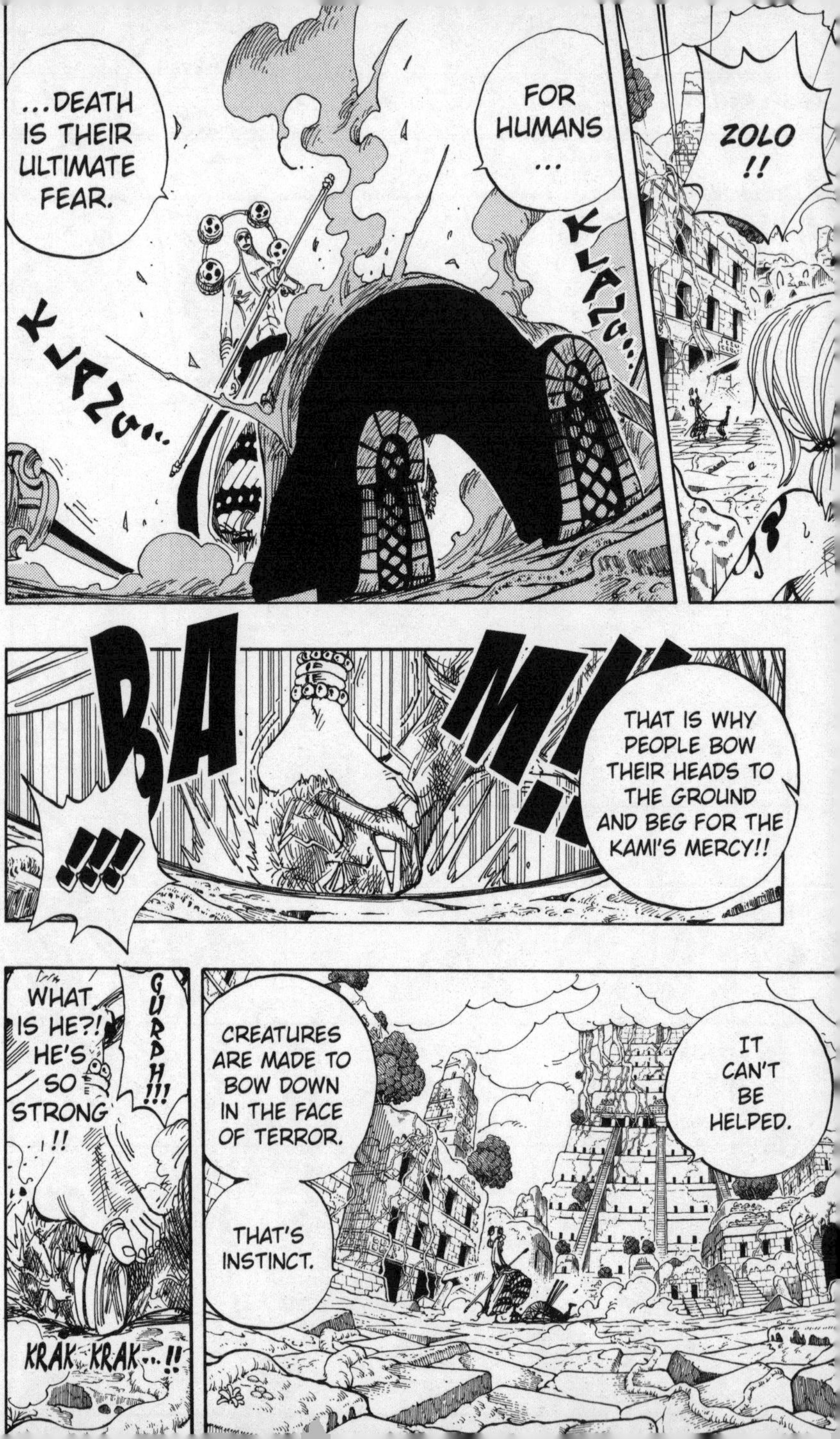
ZOLO!!
FOR HUMANS...
KLANG...
...DEATH IS THEIR ULTIMATE FEAR.
KLANG...
BAM!!!!
THAT IS WHY PEOPLE BOW THEIR HEADS TO THE GROUND AND BEG FOR THE KAMI'S MERCY!!
IT CAN'T BE HELPED.
CREATURES ARE MADE TO BOW DOWN IN THE FACE OF TERROR.
THAT'S INSTINCT.
GURPH!!!
WHAT IS HE?! HE'S SO STRONG!!
KRAK KRAK...!!

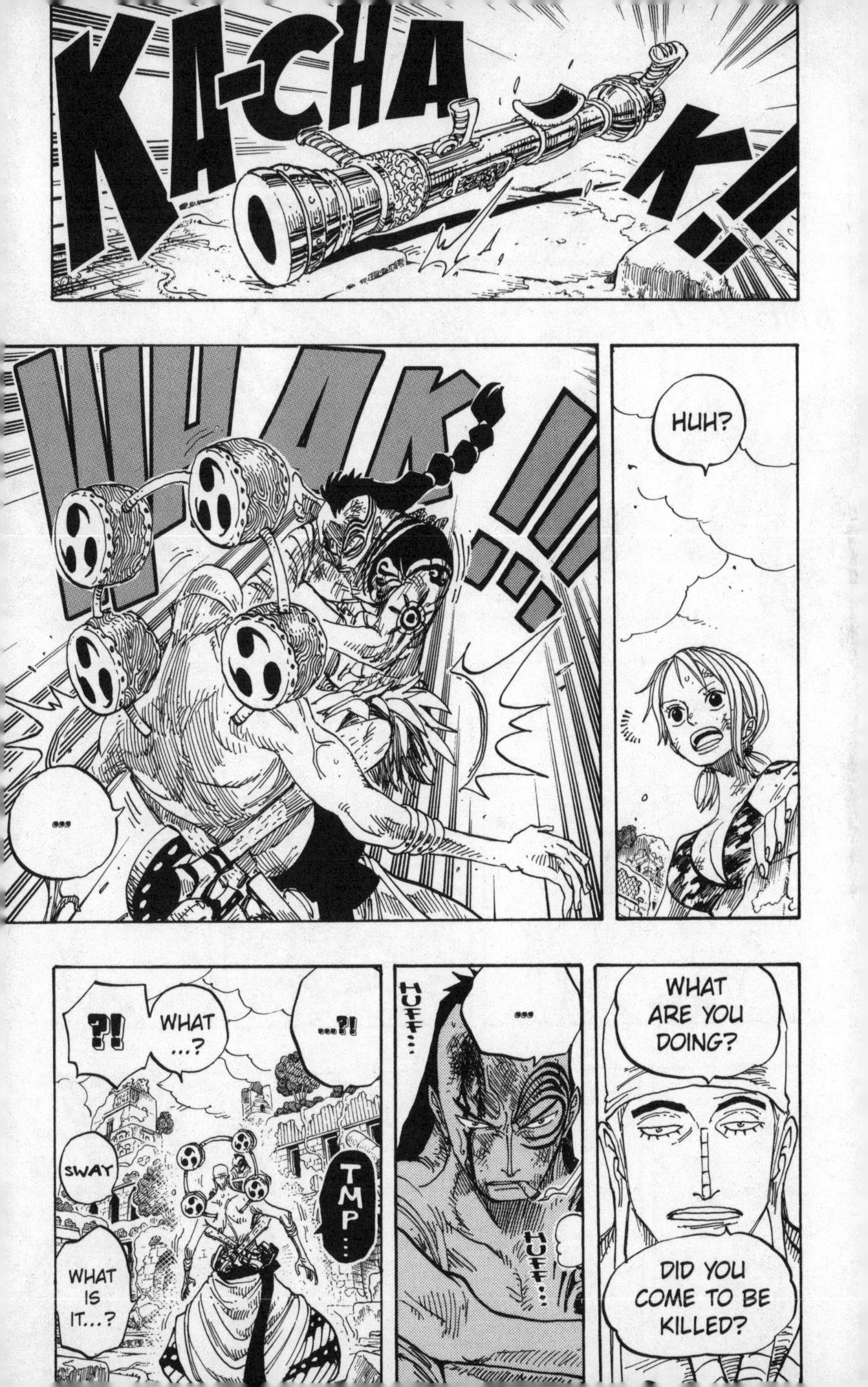
KA-CHAK!!
HUH?
WHAK!!
...
WHAT ARE YOU DOING?
DID YOU COME TO BE KILLED?
HUFF...
...
HUFF...
...?!
WHAT ...?
?!
TMP...
SWAY
WHAT IS IT...?

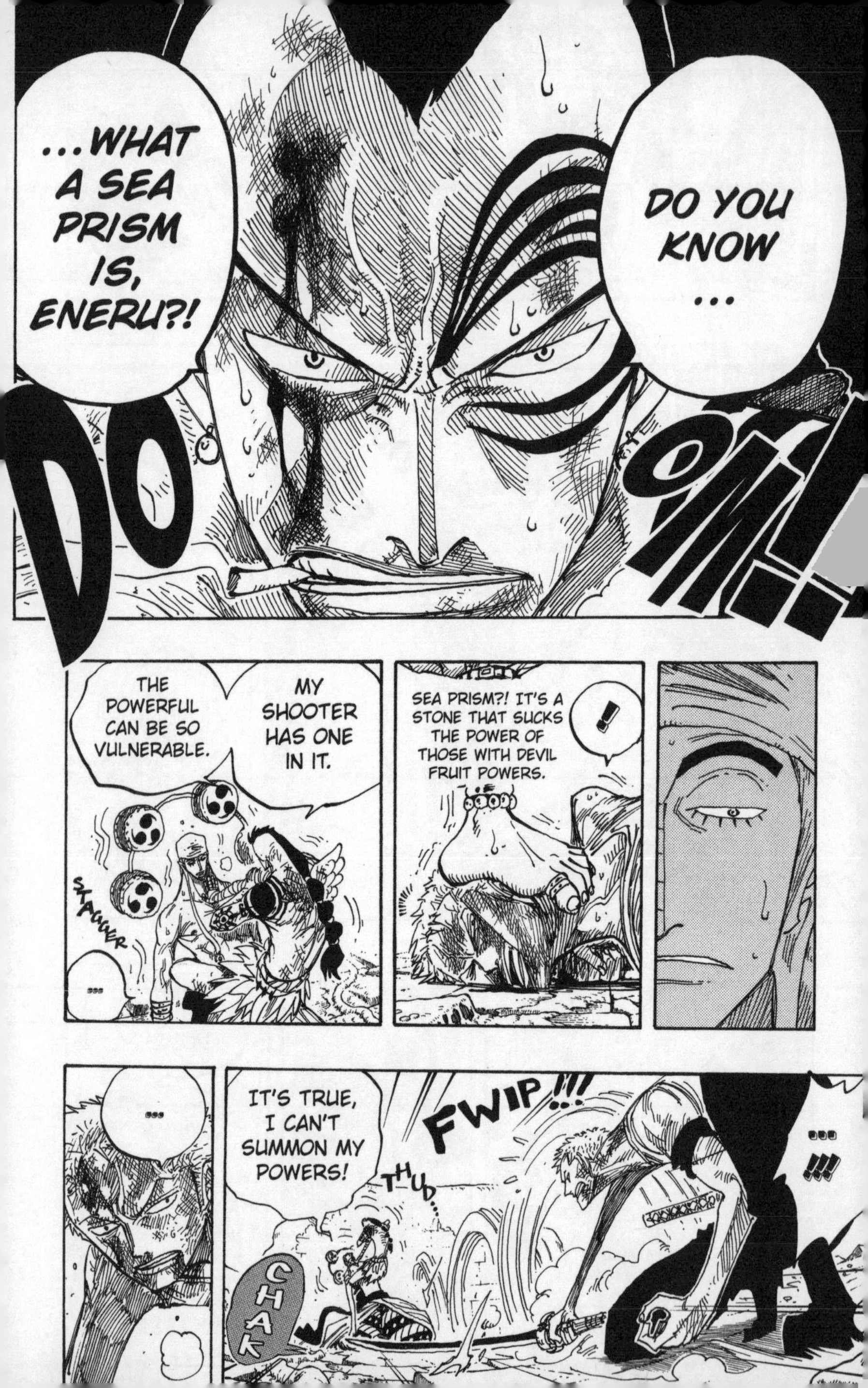
DO YOU KNOW ...
...WHAT A SEA PRISM IS, ENERU?!
DOON!!
SEA PRISM?! IT'S A STONE THAT SUCKS THE POWER OF THOSE WITH DEVIL FRUIT POWERS.
!
MY SHOOTER HAS ONE IN IT.
THE POWERFUL CAN BE SO VULNERABLE.
STAGGER
...
...!!!
FWIP!!!
IT'S TRUE, I CAN'T SUMMON MY POWERS!
THUD...
CHAK
...

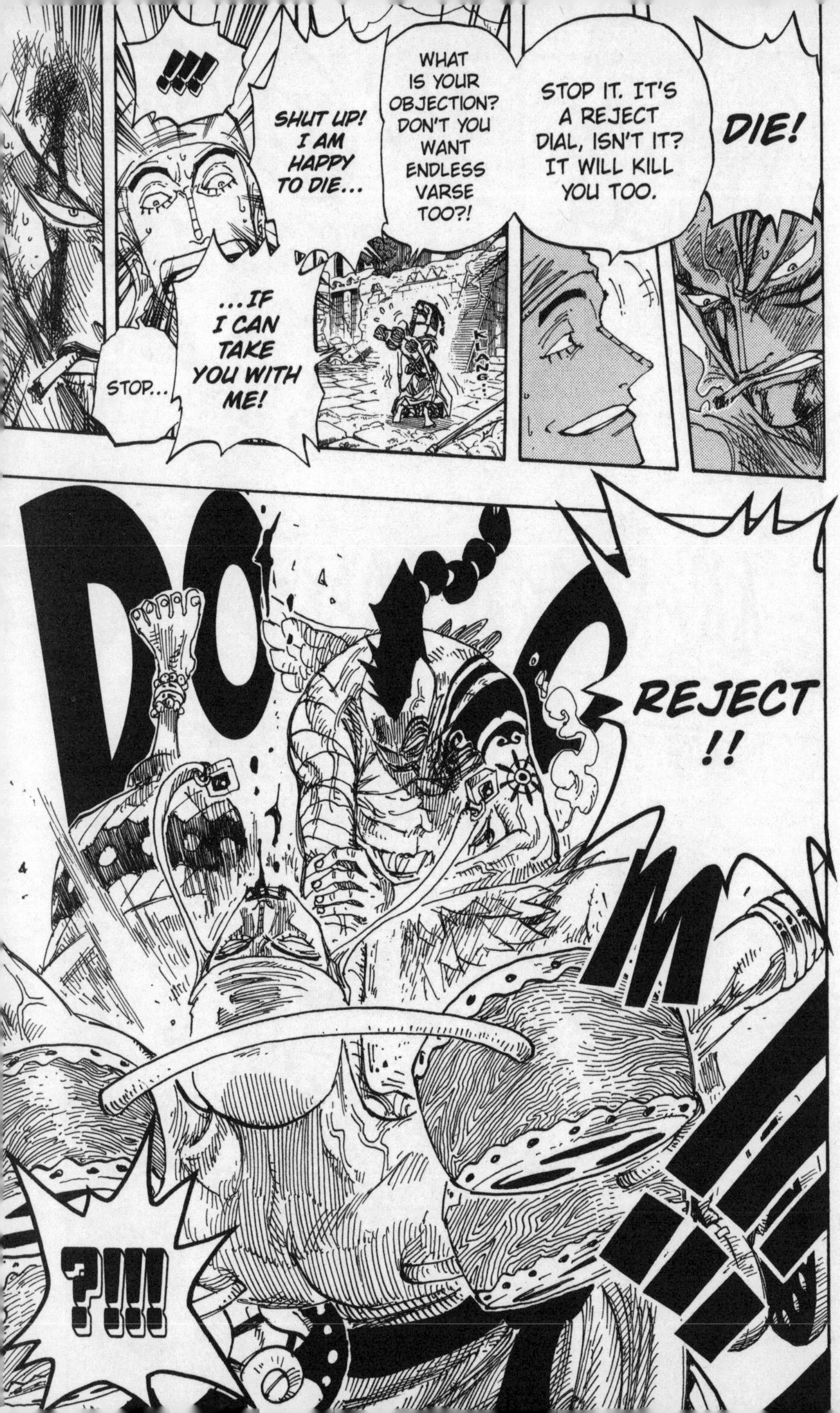
DIE!
STOP IT. IT'S A REJECT DIAL, ISN'T IT? IT WILL KILL YOU TOO.
WHAT IS YOUR OBJECTION? DON'T YOU WANT ENDLESS VARSE TOO?!
KLANG...
!!!
SHUT UP! I AM HAPPY TO DIE...
...IF I CAN TAKE YOU WITH ME!
STOP...
REJECT !!
DOOM
?!!!

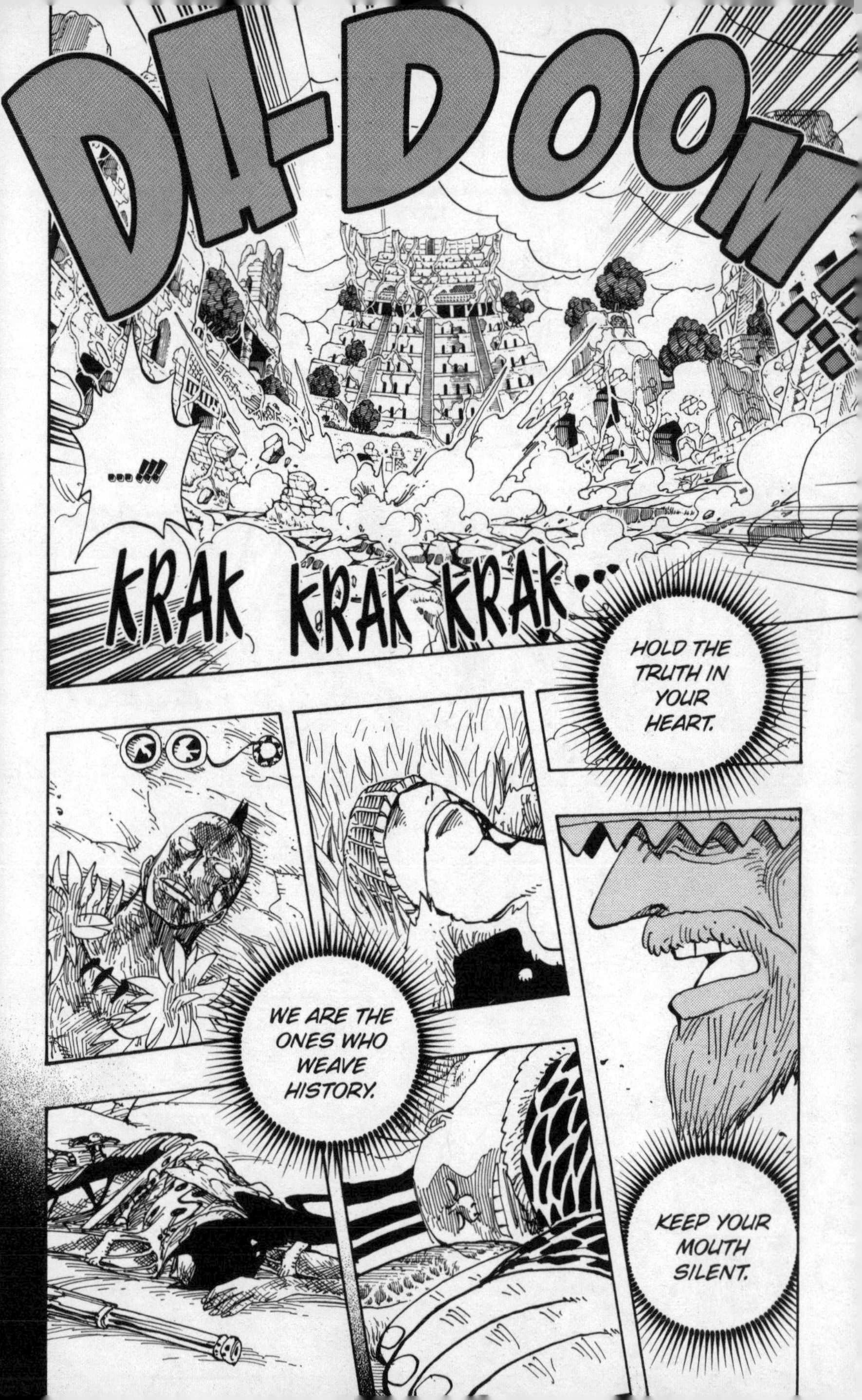
DA-DOOM!!
...!!!
KRAK KRAK KRAK...
HOLD THE TRUTH IN YOUR HEART.
WE ARE THE ONES WHO WEAVE HISTORY.
KEEP YOUR MOUTH SILENT.

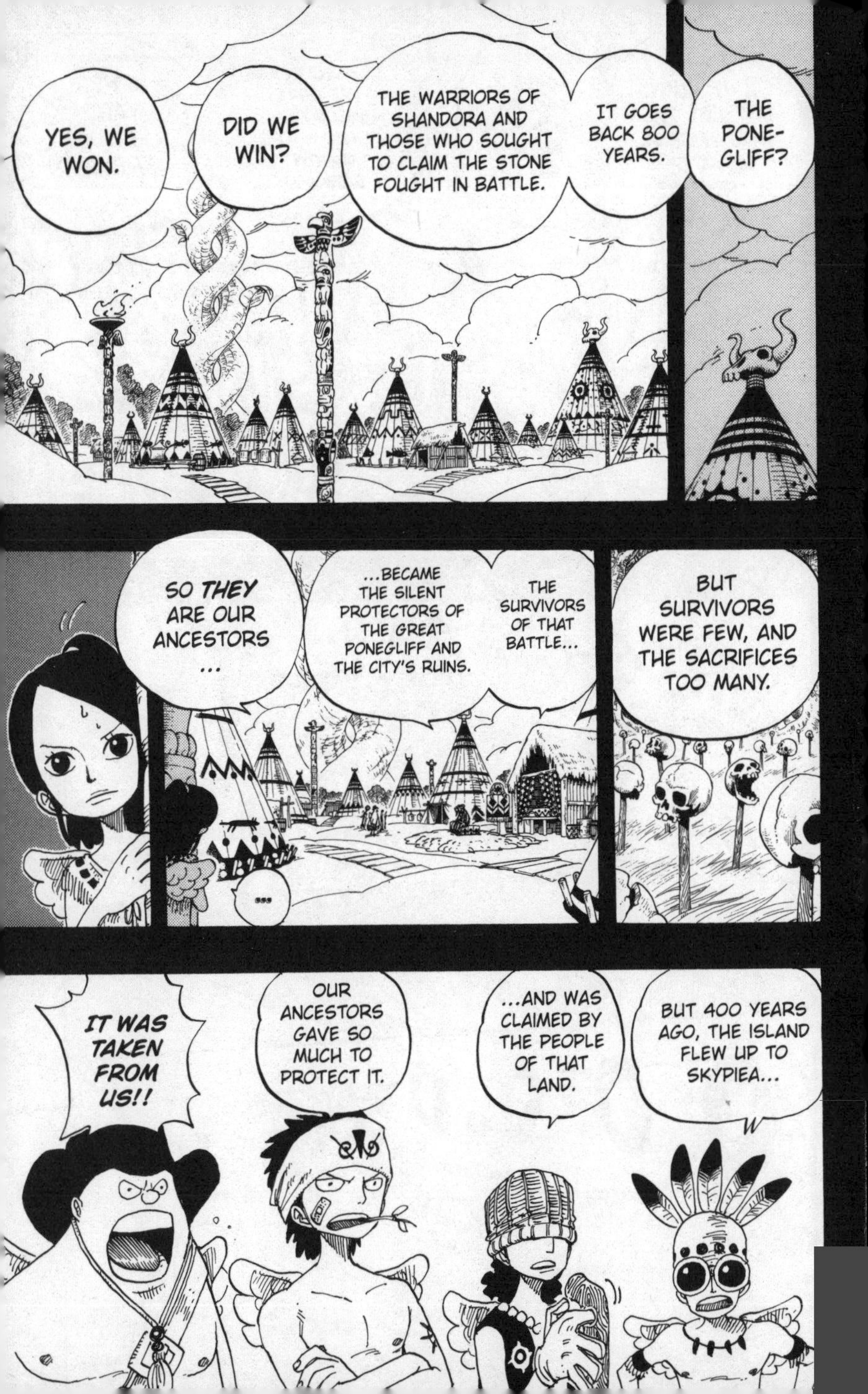
THE PONE-GLIFF?
IT GOES BACK 800 YEARS.
THE WARRIORS OF SHANDORA AND THOSE WHO SOUGHT TO CLAIM THE STONE FOUGHT IN BATTLE.
DID WE WIN?
YES, WE WON.
BUT SURVIVORS WERE FEW, AND THE SACRIFICES TOO MANY.
THE SURVIVORS OF THAT BATTLE...
...BECAME THE SILENT PROTECTORS OF THE GREAT PONEGLIFF AND THE CITY'S RUINS.
SO *THEY* ARE OUR ANCESTORS ...
...
BUT 400 YEARS AGO, THE ISLAND FLEW UP TO SKYPIEA...
...AND WAS CLAIMED BY THE PEOPLE OF THAT LAND.
OUR ANCESTORS GAVE SO MUCH TO PROTECT IT.
IT WAS TAKEN FROM US!!

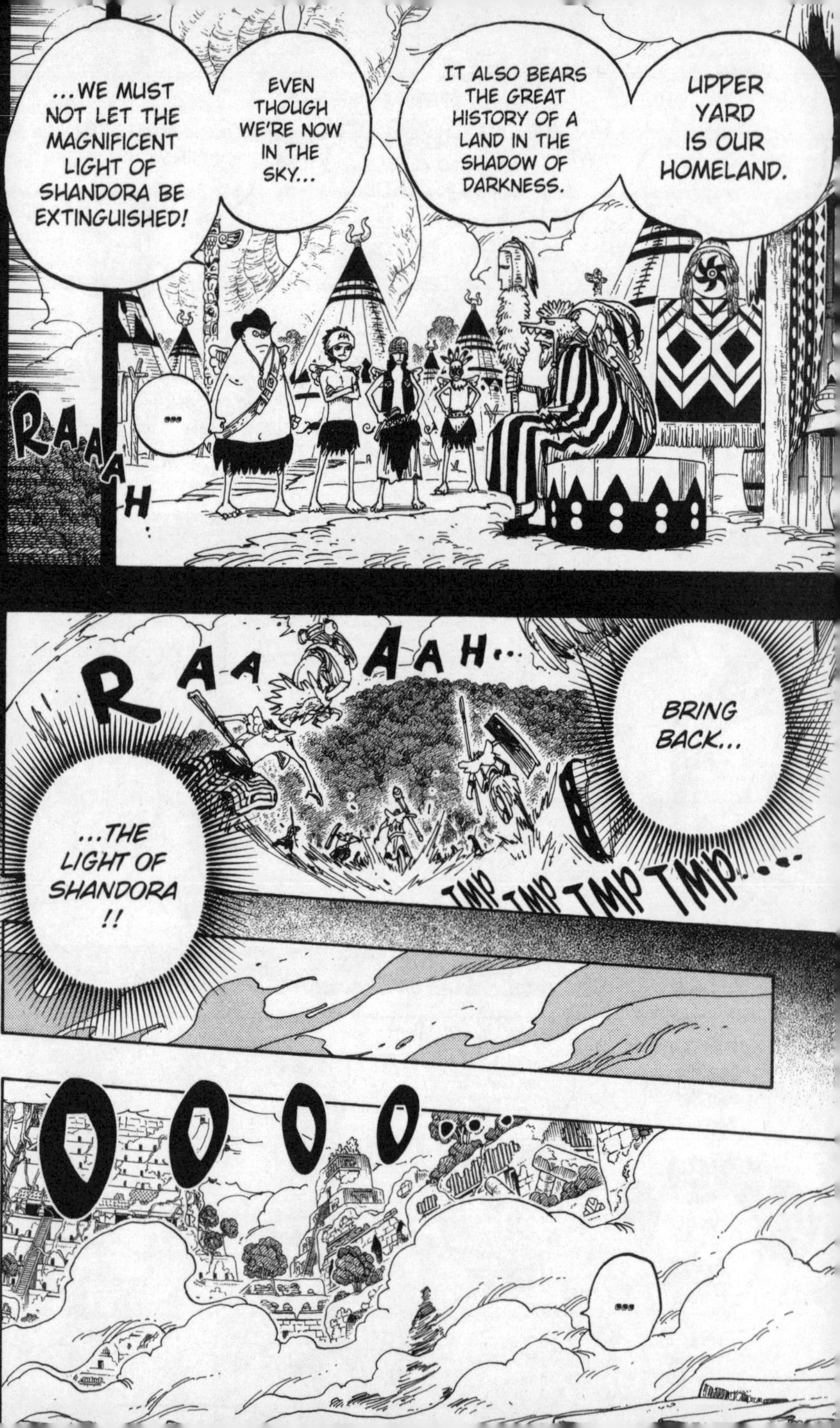
UPPER YARD IS OUR HOMELAND.
IT ALSO BEARS THE GREAT HISTORY OF A LAND IN THE SHADOW OF DARKNESS.
EVEN THOUGH WE'RE NOW IN THE SKY...
...WE MUST NOT LET THE MAGNIFICENT LIGHT OF SHANDORA BE EXTINGUISHED!
...
RAAAAH
BRING BACK...
...THE LIGHT OF SHANDORA !!
RAAAAH...
TMP TMP TMP TMP...
OOOO
...

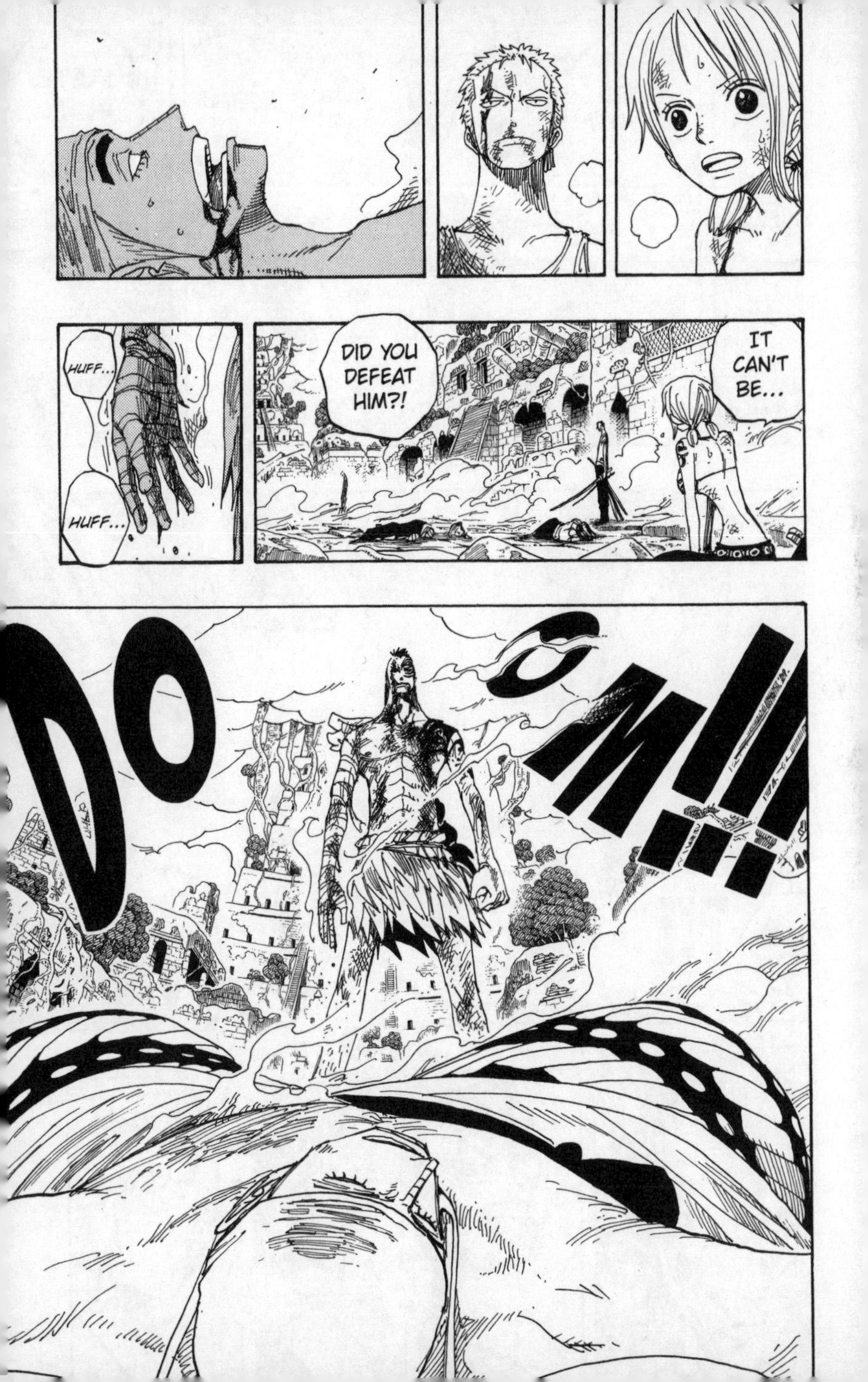
IT CAN'T BE...
DID YOU DEFEAT HIM?!
HUFF...
HUFF...
DOOM!!

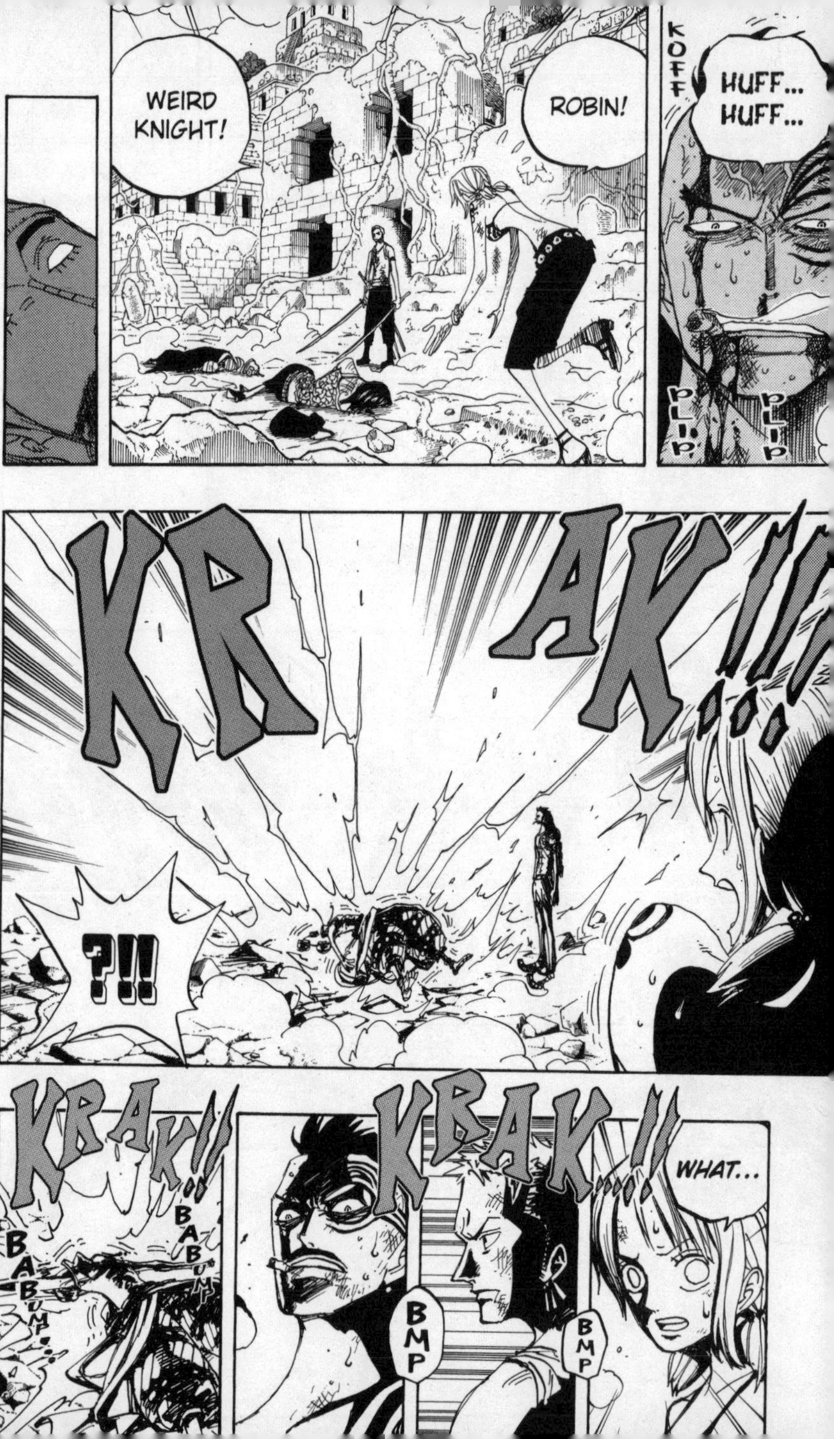
KOFF
HUFF... HUFF...
PLIP
PLIP
ROBIN!
WEIRD KNIGHT!
KRAK!!
?!!
WHAT...
KRAK!!
BMP
BMP
KRAK!!
BABUMP
BABUMP...

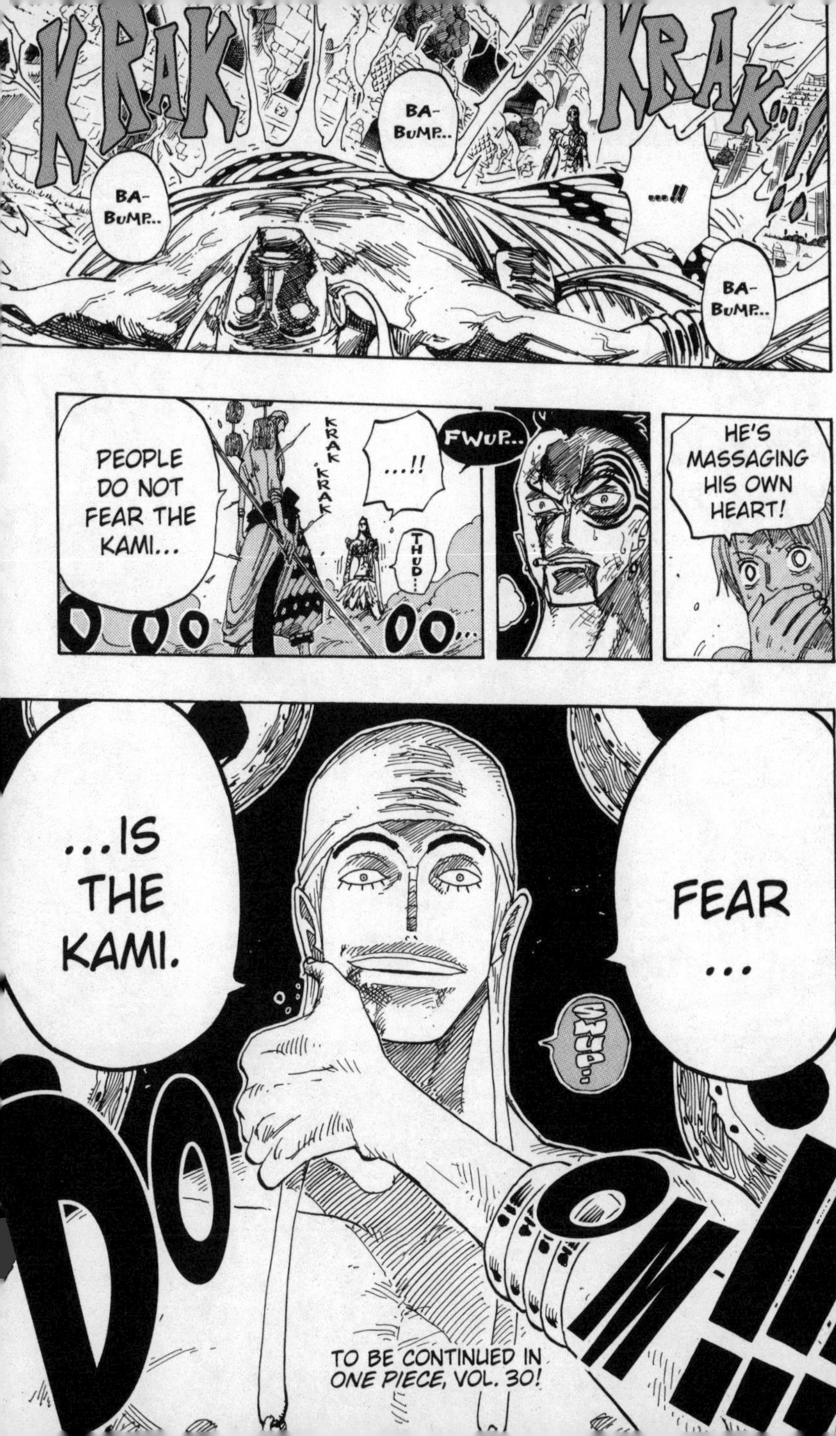
KRAK!!!
BA-BUMP...
...!!
BA-BUMP...
KRAK
BA-BUMP...
HE'S MASSAGING HIS OWN HEART!
FWUP...
...!!
KRAK KRAK
THUD...
PEOPLE DO NOT FEAR THE KAMI...
OOO OO...
FEAR...
SWUP...
...IS THE KAMI.
DOOM!!!!

TO BE CONTINUED IN ONE PIECE, VOL. 30!

COMING NEXT VOLUME:

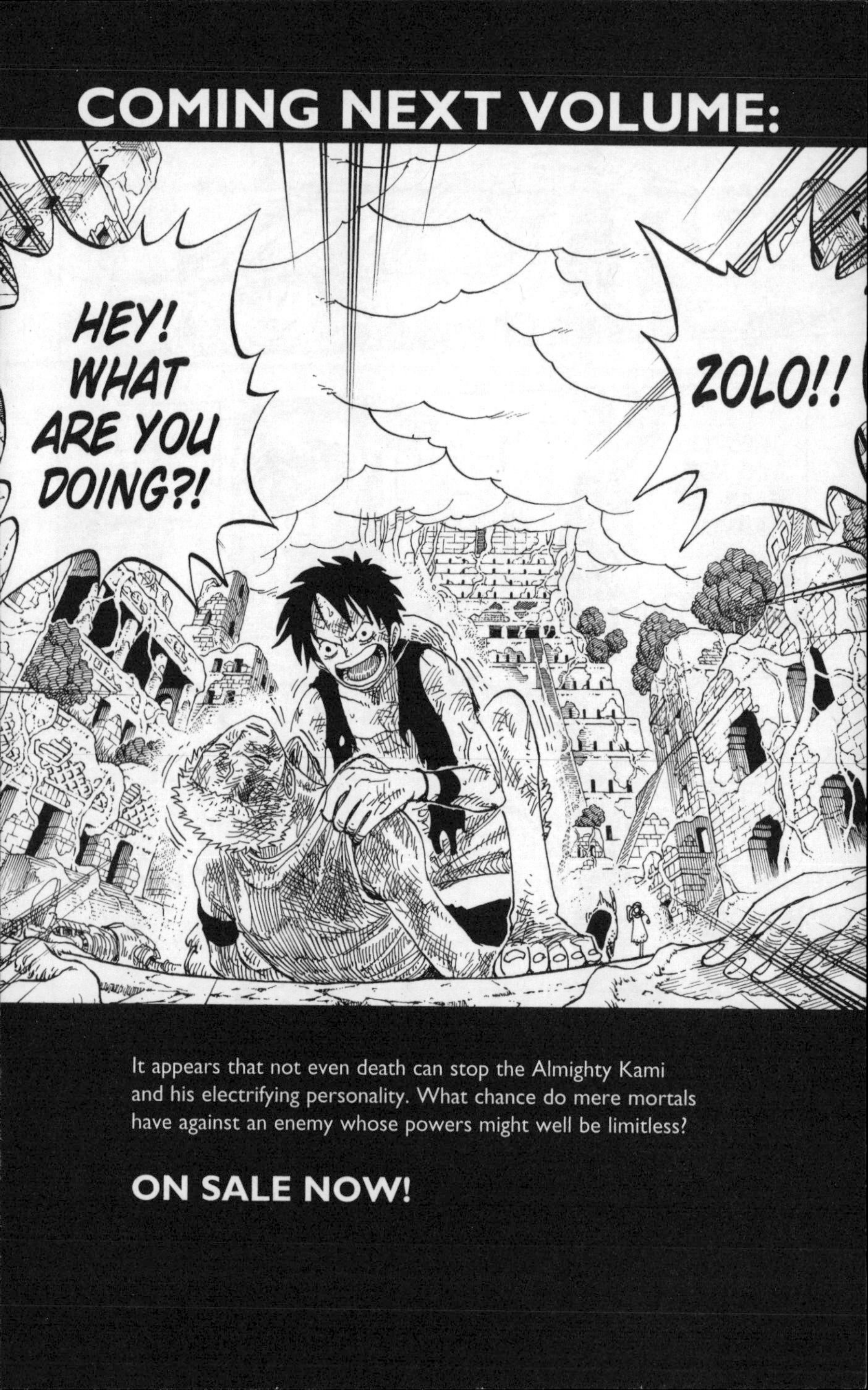
ZOLO!!
HEY! WHAT ARE YOU DOING?!

It appears that not even death can stop the Almighty Kami and his electrifying personality. What chance do mere mortals have against an enemy whose powers might well be limitless?

ON SALE NOW!

You're Reading in the Wrong Direction!!

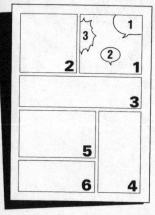

Whoops! Guess what? You're starting at the wrong end of the comic!

...It's true! In keeping with the original Japanese format, **One Piece** is meant to be read from right to left, starting in the upper-right corner.

Unlike English, which is read from left to right, Japanese is read from right to left, meaning that action, sound effects and word-balloon order are completely reversed...something which can make readers unfamiliar with Japanese feel pretty backwards themselves. For this reason, manga or Japanese comics published in the U.S. in English have sometimes been published "flopped"—that is, printed in exact reverse order, as though seen from the other side of a mirror.

By flopping pages, U.S. publishers can avoid confusing readers, but the compromise is not without its downside. For one thing, a character in a flopped manga series who once wore in the original Japanese version a T-shirt emblazoned with "M A Y" (as in "the merry month of") now wears one which reads "Y A M"! Additionally, many manga creators in Japan are themselves unhappy with the process, as some feel the mirror-imaging of their art skews their original intentions.

We are proud to bring you Eiichiro Oda's **One Piece** in the original unflopped format. For now, though, turn to the other side of the book and let the journey begin...!

—Editor